'DON'T LOOK BACK'

An Immigrant's Tale

Memoirs
Part 2: Being Who I Am

Gavin Wigginton

AD ASTRA BOOKS

First published 2022 by Ad Astra Books, an imprint of Mention the War Ltd., CF47 8RY, Wales.

Cover design: Topics - The Creative Partnership
www.topicsdesign.co.uk

A CIP catalogue reference for this book is available from the British Library.

ISBN 978 1 915335 03 6

Dedicated to Andrew, Siobhan and Brittany

Table of Contents

Part Five: Governance and Risk

Part Six: Back to Nature

Part Seven: A Parent Lost and a Parent Gained

Part Eight: Never to Retire

Part Nine: The Light of Experience

Preface

On 18 August 1986, at a muggy Heathrow airport, I boarded a plane bound for Sydney, Australia. Although, in the time following, I would return to my birthplace to visit family and friends, I would never again live in the UK. Initially, without any conviction (I choose my words carefully!), I began a new life on a continent and in a culture which would prove to be vastly different from anything I had previously known. For a few months, I did a reconnaissance. But eight months later, I would seal my fate by taking up permanent residency. And, three years down the track, on 14 September 1989 I became an Australian citizen with a Certificate and eucalypt seedling to prove it![1]

In this second book of my memoirs, I share with the reader my experience and learning from migrating to Australia, a place where I have now lived for more than 35 years.[2] This is an immigrant's tale in which my flight of fancy, borne of a fortuitous freedom to kick the traces, turned into an almost blind commitment to another place about which I had only a superficial prior knowledge. I choose the word *immigrant* advisedly. At the time, I actually saw myself as a refugee, escaping from what I saw as a toxic mixture of circumstances in my place of origin which had brought a mid-life crisis. I had become disenchanted with British politics and society, I had been made redundant following a bitterly fought takeover battle, and I had had a number of challenging experiences in my personal life that I needed to put behind me.

As is always the case with people who migrate, I would soon find out that the grass was not necessarily greener on the other side. You cannot easily escape the baggage that, if you let it, can increasingly define who you are wherever you live. And, as my time in Australia unfolded, it became very clear that the global issues of which I had become aware living in Britain were universal. In particular, in the new country I would encounter a culture in the 1980s where drivers for social cohesion were countered by an almost uninhibited pursuit of personal interests. And there was a section of society, with powerful voices, who were in denial about the finite nature of the world's resources. I would also find a very special kind of tribalism which was not conducive to national unity in a multicultural society. This was manifest in the failure by many

---

[1] It was the practice to give a seedling at the citizen presentation ceremony.
[2] In the first book of the Memoirs, entitled *"For Goodness Sake"*, I provide an account of the early part of my life lived in the UK.

inhabitants to recognise the place and prerogative of native peoples, and an obsession with holding onto colonial values and traditions.

But Australian culture also offered many positive aspects. Whilst my new life was challenging, I found that the values and passions carried from early life would enable me to flourish in a place where I was free of the class ridden constraints applicable in Britain. And what I soon discovered amongst my fellow Australians was a free spirit, a "can-do" outlook, and a genuine affinity with one's fellow man (mateship) from whatever background, which imbued the population with a sense of optimism and egalitarianism. And there were modern structures for national governance, including a federal constitution which fostered differences of outlook in the various States and Territories, and an enlightened electoral system that would ensure a fairer distribution of power and wealth than that achieved in Britain.

In this book, I relate an exciting journey of discovery, with insight into the process of settling into a new culture with only superficial similarity to the UK. Along the way, I reflect upon the successes, the failures, and the hard decisions that I encountered in reconciling myself to a different society. I give accounts of life in one of the world's most liveable cities as well as regional Australia, the challenges and rewards of working in organisations dependent on public funding, experiences obtained from ten years on the board of the nation's peak environmental organisation, encounters with water and fire, and an involvement with the administration of semi-professional sport. I also share with the reader my own peculiar version of family life. The account concludes with a new found passion to write, re-engagement with belonging, some comments on my adopted society, and a reflection on the spirit of things with a vision of the connectedness for life on planet Earth.

In preparing a book that covers the period since "the 1980s", I have relied for the early years on diaries from the period. However, since the mid-1990s, I have also had the benefit of access to electronic files which I have systematically retained in back-up systems. These are a rich source of events, facts, figures, and anecdotes. I am also a person given to periodic quiet reflection on the meaning of life and human condition, which I have recorded in various documents written and stored away for future reference. As you read the book, you will come to appreciate who I am, and what I believe. That's why people write autobiographies!

Gavin Wigginton
May 2022

PART ONE

LEGAL IMMIGRANT

1: A Toe in the Water

I left England in 1986 both as a reaction to recent events in my personal life and a response to what I saw as a deep malaise in British society. At a personal level, I had been made redundant as the result of a fiercely fought takeover battle, and I had encountered a number of other personal setbacks and traumas. But I was also deeply disenchanted with the general state of being in the country of my birth. In particular, it was my view that Thatcher's Britain had become a place where the vision of the public good in a just society had been abandoned. The commitment to small government, the paring back of social capital, and the removal of government regulations, meant freedom to pursue personal gain in a market place where the odds were heavily stacked in favour of "the haves". This increasingly libertarian society was not the kind of place in which I wanted to live and, like Socrates, I knew that if I didn't like it I should either take my life elsewhere or experience a slow death of the spirit. All the signals in my life pointed to the need to pursue a new beginning in another place.

So I determined to leave England, for a time at least, to investigate the possibility of making a new start in a place and circumstances which were hopefully more conducive to what I perceived to be a good life. My decision was a wilful act of abandon which reflected my profound belief that sometimes it is better to cut and run. But, in the first tentative steps, I was leaving my options open. On my visit to Australia in mid-1986 I set myself some relatively short-term objectives, whilst I indulged myself with some rest and recuperation from the recent rigours of daily life.

Knowing that, if I made a long-term commitment to Australia, I would probably have to live and work in a centre of population, my first objective on this visit was to discover what it was like to live in one its major cities. And I appreciated that this would be very different from being a tourist. Given my three previous visits to the country, where for family reasons I had been based in Sydney, that city might have seemed the obvious choice. But, through Australian friends, I had reason to think that the capital of Victoria would be a place that was easier to settle for someone with an English temperament, in terms of climate and culture. Indeed, despite its incomparable harbour and beaches, I felt that Sydney was a step too far from everything I had known in Britain, with its oppressive summer heat, reportedly aggressive attachment to the pursuit of wealth, and hedonistic life style. So that's why I chose Melbourne.

My second objective on this reconnoitre was to engage with the local population and form a view about whether I would be comfortable with the types of people that I would encounter in everyday life. At this stage, I had no concept of the multicultural nature of the country or its indigenous legacy. Indeed, like many British people, I thought that the Australian population was just another part of the British diaspora with the occasional non-Anglo-Celt to make up the numbers. Whilst acquainting myself with the locals, I also determined to explore the places beyond the city in a State which was the same size (in square miles) as England and Wales with only a tenth of the population.

Finally, prior to making a decision about settlement, I determined to investigate the employment market for someone with my background and experience. I also needed to discover how easy it would be in practice to obtain permission to work and live without limiting my movements and future aspirations. At this stage I had very little knowledge of the migration system.

For this fact-finding mission I decided to allocate a sum of around £20,000 from the proceeds of my redundancy from Imperial Group in London. This would cover my living and travel expenses during a six months' gap from employment. As with all previous trips to Australia, my port of entry was Sydney and I arrived there on 20 August 1986 in what was mid-winter. Sydney winters are largely mild, and the temperature wasn't that much different from the England I had just left. I got myself a hire car and, after a few days in Sydney, drove up to Newcastle to spend a week visiting my relatives, Neil and Sally Pratt. Then I began a leisurely trip down the east coast of NSW, stopping off at various coastal towns and heading for Victoria. For the final part of the trip, across the eastern part of the State called Gippsland, I had directions from my friend Chris McArthur to turn off the main road (the Princes Highway) and follow what was called the Grand Ridge Road, part of which was unsealed. This took me through a rural and farming landscape at Gormandale and up into the evergreen forests of the Strzelecki Hills. Just beyond Leongatha, I then headed north, back across the Princes Highway, to the lovely town of Emerald. After winding through the foothills of the Dandenong Mountains, I ended up at a spot called Burke's Lookout not far from Olinda. There I was greeted by Chris with a can of beer and an Australian flag hoisted up a gum tree. On a sunny spring day (4 September 1986) the view across to the city of Melbourne and Port Phillip Bay was a wonderful welcome to what would become my home town for the next twenty-five years and beyond.

For the first few weeks in Melbourne, I was very fortunate in being the guest of Chris's parents in the leafy suburb of Malvern East. In the final year of university, Chris was still living at home in a spacious single storey residence, with expansive kitchen, four bedrooms, and a homely sitting room with tastefully conservative décor and furnishings, and doors with traditional leaded lights. It sat on a quarter-acre block, with a large private garden full of native plants. Chris's father, John, was a gentle and kindly general surgeon and his mother Sally was a no-nonsense and cheerful registered nurse. They were delightful people who, together with their loyal Labrador Rufus, extended extraordinary hospitality whilst I found my feet.[3] Almost immediately, I established a bank account and registered with various estate agents in search of a flat. I also returned my rental car, and acquired my own wheels from a very accommodating fellow at a Ford dealership in central Melbourne. He offered to sell me a Laser for around $10,000, on the basis that I would be able to sell it back to him six months later less an agreed amount for depreciation. Identifying suitable accommodation took a little longer; but in early October I found a one bedroom unit in a boutique block of flats in Burnie Street Toorak for which I paid rent of $512 per month.

So now I was set up for a new, if somewhat tenuous, existence in an unknown city in a foreign land. Apart from the McArthurs, who continued to look out for my interests, I proceeded to activate a number of contacts acquired before leaving England, adopting a pretty open-minded agenda. I joined the local English Speaking Union ("ESU") which had an active bridge club, and enrolled at a local squash club where I met and played with an Englishman living and working in Australia called Anthony Bowesman with whom I was soon spending quite a bit of time on and off the court. I also joined the Melbourne Theatre Company, attended concerts given by the Melbourne Symphony Orchestra, followed bands appearing in suburban pubs, and frequented an underground jazz club which met in the basement of the Melbourne Arts Centre on a Friday night. I also did quite a bit of touring, which included visits to the Yarra Valley, the Grampians National Park, and the Mount Buffalo National Park. In late October, I made my first trip to Fiji with an idyllic five day stay on the remote Mana Island in the Yasawas.

---

[3] Amongst other things, John McArthur provided introductions to a GP in Hawthorn (Dr Negri who was an old friend of his) and a dentist in Collins Street Melbourne (Dr Coakley). The latter set me up with a newly qualified dentist in his practice named Sue King who remains my dentist to this day. He also put me in touch with another friend, Patrick Hartl, who became, and still is, my solicitor. Sadly, John and his wife Sally are now deceased.

In the first weeks, I also had a rather unnerving experience. One day, and out of the blue, I received a call from a gentleman at the Toorak *Returned Services League* ("RSL").[4] This was not an organisation of which I had much knowledge, but the fellow had acquired my name and invited me to have lunch with him. Intrigued, I accepted his invitation and met him in the reception of a rather grand Victorian building in Toorak. We had a very pleasant meal, and a discursive conversation during which he indicated that he knew that I came from a military family, and that he wanted me to know that I was welcome in Melbourne. We parted company with a warm handshake, and I never saw or heard from him again. Thirty years later, when I uncovered my father's military history, I would recall this encounter, and speculate about the long arm of military intelligence![5]

During this early period, I continued to have regular contact with the McArthur family and they made it their business to introduce me to what they considered to be the highlights of Victoria, which included a trip along the Great Ocean Road to a district where their Scottish ancestor had settled in the 19th century, a stay at a holiday house owned by friends in Lorne, overnight bush walks in the Victoria Alps, and trips down to the ocean beaches of the Mornington Peninsula.[6] To thank them for their generosity, I offered my services with a bit of physical labour and was drawn into helping with the renovation of a family property. This brings to mind one afternoon which I spent painting a significant length of fence whilst listening to the radio. In those days, the ABC broadcast proceedings from the Australian Parliament in Canberra and I was entertained during Question Time in the House of Representatives, as the Treasurer Paul Keating laid into the Opposition with some fairly colourful language. In particular, this was the first time I had heard a number of Australian colloquialisms including the expression "scumbag"![7]

With my appetite for politics, one of my most important contacts during this halcyon period was the Australian Democrats. Before

---

[4] The RSL is an organisation that supports retired members of the armed forces, and manages clubs which provide a place to eat at modest prices and pursue a variety of activities such as lawn bowls.

[5] In World War Two my father was a member of the Special Operations Executive, an organisation established to support resistance movements which later became the British MI6. My father's involvement is recorded in my book entitled *Wig's Secret War*.

[6] The Meningoort Estate near Camperdown was established in 1842 by Peter McArthur (b 1819) who migrated from Islay in Scotland in 1839. He acquired other local properties including the Glenample Station near Port Campbell owned by John McArthur's ancestor.

[7] Scumbag means "contemptible person".

arriving in Australia, I had earmarked this as an organisation with whom I might find some common political cause, and my subsequent history with them is the subject of Chapter 4. They were very welcoming. I also pursued another contact with political connections. This was a delightful woman named Deborah Towns who quickly became a firm friend. She worked for the Liberal Party in the office of State Opposition Leader Jeff Kennett. And she introduced me to a whole other side of Australian politics, including a young Michael Kroger who was later to become a major power broker in the Victorian Division of the Liberal Party, and Lorraine Elliot.[8] Deb was a divorcee with two young sons, and for a time we became quite attached. But, with my mind in quite a state of turmoil about my future, I was in no fit state to take on a serious relationship, not to mention the parenting of someone else's children. So I held back. But we spent a lot time together, having lunch and dinner, and attending sundry social events. Eventually, we drifted apart and she met another Englishmen to whom she got married. It was my loss, and I owe her a considerable debt of gratitude for being there for me during the early days of my settlement.

Whilst initially I allowed myself to drift, living the life of a visitor on an extended holiday, after a couple of months I started to feel the need to pull myself together. In my head, I was beginning to move from recovery and holiday mode into wondering whether this trip to Australia might translate into a longer-term commitment. A key factor was my ability to gain employment, and I began to investigate the local job market. I approached various members of the head-hunting fraternity and registered with a number of employment agencies. And, although people were friendly and encouraging, I soon found that my lack of permanent residency was a serious impediment. As the clock ticked by, I was beginning to think that settlement was all just a flight of fancy. But then, in November, I attended an interview at an organisation called Drake Personnel. At the time, they had nothing on their books which suited my skills. But, just before Christmas, they renewed the contact and asked whether I would be interested in joining them as a Recruitment Officer, subject to my obtaining permanent resident status. I hadn't really considered that kind of work as a career, but superficially it had its attractions. I rather naively conjured up the idea that I would be a "head-hunter", and that this activity would bring me into contact with a large

---

[8] I actually sat next to Michael Kroger at a dinner party. He was a fairly aloof guy, who quickly ascertained that I was connected with the British Liberal Party and promptly disengaged. Lorraine Elliott was the ex-wife of businessman John Elliott and became a State MP. She died in 2014.

network of potential employers. So I said that I'd think about it and get back to them in the New Year.

At Christmas, I flew up to Newcastle to spend the holiday period with my cousins Neil and Sally Pratt. Interestingly, I also planned to attend my first Boxing Day Test Match at the MCG. But the match was over before I could get there with England beating Australia within three days![9] In early January, I went bushwalking with the McArthurs, trekking from Licola up Mount Howitt. We stayed overnight at a hut, and then camped on the top of the mountain. And, as always with the McArthurs, we did this in style. After pitching tents, we drank gin and tonics as we watched the sunset, and tucked into a meal cooked on a portable stove. It was a joy and a privilege to commune with good friends in the raw character and beauty of the Australian bush. And the trip also introduced me to the vagaries of the climate. On the day of our return, we woke up in a dense fog with the temperature at around 15°C. But, within 30 minutes of walking down the mountain, we found ourselves in 25°C sunshine. Anyway, all the time I was up there, the proposal from Drake was churning around in my head. It was a big step. But, if I was settling into a world full of people like the McArthurs, what the hell. So, on my return to Melbourne, I decided to give the role of Recruitment Officer at Drake Personnel a go, and I attended an interview with a lady called Serenella Tonello during which I undertook a series of psychological tests to see whether I had the competence and personality for recruitment work. They also enlightened me on the migration rules. Apparently, there was a scheme in which a company could sponsor an incoming migrant with qualifications and/or competencies that were not readily available in the local employment market. One of the employment categories for which there was a shortage was "Economists", and they felt confident that my migration would succeed on that basis given my Economics degree. I took them at their word and made a deal. In the third week of January they then sent me a formal job offer and a proposal to sponsor me. The moment of truth had arrived.

When I look back, these circumstances unfolded in an almost casual manner. Yet the offer to sponsor me as a migrant was a pivotal movement in my life, and I seemed almost to tumble headlong into a sequence of events which became irreversible. In the first week of February 1987, I accepted the Drake offer. And, on 11 February, they lodged an application to the government to sponsor my migration. In the meantime,

---

[9] England won by an innings and 14 runs with Gladstone Small the Man of the Match.

I prepared for my return to England where I would need to make a formal application to emigrate. In anticipation of success, I extended the lease on my flat in Toorak. But I returned my car to City Ford for which I received a very reasonable reimbursement on the understanding that I could re-purchase if I returned. I said my goodbyes to all my new-found friends and, on 28 February 1987, I boarded a plane bound for Heathrow.

As I flew back to Europe, my head was buzzing with mixed thoughts and emotions. Until very recently, my trip to Australia had been a somewhat self-indulgent recuperative break. But now, my dream of settling in a new place and establishing a new way of life on my own terms had the potential to become a reality. And I was filled with an almost adolescent excitement, in which I seemed to accommodate the prospect of leaving behind all that I had known for nearly forty years in an almost fatalistic way. The reality was that I really had little idea of what I was getting myself into. Moving to another country, with a different culture and virtually no personal support system, is challenging enough when you have no other choice, as is the case for refugees. To do so when there is no existential imperative is potentially a supreme act of folly. However, with the benefit of hindsight, I would have to say that I was a prime candidate for migration. From what I now know, the things that drive many people to leave one place haunt them in the next, and that is a recipe for failure. Successful migration has two prerequisites – compelling reasons to leave a place, and a willingness to embrace the new country even at the expense of giving away most of what went before. My migration met both conditions, and a degree of financial independence did not go astray!

2: Emigration

On arriving back in England in March 1987, the full weight of my decision to emigrate was beginning to sink in. When I had left the old country in August, I was at a low ebb. The six months in Melbourne had allowed the pain to ease, with despair replaced by hope. There was the prospect of an entirely new life, where all the things that had the potential to remind me of failings and disappointments were absent. But, despite this transformation in my mental state, I did have serious second thoughts about leaving loved ones. Interestingly, my mother never sought to influence my decision. She accepted that I should do what was right for me, and I think she took pride in the fact that she had raised a son with the courage and self-assurance to take his own path. My brother had relatively little to say on the matter. At the time, he was pre-occupied with challenges in his own life. Apart from attachment to these family members, the most difficult aspect was the prospect of leaving and potentially losing long-time friends with whom I had shared values and life experience. And then there was the question of "belonging" which encompasses attachment to land and environment. I will return to this issue in Chapter 28. But suffice it to say that, despite my strong reservations about the political climate, Britain was still a country with wild places that I held dear. Australia was a blank canvass.

Notwithstanding my ruminations, having arrived back in Britain it took less than two months to process my application to emigrate, and there was never any doubt about the outcome. With the employer sponsorship process already under way, on 2 March 1987 I made an emigration application to the Australian High Commission. And this was quickly followed by an interview at Australia House in London. I then visited the Australian Consulate in Manchester to discuss the employer sponsorship proposal. I also had various medical checks from which I obtained a clean bill of health. On 23 April, the Australian High Commission wrote to me indicating that my application had been successful, and I was given my marching instructions. I had to present myself in Australia by a given date at which point I would become a Permanent Resident. In the best traditions of transportation, I would then be confined to the country for two years. I quickly organised my flight, and scheduled my departure for 11 May which was just 10 weeks after making the original migration application.

Although this was a period when I was full of hope and expectation, the final month in England was also a time of sadness. I spent a good deal of time with family and friends, going through a seemingly endless series of farewells. And at times I broke down with grief. I especially remember the final visit to my cottage in Lincolnshire where I had plotted my political escapades. Alone, and with the prospect of parting from people with whom I had cherished memories, I sat by an open fire and wept. In any event, when the time came, my mother drove me down to London and took me out to Heathrow airport. Although it was not by any means a final farewell, it was tough. And I remember my mother trailing her hand down the side of my face in an act of tenderness before we embraced. I have no doubt that, for her, this brought back memories of all the partings with her husband during the fateful days of World War Two.

After a 27 hours flight, on the morning of 13 May 1987, I arrived in Melbourne. The weather was far from welcoming. It was wet and cold and, for once in my life, I felt terribly alone. But I knew in my heart that there was no turning back. I was living life on the edge and, as I took a taxi to the city, I experienced a great surge of excitement. I was now a bona fide Australian resident with a new identity in a new environment. What happened next was up to me, and I was determined not to let myself down. In the next few days, I reconnected with various contacts, prepared myself for my new job, and re-possessed my blue Ford Laser car.

The following week, on 18 May 1987, I started work at Drake Personnel at offices located in the ANZ Tower at the top end of Collins Street in the Melbourne Central Business District ("CBD"). It was a simple tram ride into town from my flat in Toorak and, on that first day, as I walked from the Town Hall up Collins Street, I couldn't help comparing this relatively stress-free commute of 30 minutes with the endless hours of sitting behind the wheel of a car in a London traffic jam. Thus began my new working life.

I soon came down to earth. The job at Drake turned out to be anything but what I had expected. In my haste to seize the day, I had not applied some pretty basic learning from previous employment experience about the importance of organisational culture. I excuse myself because, in taking this job, I was a "fish out of water". I had no previous experience of the recruitment industry. But I should have been more discerning. Drake Personnel was a very successful private company, with a Canadian owner whose portrait hung in the entrance to their premises. The offices were open plan, with enclosed rooms available for meetings and interviews, and there was piped music playing from dawn to dusk.

As I soon found out, the mission of this business was to maximise throughput using a well-honed recruitment model. This work was a far cry from the head-hunting role that I had naively expected, where companies sought to attract appropriate senior executives from other organisations using discretely managed networks. Drake's market place consisted of a wide range of companies seeking to recruit people to fill both white-collar and blue-collar jobs. For each recruitment project, Drake would deploy a Recruitment Officer with appropriate market sector knowledge whose role was to establish a job specification, a candidate profile and, if required, some suitable advertising. Drake would then identify a short list of candidates, making use not only of responses to any advertisement but also a huge database of candidates maintained by Drake. This shortlist would be referred to the client, culminating in interviews. The client would then make a decision, subject to reference checks undertaken by Drake, and the project was completed.

In accepting this job, I really had not appreciated what an incredibly mechanistic process this was, with a focus on the appointment of relatively junior staff. Contrary to my expectations, I was to spend my day dealing not with leaders of organisations but the followers, with my senior management experience being of little account. And the work entailed routine tasks requiring little judgement, with my performance assessed according to the speed and number of placements. There were weekly "Sales Meetings" at which staff provided progress reports on current projects, targets were set, and new projects were allocated.

After a day in induction, and a few days of operational activity, it was very evident to me that I was not suited for this organisation or the role. When I set out for work each day I started to have this terrible sinking feeling. The culture, with the portrait of the owner, the background music, the commission system, and the open-plan environment, gave me the creeps. Of course, I was deeply concerned about letting down my boss, who had invested time and effort in assisting my migration. But, I knew instinctively that I did not fit, and that failure loomed. After about ten days, I plucked up the courage to meet with my boss and fess up. She was shocked, and reminded me that the psychological profiling to which I had been subjected before appointment showed a perfect match for the recruitment role. She pleaded with me to give it more time and, in deference to her endeavours on my behalf, I agreed to persist. However, a week later, I met with her again and indicated that I was still unhappy. In frustration, she suggested that I should go and see a psychologist and, a few days later, I attended some rooms at an anonymous address with a blacked-out window in Nicholson Street Fitzroy where I met a very charming fellow with whom I had a very frank discussion. His assessment was revealing, not least in that he did not try to convince me to stay with the company. He told me that I had very different values from Drake Personnel, and that I would not be happy or fulfilled in working there. He also suggested that, with my background and experience, I probably wasn't suited to a sales position. Given my recent arrival in the country, he suggested that I had a pretty straightforward decision to make. Either I could choose to accept that I had made a big mistake in emigrating and return to England. Or I could seek to establish a local support system to see me through what might be a relatively tough period in my life whilst I found a more suitable job. In either case, I should resign from Drake.

That session with the psychologist was a seminal moment in my life, and I think I have a lot for which to thank the fellow concerned. A few days later I resigned from Drake. I had been there just over a month, and it was the first time I had ever failed in a job. Notwithstanding the psychologist's advice, the decision to leave was tough. It went against all my usual instincts to be loyal and resilient. But, on this occasion, I followed my gut feeling. Interestingly, a couple of weeks after handing in my notice, I received an account for visiting the rooms in Fitzroy! I couldn't complain, but it only served to confirm the kind of organisation with which I was dealing – no room for sentiment in protecting the bottom line.

After the trauma of Drake, and with the words of the psychologist still ringing in my ears, in June I went into a kind of hibernation. Resigning from a job was one thing. But whether I should leave Australia was another. There was a lot to think about and, in the weeks that followed, I took the psychologist's advice as regards immediate survival. I extended my support system while I worked out what I was going to do with the rest of my life. And I had a stroke of luck. To keep myself occupied, I offered my services to the Australian Democrats at their offices in Melbourne and, with a Federal Election looming on 11 July, I became actively engaged in electioneering Australian style. I also signed up with a migration support programme at the ESU, and became a conversation partner for new immigrants. This led me to spend many hours talking to non-English speaking immigrants whose challenges were far greater than mine which helped put my own situation into perspective. During leisure time, I continued to play bridge at the ESU, went running most days along the banks of the River Yarra, joined a pennant squash competition playing for a Club in Prahran, went to the theatre and concerts, and renewed my connection with wild places, although the weather was far from clement in the midst of a Melbourne winter.

In reflecting on whether I should stay on in Australia, I did initially have one serious concern. My emigration had been sponsored by Drake, and I wondered whether the decision to leave them had in some way invalidated my permanent residency. But I received reassuring advice from the Department of Immigration. The various other considerations then playing through my head were far from straightforward. Were the people and values that I had encountered at Drake representative of the wider Australian society, in which case did I belong here? With only a small network of friends and contacts, did I have the mental fortitude to overcome the setback? On the other side of the ledger, there were all the reasons that I had decided to leave the UK – Thatcher's Britain, the disappointment with my political ambitions, the Imperial redundancy, the mugging that left me unconscious in a London street, and the family issues. My heart kept telling me that leaving the UK and becoming an Australian still felt right. And eventually, my head agreed.

So, after a few weeks, and although I did not underestimate the challenge, I decided to stay and keep the dream alive. And that meant finding gainful employment. After the July Federal Election was done and dusted, I prepared a new Resume. And, in the next three months, I went through all the highs and lows of over 40 job applications typed on my portable typewriter. Nothing emerged and, with a growing sense of failure, I became increasingly depressed.

3: Poacher Turned Gamekeeper

Life can be unpredictable. In the depths of August 1987, after so many failed job applications, I was certainly getting close to the thought that I was unemployable in Australia. Then, one Saturday morning in early September, I was reading the *Age* newspaper, and out popped an advertisement that seemed to speak to me. The National Companies and Securities Commission ("NCSC") were seeking to appoint a new Assistant Director in the Securities Markets Branch which dealt with the administration of the Companies (Acquisition of Shares) Act 1980 and related Code.[10] This was legislation that governed take-over activity, giving the Commissioners of the NCSC the discretion to both enforce and vary the law. In attempting to get the Commissioners to use their discretionary power, lawyers representing major Australian companies would make applications which NCSC staff would assess. The Assistant Director led the team of lawyers responsible for processing these applications.

At the time, experience in take-over activity in the UK was at a premium, and my knowledge of the City of London Takeover Code was like gold-dust. My previous experience in the corporate sector was also an asset, given that the use of discretion to vary the code involved not only legal arguments but also commercial factors. So I was tailor made for this role, and I applied and got an interview with a fellow named Geoff Robertson. I met him on 9 September, and again on 14 September, and we hit it off. He was fascinated to hear the story of the Imperial takeover, and we had an excellent conversation about all the gambits that companies deployed. A week later, I received an offer of employment. My heart sang. This seemed like a plum job providing just the sort of intellectual challenge I needed. And it was a role in a major Australian institution which involved becoming a Commonwealth public servant with all the security that this entailed. I could not believe my luck. But I also thought that it was meant to be.

The NCSC operated under what was a unique arrangement in Australia, called the *Formal Agreement* enacted in December 1978, which was designed to ensure that legislation relating to companies and the securities industry was uniform throughout Australia.[11] The

---

[10] The NCSC has now been reconstituted as ASIC. Founded in 1991, this successor body has far greater powers and resources than the NCSC had in 1987. And the Acquisition of Shares Act was rescinded in 2001 and replaced with a new Act.

[11] Some material in this chapter is taken from the *NCSC Ninth Annual Report and Financial*

administrative framework consisted of a Ministerial Council, the NCSC, the Corporate Affairs Departments in the States and Territories, the Companies and Securities Law Review Committee, and the Accounting Standards Review Board. This was quite a cumbersome structure but, as people used to say to me at the time, " ...*welcome to Australia*" and the complexities deriving from a federation. In any event, there was provision for the NCSC to delegate a range of its powers to the States and Territories through its appointed Delegates. In theory, this facilitated efficient administration within a centralised and uniform policy framework.

I started working at the NCSC on 8 October 1987, and I could not have joined the organisation at a more momentous time.[12] On 19 October, in one day, the Dow Jones Index lost 23% of its value and on Tuesday 20 October 1987 the Australian share market followed suit. At the start of trading, the ASX dropped 25% from the opening level of 2,312 and eventually closed down 27% at 1,688 on what became **Black Tuesday**. Within three weeks, Australian markets had fallen nearly 50%. The pain felt by the shareholders and the banks was palpable, and this was not to mention that devastation amongst the financial institutions. Three of Australia's largest merchant banks – Elders Finance, Tri-continental and Partnership Pacific – were more or less absorbed into their parent bodies, and many foreign banks retreated into niche activity or got out of Australia altogether. The State Banks of Victoria and South Australia had to be rescued by their respective governments. The big four Australian banks – ANZ, Commonwealth Bank of Australia, NAB and Westpac Banking Corp – were shaken for a decade.

More than anything, the cause of all this mayhem was the collapse of the US market. The Dow's decline began with general selling by investors, and this was then exacerbated by what was called *program trading*. This expression referred to the computer systems which had only recently been implemented to provide for smooth market activity. The "program" provided for the automatic offer for sale of certain equities when individual stock prices and indices hit certain levels, and this mechanism fed an already weakened market with huge volumes of shares for sale which precipitated the plunge. In Australia, the Stock Exchange Automatic Trading System ("SEATS") had been installed on

---

Statements 1 July 1987 to 30 June 1988 Australian Government Publishing Service, Canberra, 1988.

[12] The following account is based on an article by Trevor Sykes entitled *Lessons from the Crash* published in the *Australian Financial Review* on 20 October 2012.

the day before **Black Tuesday** and this efficient vehicle for selling contributed to the speed of events amongst the 20 largest stocks.

Of course, program trading was not the main cause of the fall of the markets. The central reason in October 1987 was that, after a long "bull" run, in a significantly deregulated economy, US investors perceived that the market was overvalued. And in what was an increasingly globalised world, this automatically fed through to Australia notwithstanding the reasonably healthy state of the local economy. Foreign investors quit Australian shares at any cost to bolster cash reserves at home. And, to make matters worse, on that day the Hong Kong Stock Exchange was closed. This channelled foreign selling in the Australian ASX.

This great shock to the system occurred just ten days after I joined the organisation and was of course a major talking point as I was going through my induction programme. In fact it probably gave the place a level of energy and excitement which was far from typical of its normal day-to-day existence. In a few weeks, things soon settled down.

In those days, the NCSC was based in Queen Street in the Melbourne CBD. It employed fewer than 100 people and had an annual budget of just $6 million to oversee the activities of over 750,000 companies registered in Australia. It was headed by Henry Bosch. He was an avuncular fellow with a very considerable intellect. He was widely respected in the business community and an acknowledged expert in corporate governance. He was supported by two other full-time and five part-time Commissioners.

Mine was a relatively small team of lawyers based on the 17th Floor of the building with views across the city and Port Phillip Bay. And I soon learnt that I would need to be acquainted with not only the fine print of the Acquisition of Shares Act but also the Commission's previous decisions in varying the related Code. With only a small circle of contacts outside work, I soon made some good friends including Carl Thompson who reported to me and David Danks who worked in another part of the organisation. Despite the market crash, there was no shortage of activity in the takeover field. In fact, if anything, the fall in share process fed the takeover beast and we soon found it necessary to establish the inevitable "White Board" in my office which listed all the many current takeover targets.[13] This was highly confidential information and we generally kept the window blinds down! However, when we working there, we often had the blinds up and, as we often commented, anyone

---

[13] In 1987/88 there was a 123% increase in the number of takeover applications.

with a long-range lens in an adjacent building could have made a fortune. This white board also had other uses. There was a long running joke of leaving Australian words to educate me in the vernacular and, for some reason, I remember one in particular, "drongo". With typical Australian humour the team loved this word, meaning "a stupid person", because one of our number was an exceptionally bright young guy named Dr Ong.

The takeover system in Australia at this time required that, once a company's holding of another company's share reached a certain threshold (20%), they were obliged to make a takeover bid by lodging a Part A document. And there were then provisions for the target of the takeover to respond with a Part B. Subsequent Statements by the Offeror and Target were made pursuant to provisions for a Part C and Part D respectively. Registration of applications was the business of the Commission's Delegate in each State and Territory, with those requesting variation to the Code passed to the NCSCC. The NCSC Commission then had the power to modify the "black letter law" for a takeover, on the basis of what was fair and reasonable, consistent with previous practice, and bearing in mind the public interest and the investor protection aims of the legislation. In theory, this was designed to reduce business costs and expedite the takeover, while maintaining "a level playing field".

To give some indication of the level of activity, in the year to 30 June 1988 the Commission (their meetings were called Divisions) examined no fewer than 538 applications, and some 37 other matters principally concerning enforcement, discretionary use of its powers, and requests for rulings. At the same time, the Delegates at State and Territory level were dealing with another 955 applications of a more routine nature such as amendments to information provided. The Divisions were scheduled to take place two or three times per week so there was always pressure to prepare our submissions with assessment and recommendation at relatively short notice. During that financial year, the Commission approved some 415 of these applications and knocked back 123.

As regards the work of my team, I soon formed some views about working with lawyers. It seemed to me that, whilst they applied their excellent minds to the complexities of the schemes of their counterparts representing the companies with mental dexterity, they did at times have difficulty making a decision. Often, I would be confronted with *"Well on the one hand ..... But on the other hand"* and I had to make a call. To be honest, apart from managing the workload, allocating individual jobs, and dealing with people issues, I think that was my main contribution and at times I almost relished it. Mind you, this is not to belittle the ability or the practices of the team. Indeed, I learnt a great deal from the legal profession, not least the need to understand what underpinned the law, the meaning of precedent, and the value of making a written note on every meeting, conversation, and telephone call. This would serve me well in the rest of my life.

After my extended lay-off, this hectic role was a great relief. And it was quite exciting to be at the forefront of Australia's corporate activity. Within the NCSC, there were firm views about the honesty or otherwise of Australia's corporate players and the CEO was thought to have a "black book" of potential felons which extended to the highest level of some of the biggest companies. Of particular interest in my time were the financial dealings of people like Alan Bond whose Bell Group sent him bankrupt in the early 1990s, the merchant banker Rene Rifkind, Christopher Skase and the Qintex Group, and some suspicious dealings across the Tasman. I had relatively little involvement with these suspected malfeasants, but they were the regular subject of discussion between staff. And, in late 1988, I was personally involved in making a submission to the House of Representatives Standing Committee on Legal and Constitutional Affairs who were holding an Inquiry into Mergers, Takeovers and Monopolies. The subject of this paper was the need for Consumer Impact Statements, encompassing both the need and the ability to enforce consumer and employee protection through the conduct of post-takeover audits. It was a subject close to my heart after the asset stripping I had experienced in the UK. As it turned out, I did not have to give oral evidence; but attendance at the proceedings of the Australian Parliament deep within the monumental corridors of power in Canberra was instructive, and perhaps I was not entirely surprised to see that at least one MP fell asleep at the wheel!

Whilst there was plenty of engagement with the external environment, the NCSC office was not without its internal politics. How else could it be with a complement of lawyers? The intrigue, not to mention the sexual liaisons, were at times quite astonishing. In particular, there were significant tensions between the senior management and the Commissioners about policy, and a never-ending battle with the media who were prone to criticise the NCSC for being weak and gutless. The first of these criticisms had some merit. The NCSC was but a shadow of the body that succeeded it, ASIC. The resources for enforcement were virtually non-existent, with a small team of lawyers to examine the activities of rampant entrepreneurs, and an even smaller band of law-enforcement officers (ex-police detectives) to implement court orders. And the spectacle of holding the big end of town to account was often played out in the newspapers. The accusation of being gutless was less justified. The CEO Ray Schoer was a robust character who was dedicated to "keeping the bastards honest". And he played his cards carefully to his chest. I was not directly involved, but I think he had some fairly robust exchanges with the Commissioners on whether a given potential target for prosecution should be pursued and he gave a good account of himself in the media.

Despite the political drama, working in the NSCC was not all hard graft and, although there were sometimes meetings late in the day, we did not work long hours. I used to travel to the office on the tram, and would often have a drink on the way home at the Duke of Wellington pub which was at the corner of Queens Street and Flinders Street. And sometimes we went into town for the same purpose. We also enjoyed generous lunch breaks and a particular feature of these days was my interest in Melbourne's amazing restaurants. I acquired myself a copy of the *Age Good Food Guide* and, over my time with the organisation, I systematically worked my way through most of the best. My boss was also a very amicable guy. At weekends he had BBQs at his place in Brunswick. And he was a pilot, as a result of which I had a great flight over the city one lunch time taking off from Essendon airport. And other colleagues showed considerable generosity. In December 1988, when I had not been around long enough to have extended leave, David Danks invited me to join his family for Christmas Day. David's parents lived in Glen Iris and I had a great day. This included a round of golf after lunch at the public course in Fairfield next to the River Yarra. Mind you, my Christmas Day experience brought quite a surprise. Contrary to an agreement that we would not share gifts, David and his wife-to-be Leah decided to give me a male kitten. Somewhat taken aback, I couldn't very well refuse and took him home. I decided to call him Tom and, for a while, he lived with me in Kew. Although I love animals, our time together was at times challenging. When he wasn't asleep, Tom craved company. And sometimes I took him with me as I visited friends. This gave rise to one of the more embarrassing moments in my life. One day, I naively placed him unsecured in a basket on the back seat of the car. The next thing I knew, he was crouched on the back ledge and, as I pulled up at a traffic light, he unloaded himself as the people in the car behind watched with horror! The smell of that disaster lingered on the car for many weeks and did not augur well. Eventually, Tom deserted and I concluded that I was not made for pets.

After about a year at the NCSC, I received some disappointing news. My immediate superior, Geoff Robertson, decided to leave for a job in the private sector and was replaced by a guy named Mark Dickens. Mark had started his career at the NCSC but had tried his hand in the corporate world. However, it did not suit him and he returned to the fold. I found working with him to be quite a challenge. A chain smoker, he was smart but mercurial, with an inclination to be intrusive. At the same time, I had got to the point where I was beginning to tire of the relatively narrow nature of my role. The subject material was interesting, but the issues were becoming repetitive. Luckily, I did have the opportunity in a performance review to share my concerns with an extremely nice guy named Bob Nottle who was Head of Operations and deputy to the CEO. Originally a teacher, Bob had wide experience in the business world, and he could see that I was restive. He alerted me to an impending vacancy as head of the NCSC secretariat. But this seemed to be something of a cul-de-sac. I really felt that I needed something more challenging. In December 1988, Red Cross came calling and I moved on. We pick up my employment story again in Chapter 6.

Whilst it lasted, my time at the NCSC was a wonderful experience and gave me a grounding in Melbourne which I badly needed. It was a great vehicle for transitioning to a new life in a new country, and I am very grateful for the opportunity afforded.

4: Keeping the Bastards Honest

During the initial period of my life in Melbourne, even before I migrated, I did some research into Australian politics. In the days before electronic communications, I sent a letter to the main parties requesting information on policy, and I received some enlightening replies. From my initial reading, it seemed that politics in Australia was a great deal more centrist than in Britain and the system for electing parliamentarians was much fairer. The "Liberal" Party, and their regionally based National Party "Coalition" colleagues, seemed to be centre right and not unlike the British Conservative Party prior to the ascendancy of Margaret Thatcher. The Australian Labor Party ("ALP") had a lot in common with what had been the British Social Democrats, but with the trade union links of the British Labour Party. And the Australian Democrats ("the Democrats"), founded by Don Chipp who wished to "keep the bastards honest", appeared to be squeezed between these two main protagonists.[14] But a closer examination of the Democrats suggested that they had embraced a more progressive policy position. And this was borne out by the fact that one of their previous Senators, a John Siddons, who had implemented a form of industrial democracy in his own engineering company, had recently resigned from the party because of its left leanings.[15] The Australian electoral system was a form of proportional representation with provision for transferring preferences. And voting was compulsory. There was also a written constitution which came into effect on 1 January 1901, a copy of which I obtained.

Apart from this research, I also had some local contacts. Colleagues in the British Liberal Party had given me the names of several leading Democrats and, in the spirit of bringing fraternal greetings, I made contact with the Victorian Division of the party. In October 1986 I visited their offices which were located on the ground floor of a very grand building called the Old Customs House in Flinders Street Melbourne, and met with the State President Sid Spindler.[16] He was a round-faced,

---

[14] At a media conference in the midst of the 1980 election campaign, Chipp described his party's aim as to "keep the bastards honest" - the "bastards" being the major parties and/or politicians in general. This became a long-lived slogan for the Democrats.

[15] Along with Don Chipp, John Siddons was a founder of the Australian Democrats in 1977. Although socially conservative, he believed in worker participation and a strong government role in fostering industrial development. Elected as a Senator, after Chipp's retirement in 1986 he lost a leadership contest to Janine Haines. Concerned about the Party's left leanings, he went on to form the Unite Australia Party and, in the 1987 federal election, he then lost his seat in the Senate. Retiring from politics, he died in 2016.

[16] This building was called the Commonwealth Parliamentary Offices and it was shared with

softly spoken, articulate, and welcoming sort of guy. And we had a very animated conversation in which it became apparent that the Democrats had a lot in common with the British Liberal Democrat Party, not least in my specialist field of employment and industrial relations. He also introduced me to both Senator Powell, who was a warm, friendly, and fresh-faced woman, and a number of office staff including Geelong Councillor Hans Paas who was Chair of the Democrats Victorian State Council, and a research officer named Marcus Bosch. As I left, Sid gave me a range of material on Democrat policy and activities, and I undertook to send him a similar set of documents developed by the British Liberal Democrat Party. And in November I was invited to attend a meeting of the National Executive where I met further members of the party and obtained some insight into their proceedings, with the Federal nature of the organisation very evident. Subsequently, I met Janet Powell at her office at the YWCA, for a longer discussion on current issues, and I attended the Christmas Party.

On my return to Melbourne in May 1987, and after the debacle with Drake, I was at something of a loose end. And, impressed by my first contact, I got in touch with the Democrats to offer my services on a voluntary basis. After 15 years of political activism in the UK, it had become part of my normal life to be directly engaged in campaigning on social and political and issues. I immediately felt at home, and it was a great diversion from my recent setback. Marcus Bosch was particularly welcoming.[17] He had recently been appointed as State Secretary, and I soon found myself working as an electorate officer with a variety of administrative tasks, not to mention debating political issues with other staff. Then, even as I was sitting in the Democrat offices one quiet Friday afternoon in late May, Prime Minister Bob Hawke called a Federal Election, which was to take place on 11 July.[18] It was all hands on deck.

Whilst the pretext for what was an early and Double Dissolution election was the Senate's decision to reject the government's Australia Card legislation, Hawke had more compelling reasons.[19] The political

---

politicians from other Commonwealth parties. It is now the Australian Immigration Museum.

[17] Marcus Bosch later turned out to be the son of the NCSC's Henry Bosch. This connection was entirely coincidental.

[18] The previous Federal Election had been in December 1984. In Australia, elections are scheduled to take place within three years from the date that Parliament first meets after any given election.

[19] The Australia Card was an identity card designed to standardise access to government social security payments. It was strongly opposed by the Democrats as an infringement of personal liberty. Double Dissolution meant that the whole Senate was up for election. In an ordinary Federal Election, only half the Senate are elected.

situation in Australia at that time was quite intriguing. The leader of the opposition Liberal Party was a rather uninspiring and conservative politician named John Howard. An unremarkable Treasurer under Malcolm Fraser, in September 1985 Howard had managed to wrestle the party leadership from a "small l" Liberal named Andrew Peacock.[20] Peacock was the MP for the Victorian seat of Kooyong, which he had inherited from Sir Robert Menzies.[21] After losing the leadership he agreed to serve under Howard in the Shadow ministry. But he was far from happy. Then, in January 1987, the National Party Premier of Queensland Joe Bjelke Petersen announced his intention to run for a seat in Canberra. Although he was eventually persuaded to change his mind, this triggered huge dissension between the Coalition partners. Then, in March, Peacock was recorded making some uncomplimentary remarks about Howard during a car-telephone conversation with the Victorian State Liberal Leader Jeff Kennett.[22] And he was sacked from Howard's team. These signs of disunity were a gift for the Hawke government.

The timing of the election couldn't have been better as far as I was concerned. And for the Democrats there was everything to play for. At the time, the Party was led by the first female leader in Australian history, South Australian Senator Janine Haines. Having inherited the party from its founder, Don Chipp, she had youth and charisma on her side. And in Victoria, having taken over the Victorian seat held by Don Chipp after he retired, Janet Powell was now standing for election in her own right for the first time.[23]

As the Australian Democrat Victorian Division moved into election mode, there was a real buzz in the office. In this election there were some 37 Victorian House of Representative seats in the Federal Parliament, and 12 Senate seats. It quickly emerged that Marcus was a candidate for a lower house seat (Deakin) as were a number of the other people in the office that I had already met. And, in quick order, others emerged from around the State. Whilst there were some older campaigners, most were young and enthusiastic people with a passion to overthrow the old order. To them, the Liberal Party under Howard was anathema, and the Labor

---

[20] In the 2020s, you don't hear the expression "small l" Liberal very often. After thirteen years of the Howard ascendancy commencing in 1996, the "Liberal" Party is preponderantly a conservative political force with a few progressive hangers on.

[21] Kooyong has been a seat since the Commonwealth of Australia was created in 1901.

[22] The telephone call was picked up by a journalist and broadcast on the radio.

[23] When a Senator resigns, the system provides for the Party to which the retiring member belongs to nominate a replacement to complete the term.

Party were not much better. Both traditional parties were perceived to be steeped in vested interests to the detriment of the wider public good.

In the next six weeks I threw myself into the campaign, working from the offices in Flinders Street. And I had a lot to learn, as elections in Australia were conducted in a distinctly different way from Britain. It wasn't just that campaigns were being run for both lower and upper house seats. In Australia, there was far less emphasis on canvassing and the kind of public meetings in which I had engaged as a candidate in the 1983 British General Election. Instead, there was emphasis on radio interviews, walkabouts, television appearances, press releases and distribution of leaflets. And the parties ran TV advertising with quite robust messaging that consisted of simple slogans, some of which rubbished the opposition.

My working day encompassed many tasks and I became a jack of all trades. One minute I would be meeting a candidate visiting the office for a briefing. The next I would be off to the post office with a load of mail. I helped to co-ordinate the completion and submission of nomination papers, maintained a register of candidate details and created a large map of the State reflecting the state of play on current activities. I was despatched as a courier to deliver messages and articles to the offices of suburban newspapers, and I liaised with a translator to check through the accuracy of leaflets translated into a number of foreign languages. I took and made many phone calls, and assisted in liaising with potential donors, with the raising of finance a key factor in the Party's ability to run TV commercials. And I attended gatherings of the party faithful for rousing speeches from our local leaders. I was also engaged with my local branch in the Liberal blue-ribbon seat of Higgins which was held by a man named Roger Shipton.[24] At the crack of dawn, I would stand outside railway stations handing out party literature, and in the evening and at weekends I would deliver leaflets door to door.

By the close of nominations, the Party had mustered candidates for all but two of the lower house seats in Victoria, Indi and Mallee, which were sparsely populated rural electorates on the northern boundary of the State adjoining the River Murray. It was a creditable effort given that we were such a small party. The next significant task was the preparation of what I regarded (and still regard) as the dreaded "How to Vote" Cards, and printing of posters with candidates' names.[25] I was particularly interested

---

[24] Created in 1949, the Higgins electorate had been represented by two former PMs, Harold Holt and John Gorton. It would later be held by Treasurer Peter Costello.
[25] How to Vote Cards are handed to electors as they enter polling booths by each of the main

to see how the Party came up with its preference deals. Negotiations were relatively confidential, but there was significant open debate in the office. Some in the party had strongly held views that it was up to the public to determine their own preferences. And, in any event, it seemed likely that any agreement to exchange preferences would favour the ALP with both parties relying on preference flows from the other, especially in the Senate count.

The election campaign at a national level ran what my colleagues said was a predictable course. The ALP quickly dropped the proposal to introduce an Australia Card and exploited the disunity between the Liberal and National Parties, who determined to run separate campaigns for the Senate and failed to agree preference flows.[26] And there were three-cornered fights in many electorates, the last time this would ever happen.[27]

At the official "launch" of the campaigns, scheduled for about three weeks before Election Day but already well after hustings had started, the leaders of the two main parties made their pitch at large stage-managed meetings. Howard put a brave face on it but was uninspiring, whilst Hawke spoke with passion. Thereafter, Howard quickly ran into difficulties when estimates for funding Liberal tax-cut proposals were revealed to be $900 million short. It was something he could not deny and undermined his attempt to portray the party as better economic managers. And the ALP wiped the floor with the Liberal Party in televised and radio coverage with their slogan "Let's Stick Together". They reminded the public of Howard's time as Treasurer, when he had failed to deliver promised tax cuts. And they asked how the Liberals could run the country when they couldn't manage the Coalition. In response, the Liberals tried to suggest that the ALP ran up debt and misspent tax-payers' money. The Democrats got little TV coverage and had just one advertisement which lasted 30 seconds. It referred to the people in the regions that the main parties tended to take for granted, and ended with a simple message from the Party Leader Janine Haines - *"For social and economic justice, and for a safe and secure future, you can*

---

parties, with an indication of that party's preferences.

[26] In the campaign, I secured a letter in the *Age* newspaper on the Australia Card issue. It said *"Justice is not served by instituting a new evil to tackle an old one. Even with the strictest data protection laws, the ID Card is a serious threat to our civil liberties. There are other more effective ways to deal with tax and welfare cheats."*

[27] Normally, in the House of Representatives, one coalition partner would not run a candidate against a sitting member representing the other Coalition party.

depend on us." This was very much a pitch for the balance of power in the Senate.

On Election Day I got my first experience on a polling booth, handing out the How to Vote Cards which focussed on the Senate ticket. I spent five hours at a polling station at the Malvern South Primary School in support of the Democrat candidate for Higgins, a young fellow named Clive Jackson. And I was surprised by the friendliness displayed between the representatives from opposing parties. In Britain, representatives of the main parties tended to keep their distance, with hostility to the third-party Liberals who were accused of "intervening". In this election, the Liberal and ALP workers were sociable middle-class people who were happy to discuss political issues without rancour. And some Liberal supporters made it clear that they were not big fans of John Howard. It may not have been a typical election, nor a typical polling booth. But there was a refreshing absence of class-based antagonism.

At 6.00pm the polls closed and I returned to base. I joined the Divisional team and had the opportunity to visit the Senate Count, which was held in the Melbourne Town Hall. With a system encompassing preferences flows, it was a slow process. And I was intrigued to see how party representatives were watching the ballot papers closely to see how preferences flowed between parties. Feedback from Democrat scrutineers suggested some clear patterns linking ALP and Democrat votes. In any event, with a long way to go, we returned to the Divisional offices in Flinders Street to watch the election coverage on a huge TV whilst we got stuck into some food and grog. By the end of the night it was clear that the ALP had secured a 24 seat majority in the House of Representatives, with a 50.8% Two Party Preferred vote to the Coalition's 49.2%. To me, that seemed a very small margin. But I was told that this was a resounding victory. In the Senate, the Democrats had won 7 seats with the balance of power. And this was the cause of much celebration. However, the results for the Democrats were bitter sweet. In Victoria, where two Democrat Senate seats were being defended, the water had been muddied by the aforementioned John Siddons who stood as a candidate for the new Unite Australia party. As a result, while Janet Powell was elected for a six-year term with much acclamation, the second seat was lost to the Liberals with Sid Spindler missing out. In the House of Representatives, the Democrats achieved a 6% vote with no-one elected. This was seen as a creditable performance, with Howard McCallum the top performer in the seat of Jaga Jaga, with 8.6%.

After the July 1987 election, everyone involved in the campaign took some time off from politics, including me. However, I had met some great people and made a number of new friends. And the Victoria Division were keen to retain my support and involvement. With time on my hands as I tried to find a job, my competencies were quickly put to work. As State Secretary, Marcus Bosch enrolled me as a member of the Administrative Committee, of which I became the secretary for the next three years. This body had responsibility for oversight of the party's finances, membership, branches, and fund-raising. And it had a number of sub-committees, one of which I undertook to chair, the Fund Raising and Gifting Committee. Unfortunately, just I was getting stuck into this activity, I got the NCSC job. As a Commonwealth government employee, it seemed a little inappropriate for me to be pursuing folks for donations and, after three months, I stepped down. However, I did start to attend a number of State Council and Executive meetings acting as Minutes Secretary.

Through these activities, I began to get a better handle on what kind of folk belonged to this organisation. And it did indeed have a lot in common with the British Liberal Party. There were certainly the "small l" liberals who had followed Don Chipp out of the Liberal Party following the dismissal of the Whitlam government in the 1970s. They constituted the right wing of the membership. But, in the days before the Australian Greens, the Party appeared to be a natural home for environmentalists, including people associated with the Wilderness Society, and there was a special-interest group called the Democrat Greens. There were also anti-nuclear and peace activists, to whom the ALP were anathema because that party was seen as having sold out to capitalism, supporters of radical tax policies, and United Nations activists.[28] This made the Party quite a broad church, involving considerable variation at State and Territory level. With the Victoria Division being of the centre-left variety, I felt very much at home.

Following the 1987 Federal Election, the focus switched to State politics. At the time, Victoria had an ALP government led by Premier John Cain, with Jeff Kennett the leader of the Opposition. By many Victorian citizens, this wasn't considered to be the normal order of things. In the days of Prime Minister Menzies, Victoria had been

---

[28] The Party had an uneasy electoral alliance with the Nuclear Disarmament Party which had been founded in 1984, mainly by members of the ALP who were disenchanted with the pro-nuclear stance of Bob Hawke. This party secured a seat in the Senate from WA in 1984 (Jo Vallentine) and a seat from NSW in 1987 (Robert Wood). But otherwise, with many internal party arguments, it never made much ground.

regarded as the "jewel in the crown", with 27 years of Liberal government under Sir Henry Bolte, Sir Rupert Hamer and Lindsay Thompson. However, in 1982, the government had run out of steam, with the ALP led by John Cain coming to power.[29] Lindsay Thompson stood down as Liberal Leader, with a young Jeff Kennett becoming the Leader of the Opposition. Kennett had entered Parliament in 1976 after a career in the army and then marketing. He was seen as brash and abrasive, but in the 1985 election he'd achieved a 3% swing back to the Liberals, and in 1988 was hoping for a win.[30] However, the ALP government was still seen as competent and Kennett's chances were undermined by the continuing instability at the Federal level with rivalry between Howard and Peacock.

In early 1988, we began to prepare for the State election, and there was significant debate about what kind of campaign the Democrats should pursue. Previously, the party had only contested upper-house seats and had failed to secure any, with just 4% of the vote in 1985. This time it was decided to switch our efforts to the lower house, the Legislative Assembly. This was not with any great expectation of winning a seat. Our main focus was to maintain our election infrastructure, and give the public a continuing opportunity to vote Democrat in the hope that the habit would carry through to the next Federal Election. We started to pre-select candidates and, in August, John Cain called the election to take place on 1 October. The organisation did its best to find lower-house candidates but, with few Democrat members interested in State politics, we could only find 18 candidates to stand in the 88 lower-house seats.

For this election, Marcus and I lent our personal support to Howard McCallum who had done so well in the Jaga Jaga seat in the 1987 Federal Election. This time he was standing in the State electorate of Ivanhoe, which overlapped with the Jaga Jaga seat. In planning the campaign, our activities were very similar to a Federal Election. However, I had spent quite a bit of time introducing Marcus and others to the concepts of community politics. And I convinced them to have a real attempt at canvassing (or door-knocking as they called it). This was novel for them and there was some scepticism about the reception we would get from Australian voters who were not used to people asking leading questions on the doorstep. In the event, it went quite well, particularly for the

---

[29] The Liberals lost 17 seats in the 1982 election, less than 12 months after Lindsay Thompson took over as Premier from Hamer.

[30] In these days, State elections were held every three years.

candidate himself who got to meet a lot more people than he might usually have done. But, in terms of "maximising" the vote, it had less impact than in Britain because of compulsory voting.[31] In any event, after work and at weekends, I put in a lot of time and effort into canvassing and "letter-boxing" as Australians called leaflet drops.

The outcome of this State Election was fairly close. Cain won a third term with a majority of just two seats, 46 to 44 and the Liberals actually got more than 50% of the two party preferred vote. They were ropeable. In the 18 seats where candidates stood, the Democrats secured an average of around 5%. However, Howard McCallum topped the Democrat poll with 7.51% of the vote in Ivanhoe. We were well pleased.

After the State poll, my involvement with the Democrats quietened down for a while. In late 1988, I bought and moved into a house in Kew, resigned from the NCSC and, as we will see in Chapter 6, in early 1989 I took up a job at the Red Cross Blood Bank Victoria which was quite demanding. However, I continued as a member of the State Administrative Committee and continued working at the local level. The Chairperson in my new electorate of Kooyong was a lovely lady named Jill Leisegang who had done well as a Democrat candidate for Federal Parliament, and the local team were a delightful group. In early 1989, and given my background and experience, I became involved in another area of activity. I joined a policy committee working on Employment, Training, and Industrial Relations issues which was chaired by a young fellow named Peter Taft who was Party Spokesperson for these areas of policy as well as Youth Affairs. The experience was a revelation, with outcomes sometimes questionable. The process for development and adoption of policy was highly convoluted, with the State Council debating and redrafting words and phrases in lengthy documents, and lengthy periods for membership input. This sometimes produced almost unintelligible wording. And the Committee did not have the kind of close working relationships with the Party's politicians which the British equivalent had.

In 1990, another Federal Election loomed. But then, out of the blue, there was more action at the State level. On 16 December 1989, the ALP member for Thomastown, Beth Gleeson, passed away with a by-election set for 3 February 1990. This was a part of Melbourne in which Marcus Bosch's partner, Christine Craik, lived and, after some deliberation, she

---

[31] In the UK, where turnout in local elections can be as low as 30%, one of the benefits of a comprehensive canvass is that you can win by achieving a disproportionately higher turnout amongst your own supporters.

agreed to become the Democrat candidate. Although I didn't give a lot of time to the campaign, I did make a substantial financial contribution and Christine achieved an outstanding result. Standing against ALP aficionado Peter Bachelor, she got 19.5% of the primary vote putting her just behind the Liberal candidate. But in the preference count, she overtook the Liberal and gave Bachelor a run for his money. She finished with 46.3% of the Two Party Preferred vote which was probably the best ever result for any Democrat running for a Victorian Legislative assembly seat.

After that excellent result in February, the 24 March 1990 Federal Election would see a high point for the Australian Democrats, nationally and locally. In early 1989, Howard had been struggling in the polls. And, in typical style, Keating said of his performance in Parliament that *"it's like being flogged by a dead lettuce"*. Seizing the moment, in May 1989, Andrew Peacock had challenged for the leadership and resumed the role. Keating was scathing, posing the question in Parliament *"Can the soufflé rise twice?"* Despite this ridicule, Peacock's return changed the odds and suddenly the Liberals were "back in town". In the meantime, Janine Haines decided to try and break the mould by gaining a seat for the Democrats in the House of Representatives. She retired from the Senate and stood for the South Australian seat of Kingston. It was a big gamble.

With the ALP seeking a fourth term, the 1990 Election campaign would prove to be a tight affair in which the environment would play a significant part. In particular, in July 1989, Hawke committed the Government to a collaborative land-care program with the Australian Conservation Foundation and the National Farmers Federation. And, under a strategy developed by Graham Richardson, the ALP made commitments on a range of other environmental issues, including an undertaking to ban substantial mining activity in Kakadu National Park. This would pay rich dividends in preference votes from Democrat voters. The ALP also sought to extend its constituency way beyond its traditional trade union base, with policies that appealed to women, immigrants, Aborigines, youth, and the gay community.[32]

The results of the Federal Election were tight and, despite a weakness on environment policy, Peacock performed well in the campaign. In the event, whilst the Coalition picked up seven seats, and actually won the Two Party Preferred count by 50.1% to 49.9%, the ALP won a slim majority. In part, this was thanks to the flow of preferences from the

---

[32] This paragraph draws on material published on 24 November 1997 by Dr Rodney Sullivan of the Politics and Public Administration Group.

Democrats and other parties with environmental interests in a number of key seats. The Coalition felt that they had been robbed, and were furious about Democrat preference deals with the ALP. In the Senate, the Democrats again held the balance of power, with the ALP holding 32 seats, the Coalition 34, and the Democrats 8. In addition, the WA Greens won a seat and there was an independent.[33]

For the Democrats, the results were bitter sweet. Janine Haines failed to win her seat in the House of Representatives, coming third in her electorate. And the party also lost a seat in Western Australia through a failure to conclude a preference deal with the ALP. However, in Victoria, Sid Spindler won a seat in the Senate to join Janet Powell. And across the country there was a big rise in the Democrats Primary vote, which reached an all-time peak of 12.6%. My role was modest. I delivered leaflets at weekends and manned a polling booth on Election Day. And we had a night to remember in celebration of Sid's victory. After the election, with the loss of the leader Janine Haines, South Australian Senator Meg Lees took over as caretaker, pending the election of Janet Powell as leader with South Australian John Coulter as Deputy.

Riding on this success, and with Councillor Hans Paas now its President, 1990 saw the Victorian State Democrats move out of the Commonwealth Parliamentary offices into their own premises at 71 Smith Street Fitzroy. It was great to have an independent base, although the new location represented challenges, with drug dealers at street corners. Towards the end of the year, I changed roles, retiring from the Administrative Committee and taking up a position on the Candidates Endorsement Committee ("CEC") of which I would eventually become the Chair. The CEC was responsible for vetting candidates seeking pre-selection for Federal and State seats. And, for the remainder of my time with the Democrats, this would become the main focus of my activity. At the time, we were selecting candidates for the next State election in 1991, and we endorsed a number of interesting people including the anti-duck-shooting campaigner Laurie Levy.

In the next year, Janet Powell established herself as an effective and inclusive national leader of the Democrats. But her term would be short-lived. Sadly, in response to both her way of working, and her progressive position on certain policies, there were significant forces in the Party determined to bring her down. In 1990, war was brewing in the Middle East with Saddam Hussein invading Kuwait. The Australian Democrats

---

[33] The WA Greens eventually joined with other Green groups in a national Greens Party.

had a long-standing policy to oppose war, and ensured that there was a full debate in the Senate on proposals for Australian participation. This was not well received by Australia's right-leaning media and the Democrats were the subject of sustained attacks. Consequently, in 1991 support for the Democrats started to slip with Janet's performance being blamed. And the South Australian and Queensland divisions were soon circulating a petition to have her removed as leader. When the media got hold of this, the reasons for the move against her were expanded to include criticisms of her administrative competence and suggestions of an inappropriate relationship with Senator Sid Spindler. And there was even talk in some circles that she had had secret talks with the Greens about some sort of partnership. In the first half of 1991 there was mounting pressure and then, on 19 August 1991, there was a leadership spill. With the blessing of the Democrat National Executive, she was replaced on a caretaker basis by Deputy Leader John Coulter.

Not surprisingly, this turn of events left Janet Powell's supporters in Victoria and elsewhere totally stunned. And, despite continued Democrat success in a number of subsequent elections, things would never be the same again. NSW Senator Paul McLean resigned in disgust, and the party's founding leader, Don Chipp, described the coup as the *"most tragic story to have hit the Democrats"*. Subsequently, Cheryl Kernot was elected as leader. And, in 1992, Janet resigned from the party to continue as an independent senator until she lost her seat at the 1993 election.

For loyal supporters and friends like myself, Janet's demise was a major blow. For five years, I had committed huge amounts of time and energy to a party that seemed to embrace my values and the sort of policies with which I was comfortable. And through its role in the Senate, the Party had had a real say in national policy. In all honesty, I found this turn of events and level of internal politics quite breath-taking. It made the proceedings of the British Liberal Party look like a tea party, and there was little doubt that loss of integrity was the price of personal ambition. After a long think about my values and loyalties, and along with many leading figures of the Victorian branch of the Party, in August 1992 I followed Janet's lead and resigned from the Australian Democrats. And subsequently, I well remember receiving a telephone call from a Party stalwart accusing me of treachery. It was a deeply embittering experience for all concerned.

The immediate impact of this infighting was a huge drop in the vote for the Democrats. In the 1993 Federal Election, when Paul Keating

40

defeated John Hewson in an ALP victory for *"The True Believers"*, the Democrat vote dropped to 5%. But the Party held onto seven Senate seats in a tightly contested Half-Senate election. Then, in the 1996 Federal Election, with the Coalition under Howard coming to power, Kernot led the Party to something of a revival winning 10.8% of the vote and comfortable retaining seven Senate seats. But in 1997 Kernot resigned to eventually emerge as a member of the ALP, and Megg Lees was elected as leader. In the 1998 and 2001 elections the Party held on to its seats. But, following Meg Lees' support for the GST and her ineffective leadership on a number of other issues, the Party went into terminal decline, eventually being replaced as a third force by the Greens.[34]

As a footnote, after a period as an independent, in 1996 Janet Powell campaigned for the Greens. And as the Democrats showed terminal decline with just 2.1% of the vote in the 2004 Federal election, she joined the Greens Party, citing that they were more capable of achieving the function of a third force in Australian politics. She was an unsuccessful candidate for them in the 2006 Victorian election. Sadly, she died in 2013. For me she was an inspiration and, like many Democrat supporters of the 1980s and 1990s, I followed her in supporting the new third-force although I would never again be a member of a political party. I had had enough of internecine warfare for one life.

---

[34] The Greens were formed as a political party in 1992, from supporters of the environmental movement, remnants of the nuclear disarmament movement, and sections of the industrial left in New South Wales. Dr Bob Brown was elected as the first Greens Senator, representing Tasmania, in 1996. As Democrat fortunes waned, support for the Greens increased. They now have nine seats in the Senate and have made the all-important breakthrough with a seat in the House of Representatives held by Adam Bandt representing Melbourne.

5: Out and About in Melbourne

Over the last thirty-five years, the city of Melbourne has changed enormously, with a growing skyline of skyscrapers, a regenerated river frontage, refurbished docklands and expanded cultural infrastructure. In recent times, it has been voted the world's most liveable city on numerous occasions, vying with Vancouver and Vienna amongst others.[35] In the mid-1980s, such claims did not exist and, before choosing to live there, several people had made critical comments about the place. According to my NSW relatives, it was the wet and windy capital of the wowser state, with an absence of gambling venues, and pub-free suburbs. The Yarra River was brown and polluted, and the streets were full of clattering old trams with bizarre road rules such as *"the hook turn"*. According to guidebooks, the weather was fickle, with *"four seasons in one day"*. But these were largely jaundiced views, born of envy, and, having visited in the early 1980s, I had more positive expectations. On settling in the city, I encountered an excellent quality of life in terms of infrastructure, public transport, affordability, and cultural activity. There was also a rich diversity of populations built on several waves of migration from Italy, Greece, and Vietnam. In the 1980s, there were only a few skyscrapers, and the wide streets were more akin to European boulevards with grand 19th century architecture, especially at the "Paris" end of Collins Street.

People in Melbourne showed a fanatical interest in sport, and I soon discovered that "barracking" for a local football team was a tribal rite and prerequisite for belonging.[36] The interest in sport was manifest in an abundance of sporting grounds, the biggest of which, the Melbourne Cricket Ground ("MCG" or even just the "G"), had been the Olympic stadium in 1956 and held upwards of 100,000 people. This was the home of both cricket and football. Melbourne also hosted the Melbourne Cup, run at Flemington Racecourse on the first Tuesday in November which was a public holiday, and one of the four Grand Slam Open Tennis tournaments.[37] And, from 1996, Melbourne became the home of the

---

[35] The Economist's index on the quality of life in the world's cities commenced in 2010, with Melbourne ranked the world's "Most Liveable City" for seven years in a row.

[36] The word "barrack" is an Australian term meaning "support". In Melbourne, football refers to Australian Rules Football. In the 1980s, teams played in the Victorian Football League (VFL). The main national football code, this is now called the AFL.

[37] The home of the Australian Grand Slam event moved from the Kooyong Tennis Club to what was initially called Flinders Park in 1988. The State government renamed the National Tennis facility Melbourne Park in 1996.

Formula 1 Australian Grand Prix. The city also accommodated active competition in just about every other sport you can think of, including the round ball game that Australians called "soccer" and both codes of rugby.

The part of Melbourne in which I had chosen to live during my initial foray was Toorak. I had selected this suburb on the advice of the McArthur family, and it turned out to be a very well healed place with Melbourne's most expensive property (over $1 million dollars for a mansion even in those days). And the ice-cold local supermarket had prices to match, with ladies in fur coats who abandoned their trolleys in the street to be collected by the shop later in the day. In comparison with the mansions that many of the residents occupied, my little furnished flat was a modest affair. I had a living room with a view across the expansive Como Oval, a bedroom, a kitchen, a bathroom and a laundry.[38] It was on the second floor and included a car-parking space at ground level. The centre of Toorak was within a short walking distance, where there were restaurants, a range of shops, a boutique cinema, the Trak night club, and the No 8 tram route into the city. And the River Yarra was also only a short distance away with a bike track to the city. In short, it was a highly civilised place to live, conveniently located, and with every amenity.

After surviving the experience at Drake Personnel, in October 1987 I had joined the NCSC. Now that I had a substantial job providing some security, I made one of the biggest decisions of my time in Australia which was to purchase a residence. Although I still had a cottage in Lincolnshire, with the help of my mother I had already sold the flat I owned in London and my house contents were in storage. The sale of the flat had generated a handsome financial return and I had the best part of £75,000 to spend on a new home.[39] With Melbourne prices considerably below those in London, this offered a once in a life time opportunity to relieve myself of mortgage debt. After some research into affordable inner-city suburbs, I decided to buy a property in the Eastern suburbs with connections to the city by tram. In those parts of the city there was no shortage of what the locals called units (equivalent to British town houses), and in October/November I attended several street auctions to get the hang of what was a novel house-buying process for someone from Britain. There were several properties on my radar and, after a few near

---

[38] Como Oval was the "backyard" of Como House, a national trust property dating from 1847 and originally owned by the Armytage family.

[39] In those days, this translated into $165,000. Interestingly, during my time in Australia, this exchange rate has varied considerably with the A$ worth as little as 35p and as much as 80p.

misses, on 15 November 1987 I made a successful bid for Unit 7 at 44 High Street Kew for the princely sum of $149,250. The settlement date was 60 days hence and I took ownership on 14 January 1988.

The move to Kew began an association with that part of Melbourne that lasts to this day. In 1988, the suburb was a quiet and refined kind of place. It was said that the biggest traffic risk was to be run-over by an older person's wheel-chair. There were a few undistinguished pubs, a handful of restaurants, a supermarket, a bottle shop, and a library. There were also several private schools, with Xavier College just a stone's throw away and shouts from adjacent playing fields evident on a Saturday morning in winter. My part of High Street was serviced by two tram services which went to different parts of the Melbourne CBD, with the 5 km journey taking around 20-30 minutes depending on the time of day. The 48 tram took you past the MCG, and Flinders Street station, and the 109 took you to Spencer Street Station.[40] And in those days, it was also easy to drive into town, with ample relatively cheap parking to access theatres, pubs, and clubs in the city.

My three bedroomed property was down a leafy walkway off the main road and, apart from the trundling and screeching of trams, it was a quiet spot overlooked by mature trees. A two-storey building in a terrace of three, it had patios at front and rear, and underground parking with a security gate. It was a little smaller than I was used to, but served my purpose. And, in no time, my furniture arrived from Britain. Over a long weekend in January 1988, I emptied the packing cases and set up home.

Over the next several years, Kew became the focal point of my life and, if you had to live in a city, you couldn't do much better. Apart from the convenience of public transport to the NCSC offices in Queen Street, it was close to some beautiful parkland next to the River Yarra with a café and restaurant at what was called the Studley Park boatyard. And I continued to frequent the facilities in Toorak. My taste in restaurants veered towards French (France Soir in South Yarra), Indian (Café Legend in Hawthorn), Italian (Romeo's in Toorak), and Thai (Strictly Thai in Kew).

When I look back to the first couple of years in Australia, I realise that I was fortunate to establish some important relationships that served a purpose but did not necessarily last the course. This is not to disparage the people with whom I became involved. But in the normal course of a life, most of your friends are people with whom you have become

---

[40] After substantial redevelopment, in 2015, this was renamed Southern Cross Station.

associated over a long period of time through common values and interests. When you are an immigrant, the rules are different. As an outsider, it is impossible to insert yourself into well-established groups of people of your own age. And Melbourne was a particularly close-knit community, where most of the residents spent their whole lives with the same circle of family and friends. So, I made acquaintances where I could, and mostly they were transient people that I met through work or leisure activities who were younger than myself. They were a diverse group with whom I shared a passing interest and, 35 years later, few are significant people in my life. Having said that, without these people, I would not have survived. And in this memoir they are worth more than just a mention.

I have already mentioned Deborah Towns for whom I will always have a special affection, and I am pleased for her that she is now happily married to a worthy fellow. For quite a few years, I maintained a close relationship with Marcus Bosch with whom I had endless political discussion. He taught me a lot about the Australian body politic and left me in no doubt that Don Bradman was the greatest ever batsman. Sadly, when we both left the Australian Democrats and he went to live in the outer suburbs, we lost touch. At my initial place of work, the NCSC, the most significant friend was David Danks. For quite a while, he and his partner Leah practically adopted me as a family member, and I especially remember their supporting me at my citizenship ceremony in 1989. We remained good friends for a number of years until we drifted apart.

In those early years, I met several people through participation in pennant squash. The most significant of these was Robin Brown. Robin came from the ACT and was a medical student. A highly intelligent and creative guy, he had certain eccentric habits, despised authority, and did not suffer fools gladly. But he played a mean game of squash, and we enjoyed many lengthy discussions over very long dinners. In 1988, he and I decided to attend the Melbourne Cup. It was a stinking hot day and we decided to dress with formal wear on the top half of the body and shorts and thongs below. Armed with eskies, we duly arrived at the course and walked from the railway station towards the entrance. Along the way, I was stopped by a policeman who told me that I was not allowed to take grog into the enclosure. However, hearing from my voice that I was a Pom, he said that if I walked back ten metres and covered up the alcohol with a cloth, he would wave me through. And that's what he did! With all that grog, I did not see much of the Melbourne Cup. But we had a great afternoon and my views about law and order were changed for ever. During the time I knew him, Robin got into some serious scrapes which made life interesting. And I have fond memories of visits to a property he acquired in Yarragon. Eventually, life took us in different directions. He got married to a delightful English girl named Angela, became a notable surgeon, and had three daughters. The last I heard of him, he had built a boutique brewery in his back yard.

Finally, I made several good friends through playing bridge. I learnt this game as a teenager and, during university days, I used have pretty lengthy sessions after returning from the pub on a Saturday night. Subsequently, apart from a few social games with my mother and her friends, I had given it away. In Melbourne, I joined a bridge club at the ESU in South Yarra which was run by a very well-known couple named Jim and Norma Borin.[41] Jim was a larger than life character with a load of charm that encouraged less experienced players. And he attracted some colourful clients including a middle-aged couple who were allowed to drink claret, and whose bidding got more adventurous as the night wore on! I joined up with a girl named Leonie Elphinstone, and for a time we became firm friends although nothing serious developed. She eventually got married and moved to Queensland. Through the bridge club I also met Gill Lavers with whom I played intermittently for many years. Gill was an ex-pat English lady, with a charming husband named Doug, and we became good friends. When I started to spend a lot of time out of Melbourne, and we stopped playing bridge together, we drifted apart.

Finally, throughout this early period of my life in Melbourne, I continued to see the McArthur family who were the exception to the rule as regards transient relationships. Periodically I would catch up with Christopher as he completed university, moved into a house with mates, and began to work for a company investing in Artificial Intelligence. And, every so often, we would go for bush walks with his father John. Eventually he married Anne and I attended their wedding in Swan Hill. They now have two grown-up sons, Cameron and Lachlan, and live in Sydney. Christopher remains one of my closest friends.

---

[41] The Borins were Australian Bridge champions. Jim was born in England and set up a bridge Club in with his wife Norma in South Yarra in 1970. In the 1980s they outgrew their premises and moved to the ESU. Jim died in 2003.

PART TWO

GROUNDING

6: A Blood Donation

After about 18 months of working at the National Companies and Securities Commission, I became restless. Although my appointment had been a life-saver, the corporate world in the Australia of the late 1980s was not very inspiring. And, although a fun place to work, the organisation that had been established to regulate the business community was ineffective through lack of compliance and investigatory resources. I was not actively seeking a new job but, one day in late 1988, I saw an advertisement placed by the Victorian Division of the Australian Red Cross Society ("ARC Victoria") for the appointment of a senior administrator to lead the modernisation of their blood transfusion service called Red Cross Blood Bank Victoria ("RCBBV"). This caught my eye not least because I was a long-time blood donor, and a supporter of what I perceived to be the organisation's mission.

I made an application to ARC Victoria, and was invited to an initial interview with a panel comprising members of the BTS ("Blood Transfusion Service") Management Sub Committee, and a man in his early forties who was the recently appointed RCBBV Director named Dr Gordon Whyte. They appraised me of the purpose and activities of RCBBV, which was one of a family of similar Red Cross organisations located within every State and Territory of Australia. And they stressed that, while RCBBV was a part of ARC Victoria, it relied on government financial support, currently had inadequate funding ($20 million per annum), operated in a difficult industrial relations environment with around 400 (350 Effective Full Time) staff belonging to a number of different trade unions, and had administrative systems which were in urgent need of modernisation. They then questioned me about my own background and experience and pronounced that I appeared to be more than qualified for the job. But they had a couple of concerns. They did not pay very well, and they couldn't really understand how someone with my corporate background would be happy working in a public health services organisation. In response, I explained that, with significant personal wealth acquired from highly paid jobs in the private sector, at this stage in my life I was unusually placed to give my time and experience without particular regard to the level of remuneration. And, being a blood donor myself, I conveyed my enthusiasm about working for what I regarded as a very worthy organisation helping healthy people to support the recovery of the sick. With that riposte, the interview ended on a high note of mutual regard. Ten days later, I was invited to meet with Gordon Whyte, followed by a final interview with the panel. In December, I was offered the job, which I duly accepted. It was one of the best decisions I had made in a long time and, together with the acquisition of the property in Kew, it truly marked the beginning of a new life in a new country.

I took up the role of what was initially called the Assistant Director Administration on Thursday 12 January 1989. At the time, I wondered whether this "Assistant" tag reflected a view that "administration", in an organisation led by doctors seeking to meet medical imperatives, was regarded as a necessary but lesser competency. The two senior positions were the Director (a doctor) and a yet to be appointed Deputy Director (a doctor). But perhaps their use of "Assistant" was just a way of putting me on probation. In any event, the tag was short lived and, as Director Administration, I soon became one of a triumvirate of organisational leaders. For most of my first year there was just me and Gordon Whyte. But, towards the end of 1989, we were joined by Dr Patrick Coghlan who was recruited as Deputy Director from his role as head of the blood transfusion service in Cape Town, South Africa. He arrived in October.

My first few days at RCBBV in Balston Street, South Melbourne were enlightening. On the very first day, I obtained some clear signals about the prevailing culture. I parked my car in a huge and somewhat dilapidated hangar left over from war-time days, which was located at the back of some antiquated offices in City Road that were the headquarters of ARC Victoria.[42] A brief walk took me to the relatively new and purpose-built RCBBV building, and I ascended to the first floor. My face was obviously unknown, and during this brief journey in the lift I was privy to an interesting conversation between two members of staff. To my amazement, I heard the words *Which day are you taking off for a sickie this week?* Clearly the interview panel had got a handle on the industrial relations climate! Once in the reception, I was shown to the general office on the Directors' Corridor where I was introduced to a charming group of women who provided administrative support to the Directorate. I was then shown to my office which was conveniently located between that of Gordon Whyte and the head of the nursing staff, Ruth Duffy. To my surprise, the wooden panelled room was empty, with no desk, chair or other manifestation of a working environment. With smiles and a shrug of shoulders, staff explained to me that I had arrived

---

[42] This site had been used to produce aeroplanes in the war and had a vestigial military aura. The use of the word "antiquated" reflects a distinct lack of maintenance to the extent that the floors of the office were close to giving way under foot!

a day early. And, after a coffee in the adjacent kitchen, things were quickly put to rights. I visited the stores and identified a battered old desk with a warped top, and a solid wooden chair. These items, which I gathered were army surplus, were soon delivered to the Directors' Floor and, with the help of Ruth Duffy, I carried them into my office. Finally, on this very first day, I found myself upstaging the Director. Whilst I was wearing a suit, when Gordon Whyte emerged to meet me he was wearing a short sleeve shirt, shorts, and long socks.[43] Well, it *was* summer! Before I could adjust to the local custom, on the following day the shorts were banished for ever more from the Directors' Corridor and relatively formal business attire became the normal male clothing. Talk about culture shock!

In my early days, I soon became aware of the enormity of the task ahead of me. To give just an inkling of the chronically rundown state of the organisation, I would cite the following.

a)   The organisation was "deficit funded", which meant that the operations ran "on the smell of an oily rag" with a level of funding that did not cover the demand for products and service. At financial year end, the government "funded" the inevitable "deficit" on recurrent expenditure with an additional reimbursement.

b)   Although the organisation was located in a new building, investment in the maintenance of physical facilities and equipment was at a premium.

c)   Relations between ARC Victoria and the Health Department Victoria ("HDV") were at a low ebb, with constant wrangling over funding and a lack of trust.

d)   The financial reports consisted of a General Ledger computer print-out, the first version of which did not appear until several months into the financial year. There were no budgets of any meaningful construction, little variance information, and no ability to predict year-end.

e)   The Personnel Records consisted of a series of boxes containing cards with hand written entries about employees' details including training courses attended.

---

[43] I was soon to find that the nursing staff called Gordon "Gonz". Prior to joining RCBBV Gordon had been with the New Zealand Blood Service and he frequently referred to the excellence of that organisation as in "Good Old New Zealand".

f) Staff were paid weekly in cash, and we all queued up to receive our brown paper envelope passed over the counter. In view of the risk, staff were strongly recommended to immediately make a deposit into the ANZ bank across the road, with an armed guard standing by as protection.

g) A number of the administrative services were provided by ARC Victoria with an old fashioned charm appropriate for a volunteer based charity rather than a professional medical service.

h) A number of the computer systems were in need of an urgent upgrade, and the electronic age had yet to penetrate the offices where typewritten documents were still the main form of formal communication.

At the outset, I had a relatively small group of staff reporting to me. These included an administrative officer, a building services manager, the Directorate secretarial staff, a librarian, storemen, and security guards. The most senior of these people was a man named Arthur Stevens. With a military background, he had been with the organisation for some time providing administrative support to the very long-serving and highly respected previous Director, Dr Jack Morris. And, although Arthur maintained the manual personnel records system, and liaised with shop stewards on day-to-day industrial relations issues, he relied on staff at ARC Victoria for finance and a number of other services. In any event, it didn't take me long to realise that for him my arrival was not entirely welcome. And I soon experienced what became a protracted period of passive resistance to change.

Whilst Arthur would prove to be something of a thorn in my side, the long-serving Building Services Manager named Syd Guthrie was more accommodating. Although very much of the old school, and not entirely popular with some of the nursing staff, he was a reliable man who made sure that the building structure and services were maintained in good working order. However, the best parts of my little empire were the librarian and secretarial staff. The library had been established to provide access for medical and laboratory staff to the latest scientific papers and publications. Tarangini Bansal was a very well organised professional librarian with high expectations. The head of the Secretarial staff was a delightful lady named Barbara Zion, who was both proficient as PA to Gordon Whyte, and an excellent manager of the office team.[44] She was

---

[44] Barbara had been the PA to the previous Director Jack Morris and was a fount of knowledge about the history of the organisation.

ably assisted by a lovely lady of Irish extraction named Patsy Dunne, who was PA to the Deputy Director, and was herself a very able administrator on whom for many years Patrick Coghlan came to rely.

After my first few days in the organisation, we set up an induction programme, which enabled me to take full stock of the organisation's systems and people, including ARC Victoria where I was given a whistle stop tour of all the departments by their Director of Administration, David Lewis and Director of Voluntary Services, Shirley Ambrose.[45] I then met with the ARC Victoria CEO, Colonel Frank Thorogood. Frank was an impressive man, with all the bearing of senior military rank, seated in front of a map of the world, and surrounded by various forms of military insignia including the Australian and Red Cross flags.[46] He provided a potted history of the ARC, and stressed the importance of the Red Cross symbol. He also impressed upon me the importance for donors of donating their blood to an independent and trustworthy organisation like ARC as opposed to the public health system. Finally, he took the opportunity to give me a frank account of what he saw as the issues within RCBBV and the need for significant change. And he undertook to give me every support in my endeavours.

My round of meetings within RCBVV were more relaxed, with people very willing to talk and share their perspectives. I listened carefully to each member of the management team across the whole organisation including the medical, nursing, donor records, production, haematology, testing, and distribution staff. They were a very interesting and welcoming group of highly qualified people, from very different specialist backgrounds. And I was impressed by both the competence they displayed in their respective areas of the organisation as well as their commitment to the mission and service. It was also evident that, in contrast with many other places where I had worked, a majority of the staff were women. The induction programme also included a visit to a mobile operation, where a team would collect blood at a remote location. I was impressed. And, towards the end of this process, I came to the conclusion that the part of the organisation for which I was responsible, particularly the management of finance and human relations, was the poor relation - which was of course the reason for my appointment.

---

[45] Shirley later reverted to her maiden name Shirley Caulfield.

[46] Frank Thorogood left ARC Victoria in November 1991 and moved to Queensland where he studied for a law degree and became a practising solicitor. He was replaced by Ian Lingard, a long-time member of the Salvation Army.

After completing this long series of conversations, including my first RCBBV Heads of Department ("HOD") meeting, and slowly consolidating a grasp of how the organisation functioned, I prepared an initial report for Gordon Whyte and began the long journey of modernising the administration of the organisation.[47] At this point, I retained a fairly open mind on how to proceed, recognising the need to establish trust and credibility. The scope of work was extensive and, at each stage, required a sustained period of presenting a case and securing support for change. This encompassed not only the reform of systems, but also the establishment of a new team of people with the relevant competencies. The change process would turn into a marathon and, by the time I had *done my dash* seven years down the track, RCBBV would be a very different place.

In these early days, I accompanied Gordon Whyte and David Lewis to my first meeting with HDV officers John Hayes and Brian Meehan, to discuss funding and related issues. Hayes came across as a fairly sardonic character who did not suffer fools gladly. A chain smoker, although he appeared to have a reasonable relationship with Gordon Whyte and a soft spot for RCBBV, it was clear that he did not trust ARC Victoria. Brian Meehan seemed to be an amenable and friendly sort of guy although long-suffering in his dealings with less than accommodating ARC Victoria staff. The funding model for the blood service had been in place for many years and, like many parts of the Australian health system, it involved contributions from both the Commonwealth and State governments. However, HDV negotiated the funding agreement.[48] In these early days, David Lewis took the lead in discussions. He was a well-meaning fellow, but out of his depth in terms of resolving RCBBV funding issues. And it was clear that he lacked authority in the minds of HDV officers. His approach clearly frustrated Gordon Whyte, who on at least one occasion vented his spleen in open session. In successive meetings, Gordon Whyte and I had to listen to some fairly fruitless discussions which went nowhere. And it was clear that this would have to change.

---

[47] The HOD meeting brought together quite a large number of people with different levels of seniority. A vestige of the previous regime, it lacked decision-making capacity and was used by the Director to make announcements and give everybody a say.

[48] The funding arrangement for recurrent funding derived from what was known as the 1973 Tullamarine Agreement, as revised in 1976. This provided for 60% funding from the State/Territory government, a contribution from ARC of 10% of their Charitable Donations, and the balance from the Commonwealth. By the early 1990s, the ARC Victoria contribution covered around 2.5% of the RCBBV operating budget. The Commonwealth and State governments shared the cost of capital expenditure.

After all this preparatory work, my first initiative was to establish a professional personnel function. To this end, I obtained support for the appointment of a Personnel Officer. Although I clearly needed to assume personal responsibility for industrial relations and policy development, there was a need to review the whole personnel system, computerise personnel records, and then manage what would become an enhanced personnel service to the organisation including training and education. In the absence of proper budgets, the funding for this position was quickly found and, whilst we were duty bound to advertise the position, I was blessed in having a more than adequate candidate right under my nose. On arriving, Barbara Zion had already lined up someone to act as my secretary named Pat Pappas.[49] Pat had previously been a Housing Officer in a public housing facility and, whilst she had no personnel management qualifications, she had a mature persona and excellent interpersonal skills. Although she began work as my secretary, she immediately showed an interest in the personnel role and, after consulting with Barbara, I interviewed her for this position. She met my criteria, and I offered her the job on the basis that she would extend her competencies through an RCBBV-financed training course. She would quickly prove to be an excellent choice and, apart from modernising personnel systems, one of her first tasks was to find me a new secretary. In the meantime, I set myself the task of writing up a complete range of new administrative policy and procedures. This became a hugely time-consuming exercise involving widespread consultation with all those affected and, in some cases, many iterations before approval by the RCBBV management team. The programme extended well into the next calendar year and evolved as the needs and circumstances changed. The final end product was an Administrative Manual which would become the standard reference on policy and procedures for the management team. In the meantime, there was no shortage of work in dealing with staff issues and I soon became heavily involved in dealing with the trade unions. This encompassed a never-ending sequence of minor workplace disputes resolved through meetings with shop stewards, full-time officials, and staff. Mobile Operations proved to be a particular source of disputation, with the two mobile teams encountering a variety of work places with sometimes inadequate facilities and working conditions, and supervision at arm's length.[50]

---

[49] Pat Pappas is now Pat Casey having remarried.

[50] There were two mobile teams visiting many locations across greater Melbourne.

Whilst busily establishing myself as an advocate for improving systems and policies, in this first year, I had to address some more difficult personnel challenges within my own Department. From the outset, it was clear that I would have to find a new role for Arthur Stevens. He'd already given up his responsibility for personnel and industrial relations, and I had assumed direct dealings with ARC Victoria on finance. Fortunately, I was able to create a position that avoided redundancy. The senior storeman resigned to move inter-state, and I took the opportunity to establish the more senior supervisory role of Stores Manager. After some persuasion, Arthur agreed to assume this position, providing him with a sphere of responsibility where he could run his own show with little intervention from me. In the meantime, Syd Guthrie indicated his intention of retiring as Building Services Manager in mid-1990. When he stepped down, I recruited a qualified engineer who had recently migrated from Malaysia named Orlando Ooi. He turned out to be an excellent appointment with enthusiasm and fresh ideas.

Towards the end of my first year, with significant progress in other spheres, it was time to deal with the inadequacy of the finance function. Despite the efforts of the well-meaning David Lewis, the service and reports provided by ARC Victoria were woefully lacking. If I was in any doubt about the need for radical change, in September 1989 I endured the delivery of an embarrassing year-end report to the HDV on the state of RCBBV finances for the period to 30 June with little explanation of the causes for a significant deficit in operating expenditure. HDV were scathing. The need for a fresh approach received immediate support from Gordon Whyte. But convincing the senior management of ARC Victoria would be another matter.

When I started at RCBBV, the governance structure consisted of a BTS Management Sub Committee reporting to the ARC Victoria Executive Committee. This Sub Committee was chaired by a charming gentleman with a business background named John Birrell, and its agenda was mostly focussed on medical and donor matters, with a cursory review of budgets and expenditure.[51] A particularly vocal member of the committee was the Chairman of the Donor Advisory Committee, Geoffrey Bowell, who was a powerful advocate for donor interests.[52] The main body with responsibility for financial oversight was the ARC Victoria Finance Committee. After an initial period, I took over

---

[51] In October 1993, John Birrell retired and was replaced by John Plunkett.

[52] Twenty years older than me, Geoffrey Bowell played a mean game of squash and, in the years ahead, I would play him on many occasions in hotly contested contests.

from Gordon Whyte as the RCBBV representative on this body which was populated with a wide range of well-meaning volunteers. Whilst a number were business people, I found them to have relatively little knowledge of RCBBV operations, and a top-down hierarchical view of the organisation with some fairly old-fashioned views about leadership and management. Indeed, in those early days, I well remember a meeting at which a Finance Committee Member had the temerity to propose a motion of thanks to a member of staff for the excellence of their work. The Chairman of the Committee dismissed the motion with words to the effect *"No, no. Motions of thanks are not appropriate. Staff are paid to do their work."*[53] I hasten to add that this was not the universal view of the Committee. Some, particularly a lawyer named Brian Ward with whom I would have very productive dealings over a number of years, had more enlightened views.[54]

In any event, given this structure, it was clear that any attempt to change the finance function would require the support of the ARC Victoria Finance Committee. Fortunately, we had the support of the CEO, Frank Thorogood. Gordon Whyte and I had several discussions with him and, in the early months of 1990, we arrived at the view that RCBBV should take in-house a whole range of administrative services including finance and payroll. Frank named this change "Devolution" and, whilst Gordon and I sought the support of HDV, Frank proceeded to advocate on our behalf with the ARC Victoria Officers. It took a while. Not unreasonably, the HDV view was that if RCBBV wanted to take on more staff to run a finance function it would have to be financed by savings elsewhere. But, of course, they welcomed the prospect of more meaningful financial management. The ARC Victoria nut was harder to crack. But I spent time with the Chairman, Richard Morgan, whilst Gordon Whyte and Frank Thorogood lobbied other members of the Executive Committee. Richard Morgan was initially circumspect but eventually supportive. And in May the Executive Committee agreed to the devolution proposals. This opened the way for me to recruit a finance team and discontinue payments to ARC Victoria for that and other services. It also involved an expansion of the delegation of responsibilities to the BTS Management Sub-Committee, which became

---

[53] Richard Morgan was a businessman and brother of Hugh Morgan of Western Mining fame. As a leader who volunteered his service, his attitude to staff was not that unusual for leaders of not-for-profit volunteer based organisations. Whilst he was circumspect about losing control of RCBBV, I found him respectful, charming and helpful.

[54] In 1990, Ward was a partner of Brian Ward & Associates. The practice is now known as Ward Lawyers, providing advice to the corporate sector.

a Committee in its own right reporting to the ARC Victoria Executive Committee.

In June 1990, I advertised for a Finance Manager (initially called "the Accountant"), and I undertook interviews in early July with the help of a member of the ARC Victoria Finance Committee who was a partner in a local firm of accountants, Pannell Kerr Forster ("PKF"). We selected a recent immigrant from Malaysia called Rose Chai who joined us in July. As Rose was keen to point out, she was a Chartered Accountant of England and Wales, and she was no slouch! In fact, she was an astute and charming woman whose dedication, loyalty, and skill was considerably beyond anything I could have expected. Her efforts quickly bore fruit at RCBBV, and within weeks she commenced a project to install an in-house accounting system as well as introducing some very tasty Chinese snacks for consumption at morning tea! We also set about training team leaders across all departments in the basics of cost-centre management so that they could take responsibility for their own budgets and financial performance. Within a few months, RCBBV was producing its own financial statements, had incorporated the concept of accrual accounting, and this soon flushed out what appeared to be a major anomaly. RCBBV's accounts included an ARC Victoria cross-charge for administrative services, and Rose uncovered that the annual charge was around $1 million. This fee for service had been in place for a number of years, but the quantum, embedded in the organisation's poorly constructed financial statements, was previously unknown to RCBBV management. And the amount was quite a shock to all concerned. It was quickly the subject of review through the establishment of the Cross Charges Working Party. This body comprised Frank Thorogood, David Lewis, the ARC Victoria Finance Manager Louis Jahshan, Rose and myself. And eventually we negotiated a system of fully costed payments for the provision of well-defined services and a fee in recognition of the Red Cross name. In total, following the transfer to RCBBV of the finance, payroll, and other functions, the residual cross-charge amounted to around $100,000 per annum.

As Rose began to produce regular financial statements, we established an RCBBV Finance Committee consisting of the main Cost-Centre Managers to negotiate the establishment of meaningful budgets and to have oversight of financial performance. Rose also established a project to take over the payroll function with the pro bono assistance of a Senior

Associate at PKF named Angelo di Stefano.[55] Angelo would work with us for several years supporting the implementation of a range of financial systems which included an Assets Register to manage facilities and equipment and underpin bids for capital funding, and the Treasury function. And, as time passed, it never failed to amaze me how Rose always seemed to find a source of funds to finance new projects or emergency requirements through the prudent establishment and management of reserves. Her appointment was one of the most significant decisions during my whole time with the organisation with an enormous impact.

Whilst finance was a major pre-occupation, the rest of the organisation was not standing still. In particular, with the ability to delegate financial responsibility on a departmental basis, in 1991 Gordon Whyte determined that there needed to be a complete change to the internal management structure. The old HOD model was a broad church of managers and supervisors, and not a body to which significant responsibility could be delegated. Following extended consultation, we established a Senior Managers Committee. This would eventually comprise the Directors, the Donor Services Manager covering donor aspects of blood collection, the two Senior Scientists responsible for virology, serology, tissue typing, production, and research and development, the Head of the Distribution Department (formerly Despatch), and the senior people reporting to me (initially the Finance Manager and eventually the Computer Services Manager). Later, as new functions were created, the team would be joined by a Quality Manager (1993) and a Public Affairs Manager (in 1995). This team met monthly with a well-established agenda to determine strategic direction, approve production and donor plans, agree budgets, review various aspects of performance, and adopt changes to policies and procedures. In the meantime, the three Directors continued to meet at 10.00am every Monday morning to keep tabs on weekly operational activity and consider a variety of external business.

With a leadership team firmly established, the wider structure of the organisation was the subject of many consequential changes in which I was involved as an analyst and a facilitator. These changes included the reconfiguration of the Donor Services Department, introduction of new shift systems, changes to mobile operations, several laboratory reorganisations, the upgrading of the distribution function, changes to

---

[55] Angelo di Stefano is now a Director of Coads Accounting Systems.

the medical team, the establishment of a quality function based on the haematology department, and the establishment of a Public Affairs Department with the recruitment of a Public Affairs Manager.[56]

The introduction of professional financial management transformed the relationship with HDV. By now, I had already established an easy rapport with Brian Meehan founded on honesty and transparency. Devolution within ARC Victoria had been music to Brian's ears, and the ability to provide him with financial statements based on budgets and appropriately allocated costs facilitated a relationship based on trust. Apart from the annual budget cycle and monitoring of financial performance, our "bread and butter" was the review of a continual stream of "automatic" additional funding arising from the complex web of award changes, and preparation of year-end projections at a sufficiently early stage in the year to enable HDV to make suitable financial provision for future requirements in the May State Government budget. From my perspective, it also enabled RCBBV to begin the process of identifying where and in what ways the level of funding was not sufficient to meet the level of activity and service expected.[57] With financial reporting on a sounder footing, this also opened up the opportunity to develop more meaningful relationships across the whole of HDV, and we established what was called the HDV Liaison Committee chaired by Dr Wes Rouch, which met monthly.[58] In the meantime, Gordon pursued a range of health policy issues with the Chief Medical Officer, Dr Chris Brook, and a range of specialists including Dr Graham Rouch, Associate Professor Dr Alison Street of the Haemophilia Society, senior management of the recently privatised CSL Ltd with whom we had a relationship for the production of plasma-based products, and many others.[59]

With finance in much better shape, and Rose Chai eventually establishing a small team financed by significant improvements in controlling costs, I was now able to turn to other matters. One of the more difficult areas was industrial relations. RCBBV was heavily unionised with the Health Services Union of Australia ("HSUA") representing the less qualified staff. But there were also separate unions representing the

---

[56] Yvonne Bennett was recruited as Public Affairs Manager from Yakult, a company producing probiotics.

[57] In days when both of us had moved on, Brian and I would eventually turn into firm friends and we keep in touch to this day!

[58] A senior HDV bureaucrat, Dr Rouch retired in 1991, to be replaced by Dr Chris Brook.

[59] CSL Ltd was formerly a government owned entity called the Commonwealth Serum Laboratories and was privatised in 1994.

registered nurses, the scientists and the medical technicians. All these groups had shop stewards and they operated under a system of awards which laid down pay and conditions. Over the years, these unions had negotiated an amazing set of special working conditions and payments, some of which were not well documented. It took a long time to flush them out and I think my favourite was the "Buck a Chuck" payment whereby nursing aides were paid a $1 for every time a blood donor vomited during or after a donation. In any event, my task in the early days was to meet and develop a polite working relationship, and eventually a level of trust, to enable effective negotiations with both shop stewards and full-time officials. Such things are not easily or quickly achieved, and are easily lost. I set about this challenge by developing strategies for incremental review of practices and consolidation of payments, through a series of endless negotiations. In the fullness of time, award conditions were slowly modernised, old and inappropriate practices were removed, and new working standards were introduced. During 1991, there was also a major change in the cost structure arising from the introduction of compulsory superannuation contributions, the Superannuation Guarantee, which started at 3% of basic pay and slowly rose with small annual increments. This turned out to have a significant industrial relations dimension as ARC Victoria arranged for superannuation payments to be lodged with a private sector superannuation organisation called HESTA. RCBBV unions were up in arms because they saw their staff as being part of the public sector. This triggered a long saga with RCBBV employees eventually joining the public sector Health Super organisation. Around this time, we also introduced "salary packaging" whereby employees were able to allocate part of their salary to a suite of benefits before tax.

On 3 October 1992, there was a change in the external environment which would have a major impact on the organisation. In the Victorian State election, the Liberal Party came to power with Jeff Kennett elected as Premier. Kennett had a neo-liberal economic agenda which involved reducing "the size of government". This included privatisation of publicly owned enterprises, enabling reduction in the public debt which had mushroomed during the latter years of the previous ALP government, and an attempt to drive efficiency in the public sector, particularly in the fields of education and health.

One of the first things to happen was that HDV was reorganised, with the creation of a new Department of Health and Community Services ("DHCS") under a minister named Marie Teehan. Accordingly, the HDV

Liaison Committee became the DHCS Liaison Committee, but with similar responsibility for oversight of RCBBV affairs. More significant was the requirement for organisations like RCBBV to deliver what was called "an efficiency dividend", another name for "doing more with less". RCBBV had just spent the last three years recovering from years of under-funding. And, given the public health challenges of the time, including new testing programmes, whilst there was always room for improvement in the utilisation of resources, we were not in a position to find such a "dividend". Gordon Whyte and I entered into talks with DHCS, and it was agreed that external consultants should be appointed to assess the efficiency and effectiveness of RCBBV. It was a risky strategy but, given our recent progress, and the vastly improved information systems, it was a risk that we were prepared to take. And this became a major project for my team. The consultants appointed to undertake this independent review which took place in 1993 were KPMG, and we developed some broad Terms of Reference for their project. Over several months, we worked diligently with a number of people deployed by the consultants to examine the cost and effectiveness of every part of the organisation, benchmarking with other blood services in Australia and around the world. We left no stone unturned to respond to all their requests and undertook research on our own account as input to their deliberations and assessment. The internal team did a fine job and the outcome was not what the State government had expected or wanted. According to KPMG, RCBBV was a relatively well managed organisation, and was significantly underfunded given what the government expected it to deliver. Far from justifying a cut in funding, in their final report KPMG recommended that the State government should invest more funding in both recurrent expenditure and capital projects. They also embraced the concept of output-based funding based on the products and services delivered by the organisation.

The KPMG Report would have a profound impact on both RCBBV and the wider delivery of blood transfusion services throughout Australia. In the short term, we stepped away from the deficit-based funding system which was replaced by the establishment of a Funding and Services Agreement which provided specific lines of funding to finance six activities – the Main Operating Programme, two AIDS programmes, the recently implemented HTLV1 Testing programme, the Bone Marrow Programme, and eventually two regional programmes covering Collections and AIDS Testing.[60] Although we did not yet have the means to allocate costs at a detailed level, the funding was now to be based on the submission of plans for the number of blood donations and delivery of a given set of products and services. And, although there was a clear understanding that the system would continue to be based on voluntary donation and the free supply of products, it was acknowledged that there was merit in providing price signals to hospitals on the basis that this would affect their approach to usage, some of which was profligate. To this end, DHCS established a Price Signals Working Party to develop an appropriate model for costing products. This potentially radical change became a major project for the whole organisation, although it would not reach fruition until the advent of a national blood service some years later. Similar usage-based models were being introduced for the funding of hospitals with the development and implementation of what was called Case Mix Funding, in which hospital funding was based on the number of patient admissions.

As part of a broader agenda, the government was also keen to reform the Award system and move to the establishment of an Enterprise Bargaining Agreement. And towards the end of 1993, this would become another major project with significant industrial relations consequences. Given the wide range of work in which I was now engaged, this led me to the view that there was a need to recruit someone who would focus on industrial relations and I developed a case for appointing an HR Manager with responsibility for the full range of HR services including personnel, training and development, and job evaluation as well as industrial relations.[61] The need for this appointment was eventually accepted and, in early 1994, we recruited Chris Andrews. He only stayed for six months before going into a consultancy business with his wife and was replaced by the avuncular Joe Goddard who hailed from an English mining background. In the years ahead he provided a steady hand.

Whilst all of this was unfolding, and given the direction of government policy on the funding model, in 1993 we agreed that it was time to establish a strategic plan, with objectives, strategies and performance measures, and a more robust approach to project planning which was linked to the plan. With my previous experience, responsibility for this activity fell to me, with the development of the

---

[60] HTLV stands for Human T-Lymphotropic Virus.

[61] The Hay MSL Job Evaluation system, with external input to the Evaluation Panel, was implemented in 1993 in place of an internal system and provided much needed benchmarking references.

first plan a team exercise involving all the senior managers, and undertaken over a twelve months period. Concepts of structured planning were somewhat new to most of the management team, and I introduced the various elements with great care as a learning experience. We started with some basic exercises, such as a SWOT analysis, development of vision and aims, and identification of values and associated behaviours.[62] It was a lengthy process, as I tried to establish a new paradigm in which team members had a real say in determining priorities, and it was not without its challenges. In particular, I remember one afternoon in which the Senior Managers attempted to rationalise the organisation's project plan which included some projects for which there were insufficient resources and little strategic rationale. Through an iterative process, the team ranked the projects and arrived at a much-reduced list. Sadly, though, the Director's prerogative then came into play. After the exhaustive team exercise, he made a final call in which he reinstated some of the projects that we had collectively sought to remove. The feeling of disappointment amongst the team was palpable.

Despite this kind of frustration, the planning approach did bear fruit, with the adoption of an agreed set of projects, to which resources could be allocated in a systematic fashion. Our first full Strategic Plan was completed in October 1994 for the period from 1995/96 to 1999/2000. Our vision and mission were as follows:

- *To establish and maintain a position of international pre-eminence as a provider of health services in the field of transfusion-related products and services.*
- *To develop a continuous improvement culture, through the achievement of excellence in providing sufficient safe transfusion-related products and services, fostering community involvement in the organisation, and selling knowledge-based services.*

This was to be achieved through the pursuit of the following Objectives and Strategies:

Objective A	Improve Core Business and Operations
Strategies	Achieve Sufficiency of Supply
	Improve Service to Hospitals and Medical Community
	Improve Management Control Systems
	Improve Employee Motivation and Performance
	Develop Public Affairs Role and Plan
	Extend Academic Links
Objective B	Develop More Effective Risk Management

---

[62] SWOT refers to Strength, Weakness, Opportunity, and Threat.

Strategies	Improve Management Systems		
	Reduce Recipient Risks		
	Improve Donor Safety		
	Develop Litigation Management Programme		
Objective C	**Develop New Businesses**		
Strategies	Develop Business Infrastructure		
	Undertake Research and Development		
	Develop New Business Units		
Objective D	**Secure Long Term Future**		
	Develop Greenfield Scenario		

Flowing from this over-arching plan was a detailed set of sub strategies, a production plan, financial projections, and a comprehensive project plan. After completion, we established performance measures and committed to an annual review.

As RCBBV developed, a major area of challenge was the computer systems. The organisation was fortunate to have an outstanding Computer Services Manager named John Butler and, following changes to the management structure, in 1993 this unit came under my wing with John joining the Senior Manager team, and the establishment of a Computer Steering Committee as the vehicle for determining the allocation of priorities and resources and reviewing progress. John was very much his own man and did not suffer fools gladly. Indeed, at times, he lost all patience with what he saw as the autocratic medical hierarchy and periodically urged me to "take them on" in terms of developing a more enlightened and collegiate approach to leadership and management. In many ways he developed into someone that represented the organisational conscience, and I retain fond memories of his independence of mind, his diligence, and his ability to make things work. In any event, the range of computer projects was extensive and, having had responsibility for this area of activity in a previous life, I played an active role in identifying priorities as RCBBV moved into the computer age. In addition to the administrative systems mentioned earlier, in the early 1990s, the work programme included significant laboratory projects, including the implementation of the LABEL 2000 labelling system, the ANELISA laboratory testing system, and a Local Area Network ("LAN") providing for the introduction of an email system that revolutionised internal and eventually external communications. However, the mother of all projects was the replacement of the production system, through the ERIC project.

Throughout my time at RCBBV, a significant pre-occupation was the potential for the transmission of diseases through transfusions and use of blood products, with the relentless spread of Human Immunodeficiency

Virus ("HIV") and AIDS casting a shadow over the organisation. Looking back from the third decade of the 21st century, it is sometimes hard to believe what a scourge HIV had become in the 1980s and 1990s. I had first become aware of this disease when I joined Imperial Brewing in the early 1980s, with a member of the management team became one of the first people in the UK to die from the disease. Anyway, by the time I arrived at RCBBV, and following the famous Australian TV advert featuring the "Grim Reaper", the organisation was subject to a barrage of legal challenges associated with the alleged transmission of HIV via a blood transfusion. The organisation's response was multi-facetted including screening of donors through what was regarded by some as intrusive questions about sexual activity, and the implementation of a succession of blood-testing programs designed to identify the presence of HIV. These were costly, particularly in the immediate years following introduction of a given test. And, notwithstanding our commitment to implement the latest screening regimes, the organisation was potentially subject to litigation at great expense in terms of insurance cover and possible damages if a case was proven. And the threat to the blood supply posed by this virus, and the cost of reducing the risk through screening, testing, and insurance cover, was added to the threat arising from other blood-borne diseases including various types of hepatitis, and CJD or "Mad Cow Disease".[63] To deal with issues arising from these risks, ARC had established a national Committee chaired by Dr Dick Kimber on which each of the 8 State and Territory blood services were represented by their respective Directors (all of whom were doctors) together with a full time ARC national medical director, Dr Muriel Baker. This body ensured a consistent national policy and a shared response to a succession of litigants making allegations about lack of due care and diligence. But ensuring national consistency was at times a struggle and eventually became a driver for major structural change at a national level.

One of the main developments associated with this relentless drive to maintain the safety of blood was the decision by the Commonwealth government to regulate activity through the introduction of a Code for Blood Products administered by the Therapeutic Goods Administration ("TGA"). The concept of "quality" was not lost on RCBBV. In my own area, for several years, we had made a virtue of achieving and retaining a Five Star award for the standard of our OH&S systems which was the subject of an annual external audit. But the advent of the TGA in 1992

---

[63] CJD is Creutzveldt Jakob Disease, potentially acquired from eating meat in the UK between 1985 and 1995.

required a major change in RCBBV policy and practices. And the organisation responded by establishing a new Quality Department under the leadership of a Quality Manager named Diane Hull who came from the Red Cross in Western Australia.[64] Her job was to prepare the organisation for TGA audit and to develop and maintain a "quality system". This work included not only the creation of new systems, but significant retraining of staff, and major changes to work practices, all of which were implemented through the establishment of a Quality Council. The activity caused considerable apprehension. Not least, this was because the TGA approach to compliance, which required commercial pharmaceutical companies to use some of their considerable resources to invest in safety, was not easily adapted to meet the operation of a volunteer blood service. The not-for- profit blood services simply did not have the sort of resources available to meet some of the TGA demands. And, although TGA did contribute to the improvement of RCBBV systems and work practices, implementation of the Code created huge stress for many individuals and this was not helped by the approach adopted by some of the agents of change both within RCBBV and in the TGA audit function. There was a fierce counter-point between the team-based approach to management which we had spent several years developing, and a TGA model which was inclined to be prescriptive and hierarchical. As a result, grown men were drive to tears as the new paradigm was implemented by people who had little knowledge of blood transfusion and employed adversarial inter-personal skills. And this cultural issue was exacerbated by the fact that the Commonwealth government tried to implement the Code without recognising the ability to pay for the cost of changing work practices. It was a flaw in their system which was to be repeated again and again. And this was eventually picked up by the review of the blood services undertaken some years later by the retired Governor General Sir Ninian Stephen. His recommendations, that proposals to improve safety must be accompanied by an appropriate allocation of funds, never reached fruition. There will be more on this in Chapter 12.

With significant changes in the external environment, including the advent of TGA, relentless litigation and government pressure to adopt a more commercial approach as recommended in the KPMG Report, in June 1994 Gordon Whyte initiated a review of the RCBBV governance structure. Terms of reference were established in July, and in September

---

[64] Diane Hull stayed for a relatively short period and was replaced by Pat Rayner.

ARC Victoria established the BTS Structure Working Party under the chairmanship of Brian Ward (ARC Victoria Deputy Chairman). Other members of the team were newly appointed Executive Director Ian Lingard, the RCBBV Directors, and three members of the BTS Management Committee, John Plunkett, Dr David Race and Dr Max Whiteside. Our mission was to formulate a governance structure that would enable timely decision-making in response to changes in the external environment, protection of ARC Victoria's reputation, and effective risk management. In examining options it was noted that, while the review would have a State-level focus because of current funding arrangements, it would need to leave open the possibility a significant change in the national structure for delivering blood services. This prescience proved accurate as the Working Party's deliberations would quickly be subsumed into a more general review of the blood service by ARC at a national level which would have profound implications, not least for me personally.

In 1994, ARC Secretary General Jim Carlton commissioned a review of the blood services undertaken by health consultants Ron McKay and Bernie Wells.[65] Amongst other things, the McKay Wells Report issued in early 1995 envisioned the vertical integration of the blood industry with the establishment of a national blood service. This new national body would be advised by a standing committee of AHMAC and receive "blood shield" legislation.[66] This would require a major change in the governance structure of ARC including the Royal Charter, and Jim Carlton had lengthy discussions with the ARC National Chairman, Ron Green, about the establishment of a single organisational unit for the blood services within Red Cross with a professional Board of Management capable of meeting the challenges on the 21st century. With support from the Commonwealth government, significant support from ARC Victoria, and after much deliberation and anxious internal debate within State and Territory Divisions, at the ARC AGM in November 1995 it was decided to establish a new national body to be called the Australian Red Cross Blood Service.

Once a decision to proceed with this change had been made, in early 1996 ARC established a project to facilitate implementation, and Jim

---

[65] Jim Carlton had been a minister in the Commonwealth government, and was particularly knowledgeable of the long and somewhat tortured history between ARC and Australian governments.

[66] The current risk management regime involved the National Blood Transfusion Committee. AHMAC is the Australian Health Minister's Advisory Committee, a forum for Federal government health officials to consult with their State/Territory counterparts.

Carlton called for applications to take on the role of leading the project. Coincidentally, at this time I was seriously considering my future. Having been involved in managing change at RCBBV for nearly seven years, I took the view that it was time to move on not least because, if there was one thing I had learned from previous experience, change agents often become obstacles to continuous improvement. I had already applied for other jobs including the role of CEO at the Multiple Sclerosis Society. In any event, to my surprise, I was invited to apply for the ARCBS Implementation Team Leader position. I consulted with my colleagues, and they were supportive. Unknown to me, at the same time, Gordon Whyte also put his own hat in the ring, which was not surprising given that he was a great advocate for the establishment of the national blood service. In the event, my application prevailed. I don't flatter myself. With extensive change-management experience over 15 years in many different organisations, I was more than qualified to manage a change-management project. And I also had an in-depth understanding of blood service administration. But I think I got the job because I posed less of a threat than Gordon Whyte to the ARC hierarchy and senior management in the other State and Territory blood services. In any event, in February 1996, I left RCBBV to start a new job based at the national ARC headquarters in Wellington Parade, East Melbourne. We pick up this journey in Chapter 11.

Finally, this account of RCBBV years may give the impression that it was all work and no play. This is far from the truth. I did work long hours and, at times, working with a man of vision and passion like Gordon Whyte was not for the faint hearted. In any event, there were some lighter moments. For several years, the management team on the First Floor of the blood bank ended each working week with a glass of wine and some cheese which was usually organised by the nursing staff and served up in the office at the end of the corridor. It was a time when we discussed current issues and shared a few anecdotes of the week gone by. And at Christmas, we did things in style with a Christmas party in the Lecture Theatre, and I had a special picnic lunch with the secretarial staff in St Vincent Gardens. In fact, we really needed very little excuse to have a party and I especially remember the day after I was accorded Australian citizenship in September 1989 with a special afternoon tea. I was also on call to give urgent samples of my AB rhesus negative blood to the Tissue Typing Department. I never quite found out what they did with these samples but the rarity of my blood type was useful, even after it was decided that I could no longer make a regular donation because of my potential exposure to CJD.

The Blood Bank also had a number of external social events. These included a boat trip down the Maribyrnong River into the Port Melbourne Basin, and a cricket match against ARC Victoria. The latter was intended to engender closer relations but ended in a dispute. With the RCBBV team chasing and just failing to reach a target, the scorer (the son of RCBBV Marketing Manager Peter Carolan) suddenly found that he had miscounted the overs. So RCBBV was able to bat for a further over which enabled us to overtake our opponents' score. They did not take this well!

During my time at RCBBV, I also had my first experience in Australia as a customer of the local health system. For several years in the late 1980s, I had harboured a hernia. Like most men I was in denial and did nothing about it. But my friend and squash partner Robin Brown was a medical student. He noticed my bulge in the showers, and advised me to get it checked out. Reluctantly, in early 1992, I went to see my GP. Dr Negri told me that I needed to have it fixed immediately as I could develop peritonitis, and he referred me to a specialist that I met the following week. We set a date for the operation, and a few days later I had dinner with Robin with whom I shared my plans. He asked who the surgeon was and, not a man for understatement, when I gave the name, his response was to tell me that *"the man is a butcher!"* The next day, I cancelled the operation, and told Dr Negri that I had an urgent business trip. A few weeks later, Robin gave me the name of another surgeon to whom Dr Negri was happy to refer me. The operation in April 1992 was a success and, more than thirty years later, it still holds firm. As Robin told me afterwards, and this is an important lesson to all who submit themselves to the knife, a surgeon is only as good as his sowing skills!

Meanwhile, my role in the blood bank involved me in quite a few non-core and external activities such as the annual conference of the International Society of Blood Transfusion which in 1992 was held in California. Strangely, whilst the many papers on overseas practices were enlightening, the most lasting memory from that trip was the spectre of poverty in the streets of San Francisco, with many beggars on the pavements following Ronald Reagan's closure of public welfare institutions.

Coming back to RCBBV, from the early days I was involved in managing what was called the Education and Research Trust Fund.[67] This body had been established by Gordon Whyte to act as a repository for income arising from charges for non-core activity, most of which came from the highly successful Transfusion Medicine Conference run by RCBBV and administered by Patrick Coghlan's PA the redoubtable Patsy Dunne. The committee of trustees met quarterly to review applications from staff and disbursed grants to finance the improvement of staff facilities, attendance at education courses, and acquisition of specialist equipment. In the early 1990s, I also represented RCBBV at Volleyball events for which we were a sponsor under the Victorian Health Promotion Foundation.[68] This would turn out to be a serendipitous involvement, as we will see in Chapter 8.

Finally, I have to say that the seven years that I spent at RCBBV were seminal. I am proud of the substantial and far-reaching changes to the organisation and, as became apparent when I led the ARCBS Implementation Team, many of the structures, policies, and systems we implemented were significantly in advance of those in the other States and Territories. Indeed, the ideas and initiatives being pursued by Gordon Whyte and his team would provide the bedrock for establishing the new ARCBS national organisation. And it is one of my regrets, borne of a need for me to be impartial, that this achievement was never properly recognised, valued or cherished by other members of the ARCBS management team established in 1997. On the contrary, there was a tendency to denigrate RCBBV which was neither fair nor accurate. Sadly Gordon Whyte died in April 2022.

On a personal level, when I started with the organisation in early 1989, I was still getting over the pain of all that had happened to me in the early 1980s. I had been a lost soul looking for a new life in a new country. In many respects, RCBBV became my family. Many of the staff became lifelong friends, and I was a lucky man to gain so much in return for what I gave.

---

[67] This fund was introduced in 1989. In 1994, the State government determined that much of the funds would have to be allocated to the Main Operating Programme. So we closed the fund and established a new trust fund to serve a similar purpose financed by fees received for services that were outside the State government's remit. The new body was called the Staff Welfare Trust Fund.

[68] The Victorian Health Promotion Foundation was a government agency established to provide funding to replace the loss of sponsorship from tobacco companies which was made illegal.

7: A Family Apart

Thus far, it might reasonably be deduced that when I migrated to Australia in 1987 my local roots were inconsequential. This could not be further from the truth. My mother had a brother and sister who had migrated to Australia in the first half of the 20th century. And, by the 1980s, I had over 20 relatives living in NSW. During the early years of my life in Australia this would be a source of some belonging, although it came to an abrupt and unhappy end.

My mother had four siblings and there were two generations. In her first marriage, my grandmother Edith had three children who were born at the turn of the 20th century, Edith, Ernest and William. My grandmother's first husband died in 1904 and, after a lengthy pause, in 1916 she married Charles Piper. With her new husband, she had two further children, my mother Eunice and her sister Rene. Charles died in 1926 and my grandmother died the night I was born in 1945.

When I was young, there was very little contact with my mother's half-brothers. Uncle Ernie was a ship's cook and settled in Sydney in the 1920s, and I only met him for the first time when he visited England in the 1960s. Subsequently, I did see him and his family on my trips to Australia in the 1970s and 1980s. But I had relatively little in common with them and both he and his wife Kathleen died in the 1990s. Although my uncle Bill lived in England, I only met him a couple of times in the 1970s and we had little to do with his family.

In contrast, my mother was close to both of her sisters. My Aunt Edith (we just called her Aunty) had no children of her own and played a significant part in my life as a carer and a kind of grandmother. Sadly, she died in the 1970s. My Aunt Rene migrated to Australia in 1945 after meeting and marrying Australian soldier Bill Pratt whom she met while he was billeted in London at the end of the Second World War. They settled in NSW, and had four sons, Lynn, Ian, Neil, and Lloyd. Sadly, I never met Rene because she died of cancer in the 1960s. But she figured in my life from an early age. When I was a young child, I remember letters arriving from her on a weekly basis and, in the immediate post-war years, she even sent us food parcels. When I was old enough, it was decided that I should become a "pen pal" with my cousin Ian who was about the same age as me and, in the early 1950s, I began a regular correspondence with him which continued well into our teenage years. Through this regular contact, I slowly became acquainted and enamoured with Australia as a nirvana on the other side of the planet.

Eventually, Rene's children began to fly the nest and Lynn was the first to arrive in the UK in 1969 when I was living in Glasgow. He struck me as a larrikin. But he was a likeable fellow, and I did my best to entertain him, driving him around half of Scotland and down to Newcastle where he wanted to see Hadrian's Wall. That was the only time I ever met him but, from time to time, news of him filtered through. And eventually he settled down with a partner in a remote part of Bali where, to my knowledge, he lives to this day. The second of Rene's sons, Ian, turned up in England in July 1971, and I remember travelling down from Grimsby to London to pick him up at Heathrow airport. He was a charming and good looking lad, and I did my best to entertain him for the week or so. Afterwards, we continued to keep in touch until I eventually ventured down to Australia. The third of Rene's sons Neil and his wife Sally visited the UK whilst I was living in Bristol in 1977. They were doing the classical "European Trip" and had left their two young children with Sally's parents. They stayed with me and I took them around a variety of local haunts in the West Country. They also visited my mother in Nottingham and my brother Michael in London. We hit it off very well, and thereafter, I kept in touch with them on a regular basis.

Eventually, the time came for me to realise a lifelong dream of visiting Australia. I made the first of several trips to NSW in 1978 and, as recounted in *For Goodness Sake*, this holiday was full of surprises. Apart from becoming acquainted with Sydney and its wonderful harbour, beaches, restaurants, and adjacent bushland, I was able to visit my relatives in their home environments. Ian took the biscuit as I found he was living in a flash Bronte Beach mansion with George who was his partner in life as well as in a lucrative plumbing business. In contrast, my Uncle Ernie and his family lived in modest dwellings in the western suburbs of Sydney. My journey of discovery finished with a drive up to Newcastle where I stayed with Neil and Sally. At the time, they lived in a small weatherboard house in Belmont, where Neil worked as an engineer for the water board whilst Sally was a teacher. They extended great hospitality and introduced me to a number of their friends and the youngest brother Lloyd who lived next to Lake Macquarie and was employed as a roof tiler.

That first visit to Australia left me with very mixed feelings about the country and the family connection. I didn't know how I felt about Ian and his partner George and their lifestyle was challenging. But Neil and Sally seemed to me to be the sort of people with whom I could develop a natural family tie if ever I moved to the country.

I visited Australia again in 1980 and, although I caught up with all the above family members again, I spent a great deal more time with Neil and Sally who had now moved to a larger house in a suburb of Newcastle named Adamstown Heights. In particular, they took me to meet Sally's folks who farmed in Wellington near Dubbo which was a good four hours' drive to the west. Back in Newcastle, Neil also introduced me to his father for whom he had a watching brief on certain business interests. Uncle Bill lived in the outback, but occasionally stayed with a female friend in Newcastle. He was a strange fellow and, from talking to him, it seemed that he did not have much time for my mother but Neil told me to take no notice. On a further trip to Australia in 1982, I explored more of the country, visiting the Northern Territory, and southern NSW. I also visited Melbourne. It was a superficial view, but I was struck by what seemed to be a very different culture from NSW which sowed a seed for what was to follow.

The next time I travelled to Australia was in 1986. As already recounted, this was a time of great challenge and uncertainty for me. I had left England for good reasons, and had an expectation that Australia would offer me a new life. And the connections I had made, particularly with the family in Newcastle, certainly helped. By this time, Ian had become distant and a person with whom I had infrequent contact. In the first couple of years of my life in Australia, I had excellent relations with Neil and Sally in which they more than repaid my hospitality to them when they had visited the UK. I not only enjoyed their company, but also that of their two boys, Matthew and Ben who were heading into their teens. And Sally wrote to me on a regular basis and occasionally called me on the telephone. They seemed keen to have me visit, and made a special point of inviting me for Christmas. At Sally's suggestion, and with the aim of getting him to write properly, I also started to correspond with Matthew and I exchanged a series of amusing letters with him establishing an excellent rapport.

After I bought my house in Kew in January 1988, I didn't get up to Newcastle until Christmas. But during that trip, and keen to reciprocate their hospitality, I invited them to visit me for a weekend in Melbourne. Eventually, they took me up on this offer and in mid-August 1989 they drove down from Newcastle staying overnight along the way. Despite my best efforts, including tickets for an AFL match between Sydney and Melbourne at the MCG, and a good deal of touring, this visit ended on a sour note. At the time, I was in the early stages of my time at the Blood Bank and my work involved long hours. On the Monday, I was due to return to work while they were scheduled to return to Newcastle. However, Neil asked if they could stay on for a while. If I'd had a bigger house, I wouldn't have hesitated. But I had vacated my own bedroom for them and was sleeping on a couch in the study. I was exhausted. So I said that I would prefer if we stuck to the original plan. At the time, Neil seemed to accept this and they left on the Monday. But a few days later I received a curtly worded note from him requesting that I mail him something they had left behind. At the time, I didn't read too much into the tone of that letter, but I later discovered that Neil was offended by my unwillingness to extend their stay. And this would become a source of discord that would be prove to be a turning point in what, up to then, had been an important relationship in helping me to settle in Australia.

In the months that followed, I continued my contact by letter with Sally, and with Matthew who asked whether he could visit me in Melbourne. Although I assumed it would be a formality, I told him that I'd need to ask his parents. A few weeks later, my mother was visiting from England and we were invited to visit Newcastle. On arrival, whilst she was well received, I was told that I would need to stay in a motel in town. Initially taken aback, I shrugged it off. But worse was to follow. In conversation with Neil and Sally, I raised the matter of Matthew visiting Melbourne. Neil dismissed the suggestion in peremptory fashion. While I was trying to work out the reasons for this hostility, my mother had a word with Sally. Apparently, Neil was harbouring a grudge because I'd not allowed the family to stay longer on their visit to Melbourne. Then, Matthew shared with me what I now realise was just some typical teenage angst about coping with parental authority. At the time, though, it was all looking a little ugly. And to make matters worse, Matthew then raised the question of going to Melbourne in front of his father, and Neil asked me to come outside with what I interpreted as extremely aggressive intentions. Unaccustomed to fisticuffs, I declined the offer to meet on the veranda, but was left in no doubt that my relationship with this family was on the rocks. It was a rude awakening. Later, Sally said I should just let it go and that Neil would come around.

When my mother and I left Newcastle on what would be my last visit to the Pratt family, I was deeply upset. Given Neil's evident hostility, my mother strongly cautioned me to cut my ties. But I thought I knew better. In the spirit of trying to provide some support for Matthew, who seemed to be doing it tough, I continued to keep in touch with him through correspondence and the occasional telephone call at a time in the morning before he went to school. This went on for some months, without misadventure, and I honestly thought I was helping the boy through a difficult patch. However, in early 1991, the wheels fell off. On one occasion when I rang Matthew, a woman answered and I thought I had a wrong number. A few weeks later, I found myself talking to Neil. In not so many words, he told me that my contact with Matthew should cease, and that the family never wanted to hear from me again. And, a week later, I received a letter from Sally, in which she accused me of keeping in touch with Matthew behind her back. She wished me well, and left me in no doubt that she supported Neil's "coup de grace". Finally, I got a very sad letter from Matthew telling me that he could not speak or write to me anymore. In response to Sally's letter, I wrote back to apologise and take upon myself full responsibility for what I naively regarded as my helpful contact with Matthew. I hoped to absolve him from any blame; and I can only hope that he was forgiven for innocently liaising with someone he regarded as a friend.

The trauma of this turn of events has never completely left me. It happened at a time when I was beginning to feel that Australia really was my home. And the Pratts were an important part of that. I have occasionally thought of trying to get in touch with Matthew who probably now has children of his own. The time may come. In the meantime, there is much learning that would serve me well in years to come. My mother's instinct was correct. I had presumed upon a family connection that was clearly not as strong as I had thought. And I resolved that, whatever the circumstances, I would never again place myself in a position of potentially coming between a parent and an unhappy teenager.

But it wasn't all bad. In the relationship I developed with Matthew, I discovered something which was clearly missing in my life. I had enjoyed what was almost a fatherly role, and I realised that by not getting married I had deprived myself of the joys and challenges of parenthood. This would resonate with me in another significant relationship that would change my life. And that is the subject of the next chapter.

8: My One, My Only Son

About five years after moving to Australia, and while I was still recovering from the break-down in my dealings with my relatives, I was fortunate to encounter someone who would become "a significant other". As is often the case in life, I never set out to acquire this relationship. It was serendipitous. Given the profound impact it would have on my personal life and well-being, the development of what would become an unconventional form of family is a centre-piece of my immigrant's tale.

I first met Andrew one Sunday in February 1991, when we both happened to be working at the Red Cross Blood Bank Victoria, in Balston Street, Melbourne.[69] I was in the office at the weekend because it was the only way to get through the heavy workload of writing plans, policies, and procedures without the inevitable intervention of normal weekday operations. Early in the afternoon, I was interrupted from my deliberations by a knock on the open door to my office. Standing there was a tall lad with long fair hair, wearing a white laboratory smock, shorts, and sneakers. He announced that he thought I should know that he had had an accident in the laboratory and spilt some acid. He said that he had cleaned it up, but he felt he should report it to someone. I thanked him, and asked him if he was OK. He said he was fine, and we then struck up a conversation during which I asked him for his name. Intrigued by his surname of "Kleinig", I enquired about his origins. And he told me that his grandfather was an engineer who had come to Australia from Germany before the Second World War, and had been involved in motor racing. So began one of the most important relationships in my life.

In continuing this story, I need to explain something. Throughout my life, I have been interested in all forms of sporting activity, as a player and as a spectator. And, as I sometimes reflect, it was no coincidence that I should end up living for a good many years in a city which is arguably the sports capital of Australia. In the early 1990s, as someone with a bit of spare cash, I was seriously thinking of becoming the sponsor of a budding sports star, perhaps in search of some reflected glory! I had acquired this sponsorship concept through my friend from NCSC days, David Danks. One day, he had idly suggested that I might like to sponsor him in indulging his passion for motor-cross and even offered to have

---

[69] These days, the Victorian branch of what is now called the Australian Red Cross Lifeblood organisation is based in Batman Street, West Melbourne. The custom built building in Balston Street has been replaced by apartment blocks.

me as a co-driver. But getting seriously injured in a crash wasn't on my agenda. Nevertheless, he had planted an idea that was gestating, and my mind was open to other opportunities.

In the weeks after our initial encounter, I bumped into Andrew on several occasions and we had further conversations. He attended team meetings in the Lecture Theatre which was adjacent to my office. And I would often meet attendees in the kitchen during tea breaks which were a regular feature of blood bank life. Andrew was a friendly and thoughtful young man with a natural charm, an inquisitive nature, and little inclination to defer to those in authority. I also think that, apart from the social interaction, he found life in the Blood Bank's laboratories profoundly boring. So he sought intelligent conversation. In any event, one morning, in idle chatter, he shared with me that he had a passion for the game of volleyball. As it happened, this was something in which I had more than a passing interest. RCBBV sponsored the sport under the Victorian Health Promotion Foundation's tobacco advertising replacement programme, and Gordon Whyte had asked me to attend competitions on behalf of the organisation and occasionally hand out trophies.[70] So I listened intently to what Andrew told me about the sport.

A couple of weeks later, I attended a volleyball competition which was being held at courts in Bundoora. Surprise, surprise, I once again encountered Andrew and we had a further chat. From memory, it was on this occasion that he told me about the rigour of training for what was a very demanding sport. And he also shared with me that he was thinking of switching to the beach version of the game. Beach volleyball involved two person teams. And there were both local competitions and a national circuit which included semi-professional players. As I digested this information, a few things began to gel in my mind. I was intrigued about the beach version of the game, and I was wondering whether this was an opportunity to support a budding sportsman. In May, I visited Andrew in the RCBBV laboratories and suggested that we have a chat outside work. I think he was a bit taken aback, but perhaps he was also intrigued. Anyway, he agreed to meet me, and on 22 May we rendezvoused at a pub called the Bleeding Wolf on Beaconsfield Parade in St Kilda.[71]

---

[70] Following the ban on tobacco sponsorship of sport in December 1989, the Victorian government established the VHPF with funding to replace that provided by the tobacco companies. RCBBV was keen to be involved because sports men and women were seen as potential donors. So we sponsored volleyball and lent our name to various trophies.

[71] This somewhat gloomy hotel, with dark wooden benches and tables, no longer exists.

At this point, volleyball, let alone beach volleyball, was not a sport of which I had much knowledge, and I had a genuine interest in learning about the finer points of the game. But I also wanted to form a view about whether this young man was someone whose sporting ambitions were worthy of support. After all, I didn't know him from Adam. Anyway, our conversation in the pub was fruitful and we got to know a bit about each other. And, during our chat, he also told me that beach volleyball was about to make it to the Olympics. This both surprised me and heightened my interest.[72] And, at his suggestion, I subsequently went along to watch an event down at St Kilda beach where I met his partner Tim Burrows who seemed to be another friendly and intelligent fellow. To the uninitiated, it was a spectacular sport, with athletic bodies flying through the air. And I could see why it had potential for drawing spectators already enamoured with beach culture. My mind ticked over, and I did a bit more research on the sport, with its international reach very evident. I got the bug and, with my interest in supporting a professional athlete, the next time I saw Andrew at the blood bank I took him to one side and put a proposal to him. In short, I offered to support him and his partner in becoming serious competitors on the national stage. I could already see the Olympic rings! Andrew said he'd have a chat with his partner. And he wanted to know more about what it would involve. But in principle he accepted my proposal.

During the next few months, I committed some serious time to educating myself about beach volleyball, and getting my head around what might reasonably be expected of someone in a management role. And Andrew and I met regularly, sometimes during tea breaks at work, but mostly over dinner at a series of restaurants, with Romeo's in Toorak eventually becoming the most frequented venue. In August, we had a setback because Tim became unavailable. But Andrew soon found a new and more experienced partner named Simon Yudelivich, whom I met for the first time in September. He bought into the concept of having a "team manager" and it was all systems go. And we subsequently had a series of meetings to establish a form of contract and to plan the campaign. I also put up the cash to employ a sports psychologist with whom Andrew and Simon had several sessions, we developed a brochure which I hawked to several potential sponsors, and I acquired a video camera to film games for the purposes of recording and analysing play. Andrew also did some photo shoots to pursue some marketing opportunities.

---

[72] Beach Volleyball was introduced at the 1992 Barcelona Olympic Games as a demonstration event, and became an official Olympic sport in 1996.

Once the season was underway in mid-November, I was soon travelling with the team to inter-state events commencing with a tournament at Bondi. The lads focussed on their competition whilst I handled the entry fees, flights and accommodation. And once I appeared on the beach in a "managerial" role I met a number of other players. This led me into a whole other adventure in my life, with the establishment of a players' association, and eventually to a serious commitment to the administration of the sport, which is the subject of Chapter 9.

I am not quite sure how this sporting-based association with Andrew led to a lifetime family commitment. It's quite a leap. But these things can creep up on you, and there were special circumstances. Spending significant time with a sports person before, during, and after competition can become quite intense and inevitably you become involved in their personal life. And therein lies the rub. Andrew came from a family which was very similar to my own, consisting of his mother and a brother who was five years older. His biological father had walked away when he was only two years old. So, like me he had been raised in a single parent family in which his mother had found the raising of two boys quite challenging. During his early years, there had been several step-fathers, and during his teenage years, his brother had left home and eventually moved overseas. Following his graduation from Monash University as a medical scientist at the end of 1989, his mother had found a new partner and had taken up a life of managing motels as a locum which took her all over Victoria and NSW. So Andrew was of no fixed abode, and started to live with mates. So, when I got to know him, he seemed to be very much on his own, driving a succession of much beloved old cars, with only his mates to support him.

After dealing with me as a manager, and receiving financial support for his sporting ambition without any strings attached, I think Andrew saw me as an older person that he could trust in a world where he had no roots. For my part, I really enjoyed the company of a younger person who challenged my views. He was honest and open, not averse to lengthy conversations about practically anything, and had values very similar to my own. And the shared experience of coming from a small nuclear family meant that we had a lot in common. So, what started off as being a business relationship gradually turned into a friendship. And, moving between rented accommodations shared with mates, on several occasions he came to briefly live in the spare bedroom at my place in Kew. Strangely, during these visits, we didn't see much of one another. We lived in different time zones. He worked shifts at RCBBV, and often in the morning he would be returning from a night out on the tiles when I was going to work. In any event, I think that my place offered a sanctuary, and I have always considered it a mark of the trust between us that he chose to leave some cherished personal belongings with me for safe keeping which are still with me to this day.

Despite our diligent preparation, the 1991/92 beach volleyball season wasn't all plain sailing. The team was moderately successful but they were competing against guys who had a great deal more experience. In Adelaide over the New Year period Andrew got sick with a virus, and at other events he had the odd niggle with a shoulder injury. As the later tournaments loomed, his girlfriend also started to emerge as a significant figure and she began to travel with us. This presented certain challenges, not least in retaining the commitment of his partner Simon. However, at the end of the season, the team hit success in the Victoria State Open and won the tournament beating some old foes Skip and Eddy. In our beach volleyball journey, 23 February 1992 was a day to remember.

In the months that followed that first season, we took stock, and Andrew indicated that he was seriously thinking of advancing his career by moving to California which was the home of beach volleyball. In fact, Andrew and his girlfriend had set their hearts on moving to Manhattan Beach so that Andrew could obtain some professional coaching, play in local competitions, meet some the legends of the game, and enjoy the unique lifestyle of one of the most glamorously chic places in the world. I was pleased for him, and I hoped that it would give him the boost he needed to make the next step as a professional sportsman. But it meant that for a while he would have no involvement in the domestic beach volleyball season, with the future of our "contract" left open. In April 1992, he and his girlfriend boarded a plane for Los Angeles.

For the next little while, I did not see a lot of Andrew, and our paths might well have gone their separate ways. But we kept in touch and he sent me the odd postcard. Later in 1992, it was agreed that I should visit him in Los Angeles on the way back from an extended holiday in the UK. I found him and his girlfriend living in a comfortable apartment in Manhattan Beach with a kindly landlady looking out for them. And they were having a ball. Mind you, life in Los Angeles had its challenges. In late April 1992, there had been riots in the down-town area, arising from police beating an Afro-American called Rodney King. And in June there had been an earthquake. In any event, his girlfriend was working in a fashion shop and Andrew was playing with various partners on the local beach volleyball circuit. After a couple of days soaking up the beach culture, we had an interesting trip up to San Francisco and then to Yosemite National Park where we stayed overnight in one of the canvas cabins. And on our return, I stayed for a few days at the Sea Sprite Motel in Hermosa Beach and enjoyed mixing with the constant flow of beautiful people on skateboards along the boardwalk. In late June I returned to Australia by way of Hawaii. And back at the blood bank, normal life resumed. At the end of September, with resources running low, Andrew and his girlfriend left Los Angeles to spend time in Europe where they would stay for the next twelve months. Initially, they based themselves in London, and visited friends in England, including my mother in Nottingham. And they saw the winter out in Blackheath and Woolwich in London where Andrew got a job at a local blood bank.

Back in Australia, my life at RCBBV was as busy as ever. But by now I had been drawn into establishing the Australian Beach Volleyball Players Association. In late October the beach volleyball season got under way and I was increasingly involved with the politics of the sport. Andrew kept in touch and in April I received a rare letter from him to tell me that he and his girlfriend were slowly touring Europe. Eventually they made it to Turkey where they were laid up for some time as Andrew recovered from a shoulder injury. In June, Andrew and his girlfriend then took separate paths, with Andrew returning by himself to resume his beach volleyball activities in LA. I visited him on the way back from a holiday in Canada, whilst also liaising with people at the headquarters of the AVP.[73] During this trip, I had a long chat with him about his future. He seemed unsettled, and he was continuing to struggle with a shoulder injury for which he was contemplating some unconventional treatment. I advised him against it and he took my advice. But I was worried about him. In late November 1993, he returned to Australia and resumed life in Melbourne re-joining the blood bank. After two years, with what was now a chronic injury, his dream of playing competitive beach volleyball was at an end.

In early 1994, Andrew's girlfriend returned from Europe and the couple settled into a kind of family life in a unit in Mordialloc. In the next two years, our friendship continued through telephone calls, the occasional dinner, visits to the houseboat I had acquired on Lake Eildon, and very competitive games of croquet played on cricket ovals in various parts of suburban Melbourne. During this period, he shared with me that he was heartily tired of working at the blood bank. And he was

---

[73] The AVP is the Association of Volleyball Professionals which runs the professional circuit in the USA.

considering a number of options. We spent some time discussing a variety of career paths with something "environmental" seeming to be his preference; but that would probably require further education. In the meantime, no longer able to play volleyball, he was thinking of becoming a sports masseur. And, a while later, he enrolled in a part time course and duly qualified with a Certificate in Advanced Sports Massage. He then set up a practice called Klein's Tactile Therapies, for which we developed a business plan, and he got a spare time job as a masseur with a football club.

Towards the end of 1994, Andrew's life was thrown into turmoil as he split up with his girlfriend Nikki. And, with his life in a bit of spin, he came to live with me for a while. As before, we didn't see much of each other except for a weekly trip to a restaurant. Eventually, he moved in with mates in a house in Danks Road in South Melbourne. He was now a free agent and a few months later he met a girl named Siobhan, with whom he shared a lot of interests including a love of animals, and who would eventually become a significant figure in both our lives. Meanwhile, my own life reached a bit of a turning point. With my mother migrating to Australia in mid-1995, I had another extended trip to the UK to help in her preparations, and I was seriously considering a change of direction in my own career.

In 1996, what had become a friendship would change for ever. One evening in February, I received a call from Andrew in which he told me that Siobhan was pregnant. It was a seminal moment, if you'll excuse the pun. My immediate reaction was to be supportive and the rest, as they say, is history. From that moment, I found myself increasingly involved in Andrew's life in ways that went considerably beyond what might be expected of a friend. And, becoming a father would transform Andrew's life. Although initially parental responsibility laid heavily upon him, he took it in his stride knowing that his days as a free spirit were numbered and rising to the challenge of establishing a happy family life.

In the period immediately before the birth of his daughter Brittany in November 1996, and for six months after, Andrew moved in with Siobhan. It was a challenging time for all of them. In the circumstances, we discussed the need for him to have a permanent home which would enable him to have some independence in fulfilling his parental responsibilities. And, since I had the means, I helped him to establish a stable environment with the purchase of a unit in Elwood. For the next nine months, Andrew's life settled down into a holding pattern. Siobhan moved in to live with her parents, and Andrew had Brittany to stay with him at weekends. However, in early 1998 he came to what would be a cross-roads. With a lot going on in his head about his family responsibilities and his career, he decided to take time out and think through the future direction of his life. He had long wanted to go to South America and in June 1998 he commenced an odyssey which would be the last great adventure of a free spirit. For the final weeks of this trip, I joined him in Chile and we went walking down in the Torres del Paine National Park. As we travelled we talked through many issues, and by the end of our journey it was clear that he had arrived at some important decisions about his career and his family.

Initially, on his return to Australia, for a few months Andrew resumed his previous existence, working at the blood bank and having weekly custody of his daughter.[74] I would catch up with him every weekend when we would spend a couple of hours in playgrounds and parks, and visiting small cafes for a bite to eat. During this time, we spent quite a bit of time talking about his career and I provided advice which helped him to identify a vocation that fitted his values. As a consequence, in late 1998, he resigned from the blood bank and enrolled in an environmental science course at Deakin University. In early 2002, he emerged with a First Class honours Bachelor of Conservation Ecology degree with an award for top of year. In the final stages of his studies, we had a lot of fun with his major assignment for a thesis on the habitat of small mammals. It was based in the Green's Bush reserve in Mornington, and I assisted him with a trapping programme.

After graduating, finding employment in the environmental sector proved challenging, and he had several short term jobs eventually ending up with a small company maintaining Council nature strips based in Mornington. To accommodate this work, in 2003 we acquired a house close to the beach on the road down to Mount Martha, whilst we rented out the unit in Elwood. But after a couple of years of relatively unrewarding work, in 2005 he successfully landed a significant role with Melbourne Water based back in Melbourne.

During this period, Andrew made a firm commitment to family life. In the short term, he regularly caught up with Siobhan, and at the weekend Brittany came to stay in Mornington. But then the three of them began to live together as a family. On taking up the job at Melbourne Water, for a short time they lived in rented accommodation in Melbourne, while we sold the properties in Elwood and Mornington.

---

[74] Interestingly, during this period, an angelic picture of Brittany would feature on a leaflet produced by the Blood Bank to promote the Anti D Programme.

Then, in 2006, we used the proceeds to buy a family home at Crete Avenue in Ashburton.

By now, I think it would be accurate to say that Andrew and I had become a version of family. And, happily settled in Kew, my mother certainly regarded him as a grandson with whom she had a loving relationship. For several years, Christmas lunch at her place became a family fixture. I was also learning how to provide a form of parental support, where I helped him to be the person he wanted to be whilst trying not to interfere in his life. I can't claim to have been the perfect parent, but I gave it a good shot.

One of the most important things that has linked Andrew and me since the very early days has been our commitment to the environment and, for a number of years, bush walks were a regular feature of our existence. This interest eventually led to our acquisition of a conservation property. The search for our "block" in Callignee would consume a huge amount of time, and test our relationship in many ways. The full story emerges in later chapters. But it would never have happened without our joint commitment. In brief, we started this project in 2002, and it took 5 years to find the right block. In 2008, this was followed by a building project which is enough to test anyone's patience. And then in 2009 the property was consumed by fire. This was a seminal moment in my life. During the conflagration, it is no exaggeration to say that Andrew saved my life and, afterwards when talking to the media, he surprised me by saying that I was a kind of father. He had never shared that view with me. But ever since, I have had no compunction about referring to him as my son. In the meantime, I also became bonded with Siobhan and Brittany. And, together with Andrew, these are the people I have now regarded as my Australian family for more than ten years.

Finally, I could not give an account of this very important relationship without referring to Andrew's health, which in recent years has become a significant issue. For a long time, things were not quite right. His Graves disease became apparent twenty years ago, during his university course at Deakin in 2000. At that time, I well remember his getting into the car and the inside windows steaming up as he emitted heat from his skin which seemed to be on fire. Later he would have significant back issues and, after corrective surgery in 2017 he was diagnosed with an auto-immune disease. I don't need to relate the many twists and turns, but all of this has at times taken a heavy toll on him and all those around him. And it has often caused me to reflect on how relatively fortunate I have been with my own health given my pace of life and sporting activities. Amazingly, and despite considerable frustration in terms of impairing his ability to have an active life, he has borne all of his ailments with great fortitude, which is the mark of a brave and resilient man. Indeed, I am proud of him, and committed to providing support as long as I am physically and mentally able.

The account I have presented above has largely focussed on the paths of two lives over three decades during which we were slowly drawn together. I doubt that there is a similar story to be told. But then there are many models of what constitutes family. The thing that's unusual is that I had no hand in Andrew's upbringing. In the absence of his biological father, I came to occupy a natural place in Andrew's life. And he became the son I never had. For my part, as a kind of parent, I applied the model which I learnt from my mother. Unconditional love, belief in him, unreserved support, and an abiding wish for him to be happy. On a different plane, there is a very special feeling which comes with knowing that you have made a positive difference to someone else's life. I did not bring him into the world and so I have never owed him the kind of duty that comes with that creative act. So I would argue that my version of parental care is more selfless than many. And I have told myself repeatedly over many years that this is one person in the world that I will never let down. I do that not because I have to do it through biological duty, but because it fulfils some greater mission of caring for someone else above yourself. He has also become my best friend. We have come a long way since that fateful day in February 1991.

To conclude, I do think back to Redfield's concept of a *"birth vision"* about which I wrote in *"For Goodness Sake"*.[75] In my case the vision is characterised by the absence of a father in my own life. And Redfield's theory has led me to the conclusion that I have had a mission to play a significant male parent role in the life of someone else who did not have a father. As will be evident, this is not about having one's own children. It is about standing in for the missing male parent of another. This has huge resonance in the very strong relationship that I have with Andrew, who in the second half of my life has certainly become the son I probably don't deserve but I am eternally grateful to have. Through him, I have become the person I was meant to be.

---

[75] American author James Redfield wrote a series of spiritual books, the Celestine series, in which he refers to *"Birth Vision"* as being *"What we are called to accomplish"*. If we follow this calling, we help spiritualize the planet.

9: Beach Manoeuvres

In the course of supporting Andrew's beach volleyball activities in the summer of 1991/92, I started to appear regularly on local beaches in Victoria and inter-state. Andrew and his partners were participating not only in State events but also on a national beach volleyball circuit organised by the Australian Volleyball Federation ("AVF"). During the period from October through to March, this involved *Pro Tour Grand Prix* tournaments in Queensland (Surfers Paradise), NSW (Manly in Sydney), Victoria (St Kilda), South Australia (Glenelg in Adelaide) and Western Australia (Cottesloe in Perth) and a National Championship. Meanwhile, each mainland State Volleyball Association organised a State Open tournament and there were other events including 4-a-side competitions. Finally, on 19 January 1992, there was an international *World Series* tournament at Bondi Beach run by the FIVB ("Fédération Internationale de Volleyball"), and a Champion of Champions event held indoors at Rod Laver Arena in Melbourne. The FIVB event was an amazing spectacle, with stands on the beach, and a strong international contingent amongst the crowd, including Brazilians who made quite a racket with their drums.

In the initial stages, my role in all of this was to support Andrew and his partner. Behind the scenes, I organised travel and accommodation, handled tournament entry, and pursued sponsorship by a number of relevant companies retailing products such as beach clothing, sunnies, sunscreen and soft drinks. During tournaments, I watched and recorded both Andrew's matches and those of opponents, with the use of a video camera. We used this material to analyse play, and develop tactics.[76] And I also engaged a sports psychologist who provided advice on developing team work and performance. Whether all this effort bore fruit for Andrew and Simon is a moot point. But, during the season, they did advance through several rounds at each tournament and, in February 1992, they won the Victorian State Open. In any event, at the end of the 1991/92 season, Andrew decided to try his hand in the USA and my managerial role became redundant.

Coming back to the bigger picture, my appearances at successive events in the 1991/92 season, dressed in appropriately trendy beach gear

---

[76] I often left my video equipment unattended for a break and, to my amusement, players would take the opportunity to make some unscheduled recordings of a somewhat salacious nature which I then found later including close-ups of various body parts!

about which I had to be educated (!), had an unexpected consequence.[77] My activity, including the video filming of both Andrew and his opponents, did not go unnoticed. In particular, I met with a number of the other players including a South Australian guy in his late twenties called Andy Burdin. Andy was the top ranked Australian player, and also a budding entrepreneur. At the time, he played with a young partner named Julian Prosser and was based in Perth. One afternoon in late 1991, he sidled up to me during a break and asked me what I was up to. I explained my interest and he was intrigued. I guess that I was the first outsider to appear in such a "player management role". At a subsequent event, I had an off-beach meeting and chat with him and he took my telephone number. After the end of the season, he called me for several longer conversations, and I soon struck up an association with him which led to my involvement not only in the administration of the sport but also in his personal business activities. He also highlighted that beach volleyball had huge potential not only in Australia but around the world. He shared with me his participation in a professional circuit in the USA which was managed by a very strong player organisation called the Association of Volleyball Professionals ("AVP"), the growth of the sport in Brazil, and the impending inclusion of the sport in the Olympic Games. This was all very interesting stuff and bore out much of what Andrew had previously told me.

A key part of my conversations with Andy related to the manner and extent to which players had input to the conduct of the sport in Australia. At present, beach volleyball was administered by the AVF Board with the Beach Commission responsible for operational management. This body included three senior players (Andy Burdin, Jacqui Vukosa, and Paul Smith) who provided a player perspective on a personal basis. Under the AVF's Five Year Plan, it was proposed to facilitate the establishment of a players' association the aim of which would be to provide a formal structure for player input to the management and development of the sport. Andy told me that, to implement this concept, the AVF had requested that the players submit a proposal and, to this end, a Players' National Working Party had been established. A formal document had then been submitted to the AVF on 12 April 1992. He shared this document with me and asked whether I would be prepared to assist the players in establishing the organisation. After some reflection, I agreed. As a consequence, in May, I flew up to Sydney to attend a

---

[77] I really did have to learn how to dress, replacing floppy white hat, shirt, shorts, socks and sneakers with a peaked cap, T shirt, beach shorts, and thongs.

meeting with Andy and two AVF officials, the General Manager Ken Breen and the Beach Volleyball Tour Manager Blair Harrison. We met at Ken Breen's home in Sydney on 11 May 1992.

At the AVF meeting, Ken Breen provided background to the growth of the sport, plans for the 1992/93 season, the current parameters of delivering the sport through a professionally managed and sponsored national tour, and the AVF's expectations of a players' association. As regards the development of the sport, Ken explained that in the last three years the participation in indoor/beach volleyball had expanded rapidly, with the number of players between 19 and 29 expanding from 400,000 to 700,000. In recognition of this expansion, the Federal government was providing financial support of $400,000 with a further $600,000 coming from State governments. The AVF had also established substantial sponsorship agreements to generate income of another $2.5million so that the organisation's current budget was in the order of $3.5million with the employment of ten staff. An important part of the sponsorship in 1991/92 had been a contribution to beach volleyball from Diet Pepsi of $800,000. This had covered the national Grand Prix circuit, and the World Series event. The AVF had also secured media coverage with a payment of $80,000 to the ABC.

As regards plans for 1992/93, Ken Breen indicated that it might be necessary to reduce the scope of events because Diet Pepsi had cut its sponsorship by 50%. The AVF was endeavouring to find new sponsors, but sponsorship for sporting events was highly competitive. In any event, there would be no World Series event, with the focus on 6 Grand Prix events and an Open in each State. There would also be three events in which players could qualify for the national circuit. Breen then went on to describe the arrangements for managing the national tour. Mindful of its own lack of marketing expertise, the AVF had established a licence to deliver the sport which had been awarded to a company named Venture Marketing Group ("VMG"). VMG would be responsible for raising sponsorship, with the AVF taking a 15% cut.

Breen then indicated what the AVF was hoping to achieve by establishing a players' association. Under current arrangements, the input from the three players on the Beach Commission was provided on a personal basis with no obligation to represent anything other than their own views. He envisaged that a players' association would significantly upgrade player input to the development of the sport in Australia and internationally, and proposed a set of ground rules as follows:

a) The Association should be for players participating in the national circuit, with a potential membership of up to 100.

b) Men and women would have equal status.

c) The Association would handle communication with players and provide a mechanism for player input to the management and development of the sport.

d) The Association would establish a player Code of Conduct.

e) The Association would develop proposals for the establishment of a ranking system which could be used for the purposes of seeding specific pairs.

f) The AVF would allocate to the Association the Player Registration Fee of $40 per head, generating a potential annual income of $4,000.

g) The AVF would retain the right to events sponsorship, but the Association was free to get its own sponsors for the benefit of players.

h) The level of prize money would increase as the level of event sponsorship increased.

i) The Beach Commission would supply a full list of all players who had played on the circuit in 1991/92 to facilitate communication about formation of the Association.

j) It was noted that foreign players would not be allowed to play in Grand Prix tournaments in the 1992/93 season.

The response of Andy to these proposals was one of general acceptance, subject to the agreement of the Association as and when it formally came into being. Given that this was my first exposure to the national body administering a sport in Australia, I am sure that some of the finer points and nuances were lost on me. In any event, I was relatively impressed with the fact that the AVF had a strategic plan and that it had the foresight to see the benefit of tapping into the ideas of players many of whom were highly educated people who happened to have an athletic ability. And I found Ken Breen to be a highly articulate and persuasive guy. It was too early to know whether I could trust him. But he seemed to have a close working relationship with Andy which augured well. As the person responsible for managing operations on the beach, Blair Harrison appeared to be a reasonable man who had the respect of the players and with whom I could work. At the end of the meeting, we all parted in good spirits and so the journey began.

Following this initial meeting I had a number of conversations with Blair Harrison and the players' National Working Party. This team consisted of Andy and myself together with representatives from three other States - Jacqui Vukosa (NSW), Paul Smith (SA), and Robert Agnew (Victoria). However, with Andy and Jacqui travelling overseas for international competition, the work of this group largely fell on Robert, Paul and myself. And, in practice, Robert and I had carriage, with Robert keeping Paul in the loop by telephone. I met with Robert for the first time in June 1992 at his flat in South Yarra. At the time, he worked as a stock broker and, separated from his partner, he often had his five-year-old son Toby in tow.

In our initial conversations, Robert provided me with a distinctly different view of the beach volleyball world from the one that I had obtained from the meeting with the AVF and my conversations with Andy. He was persuasive, and I gradually came to the view that his assessment was an accurate reflection of the views of the majority of players, most of whom did not have access to international circuits or organisational politics. In particular, he indicated that the AVF was managing the delivery of the beach version of the sport as a poor cousin of the indoor game, which had a much stronger international profile, including recognition as an Olympic sport and greater public funding. Accordingly, it had determined to operate at arm's length. In return for a fee, it had passed significant control for delivery of the sport to the marketing company VMG who actually had little regard for player input or interests. This provided the opportunity for VMG to generate a significant return through sponsorship contracts with companies such as Diet Pepsi, and Vitari (which made dairy-free sorbets). Given that this was a commercial arrangement designed to provide a living for the operator, the payment to players was minimal which made the concept of a "professional" tour questionable. Robert also alerted me to the existence of some potentially significant competition in organising beach volleyball, including a group of players in NSW who had established an independent body called the *Northern Beaches Volleyball Association,* based in Manly and an off-shoot on the American AVP called Pro Beach.

Bearing all this in mind, Robert held the view that the AVF's proposal regarding a players' association should be treated with some caution. Whilst he acknowledged that the AVF had a genuine wish to accommodate player views, he suggested that this was window-dressing with little intention of giving players a substantive say in the management, delivery, or the development of the sport, and minimal financial reward in terms of prize money. Nevertheless, Robert thought that the AVF's initiative presented an opportunity to advance the role of players. In particular, once established, there was real potential for an independent players' association to become not only a voice for the players but also genuine partners in the management of the sport at strategic and operational levels with the ability to generate its own line of sponsorship. Of course, he realised that this approach would not necessarily be welcomed by the AVF and their marketing company, who might well respond by treating the players' association as if it were a union rather than partners. But this held no fears for Robert. And, even though my participation represented a significant departure from my previous industrial relations roles, the concept seemed to have considerable merit in advancing the rights and rewards of players. So began an extraordinary five years in which I became something between the administrative officer of a professional association and the general secretary of a small trade union.

Armed with this perspective, and still maintaining contact with Andy and his more generous view of AVF intentions, Robert and I initiated the process of forming the players' association. Following the meeting with the AVF, in good faith Blair Harrison had passed me contact information for some 80 players who had participated in the 1991/92 season and, in June 1992, we sent a survey to this group to gauge the level of support. There were no detractors, and there was a positive response from 50% of the males and 65% of the females. I then drafted a constitution, consulting with David Anthoness of the NSW Volleyball Conference, a contact provided by Jacqui Vukosa. We also considered a name for the organisation that would lend itself to a catchy acronym suitable for marketing purposes. At this stage, we came up with the *Australian Beach Volleyball Players Association ("ABVPA")*.

On the evening of 24 August 1992, Robert and I had a meeting with Ken Breen which was held at my home in Kew. The aim was for the National Working Party which we represented to report on progress, and for the AVF to share their plans for 1992. This turned out to be quite a revealing session which would significantly affect the way in which the Association would handle matters in the years ahead. In particular, Ken Breen divulged the following information:

i. Over the last three years, the AVF had made a major investment in beach volleyball because it was regarded as a sport with great potential. Finance from sponsorship had risen from $89,000 in 1989/90, to $350,000 in 1990/91 to $650,000 in 1991/92. However, the AVF acknowledged that the budget was considerably less than the $3 million invested in Indoor Volleyball.

ii. Over the three years, the sport had incurred a trading loss of around $80,000, due to the cost of TV coverage at $60,000 and an $80,000 "Sanction Fee" paid to the FIVB for staging the World Series event at Bondi in 1992.

iii. The AVF saw 1992/93 as a year of consolidation. VMG had been given a five-year contract with rights to manage the sport for a fee of $30,000 per annum and a share of sponsorship funding. At this stage player prize money would be frozen at 1991/92 levels.

iv. The 1992/93 season was to encompass six Grand Prix events, including the Australian Open. Because of the cost, the World Series event would be dropped. Ken Breen provided provisional dates.

v. Ken Breen said that Pro Beach was not seen as a threat to the AVF's rights in Australia.

vi. The AVF intended to establish an Australian Volleyball Magazine with Anthony Edgar as editor. Copies would be available to the Association at a discount.

Robert and I provided Ken Breen with a progress report on the formation of the players' association, including the favourable response to the survey of players, the likely name, and the timing for establishment and incorporation by year-end. Breen re-iterated his commitment to provide funding to the organisation. He said that this would take the form of $35 for each player registered with the AVF.[78] Finally, Robert raised the contentious issue of the requirement for male players to play with a singlet to which many players objected. Breen suggested that this was a matter for VMG to determine, depending on sponsorship arrangements, and suggested that the Association might like to take up the matter with VMG CEO John Winters. However, he indicated that failure to wear a singlet might well be the basis for excluding a player.

Following this meeting, Robert and I briefed the other members of the National Working Party, and laid plans for the important first gathering of the players scheduled for mid-November, during the Grand Prix event

---

[78] Interestingly, this was a back-track on the $40 promised in May.

in Sydney. In the meantime, in early September, we conducted a survey of players regarding a number of current issues, including options for a points-based ranking system, proposals for membership and tournament entry-fees, the type of ball to be used in competitions, an Association logo, the system for international qualification, the proposed programme of events, the status of foreign players, the level of prize money, and reimbursement of travel expenses in the event of tournament cancellation. This engendered a considerable correspondence and enthusiasm for what we were trying to do. Finally, on 16 September 1992, the National Working Party convened to adopt a Constitution and so the ABVPA came into existence.

On 18 September, VMG proceeded with a communication to players about arrangements for the 1992/93 season. Even though the AVF had briefed them on the establishment of the ABVPA, in preparing its plans they had made no attempt to involve the players. Ignoring this oversight, on 28 September the National Working Party submitted a response to VMG's communication, referring to it as a Discussion Paper rather than accepting it as a "fait accompli" announcement. In particular, the National Working Party suggested amendments to some of the "proposals", rejection of others (eg change to the Double Elimination system, schedule of prize money, and the introduction of a 4-a-side competition), and an assertion of its rights in respect of a number of policy matters as agreed with the AVF (such as the player registration and ranking systems). The National Working Party foreshadowed a range of other proposals and initiatives. One can only imagine how all of this was received by VMG who appeared to think that they had a *carte blanche*. In any event, this early exchange of material very much characterised all that would follow. It was clear from the outset that VMG had no intention of accommodating a role for players and would proceed as if they did not exist except as participants. And from the outset, the players gave a clear signal that they were partners whose views would be ignored at VMG's peril.

On 7 October 1992, the National Working Party issued a progress report to all those players who had responded to previous correspondence. And on 31 October 1992, midway through the Grand Prix event at Bondi Beach, we held the first general meeting of the players at the Bondi Pavilion. At this very well attended gathering, which I chaired, Robert explained the genesis of the ABVPA, the aims of the organisation, and the importance of obtaining recognition of players' rights to have a say in the development of the sport, the organisation of events, reasonable prize money, and a range of other issues. I tabled copies of the ABVPA Constitution, and we discussed the results of the recent survey, with particular emphasis on the format of tournaments (Double Elimination vs Pool Play), type of ball, ranking system including impact of foreign players, cancellation of events, and proposals for 4-a-side events.[79] Finally, we foreshadowed the first AGM to be held during the second tournament of the season, at which the Constitution would be formally adopted ahead of concluding an application for incorporation, and we enrolled virtually all those present as members. Amazingly, ten days after this meeting, and without consultation, VMG sent a letter to all players indicating that John Winters would be attending the AGM to address the players. The National Working Party responded with an indication that this was a private meeting and that, once established, elected ABVPA officers would be only too pleased to commence discussions with him about a range of matters.

As planned, the ABVPA proceeded with its first AGM on 28 November 1992 at the Esplanade Night Club in Surfers Paradise. It was attended by 52 members and, within a few days, membership had climbed to 80 with 50 men and 30 women. At this meeting, I was confirmed as Public Officer and the following Officers were elected:

President	Robert Agnew
Vice President	Paul Smith
Treasurer	Jacqui Vukosa
Secretary/Membership Secretary	Andrew Molo

The other members of the Executive Committee were the following State Representatives:

New South Wales	Cassie Drew
Queensland	Glenn Robertson
South Australia	Mark Frisby-Smith
Victoria	Phil Roberts
Western Australia	Annette Huygens-Tholen

---

[79] Rather akin to the repechage system in rowing competition, a traditional format for beach volleyball events allowed for pairs who were eliminated in the first round to have a second chance by playing losers in the next round. The aim was to assist pairs who might have been drawn to play the top seeds in that first round. This extended the competition and VMG were keen to adopt a pool system with no double elimination.

Following the AGM, I concluded a number of administrative arrangements, including formal registration with Corporate Affairs, the establishment of a bank account, and a registered address with a PO Box in Kew. Ahead of the next Grand Prix, scheduled to take place at Glenelg Beach in Adelaide over the New Year holiday, Paul and Jacqui had a meeting on 27 December with John Winters to establish some sort of working relationship. At this meeting, it was made clear that the ABVPA were now formally representing the interests of players and that VMG would need to work with the President and Vice President in achieving a successful delivery of the national circuit. A formal communication on a range of issues was also foreshadowed.

A few days later, on 30 December, the Executive Committee had its first meeting, which took place at Paul Smith's home in Glenelg ahead of the SA Grand Prix. At this and two further meetings during the tournaments at Manly and Cottesloe, it was resolved to write to VMG requesting a copy of their contract with the AVF and requesting a meeting in March 1993 for a full discussion on the scope and content of the 1993/94 season. The Committee also identified a number of other issues for discussion with VMG, including tournament formats, reimbursement of expenses in the event of tournament cancellation, opposition of male players to the wearing of singlets, abolition of tournament entry fees, and need for a fairer system for distributing sponsorship benefits. The Executive Committee also considered a range of other matters which would become the core business of the organisation in the year ahead. These included the development of a Player Code of Conduct, a Seeding System, Most Valued Player Award system, review of the Association's name which some thought was too long, design of an Association logo, conclusion of a budget, search for Association sponsors, development of a written Player Guide, need for player facilities on the beach, ethics in obtaining personal sponsorship, and a Wild Card Entry system. Finally, it was decided to appoint two Honorary Vice Presidents. Andrew Burdin became Hon VP responsible for "International Relations", and I became Hon VP with responsibility for "Administration". In this role, I undertook to operate as a kind of General Secretary with responsibility for financial management, recruitment, organisation of meetings, and the publication of an association newsletter called TIMEOUT, the first edition of which was published on 6 January 1993.

1993 turned out to be quite a roller-coaster. When I look back, I never cease to be amazed at how I became involved in such a momentous set of events. I would be the first to admit that I started with little or no knowledge of sports administration, marketing and event management, not to mention the politics involved. What I did bring was my managerial and administrative skills, a commitment to due process, and my experience in the development of plans, strategy, and policy. I also brought a moral compass to a field of human endeavour that was dominated by a culture of administrative bureaucracy and financial self-interest.

In the next twelve months, the ABVPA made strenuous efforts to contribute to the management and delivery of the sport. By mid-year, membership had expanded to over 90 and even the most faint-hearted players had joined the organisation because the organisation was seen as a vehicle for ensuring player input to successful outcomes. Mind you, it was a struggle. In being called to account, VMG resorted to all manner of tactics to ignore or resist player proposals. In the meantime, the AVF endeavoured to maintain a low profile. From the papers I hold, I could write a book on a remarkable saga but, in brief, the main events and developments during the next four years were as follows.

1993

On 29 March, the ABVPA was invited to join a meeting organised by the AVF to review the 1992/93 season. This was held at the Sydney Boating Club at Elizabeth Bay and was attended by AVF representatives, Executive Directors of State/Territory Volleyball Associations, and VMG. The ABVPA was represented by Rob Agnew, Paul Smith, Jacqui Vukosa and myself and we turned out in business attire which somewhat upstaged the more casually dressed volleyball fraternity. Ahead of this meeting we distributed a paper in which we provided an assessment of the 1992/93 season just finished and identified a range of issues for discussion. Ken Breen outlined plans for 1993/94 and announced that the beach volleyball national tour would in future be delivered by a new subsidiary of VMG named Beach Volleyball Professional Tour ("BVPT"). Of significance, and to our dismay, it was proposed that the national tour would be restricted to four mainland States with Adelaide excluded. These events were to be complemented by State run Open tournaments. BVPT was also unable to finance an FIVB World Series event. However, there was a tentative commitment to improve player facilities at events, tournament presentation, and prize money subject to the outcome of sponsorship negotiations. Whilst this showed that some attempt had been made to respond to issues raised by ABVPA, it left a lot of issues hanging in the air.

During the off-season, the AVBPA pursued a number of matters including the following:

a)   We successfully lobbied for the reinstatement of the Grand Prix in Adelaide.

b)   We submitted a policy on Ranking for adoption by the AVF.

c)   We adopted a policy on the ethics of obtaining individual sponsorship.

d)   We established a partnership with Volleyball Magazine to manage the Most Valued Player Awards, encompassing a range of separate awards for men and women reflecting the various skills associated with the sport.

e)   We sought to improve the delivery of the national tour, including installation of electronic scoreboards, and provision for a Wild Card Entry system

f)   We pursued the AVF to honour their commitment to provide an annual grant based on the re-allocation of the per-capita player registration fee, and they agreed that we should register players and collect the fee.

g)   We submitted proposals to the AVF for international selection, following admission of beach volleyball as a sport to be included in the 1996 Atlanta Olympic Games.

h)   We sought to establish a new Player Contract that would encompass player interests including ownership of body signage, an equitable distribution of prize money, First Aid and masseur services, a players' tent with security for personal belongings, and compensation in the event of tournament cancellation.

i)   We continued to resist the introduction of a 4-a-side series.

j)   We offered to work with BVPT in developing promotional material.

k)   In July, I visited the AVP in California and met with the President, Jon Stenson, who provided valuable advice on a player based approach to the development of the sport.

l)   The Executive established a marketing strategy designed to secure a sponsorship deal for the ABVPA.

m)   Members voted to change the name of the Association to the Australian Volleyball Professionals Association ("AVPA") and to adopt an associated logo. The new name came into force on 9 December 1993.

As the start of the 1993/94 season approached, BVPT remained tight-lipped about the national tour. Frustrated, we wrote to the AVF to register our serious concerns about BVPT's abilities to meet their contractual obligations. In particular, we indicated their unwillingness to consult with players, and their apparent inability to attract significant sponsorship following their loss of the contract with Diet Pepsi. We also noted the failure to confirm the details of the tour which deprived players of the ability to plan their participation in a cost-effective manner. In response the AVF prevailed upon BVPT to meet with AVPA representatives. At a meeting with VMG which took place on 12 October, they refused to recognise the AVPA, dismissed our offer to negotiate an agreement with them, and rejected virtually all our proposals regarding a player contract apart from our ideas on a ranking system. They then proceeded to unilaterally launch the season with just three weeks' notice ahead of the first event at Surfers Paradise in early November.

As the start of the season loomed, it was clear that there would be a rocky road ahead. The AVF appeared to have retired from any direct involvement in the delivery of the sport and seemed unwilling or unable to honour their commitment to facilitate a meaningful input from players by intervening with VMG/BVPT. The AVPA was faced with either taking industrial action against BVPT or pursuing a rear-guard campaign of attrition. Given that industrial action would deny players the ability to play the sport they loved, not to mention simple logistics in the days before social media, we chose the latter.

In the meantime, there was one really important development which would have a major long-term impact on the future of the sport and significantly change our approach to representing player interests. In September 1993 it was announced that beach volleyball was to be upgraded from a demonstration sport to a full Olympic event for the 1996 Olympic Games in Atlanta. At the same time, Sydney was selected as the venue for the 2000 Olympics. This augured well for the status that the AVF would give to the sport, and the availability of government funding. In response, in late November, the AVF convened a meeting with the AVPA in Sydney to discuss plans for Australia's Olympic programme. In preparation for this meeting, the AVPA put forward criteria for Olympic selection and access to Australian Institute of Sport ("AIS") scholarships. Our input was welcomed and treated with respect.

Spurred on by the AVF approach to dealing with us, we redoubled our efforts to achieve improvements in the presentation of the sport on the BVPT circuit. As the season began, we implemented a system of comprehensive feedback to BVPT after each event and, in initial comments, we highlighted concerns about the standard of refereeing, the restriction of entry to just 16 players, the unilateral introduction of a system of fining for misdemeanours, and the lack of a Tour Guide despite AVPA input.[80] On the positive side, we welcomed the installation of an electronic scoreboard and the introduction of a relatively secure players' area on the beach.

1994

At the turn of the year, we were hopeful that 1994 would deliver a real change in attitudes, and we were delighted to receive the long-promised financial support from the AVF in the form of a capitation fee. However, despite improvements in event management in the initial Grand Prix Events of the 1993/94 season, by the time we came to the final event in Cottesloe the standard of presentation was very much below par with no players' secure area, no stands, and no scoreboard. It was as if the wheels had fallen off, and we suspected that BVPT had just run out of money. We sent a comprehensive report on performance to the AVF and renewed our campaign for an agreement between BVPT and the AVPA designed to ensure greater accountability. In our feedback, we continued to press for the re-introduction of Double Elimination, expressed our disappointment with TV and media coverage, and indicated concerns about inconsistent umpiring, poor on-court presentation, inadequate scoreboards, and poor player facilities at some events.

Following our representations to the AVF about BVPT performance, on 19 February 1994 Robert and I met with the AVF Board. The Board were sympathetic to our concerns about BVPT and indicated that they had decided to institute tighter control over the delivery of the sport. In particular, they announced that Greg Lehmann had been appointed as Director responsible for beach volleyball and that the Beach Commission was to be re-established to manage beach affairs, with the AVPA

---

[80] The feedback was prepared by Rob, based on consultation with players, and was delivered with suitable relish.

recognised as the body representing player interests.[81] They also announced plans to establish a professional referees group, to finalise international selection rules, and to expand the number of events on the domestic circuit. In the meantime, VMG/BVPT reinvented itself as a new organisation named Sports Management Group ("SMG").

In the off-season, the AVPA concluded a Player Code of Conduct and also conducted the first MVP Ballot, with Julian Prosser and Anita Palm taking out the top Awards. And, on 31 March 1994, the AVF convened the first meeting of the new Beach Commission. Membership consisted of Greg Lehman as Chairperson, Ken Breen, John Winters, and Rob Agnew, with the appointment of a Beach Director pending. At this meeting, the AVF issued a policy document that indicated the basis on which it was proposed to measure SMG's performance in delivering the national tour. The AVPA had significant input to this document, and was well pleased with the final version which encompassed a number of goals including the following.

a)   Inclusion of all States on the national tour.
b)   Establishment of a national ranking system.
c)   State managed events to be used as qualification for participation in the national tour.
d)   Role of players on Beach Commission to be strengthened.
e)   Commercial TV coverage to be achieved.
f)   International component to be stressed.
g)   Journalists in each State to be targeted with press releases to ensure maximum exposure for the sport.
h)   Presentation standards to be maintained.
i)   Maintenance of leadership of Australia in the Asian region.
j)   Position of Australia internationally to be assured by close liaison with FIVB, and by support for Australian players in qualifying for overseas events.
k)   Australian Open to be developed as major event.

The document also introduced a set of performance indicators for SMG covering the need for at least six Grand Prix events, adequate promotion, maintenance of existing levels of prize money, and professional presentation of events including: an enclosed Centre Court, electronic scoreboards, well-informed commentaries, and professional

---

[81] The Beach Commission had been abolished when the VMG contract was established.

umpires. SMG was also to institute appropriate facilities for players including: shaded area with chairs on the Centre Court, a secure area for storage of belongings which was out of public sight, facilities for massage/physiotherapy and first aid, full first aid equipment and plentiful supplies of water. It was a big step forward for which the AVPA could take some considerable credit.

Despite the promulgation of this comprehensive set of guidelines, and the implied need for a co-operative approach to managing the national tour, SMG treated the AVPA with complete disdain. With mounting frustration, in September 1994 the AVPA again wrote to Ken Breen, citing our concern about the unwillingness of SMG to work with the AVPA, and the apparent failure of the Beach Commission to supervise the implementation of the SMG contract. We did not receive a meaningful response, and it seemed to us that the AVF had now abandoned its support for the AVPA.

1995

Ahead of the 1994/95 season, the AVPA received some good news regarding sponsorship. For some time we had been marketing our credentials to a wide range of organisations and, eventually, we obtained support from the local subsidiary of the German electronics company Blaupunkt. It was a modest deal with just $15,000 on offer in return for the players showing body signage. But this enabled us to establish a Bonus Pool with cash to be shared between the best-performing pairs. And we also proposed to invest in scoreboards for side courts, to improve presentation. The contract with Blaupunkt had been signed in early November 1994, in time for the NSW Grand Prix at Manly commencing on 11 November, and implementation presented quite a challenge. First of all, although the AVF were on side, SMG were highly reluctant, and we had to negotiate placement on the available clothing worn by the men and the women. In the case of the men, this was resolved by getting the guys to sow a patch on their singlets just below the main sponsor, Vitari. For the women there was scant clothing available for signage, so we obtained acceptance that they would wear an arm band. This arrangement worked well and signage was very evident on the TV coverage. The learning from the first outing was applied to the remaining tournaments and Blaupunkt were happy with the outcome. As the only non-player, the onus fell upon me to implement requirements, which was a far from enjoyable task. I had to obtain and issue the patches and arm bands, and then police the wearing which, for a while, did not make me the most popular person on the beach. At the end of the season, the AVPA was able to significantly supplement SMG prize money with Lee Zahner/Jeff Grocott and Kerri Pottharst/Anita Palm earning the top prize money. The runners up were Burdin/Prosser and Huygen-Tholen/Cook.[82] In the meantime, we were far from happy with the presentation of events. At Cottesloe, the end of season event was again run on a shoestring. There was no advertising for the event, no stands, no medical facilities, and no masseur. But there was a professional commentator and we improved his performance by supplying him with biographical details of all players to which he was able to refer in his commentary. We also established a good working relationship with the Chief Referee, and agreed with him the establishment of a liaison committee to ensure that any issues arising from tournaments were addressed in a timely and systematic way.

A major bone of contention to arise during this season was the existence and operations of what was called the Northern Beaches Volleyball Association ("NBVA"). They had been in operation for some years, and Robert and I had maintained regular contact with them. In late 1994 the AVF called on them to desist from organising events and, in early 1995, this escalated with threats to ban players participating in NBVA events from the AVF circuit and international selection. The AVPA did its best to intervene citing "restraint of trade" but the AVF were adamant and it was a continuing bone of contention. Sadly, from the AVPA perspective, the reality was that the NBVA presented events in a far more professional manner than SMG.

At the end of the season, we again conducted the MVP vote and this time the top female was Anita Palm with Lee Zahner and Julien Prosser equal top male player. And mid-year we conducted a vote on the introduction of an AVPA membership fee. 94% of the 86 members voted in favour of a $10 fee which we regarded as a real vote of confidence in our efforts. We also prepared a comprehensive review of SMG's performance during 1994/95, with proposals on a number of matters as follows.

---

[82] The subsequent Pottharst/Cook pairing went on to win the Gold Medal at the Sydney Olympics! Playing with a younger guy named Mark Williams, at the 2004 Athens Olympics, Julian Prosser obtained 4th position in a Bronze medal play-off.

a) More events in the 1995/96 Season, with more players in the draw.
b) Increased level of prize money.
c) Recognition of AVPA sponsorship requirements, including player rights over use of their bodies for promotion.
d) Commitment to a World Series event in Australia.
e) National tour to avoid clash with overseas events.
f) AVPA signage on court, including umbrellas.
g) Improved on-court player facilities.
h) Improved presentation of events, including centre court stands, scoreboards on all courts, and well-informed commentary.

In the absence of John Winters overseas, in June 1995 we met with SMG/BVPT's Russell Hanna to talk through all our input. For once, the meetings were amicable and some progress was made, particularly on player rights. However, there was no news on sponsorship for the 1995/96 season and this did not augur well. On 13 October, the AVF then informed the AVPA that SMG/BVPT had withdrawn from their contract because they had failed to obtain sponsors. Legal action was pending. In the meantime, the AVF was endeavouring to find sponsors through its own in-house marketing company called Sports Marketing and Management. The AVF also started talking to the Northern Beaches Volleyball Association about their picking up the NSW part of the National Tour. The support and co-operation of the AVPA was sought and we made a major submission outlining our requirements to consolidate previous achievements including the following:

a) Prize Money no less than previous levels.
b) A Grand Prix in every main-land State.
c) Maintenance of adequate player facilities.
d) Recognition of player rights to body signage.
e) Pre-event qualifying competition or extended draw.
f) Joint AVF/AVPA Committee to monitor event management and presentation.

In the meantime, in an open letter to the AVF, the AVPA reflected on the collapse of the SMG/BVPT contract with some telling views as follows.

"The collapse of the BVPT contract probably comes as no surprise to anyone who has regularly attended events on the national tour over the

last three years. *Although it's fair to acknowledge the benefits of commercial TV exposure and improvement in presentation of Sydney based events, the overall quality of the Pro Tour has languished, and BVPT has lacked the vision to capitalise on the potential of the sport and sustain sponsorship support. This was evidenced through poor selection of TV material, inconsistent standards of event presentation across the country, an insufficient number of events, and declining prize money in real terms. Furthermore, this demise occurred during a period of sustained economic growth where, at times, advertising and marketing revenues grew at over 10% per annum.*

It has to be said that responsibility for the current situation lies firmly with the AVF. When the sport in Australia was beginning to attract genuine public interest, the AVF decided to delegate much of their responsibility for development of beach volleyball to BVPT and did not accommodate the only source of competition, the Pro Beach Tour. Since then, it would seem that they have given insufficient time to monitoring the performance of the promoter they appointed. They have also been slow to establish an effective management structure for the sport. The Team Australia Beach Program is still at an early stage of development, and in the meantime the national tour has come close to disappearing.[83]

Changes to the way in which the sport is managed are urgently needed, if we are to turn this situation around. The AVPA has already submitted proposals to the AVF, as previously released to AVPA members.

By November 1995, there was still no news of a national tour to replace the collapsed SMG/BVPT circuit. In the circumstances, we urged players to support their local State-run competitions. In the meantime, the AVPA made very strong representations to the President of the AVF, Barry Couzner, to take a long hard look at how beach volleyball had been managed. In December 1995, the AVPA published a document reflecting on its aims and achievements.

1996

1996 saw a major upheaval in the organisation of beach volleyball in Australia. Just as the sport had gained international recognition and Australian players were qualifying for the 1996 Olympic Games, the

---

[83] The Team Australia Beach Program had been established as the vehicle for Australia's participation in the Olympic Games.

collapse of the AVF's model for delivering and developing the sport in Australia was a major embarrassment. The promoter had stepped away and there were major changes at the AVF. At Board level, several Directors resigned and a new Board was appointed by the AVF Council which was the sport's governing body. The new Directors were Senator Chris Schacht whose son was a player on the circuit, Hans Schmerlaub, and Kevin O'Flaherty, with Barry Couzner retaining his position as President. At the management level, Ken Breen resigned to take up a volleyball position overseas and a new CEO was recruited. Significantly, the new Board decided to establish a new management structure for Beach Volleyball which met FIVB requirements. This involved the reconstitution of the Beach Commission, with a Permanent Committee and Beach Director. The Beach Commission was to consist of representatives from all stakeholders in the sport, including the AVPA, with meetings twice yearly. Its Permanent Committee had its first meeting on 16 June 1996 with the following members appointed by the AVF Board: Chris Schacht (Chairperson), Andrew Burdin, Craig Carracher of the Northern Beaches Volleyball Association, Blair Harrison, Annette Huygens-Tholen and me.

At first, my response to this turn of events was positive. My membership of the Permanent Committee was recognition of five years' voluntary work. And I also felt that the AVPA had been totally vindicated in all that we had sought to achieve. However, on reflection, I had some qualms about taking up this role. It was a very different set of responsibilities, with significant politics, and a long way removed from what I had set out to achieve when I became involved in 1991 in support of Andrew who had now retired from the sport. In mid-1996, I was also taking on significant responsibilities with the Australian Red Cross Blood Service. Even as the sport was getting its first exposure at Olympic level at Atlanta, I had a long chat with Rob Agnew. Although he intended to play on with his partner Mark Janssens for several years, he had got to a point where he had had enough of the politics and the burden of player liaison. For our various reasons, both of us concluded that our involvement had run its course. So, in November 1996, I resigned from the Permanent Committee. Needless to say, my decision was not well received by the fraternity and the Chairman actually told me that I wasn't able to resign! Nevertheless, I walked away. In early 1997, I also handed over my role with the AVPA to new folk and Robert Agnew stood down as President.

Thus ended a most remarkable episode in my life. When I now look back, I have to say that I am astonished by my five years in the sport of beach volleyball. It is almost like a dream. I do of course owe my initial involvement to Andrew, and even the journey with him and his partner was quite an adventure in its own right. But the creation of a players' organisation was a significant achievement. I am proud that we gave the players a voice, made a real difference to the management and marketing of the sport, and set benchmarks for the delivery of events. In another version of my life, I might have contributed for many more years. But life moves on and what remains are fond memories and some good friends. In particular, Robert Agnew has figured in my life ever since. Sadly, I have lost touch with most of the others although I do have some knowledge of the redoubtable Andy Burdin who first drew me into the organisational side of beach volleyball. After being the country's top-ranked player for so many years, Andy did not make it to the Olympic Games as a player. At the 1996 Atlanta Games, his long-time partner Julian Prosser played with Lee Zahner. However, he was there in a supporting role. And for some time he would continue his involvement through the AVF's Permanent Committee in running the Australian national circuit. His contribution to the sport in Australia has been marked by a trophy awarded to outstanding junior players. However, through his international competition, he became closely involved with senior people in the FIVB with whom he eventually took a role in Geneva. On a personal basis, I learnt a great deal from him about the demands of being a professional athlete, and I provided financial assistance to his participation in overseas events, as well as providing input to some of his business ventures. I have no doubt that he is still out there somewhere in the beach volleyball firmament. He was a worthy fellow and, if there were a Beach Volleyball Hall of Fame, he would be up there.

25 years on, the AVPA is long gone. But I am pleased to report that some of the people involved in organising the players associations in the 1990s have emerged as leaders of the sport. In particular, Craig Carracher of the Northern Beaches Volleyball Association is now the President of Volleyball Australia as the AVF is now known and also a member of the Australian Olympic Committee. The AVPA's Anita Palm is Vice President, and the Director of Volleyball Australia is previous AVPA member Kerri Pottharst.

10: Boats in the Bush

Through my association with beach volleyball, I formed a particularly strong relationship with Robert Agnew. Apart from his beach volleyball, Robert had two main preoccupations and an abiding interest. For a living, having obtained a degree in Economics from Monash University, he had become a stock broker and, when I first knew him, he was working for a Japanese company based in the city. In his personal life, he had a young son named Toby, and an ex-partner called Linda who was a music teacher. Given that he wasn't living with his son's mother, his personal arrangements were at times challenging. To fulfil his parental commitments, Toby spent three days a week with his Dad and the rest of the time with his Mum. Robert also had a passion for houseboats which derived from time spent as a kid on Lake Eildon in the 1970s. This leisure-time activity involved swimming, fishing, and water-skiing, not to mention eating, drinking and otherwise relaxing, in a relatively pristine bush environment.

Although popular for recreational purposes, Lake Eildon was established in the early 20th century as a head of water for irrigation across northern Victoria. It is situated about 145 km to the north-east of Melbourne at the upper reaches of the Goulburn River, and is administered by the Murray Goulburn Water Authority. Construction of the original storage, which was known as Sugarloaf Reservoir, took place between 1915 and 1925, with extensions in 1929 and 1935. Between 1951 and 1955, it was again extended to its current capacity (3,334,158 megalitres) and renamed Lake Eildon. The current lake is six times the size of Sydney Harbour with a perimeter shoreline at high water of 515 km. In the final phase of development, a small 135 MW hydro-electric plant was established next to the main dam, which is close to the township of Eildon. This settlement was built for the construction workers, and is now a small tourist destination with shops, motels, a pub, and boat storage and maintenance businesses. On the perimeter of the lake is the Eildon National Park (previously Fraser National Park) and significant State forests as well as moorings for some 750 houseboats and other craft. The level of the lake varies considerably, depending on climate and the need to release water for irrigation. During my time on the lake, the level varied between 100% in the early 1990s and a low of 5.3% in 2007.

In the spring of 1993, Robert engaged my interest in boating on this lake. To reconnoitre, we went on a camping trip up to Mount Torbreck which is at the western end of the lake, and we visited several moorings to view a number of houseboats.[84] At the time, I had already had reserves arising from the sale in September 1992 of my cottage in Lincolnshire, and I had the proceeds of around $90,000 to invest. On a subsequent visit, we found a boat called *Slice of Heaven*, which was jointly owned by a couple of gentlemen from the south-eastern suburbs of Melbourne named Bill Baberton and Ted Hawking. They had owned the boat since its construction about 10 years previously, and the asking price *including contents* was $85,000. A further $15,000 was required to purchase shares in a club named Darlingford Waters Boat Club which would secure a mooring in Jerusalem Creek.

To the uninitiated, the purchase of a houseboat is a somewhat disconcerting experience in that, despite the relatively large sum of money involved, the process is more akin to buying a car than a house. Before proceeding, and with no previous experience of boats, I had someone look it out. It got a clean bill of health, and I then tried to negotiate a price. But the vendors were not budging and, after some deliberation, I accepted their price. Then came the transaction, which took place at Bill Baberton's home in deepest Langwarrin. I fronted with a bank cheque, we signed the change of registration for despatch to the authorities, and they handed over the keys.[85] That was it. On Tuesday 1 March 1994, I took ownership of the boat and made my first visit the following weekend. For six months, I rented the mooring, before securing ownership on 22 November 1994.

Slice of Heaven was a forty-feet-long and fifteen-feet-wide single-storey boat, powered by an outboard engine which at full power could get the 10 ton hulk up to a speed of around 10 knots. The infrastructure consisted of wood and fibreglass sections with full-length windows at the front and rear, and half-length windows down the sides. You entered by stepping onto a wooden deck positioned at the front, with sliding doors giving access to the open-plan living area. This space included a spacious beige-coloured three-piece suite, the driving column and steering wheel at front left, a well-kitted-out kitchen, and a dining area. In the centre of the boat were two bedrooms, and a bathroom with shower. At the rear, there was a small lounge which could be converted to another sleeping area, and a toilet accessed from the back deck. Also

[84] On that camping trip, I learnt how really cold it can get in the Australian bush and, for the first and only time in my life, I caught pneumonia.

[85] I was accompanied on this trip by my mother who provided moral support. She was equally bemused by the almost casual process of handing over $85,000.

astern were two cupboards for storage of the batteries, ropes, and other equipment, and a landing deck called a *duckboard*. Finally, around the whole of this lower deck was a narrow walkway and, from the back deck, there was a stairway up to the roof which was open to the elements. On this upper deck, which was enclosed by two-feet-high metal cladding, were solar panels, and a cupboard containing a generator.

There is little doubt that the acquisition of this *caravan on the water* was one of the best things I ever did in my life. With turbulent events at the blood service in the mid and late 1990s, the flight to Lake Eildon on most weekends was what kept me sane. Apart from the change in the scenery, the challenges thrown up by boating at the weekend enabled me to keep the rest of my life in perspective. And it facilitated a firm friendship with Robert, Toby, and subsequently his younger brother Oliver.[86]

In the first few weeks of owning the houseboat, my visits to Lake Eildon were always with Robert. He knew how to drive what was effectively a ten ton caravan sitting on two pontoons, one of which held fuel and the other of which held waste fluids which could be periodically pumped out at a pumping station on the lake that we called the Poo Barge. Apart from driving the houseboat on the open stretches of water, there was a huge amount to learn about manoeuvring this beast in the constantly changing weather conditions on the lake. When moored at the boat club, it was situated next to a four-feet-wide galvanised steel walkway from the shoreline to which it was tightly secured by ropes. Manoeuvring in and out of the mooring required considerable skill to avoid other boats. Once in the main body of water, there were rules of the road regarding interaction with other craft and great care was required to avoid dead trees which were lurking just below the surface of the lake. These had been left when the lake had been formed by inundation of a river system, and collision could cause serious damage. Then there was the issue of mooring the boat in the bush. To do this you had to approach the shoreline until the front of the boat made contact with the bank. You then used the engine to hold the vehicle in place, whilst you skipped on to dry land along a plank extended from the front deck. Once ashore, you sought to secure the boat to right and left with very strong ropes which linked the back of the boat to trees or pegs

---

[86] Ollie is the son of Toby's mother and an itinerant Irishman. Robert took responsibility for this child and, to his eternal credit, has supported him as a father. He is now a fine young man in his early twenties, as is his older brother Toby who is now in his thirties and married to Cat with three children of their own living in Perth.

banged into the bank. Finally, with the boat firmly moored, you went back on board, turned off the engine, and collapsed with relief!

A month or so after buying the boat, Robert helped me find a run-about in Melbourne which I acquired for around $5,000. This small boat had various functions. It was a means of rapid return to base in an emergency, enabled visits to other parts of the lake for picking up supplies, and could be used for fishing. For some people, such craft were also used to tow water skiers and other pleasure craft such as rubber rings. My first runabout was a very basic model, and came with a cover which was fastened by studs around the rim. It was capable of 20 or 30 knots and highly manoeuvrable. The only issue I had with it was that, in the cold weather, it didn't always want to start. But it never let me down, and lasted for several years until I upgraded to a more comfortable model with a canopy and small sonar fish-finder on board. In using the small boat came the need to acquire and wear life jackets. These were compulsory on all small craft although this requirement was often ignored except for small children.

The traditional outboard engine runs on leaded petrol. *Slice of Heaven* had a 200-litre fuel tank that could be topped up from one of two petrol stations on the lake or by carrying on fuel. From an environmental point of view, use of this leaded fuel is one of the less attractive aspects of the traditional houseboat. And, given that leaded fuel was no longer available from service stations, you had to purchase bottles of a lead product to add to your unleaded petrol.

The main source of electric power, required for light and appliances, was either batteries charged by the solar panels and the engine, or a generator. The other source of energy was LPG gas which came in large bottles that were secured by chains on the back deck, and replenished by the Boat Club when they ran empty. Gas was used to run the stove, two refrigerators and a heater. All of these basic systems worked tolerably well, although I never felt 100% confident in the efficacy of the batteries. The real problem was that the solar panels were not sufficient to the task. If only I had had the knowledge about these things that I acquired ten years later from living off the grid in Gippsland!

Another important aspect of living on a houseboat is communications. All houseboats had a CB radio which, for many people, was the traditional way of talking. However, in the late 1980s, the first prototypes of a mobile telephone had come onto the market. These *portable* phones did not bear even a faint resemblance to the modern Smart Phone but they did operate independent of a land line. My equipment consisted of a traditional handset sitting in a cradle in a padded box which looked like, and was often called, *a brick*. It was powered by plugging it into the boat's electricity supply which worked fine except that the reception in many corners of the lake was notoriously poor. The eventual advent of modern mobile phones was a godsend.

The other thing about boating, which I did not fully appreciate until I had acquired the houseboat, is that I needed an operator's licence. Identical in appearance to a car drivers' licence, it was much easier to obtain. You did not have to demonstrate an ability in driving the boat. You just had to sit a written exam about maritime rules, with most of the questions relating to the operation of sea-going vessels! Thankfully, the knowledge was quickly acquired after a few hours' study of a small booklet, and I passed the test on my first attempt. Strangely though, apart from needing to be at least 16 years old, you only needed this licence if you were taking out a boat which you actually owned. People could hire a boat without a licence, and you could often identify a rented boat by the erratic way in which it was being operated!

Even when I had acquired my operator's licence, I was reticent about taking out the boat by myself. But, after a learning period, I eventually plucked up courage, and so began a great series of adventures. Cruising around Lake Eildon offered endless opportunities, with a mix of relaxation, mishap, and entertainment. And the anecdotes acquired over a period of twelve years are sufficient to fill a book in its own right. I will mention just a few.

Lake Eildon

A good place to start is the initial journeys of discovery. *Slice of Heaven's* base was in Jerusalem Creek, which is off the main arm on the southern side of the Lake. This was a relatively small inlet (to the right of the word Eildon on the map above) pointing almost due south with a view of Mount Torbreck, which was snow-capped in winter.

Before venturing very far from this relative haven, I acquired a number of survey maps for the area which showed contours and water depths, knowledge of which was critical in traversing long stretches of water. In particular, it was useful to know the original line of the rivers on which the lake was constructed as these represented the deepest channels. It was also essential to be watchful for submerged obstacles. Over time, one acquired knowledge of the location of the trees lurking just below the surface. But there were other obstacles such as submerged buildings and even bridges, and you had to take special care in waters previously not visited.

As you departed the mooring at the boat club, the tentacles of the lake extended in all directions. On coming out of Jerusalem Creek, there were several options, travelling to the east and then south or west and then north up the Main Arm. If you travelled east, the first main option was a trip south along a 10km navigable waterway called Big River. There was a bend well down this arm which formed a natural mooring spot beyond which the water level became too shallow for a houseboat. However, the higher reaches of the river were accessible by run-about and it was possible to land a small craft well up the river and then wade through bubbling waters for the purposes of fly fishing.

On a much longer trip travelling east, and following the original line of the Goulburn River, it was possible to visit the small township of Gough's Bay for provisions, and the outskirts of the towns of Jamieson and Howqua. Access to Jamieson which was a good three-hour trip from base, involved following a long and winding river route which eventually brought you to a road bridge which blocked the way. However, it was possible to moor the boat next to a paddock and walk across to a pub that in those days was called The Junction. At the far east of the lake was the Howqua Arm leading up to a small mooring where there was a shop and a recreational area which we occasionally visited for our own and Toby's amusement. These waters were relatively shallow and, on one occasion, we managed to ground the boat on a sand bank from which we had to be ignominiously towed by a couple of smaller boats.

The waterway to the west of Jerusalem Creek took you up the Main Arm of the lake, and under huge electricity pylons. This stretch of water became very busy in the summer, with all manner of craft, but there were many options for mooring including some favourite spots in inlets opposite the dam wall. These were particularly convenient for a quick trip across to the dam from where you could walk down to Eildon Village for provisions. This area was also excellent for TV reception, and watching Test Matches on a lazy summer afternoon! Further up the Main Arm, there was access to Fraser National Park which encompassed a number of inlets including Coller Bay, Wallaby Bay, Aird Inlet, and Stone Bay with a headland named Cook Point. This area of the lake, which was 20km and a good two hours journey from base, was probably my favourite place. You could park the boat tucked away from wind and boat traffic. And there was easy access to walking tracks up adjacent hills including Mt Blowhard from where you could obtain magnificent views across most of the lake and mountains in all directions. Nearby, there was a well-maintained trail around the perimeter of the lake called the Wallaby Track (or Wobbly Track to the kids). It had this name for a good reason. It was not unusual to meet roos coming towards you, and the best you could do to avoid a head-on collision was to step aside as they hopped through. The walk up Mt Blowhard was relentlessly steep, and excellent exercise. It became a regular feature of my visits to the lake.

Finally, at the northern end of the lake, the waters stretched up to the small township of Bonnie Doon, with a bridge carrying traffic from Alexandra to Mansfield, and the Maintongoon inlet where the Delatite River flowed into the lake. In winter, a trip up this arm of the lake offered fantastic views of a snow-capped Mount Buller to the east. At high water, it was actually possible to pass under the bridge, and on a couple of occasions in winter we moored on the east side to walk across a paddock to the Bonnie Doon Hotel for a counter tea and some Saturday night football on the TV.

When I look back over more than a decade of boating it is difficult to pick the special moments. Although for half of my visits I was on my own, I was frequently accompanied by visitors. My most regular companions were the Agnew clan which included blue heeler dogs Les and Bev. The dogs were a hoot. Les in particular found it necessary to bark at the engine, but was a total wuss when it came to entering the water. Bev, on the other hand, swam with gay abandon. Toby had his moments, with the odd accident. His time on the boat was during formative years when he was at Primary and Secondary school and, in my estimation, Robert was a hard taskmaster. If Toby transgressed, which was usually through excessive zeal and a failure to follow orders, he would be sent to his room to have a long hard look at himself in "the wall of long mirrors". But Toby's exclusion never lasted long, and he seems to have survived with a very sound mental state so I guess that Robert knew what he was doing. In later years, when he was old enough, we also included Ollie, who did not like wearing a lifejacket!

Life on the boat with Rob's team was full of endless good fellowship. During the day, there would be swimming, canoeing, or fishing off the back deck. Often we would leave the boat and take extended walks along creek valleys and up the nearest hill for great views across the Australian Alps. In the late afternoon, we might slip into one of the floating chairs and knock back a drink or two. In the evening, there were endless games of Backgammon, Blokus, and Risk, and Robert would usually do the cooking. Making a fire on the shoreline was always a special treat for Toby, as was the cooking and eating of the trout, and yabbies that we caught overnight in a cage thrown off the side of the boat. We also watched quite a bit of sport on the TV, although the reception in some spots was a challenge. One particularly memorable night was New Year's Eve at the turn of the century. Fireworks were not allowed on the lake, but this didn't deter Robert who had access to a supply from Canberra. We had a spectacular 31 December 1999 as did many other houseboats. And the supply of bangers lasted well into 2000, with many a surprise for the unsuspecting visitor.

On visits involving Robert, I also have another amusing story. Over the years, Robert owned quite a few cars, including an ivory coloured Mercedes 280 SE Coupe.[87] This was a beautiful low-slung beast and he decided to give it a run into the bush. We set off from Darlingford and ventured up the track to Mount Torbreck only to find ourselves stuck with the wheels in ruts and the bodywork firmly grounded. Fortunately, we were within walking distance of a camp site and were able to get a tow from a friendly bearded fellow with 4WD.

Apart from Robert, the next most common visitor was Andrew. We drove up together every few months, and had many happy weekends walking, swimming, playing games, and talking well into the night. Unfortunately, more than one of these visits was marred by issues arising from Andrew's back condition. And, to my amusement, he had a real problem with spiders which lived in quite large numbers in and around the boat and out in the bush. On several occasions, during a walk, I remember him taking off at a rate of knots to free himself from some

---

[87] This car had previously been owned by Tammy Fraser, the wife of the ex-PM Malcolm Fraser. He reckoned there was still plenty of Fraser DNA in the leather seats!

great crawling beast that had attached itself to him. Sometimes, he also visited the boat by himself with his mates, and he had his fair share of incidents. Once, while parking the boat in a remote spot, the steering wheel came off in his hands and he had to think quickly to avoid a major bingle. Another time, he managed to cause a small explosion with the batteries by connecting the wrong terminals. However, these were minor escapades compared with the drama that I brought upon by myself whilst alone.

The most dramatic event on my solo voyages occurred one stormy night in the early autumn of 1998. As always before leaving the mooring, I had checked out the weather forecast, paying particular attention to the direction and level of wind. There was a front going through, but it didn't look that dramatic on the weather chart. So off I set and parked in Coller Bay, which is in Fraser National Park. As I had been accustomed up to that time, I secured the boat by ropes attached to two pretty large metal stakes which were hammered into the solid earth bank. I settled in, had a meal, and retired for the night. At about 3.00am I awoke to the sound of a huge and quite alarming storm with much thunder and lightning. Of more concern was that I was adrift, with the boat rocking from side to side, and travelling at some pace into the middle of the adjacent main channel! Feeling somewhat dazed, I went onto the front deck and quickly realised that I was adrift because the stakes had pulled out of the ground and the ropes had come free. I was immediately fearful of capsizing and my predicament was not helped by the fact that, in the absence of my contact lenses, my long-distance vision was blurred. But I kept my wits about me, knowing that I must not start the engine because of the danger of wayward ropes catching around the propeller. Fortunately, a large tree loomed up ahead, and I grabbed hold of one of the loose ropes still secured to the boat and wrapped it round the trunk, hanging on for dear life. The boat slowed, giving me enough time to fully secure myself to the tree with several ropes. Then I took a few deep breaths and let out a sigh of relief. Content that I was firmly anchored, I went back to bed and slept until daybreak. At dawn, the scene was transformed. The lake was still as a mill pond with the sun soon beating down. I recovered the ropes, started up the engine and returned to the bank, finding a spot where there were trees to which I could tie up. Whilst chastened, I enjoyed the rest of the weekend in a state of euphoria that I had survived without serious misadventure.

A second serious episode happened in the year 2000. Having moved to Australia in the 1980s, in the years that followed I was fortunate to receive many visits from English friends and their offspring. One such was a young man named Oliver Moore who was at school with Jonathan Dixon, the son of my dear friends Clive and Kathy. Oliver was touring Australia with a couple of friends, travelling in a VW campervan. And, afterwards, he stayed with me for several weeks to follow the Australian Open. Anyway, when he first arrived, he came down from NSW and we met in Eildon township late one Friday afternoon. We quickly transferred to the lake and off we went down the Main Arm to a favourite spot in a bay tucked behind Cook's Point. We settled in for the night and got into a serious game of Risk. The next day, we went walking, following which the young folk decided that they wanted a bit of fun on the water with the rubber ring. The "fun" consisted of sitting in the ring and being towed at speed by the run-about which took a zig zag course creating waves with lots of bumping for the ring and its occupants. On about the third of these runs, we narrowly avoided a horrific accident. The run-about had just been returned to me after an off-lake service. Unfortunately, the engineer had not properly secured the engine to the boat. And, after several trips across the water, the engine had slowly worked loose and the inevitable happened. In the middle of a run, it detached itself from the back of the boat and flew through the air, landing in the water about half a metre from where Ollie was clinging on for grim death in the ring. If it had landed on him, he would probably have been killed. Obviously, by now the boat had come to a stop, as the engine began to sink into the lake. However, it was attached to the boat by two steel ropes. Ollie swam to the runabout and climbed on board with the calm and certainty that only a 20-year-old would have. He and I towed the engine in from the depths and man-handled it on board. We then rowed back to the houseboat with oars which you were always required to keep on board for such emergencies. With relief, Ollie had a huge laugh. But I was not amused. The following week, I gave the service guy a major serve. This wasn't the first time that his negligence had caused a mishap. Previously after a service, I had launched the boat back into the lake only to find myself sinking because he'd left the bung out!

The third and final story of close shaves involves my friends Patrick and Jackie. They visited on several occasions when the water level on the lake was high and we were able to park in Barnewall Inlet opposite the dam. On evening, after dinner and as dusk fell, we were sitting on the back deck having a drink and reflecting on how lucky we were to have the place to ourselves. Then we heard music and saw a glow looming beyond the headland. Before long, a huge two-storey boat came into

116

view, with a party in full flow, disturbing our peace as it proceeded up the inlet. As the boat had passed us and then disappeared up the end of the inlet we saw someone in the water with an upstretched arm. Patrick and I jumped into the runabout and motored over to what turned out to be a young girl. Patrick dived in and we lifted her into the runabout. Thankfully, she appeared to be OK and told us that she had fallen from the boat. We quickly set off down the inlet and hailed the houseboat. With some annoyance, the driver cut engines and then looked in amazement as he saw the girl. We passed her to him and he expressed a hasty thanks. Then, without further ado, he resumed his journey. Astonished by this behaviour, we returned to the houseboat and had another drink. The next day, we did get a visit from the man who came to thank us. Clearly embarrassed, he explained that the girl had fallen through a window in her bedroom. That was it, and he disappeared never to be seen again.

Fortunately, not all mishaps were so dramatic and there were many minor amusing incidents. To give just one example, one weekend I had moored myself in Big River which was handy because it was relatively close to base and there were quite a few places where it was easy to park. Making my way back to base one Sunday afternoon, with not a care in the world, I saw some people waving from the bank. I waved back thinking nothing of it, but they kept waving and pointing behind me. I put the boat into neutral and ambled to the back deck to find that the runabout which was normally attached by rope to the back of the houseboat had disappeared. Then I saw the craft bobbing around about 400 metres behind me. With relief, I turned tail and collected it. Without seeing those people, I doubt if I would ever have seen that runabout again.

For the first five years on the lake, I kept a very low profile at the Club that owned and managed the mooring and related facilities.[88] While many of the boat owners spent the weekend parked in the marina socialising, I would arrive on Friday night and slip out early on a Saturday morning. It was anti-social, but I didn't go to Lake Eildon to make friends. In the early days, the only person with whom I had regular contact was the Site Manager, who was a rustic bearded fellow named Billy Ferris. He lived on the lake in an antique houseboat called *Progress*

---

[88] The Darlingford Waters Boat Club had been established in 1983, as an organisation owned and managed by its members who had broken away from the privately owned and operated Jerusalem Creek Marina.

Hall.[89] He was paid a small fee to provide security, adjust the walk ways as the water level rose and fell, and replace gas bottles which you left on the duck board when they were empty. He also did odd jobs, particularly for members like me who were of the less handy variety. Amusingly, Billy was known to Robert from his youth as *"Billy the Fair Arse"* because he reckoned that he was sweet on his mother during her boating days.

Following the death of Billy, the Club took stock and the Board decided to employ a full-time Site Manager, and erect a house on site in which he and his wife could live. And there were other projects mooted. With all this going on, I decided that it was time for me to make a contribution. So, when the AGM came around in 2000, I stood for election to the Board. People weren't actually fighting to assume this kind of responsibility, with most Club members being free riders, so I was elected uncontested. I took on the role of Minutes Secretary. But I also agreed to revise the Constitution and update a number of operating policies including the Club Manual. This turned out to be a significant log of work, but I found it rewarding not least because it was a real way of contributing using a skill which no-one else had, and compensating for the fact that I had less to offer in undertaking the more practical tasks involved in managing the Club.

Membership of the DWBC Board opened up a whole new dimension to life on the lake. I soon learnt that boating activities were the subject of manifest regulations established and managed by the Goulburn Murray Water Authority operating under the 1989 Water Act, with waters shared by a number of competing clubs, camp sites, and day trippers launching boats for fishing and water-skiing from a number of ramps. Although the lake was huge, the multitude of users had its challenges with many conflicting interests. To deal with all these issues, and manage club finances and development, the Board comprised a diverse mix of personalities, most of whom had a small-business background. When I started, the Chairman was Jos de Klijn who was a dental technician. He was a real gentleman and a widely respected leader who had been around since the Club had broken away from the Jerusalem Creek Marina. However, after my first year on the Board, he stood down as did the Secretary and Treasurer. The new officers were very

---

[89] The name of this boat was a reflection of Billy's trade union past. Strictly speaking, living on the lake was not permitted. But his presence was tolerated. He eventually died on board in 1998. It was the end of an era, and his boat was eventually sold and removed from the marina to pastures new.

representative of the kind of people who had houseboats at that time. The new Chairman was a retired policeman named Greg Boland who had taken up a job as Manager of the Inspectorate at the RSPCA. He was a lovely guy, and I spent a good deal of time with him talking through many organisational issues. I also formed a real friendship with the new Secretary, Richard Pensa, who owned a business that made various plastic goods including signage. The Treasurer was Greg Tieman, another thoroughly decent fellow whose father had created the Tieman Tail Lift business. Finally, the Site Director was another great guy and long standing member named Ron Mullholland. He owned the boat moored next to me, and had responsibility for day to day oversight of the Site Manager. This team was augmented by a number of other boat owners nearly all of whom were small businessmen or tradies. So there was no shortage of experience in managing the practical aspects of the Club's affairs. And by and large the team worked well, although there were tensions over certain projects, and some latent personality conflicts. However, on the whole, there was a unity of purpose to ensure that members of the Club obtained the best possible experience from cruising the waters of Lake Eildon in a manner reflecting both mutual respect and orderly behaviour, despite the inclination of some members to over-indulge!

The Board met monthly and we also had regular General Meetings with the wider membership. These gatherings took place at various venues on the eastern outskirts of Melbourne, including at one stage the premises of the Hawthorn Football Club. Apart from the governance and administrative work for which I had personal responsibility, during my three years on the Board, we dealt with many other matters including the following:

a) Improvement in the main entrance to the site with a new gateway and electronic pass system.
b) Construction and allocation of new sheds for storage of run-abouts.
c) Relations with the neighbouring Water Skiing Club.
d) Organisation of numerous social events including the Annual "Sail-Past" which was a weekend party.[90]
e) Sealing of the access road.
f) Longer walkways to accommodate expansion of membership.

---

[90] There was usually a theme for this event which was often held at Big River, and often involved cross-dressing.

g) Issues with the Goulburn Murray Water ("GMW").[91]
h) Plans to remove the mooring system out of Jerusalem Creek as water levels reached fell below 10% in the early 2000s.
i) Employment of the Site Manager and the maintenance of his dwelling on site.
j) Resolving disputes between members.
k) Acquisition and maintenance of club equipment.
l) Organisation of working bees to maintain the site.

My time on the Board was largely uneventful. I never had any issues with the other Board members and they seemed to respect the particular skills that I brought to the team. I didn't consider my contribution to be anything special. So, in 2006, I was genuinely surprised when I was awarded the Delia Shield as the most outstanding member of the year. This was a perpetual trophy that you retained for one year. When you returned it for passage to the next winner, your name was entered on the Club's Honours Board. My name is there to this day.

Returning to my personal experience of boating, I think anyone who has owned a boat will attest that you need to have deep pockets to maintain a fully operational craft. In the case of boats on Lake Eildon, GMW regulations required that you slip your boat every five years for audit of the pontoons, electrics, and sewage system. This was quite a drama and required transport of the boat on a trailer owned by the Club to maintenance sheds near Eildon township. On the first occasion that the boat was slipped, I took the opportunity to repaint and remove the *Slice of Heaven* signage. Concerned about superstitions associated with changing boat names, thereafter the boat had no name displayed on the bodywork. On the second occasion, I had quite a bit of remedial work on internal panelling damaged from a leaking roof. Needless to say, this slipping was quite an expensive exercise, costing upwards of $10,000 on each occasion.

No account of the years on Lake Eildon would be complete without reference to the trials and tribulations arising from the level of the lake. In a normal year, the water level rises in autumn, winter and spring and falls during the summer. A critical point each year is the start of the irrigation season in May when water is released through the spillway into the lower reaches of the Goulburn River. When I started boating in 1994,

---

[91] GMW were custodians of the lake. The DWBC President and I visited their premises at Tatura to discuss various issues, including their fees, their policy on releasing water for irrigation and a proposal to require all boats to have on-board grey-water processing.

the lake was at around 95% full, with water lapping at the upper steps of the Club leading down to the mooring. For the next couple of years, the water level moved between around 50% and 100% depending on the season. In the years that followed we entered a ten-year drought with the water level eventually reaching an historic low of just 5.3% in May 2007. This should never have been allowed to happen as it seriously compromised the stability of the dam wall. In any event, one might imagine that with such little water there would be no place for houseboats or any recreational activity on the lake. However, Lake Eildon is constructed on a configuration of deep river beds and, although the shallower inlets were all dried up, there was still plenty of deep water. With Jerusalem Creek completely dry, Darlingford Water Boat Club had a contingency plan which involved relocating the walkways out to a point on the shoreline where the water was still deep. Access was obtained by driving across mud backs to a barge stationed at a small landing situated at the mouth of the Creek. With two barges, to cover traffic to and fro, this worked remarkably well, and life on the lake continued throughout the drought. But it was challenging as the number of destinations for weekend mooring was restricted. One upside of these difficult circumstances was that various settlements and infrastructure, which had been inundated when the lake was formed, re-emerged from the waters. In particular, there were signs of habitation at the mouth of Big River and in Coller Bay with brick walls, chimneys, toilets, stone cookers and numerous personal effects surfacing to the delight of onlookers and scavengers.

Finally, after about twelve years, when other priorities emerged, my days of boating came to an end. In the early 2000s when the drought was at its worst, Andrew and I began a conversation about making a serious commitment to the environment. Eventually, this took the form of buying a nature reserve in the south of the State and this made continued visits to Eildon impractical. So, reluctantly, in the mid-2000s, I decided to sell the boat. With the drought and low waters still evident, this was a far from ideal time. I put the boat on the market and for a few months there were few interested parties. But eventually an offer of around $120,000 emerged and, in 2007 the deal was done. I subsequently sold off my shares in the DWBC and disposed of the runabout. It was the end of an era of which I continue to have fond memories.

PART THREE

BLOOD AND GORE

11: Agglomeration

In February 1996, I left my job as a director of the Victorian blood bank to take on a radically different role. After much debate, in 1995 ARC had decided to integrate the State and Territory blood services into a national body to be called the Australian Red Cross Blood Service ("ARCBS"). I was invited to an interview by a panel consisting of ARC officers and the Secretary General, Jim Carlton, and was subsequently offered the position of ARCBS Implementation Team Manager.

While I reported monthly to the ARCBS Steering Committee chaired by the ARC National Chairman Dr Rob O'Regan QC, my direct boss was Jim Carlton who turned out to be a wonderful person with whom to work. After his political career, he had spent some time as a consultant with McKinsey, and he talked the same language as me. He also understood the word *delegation* and worked on the basis that I would get on with what I had been asked to do with overall direction but minimal interference. Mind you, he did have an insurance policy. To assist in making the case to ARC for the establishment of ARCBS, Jim had taken on a young McKinsey consultant named Bill Kelsall. Although lacking in experience, Bill proved himself to be smart and diligent, and he had played a key supporting role in convincing ARC to proceed with the establishment of ARCBS. Following that success, Jim retained his services, and allocated him to work with the Implementation Team, contributing a significant resource as well as providing reports on my performance!

Apart from Bill, the Implementation Team had two other permanent members, Dr Sally Thomas, who was a senior manager from the WA Blood Bank, and Colin Speller, who was the IT Manager from the NSW Blood Bank. We also seconded for specific tasks a number of other people such as Terry Selva who was head of administration at the Queensland blood bank. And we were assisted by the ARC National Medical Director Dr Muriel Baker, and the ARC National Finance Manager. The final member of our team was my very loyal and competent administrative assistant, Dianne Love. In late 1995, I had recruited her as my secretary at the Victorian Blood Bank and she transferred with me to the Implementation Team. She was a tower of strength, turning her hand to anything, including cleaning the offices!

After a briefing from Jim Carlton at our first meeting, and some initial discussions about the logistics, the Implementation Team established a work plan. Our main task was to complete a review of all the current

State and Territory blood services and compile what we called a *Fact Pack*. This aim of this document was to provide a resource for the Board of the new organisation, with data on all aspects of the respective State and Territory organisations, and identification of critical issues associated with integration. At the same time, it was recognised that a significant feature of the national blood service would be its funding system. To this end, Sally Thomas had already commenced some research on an activity-based costing system which had the capability to provide a model for output-based funding. This became a significant sub-project, and computer software was acquired through the team's budget to facilitate further research. All of this work was to be completed by July, when the new organisation was due to commence its life.

After some debate, we determined that the only way to collect the kind of information we needed was to visit all the major blood service sites around the country. This would include not only the headquarters of each State and Territory operation, but also a range of outposts. We decided to travel as a team, and divide up our fact-finding activities according to our respective fields of knowledge and experience. This involved considerable travel, especially for Sally, and took us to all corners of the country. We also met with a number of public servants, although this was largely confined to people at the Commonwealth level who were funding the project.

Our activities proceeded post haste. We assembled and circulated a briefing, and then quickly landed on the doorstep of blood banks all around the country. The reception was not universally welcoming and it soon became clear that not all blood bank executives and/or ARC officers were in favour of this national initiative. However, for the most part, people were co-operative and we started to accumulate details of policy, people, finances, infrastructure, and activity, which quickly revealed amazing diversity. In allowing the blood services to be governed by the independently minded ARC State and Territory Divisions, people had found eight different ways of doing the same thing and this did not augur well for trying to integrate the organisation into a homogenous entity.

In any event, our work proceeded largely on schedule, and we began to consolidate the Fact Pack which was eventually completed in early July. As a team, we had our moments, but we got on pretty well, and we managed to have quite a bit of fun and games along the way. Bill in particular was determined to visit every Casino in Australia and we duly achieved a Full House. During this period, ARC also selected the

Chairman of the new organisation, a man called John Hasker who came from a manufacturing background at Orica, and commenced the recruitment of the first ARCBS Board. John, Bill and I had a separate project to find premises for the initial HQ of the new organisation. We identified a small suite in Johnstone Street in Fitzroy, chosen in part because of its ease of access to the airport. Notoriously, the first-floor offices were located over the top of a shop front displaying naked mannequins, and opposite a row of terraced houses where potentially nefarious activities were seen to occur. But it did the job, being cheap and convenient. And it gave us access to the delights of the local restaurant scene down Brunswick Street. In keeping with what was to be a frugal culture, our fit out consisted of second-hand furniture from Ex Government Supply shops.

The delivery of the consolidated Fact Pack to the first meeting of the ARCBS Board in July 1996 was a major event. The document covered a very wide scope including factual information and softer data on the following: Culture and Values, Strategic Planning, Management Culture, Finance, Activity Levels (including donations and blood products), Infrastructure, Human Resources (including data on staff, employee and industrial relations, union pay rates, and training and development), IT, Research and Development, Regulatory Framework, Risk Management, Government Relations, and Public Relations. The final report identified a number of key issues as follows:

- The establishment of ARCBS had been achieved with the active support of the Commonwealth Government. But State/Territory Governments had been insufficiently involved, and this was a particular concern in NSW where the blood service was managed as a Schedule Three Hospital within the NSW Health Department.[92]

- The service was seriously underfunded for both recurrent and non-recurrent expenditure, and the current system of funding did not meet the demands of financing an increasingly complex set of activities. There was also an absence of a policy framework for managing significant unfunded liabilities such as leave provisions, superannuation entitlements, and depreciation.

92 A Schedule Three Hospital was a medical institution administered by a charitable or religious body with public funding.

- In making changes to the funding system, it was important not to abandon the organisation's core community values and lose its connection with the volunteer blood donor population.

- The government regulator, the Therapeutic Goods Administration ("TGA") made decisions on quality and safety issues which were inconsistent between jurisdictions and without regard to the financial consequences.

- The senior management teams of the State/Territory blood services were concerned about their loss of autonomy.

- There was the risk that militant health unions might seek to exploit the strategic nature of the new national body, and this was a particular threat given that the new national body might rationalise facilities and operations.

- There was a risk that the new body might become captive of government with ARC losing influence and control.

- There was an urgent need to consolidate and preserve strategic alliances for research and development.

- The computerised production systems were in urgent need of modernisation, and development of a national system presented both an opportunity and a major risk.

These issues, and some others that would emerge at a later stage of the new organisation's development, would set a significant agenda for the incoming Board and national management team for the next five to ten years.

In the next three months, the work of the Implementation Team was slowly wound back ahead of the arrival of the newly appointed CEO. The Team was formally disbanded on 28 October 1996.

12: The Whole Bloody Story

The work of the ARCBS Implementation Team in the first half of 1996 easily morphed into the formal establishment of ARCBS. The next part of my working life came in two parts. In the early years of the new organisation, it was a time of great achievement by a small and close-knit group of people, most of whom were sourced from the blood services across the nation. But, in the final years, the promise of that period in terms of positive outcomes was somewhat eroded. Over this extended seven-year period, there were significant challenges in both the external environment and my own fortunes, and a full account is available in an as yet unpublished history of ARCBS I was commissioned to prepare in 2005. What follows is a more personal history reflecting my own journey, and my considered views about a number of the events and people with whom I worked.

I first met the inaugural ARCBS Chairman, John Hasker, at the Australian Red Cross Society ("ARC") national offices in East Melbourne. A lanky fellow in his fifties, who would often carry his papers in a plastic carrier bag, he initially struck me as shy and diffident. But, after a few meetings, I found him to be an intelligent man, with a dry sense of humour. And he was a kindly and instructive mentor. If he had a failing, it was that he did not welcome confrontations with people unwilling to accommodate his usually rational point of view. After a career culminating with the role of General Manager of the explosives division of ICI (now called Orica), Hasker viewed his appointment as ARCBS Chairman as a "feather in his cap" and he took great pride in the role. He also brought from his previous business experience not only progressive ideas about governance, but a keen awareness of health and safety issues. Having been selected by a team of senior ARC officers, including Jim Carlton, who were advised by an external consultant Nobby Clark, Hasker set about recruiting the ARCBS Board.[93] This team of ten, of which he was the independent Chairman, comprised the ARC National Chairman, the Chair of the ARCBS Advisory Council, the CEO, and up to six others of whom two were members of the ARC Council.[94] The inclusion of the CEO as a full member of the Board was

---

[93] Neil Nobby Clark had been CEO of the National Australia Bank.

[94] The ARCBS Advisory Council was appointed by ARC to provide advice to the Board on medical and technical issues. It provided an extra level of assurance to the governing body that, in delivering a well-managed blood service, the Board was giving due account to those matters. Jim Carlton referred to it as his "canary in the cage".

mildly controversial as it had the potential to confound his/her accountability. In any event, the people appointed were an outstanding Board for the time and purpose. Each was qualified in their own sphere of knowledge and experience. And they were also a highly effective team, led by a man who behaved like the first amongst equals. For the first three years of ARCBS's existence they provided a standard of governance and leadership equal to any I have experienced before or since. And they were also delightful people with whom to deal on a personal level, with considerable good humour and generosity of spirit. Probably my favourite, a man who died in 2005, was Ron Green. He was the ARC National Chairman, who had steered the creation of the national blood service through the crocodile-infested waters of ARC in late 1995. And, in his role on the ARCBS Board, he constantly sought to ensure that the independent members of the Board understood and took account of the ARC perspective. In the early days, he headed off many an issue which could have brought a serious crisis. And he imparted many pearls of wisdom from his long career with the International Committee of the Red Cross ("ICRC"). A prime example was his recipe for achieving successful outcomes in the face of what seemed like insurmountable odds. He told me that he always worked on the basis that *"you should allow people to think that you are less smart than you are"*. In an environment that was sometimes characterised by high politics and significant ego, this was wise counsel indeed, and an echo of what my mother had told me many years before.

The new Board met for the first time on 26 July 1996 in the temporary Implementation Team offices in Johnstone Street, Fitzroy. Having completed my work as ARCBS Implementation Team leader, I had already been asked by John Hasker to act as Board Secretary. This was a role for which I was more than qualified from my days at Imperial Group in the 1980s. Mind you, not everyone agreed with my appointment. The ARC Medical Director, Dr Muriel Baker, had her reservations about the encroachment of what she saw as a *"Johnny Come Lately"*. According to John Hasker, she told him that I was "hopeless" and should be returned to sender (ie the Victorian Blood Bank). Fortunately for me, there were others in the ARC national office who thought otherwise!

The agenda for the new Board was almost immediately hijacked by a blood transfusion litigation issue to which the blood service was intermittently prone. But our pre-existing disaster management arrangements, involving a response from the National Blood Transfusion

Committee chaired by Dr Richard Kimber, were quickly enacted.[95] In a hastily convened press conference the matter was kicked into touch. Thereafter, the Board's initial priorities were to receive and digest the Implementation Team's Fact Pack and recruit a CEO.[96] This was obviously a key appointment and there were both internal and external contenders. After an extensive process, in August the Board appointed Dr Robert Hetzel and he joined the organisation in October. In the meantime, I spent my time putting together a whole range of policies and procedures designed to provide for the effective administration of the Board. This included the development of a Board Administration Manual, a Board Accountability Statement, and a Delegations Matrix to clarify the respective responsibilities of Board and Executive. I also developed policies on Independent Professional Advice, Conflicts of Interest, Director's Indemnity, and a competency-based protocol for Board selection. To provide advice on current best practice, we engaged a consultant from the Institute of Chartered Secretaries, a wise and helpful fellow named John Green.

On his appointment, Robert Hetzel hit the ground running. He was a GP by training (including a specialism in the use of hypnosis), but in his immediate previous job he had been the head of the Monash IVF program for three years and had also spent some time as a management consultant working in the health sector. Anything he lacked in general management experience was more than adequately compensated by energy, passion and drive. In the early days, I found him a charming fellow with whom it was easy to work. He was a tall and well-built man, prone in winter to wear an overcoat that stretched down to his ankles. He came from a South Australian family of notable doctors, and had a keen sense of humour and a sharp mind. However, as time passed, the weight of responsibility, working in what was often a hostile environment, would test him. And, as time passed, I slowly formed the view that the initial ease of his relationship with his management team during the organisation's formative period might be driven more by necessity than inclination. Initially, he relied on what insiders had to offer him in terms of knowledge of the blood business. Down the track, he became his own man, perhaps with less inclination to accommodate the views of people whom he sometimes saw as presenting obstacles to his vision for change.

---

[95] Dr Richard Kimber was appointed as Chair of the new ARCBS Advisory Council and thereby a member of the Board. In 1998, he was succeeded by Dr Alison Street who was chair of the Haemophilia Society and an Associate Professor at the Alfred Hospital.

[96] Pending this appointment, John Hasker was acting CEO.

He also developed an ego-centric way of working which created a management dynamic that could sorely test his subordinates. I would characterise this as a model in which the leader occupies the quiet centre of a swirling vortex. It would put mounting stress on all around him, and would eventually take its toll on my own wellbeing.

On assuming responsibility in October 1996, Hetzel did a whirlwind tour of the country, visiting the main facilities and meeting key staff. He was by no means universally welcomed by State/Territory directors. He also assumed leadership of what was called the National Executive Committee. This body initially consisted of the heads of all the State and Territory blood services and the ARC Medical Director.[97] One of his first acts, in early November, was to appoint me as Manager Corporate Planning and confirm me as Board Secretary, both of which were full-time permanent positions. My "permanent" status was significant as many around me later found themselves on short term contracts. I also acted as ARCBS finance officer, with the ARC Finance Department initially providing an accounting and payroll service. At an early stage, it was decided that the ARCBS National Office would be a relatively small group of no more than 20 people, setting policy, and coordinating change through a series of projects to be undertaken by existing staff based in the State/Territory operating units. This was in keeping with a model that had already been mooted by ARC in obtaining the support of State and Territory Divisions for the establishment of ARCBS, and was seen as a strong selling point with State/Territory governments. In December, Hetzel obtained Board approval for some key appointments and, in the early months of 1997, he proceeded with the recruitment of his national team. In addition to me, this comprised a Director of Intellectual Capital (Patrick Coghlan from RCBBV), a Human Resource Coordinator (Marie Sellstrom, who was an external appointment), a Finance Manager (Rose Chai from RCBBV), a Quality Coordinator (Vee Armstrong from the WA Blood Bank), an IT Coordinator (Myles Hourn from the Queensland Blood Bank), and a Public Relations Coordinator (Carol O'Shea from the NSW Blood Bank). As will be apparent, this was truly a national team with representation from nearly every ARC jurisdiction and, given the likely process of significant organisational change, the appointment of an outsider to fill the HR role was a wise move. The word "Co-ordinator" in some of the job titles was deliberately

---

[97] In late 1997, Robert reconstituted this team, to include the Manager Corporate Planning, the Director of Intellectual Capital, and the National HR Coordinator.

chosen to reflect the fact that this team had the task of implementing change by force of argument not through line authority.

After some months, and with Rose Chai as my able first lieutenant, I was eventually appointed as Chief Financial Officer ("CFO") as well as Manager Corporate Planning and Secretary. From an early stage, the organisation was also advised by an external risk consultant, David Jewell, whose mission was to rationalise the organisation's insurance arrangements, and develop a proposal for self-insurance that eventually materialised as the National Managed Fund. Finally, I should not overlook the administrative support team. During the Implementation Project, I had been ably supported by Dianne Love, and she was confirmed as my Personal Assistant. Initially she worked for John Hasker, Robert Hetzel and me. But, after about six months, with a mounting workload, she accepted an offer to become Hetzel's Executive Assistant. I then recruited a new PA, Gabrielle Hewitson, who had previously worked as a Laboratory Manager at RCBBV. Gabrielle wanted a change of career and turned out to be a more than able choice. And, down the track, after acquiring a company secretary qualification, she would eventually succeed me as Board Secretary serving with distinction.

In one of our earliest tasks, we gave serious thought to some new premises for the organisation. The offices in Johnstone Street Fitzroy were only a temporary arrangement. At this early stage, the geographical location of the facility was still an open question, with both Sydney and Melbourne being options. The respective State governments were approached about the possibility of some financial assistance towards the establishment cost, and only the Victorian government responded, with an offer to help with rent. So, to my relief, Melbourne got the prize. And, given the need to fly around the country, we decided to secure a site north of the city with easy access to the airport. I soon found myself visiting a range of premises in a variety of northern suburbs. And eventually Hetzel found a building with a five-year lease at 88 Nicholson Street, Fitzroy not far from our perch in Johnstone Street.[98] In March 1997, we took the first floor, with an option on the lower floor which we exercised in October. For the next few years this would become my second home.

By now, the ARCBS Board was well into its stride, with monthly meetings. For Gabrielle and me this meant a relentless cycle of preparing and distributing Board papers as well as providing support to the ARCBS

---

[98] According to Rose Chai, and her understanding of Chinese numerology, the number 88 augured well for our wealth and prosperity.

Advisory Council, the Finance and Audit Committee, and the Nominations Committee, which had responsibility for both recommendations to ARC on Board appointments, and the conduct of periodic reviews of Board performance. In keeping with our commitment to connect with the organisation's staff, and promote the national profile, it was agreed that over the course of a year the Board would meet in every jurisdiction. This required considerable logistical work and, wherever possible, the Board met on the premises of the local operating unit. But in the absence of a suitable room, we convened in a neighbouring hotel. And the Chairman took a personal interest in selecting low-cost accommodation, including the use of Clubs for which he had reciprocal membership. It also became a regular practice that, on the night before a meeting, the Board would assemble for dinner, to entertain stakeholders and have a preliminary discussion about key issues on the agenda.[99] As well as being inexpensive, some of the clubs we used proved to be archaic, with a need for women to be accompanied by a male partner![100]

Based in Fitzroy, the new national management team soon became known as the National Office Group ("the NOG"). But they were not all located in Melbourne. On the contrary, those from inter-State remained at home. Apart from enabling the CEO to recruit the best person available for a particular national job with minimal relocation cost, this approach also enabled National Office to keep its collective ear to the ground. The NOG had a monthly face-to-face meeting in Melbourne and, in the early days, these gatherings were used to develop strategy and share intelligence. The team developed a close-knit camaraderie, and members were encouraged to prepare "Narratives" in which we recorded learning and experience which was shared between us on a regular basis. It was a great model which worked well during the formative years of the new "learning" organisation.

Commencing in early 1997, the next three years proved to be one of the most productive periods of my life, in which much of the experience I had acquired in previous roles became fully utilised. And it was a natural extension to the seven years of rolling change that I had spent at RCBBV. Much of the learning acquired in modernising that organisation

---

[99] In the early days, at least one Board member unexpectedly invited his wife to dine with the Board who proceeded to request that we didn't spoil the evening by discussing work! The Chairman was not amused.

[100] Almost invariably, these clubs included a snooker room, with games becoming a regular feature on the eve of Board meetings. In at least one club, women were barred from playing snooker!

would now become acutely relevant in establishing a national body, although I had to take care not to be seen as bestowing favour on RCBBV.

In this early period, the most immediate challenges were financial. When the Commonwealth government decided to support the establishment of ARCBS, it provided a $5.7 million line of "seed funding" to cover the first three years of "implementation", commencing in 1995/96 and ending in 1997/98. However, they had made this commitment without obtaining the agreement of State and Territory governments. And this was to become a major bone of contention, with the potential to unravel the whole national project. Reversing a "gentlemen's agreement" with ARC, the Commonwealth government eventually determined that this funding was really just a loan. And they attempted to impose on the State/Territory governments a requirement to contribute to the new national overhead, according to the time-honoured principle of "matched-funding". This was a provision where 40% came from the Commonwealth and 60% from the States/Territories. Some of the State/Territory Health Departments would have none of this. And I well remember a meeting with senior bureaucrats from the NSW Health Department who told me in no uncertain terms that NSW was a sovereign State and the Commonwealth had no power to impose any such agreement. So, for some time, we soldiered on without security of funding. And, with some initial resistance at the local level, we financed our relatively small National Office budget by putting a levy on each State and Territory blood service which they then claimed from their respective Health Department. Eventually, with the passage of time and persistence on our part, this approach was accepted. But it caused me sleepless nights.

Another major funding issue was what was called "Broad Banding." In 1996, a new Commonwealth government was elected under Prime Minister John Howard and, like his Coalition counterpart in Victoria in 1992 (Jeff Kennett), he adopted a neo-liberal economic agenda which included cuts to public expenditure. His Health Minister, Michael Wooldridge, was quick to review the long-standing "matched-funding" model, and impose a 10% so-called *"Efficiency Dividend"*. This posed an immediate threat not only to the embryonic national organisation but also to the delivery of blood services at an operational level. Thanks to interventions by Jim Carlton, at AHMAC meetings in October 1996 and May 1997, arguing that ARCBS must be given time to establish itself and introduce output-based funding, this proposal was deferred pending a wider government review of funding arrangements. But again, the saga caused several months of angst.

With these financial imperatives playing out, a significant part of my work in the first half of 1997 involved the development of the first ARCBS Strategic Plan. The building blocks for this were established in early 1997, with the completion by the National Executive Committee of a traditional SWOT Analysis, a risk analysis, and the development of Vision, Mission and Values statements in which all ARCBS staff had input. This latter exercise, which also involved the identification of values-based behaviours, became a major task for Marie Sellstrom. And her success in this venture, and subsequent projects designed to generate a new national "culture" for the organisation, stand as a significant achievement during the early years. Sadly, some tenets of this culture eventually struggled to survive in what eventually became a more bureaucratic and hierarchical organisation.

The first version of the Strategic Plan was presented to the Board in April 1997. It was inwardly focussed to provide for the establishment of an integrated national blood service within a three-year period running through to 2000. The plan recognised significant barriers to the achievement of such an objective in such a short time frame, but the milestones in the related change programme stood the test of time.[101] In essence, the initial plan provided for the consolidation of a national organisational structure, establishment of a centralised funding model, the continued provision of a sufficient supply of blood and blood products, the embedding of what was called "best-practice" leadership including the development of a *learning organisation*, more effective risk management, an expanded commitment to research and development, and diversification of operational activity. The Plan was notable for having well-defined performance measures designed to enable systematic reporting on achievements both within the organisation and to external stakeholders. For the next three years, implementation became a major part of the organisation's work, and I provided periodic progress reports. It was not without some serious challenges. Significant activities included:

---

[101] Board member Jean Paviour-Smith counselled that three years was an ambitious target, with five or even ten years being a more likely timeframe. And, Robert Hetzel was keen to quote a line from Peter Drucker that *"culture eats strategy for breakfast"* meaning that the best laid plans may be confounded by long standing practices.

a)   The development of an output-based funding model,

b)   The introduction of a national computer-based production system with an ever-expanding budget,

c)   The implementation of a regional organisation structure, designed to achieve consolidation of functions and economies of scale, and

d)   The resolution of significant industrial relations issues as some functions were consolidated and testing laboratories in some States were closed.

At the same time, we had to implement a new testing programme, and ensure continued compliance with ever tightening TGA regulation.[102] In the early days, the latter became a serious issue in South Australia where the organisation had failed a TGA audit which required an urgent intervention to avoid operational closure.

Within my own sphere, two of the more important challenges were the implementation of a standardised national financial management system and the development of the new funding system. Rose Chai had carriage of the first of these projects, with a number of options available in terms of commercially available software. As it happened, although it was not the optimal choice, the NSW blood service had recently implemented the Sun system which met most of our national requirements. And, after a good deal of inter-state manoeuvring, this and an associated payroll system were rolled out in all jurisdictions. For the first time, we now had standardised financial information which was an essential building-block for national budgeting, systematic management of financial performance, and collection of data for evaluating funding models. Under Rose's leadership, and through the workings of a new national Budget Planning Team and a National Finance Committee, this facilitated the preparation of the first output-based budget (for 1999/2000).

As regards the funding model, ARCBS had inherited from the State/Territory arrangements the antiquated "deficit-funding" system with the Commonwealth "matching" State/Territory government contributions, and additional funding released at the end of each financial year to cover accumulated deficits. For an organisation with an increasingly complex range of products and services, operating under TGA regulation, this was totally inappropriate. The need for a new

---

[102] Implementation of Nucleic Acid Testing (NAT) was the subject of a highly successful project led by Dr Anne Fletcher, the Deputy Director Intellectual Capital.

approach had been highlighted by the ARCBS Implementation Team in 1996, building on the work undertaken by RCBBV following a review by KPMG in 1994, and some ground-breaking research on activity-based costing undertaken by Dr Sally Thomas at the WA Blood Bank. To provide a sound basis for the development of the new funding system, in April 1997 we engaged consultants KPMG to undertake a fresh review of options. They reported their findings in September, which focussed on an output-based funding approach. The main KPMG proposals encompassed the following:

- Single stream of funding for operational activity
- Three-Year Funding and Service Agreement
- Mix of fixed grants and output-based funding
- Efficiency Dividend mechanism
- Range of product clusters for costing and pricing
- National price schedule
- Price signals and data on product usage provided to clinicians
- Funding to cover contingencies and working capital
- Separate line of funding for capital programmes

In response to this report, I established terms of reference for the Funding Project which both accommodated these recommendations and commissioned further research including a survey of clinicians to obtain their response to the use of price signals. And we recruited a Project Manager, David Rehe, to have carriage of a project that would continue to a successful outcome in 2003. We also did a road show in which we presented the results of the KPMG Review to all State/Territory governments to test their reaction and obtain their support. Subsequently, in 1998 AHMAC established a funding project of their own called the CEO's Working Party, which ran in parallel with our activity. In October 1998, they presented proposals which would involve plasma production being financed by the Commonwealth government, and so called "fresh blood products" being financed by State/Territory governments. In our view, this concept was flawed because it did not accommodate the fact that plasma was sourced from both plasmapheresis and whole blood collections.[103] And such a model did not deliver the kind of centralised funding that we regarded as being essential to facilitate the rationalisation of facilities and operations independent of parochial

---

[103] Plasmapheresis is a process in which plasma is separated from blood cells.

137

State/Territory considerations. After some debate, AHMAC commissioned further work as a result of which, in April 1999, they endorsed the concept of national output-based funding. The CEO'S Working Party was then replaced by a new government team called the Shadow Pricing Working Group which focussed on the needs of blood product customers, building on research previously completed in Victoria. In the meantime, ARCBS pursued its own proposals as follows:

a) Funding for "core" products using a National Price List.
b) All funding to come from one centralised source (preferably the Commonwealth government).
c) A separate national capital investment programme.
d) Inter-State transfer of products.
e) Cost recovery of non-core activities.

With ARCBS now registering as a significant national activity, in May 1999 the Commonwealth government appointed a Review Panel under the Chairmanship of Sir Ninian Stephen to undertake a comprehensive review of the blood industry.[104] This was to be undertaken with the recognition of some key assumptions. ARC would continue to have responsibility for the volunteer donor system, hospitals would not be charged for blood products, and the industry should be geared to national self-sufficiency. Given the inadequacies of current systems, we welcomed this initiative.

The Review Panel had extensive Terms of Reference, and was optimistically scheduled to report back in mid-2000. In the event, and as a result of the complexity of the task, the Stephen Report was not issued until mid-2001. The Panel was asked to consider the following matters:

i)   Safety and quality of the blood supply.
ii)   Ability to achieve vertical and horizontal integration.
iii)   Decision- making systems, particularly as regards consistency across the various arms of government.
iv)   Strategies for increasing supply, including the possibility of using imports.
v)   Capacity of the plasma fractionation business to meet future requirements.

---

[104] The Rt Hon Sir Ninian Stephen, who was also Governor General between 1982 and 1989, died in October 2017 aged 94.

In the next two years, co-ordination of the ARCBS submission to this Review became a major part of my work. And the issues on which we focussed included the following:

- Replacement of the joint Commonwealth and State/Territory funding system with centralised funding,
- Integration of the government decision-making system, with TGA decisions on safety appropriately funded,
- Development of a framework for achieving sufficiency of the blood supply,
- Investment in run-down facilities, and
- Implementation of a comprehensive government indemnity covering ARCBS operations.

The preparation of the supporting arguments for all these proposals obviously required a huge effort by the ARCBS national team. In response to these submissions and proposals from many other bodies, the Stephen Report issued in June 2001 contained some hugely significant recommendations including the following:

- Establishment of a new government body to be called the National Blood Authority ("NBA"), with a Board of Management having powers to supervise ARCBS activity.
- Centralised Commonwealth funding, with the ability to respond to emerging issues, out of cycle.
- Stronger liaison between this new body and TGA on regulatory policy.
- Nationally uniform statutory defence laws.
- National self-sufficiency using volunteer donors.
- National approach to import of blood and commitment to a National Plasma Reserve.
- Commitment to Research and Development, according to priorities agreed between the NBA and NHMRC.[105]

The recommendations were broadly welcomed by ARCBS and, after two years, the government implemented centralised output-based funding which was a major achievement. However, by the time I left the organisation in early 2003, the NBA had yet to be established. And the

---

[105] NHMRC is the National Health and Medical Research Council.

form it eventually took was some distance from the Stephen recommendations. The biggest flaw in the new arrangements was the failure to integrate government decision-making. Under the new NBA regime implemented in late 2003, TGA were still able to mandate safety standards without regard to ARCBS's ability to pay. This perpetuated a failure to understand that ARCBS was not just another commercial operator that would find the funds from other parts of its business to meet the cost of improved safety standards. And ARC had to make strenuous representations to eventually acquire an associated indemnity. However, despite these deficiencies, on a number of other issues the recommendations of the Stephen Review were adopted. And the establishment of the NBA completed the overall structure required for delivering the ultimate objective of a national blood service with output-based funding. In the scheme of things, it was a notable achievement. The main down-side was that the NBA heralded a huge change in the level of reporting required by ARCBS, a consequent expansion in the size of National Office, and the onset of a more bureaucratic culture which had the potential to confound the commitment to a learning organisation.

Even before the advent of the Stephen Review, my world was showing considerable signs of stress. On 5 February 1999, and three years after I commenced my ARCBS adventure, I had a health episode which left me in hospital for 24 hours. By now, the work involved in the three jobs of Secretary, Manager Corporate Planning, and CFO was taking its toll. I was working all hours of day and night. And, in those days, we did not have the facility for electronic meetings. The only respite, which kept me sane, was frequent weekend visits to my houseboat on Lake Eildon. But during the week, I was flying around the country, with sometimes two or even three trips, staying in hotels, and eating on the run with snacks obtained in the Qantas Club, or the Chairman's Lounge if I was travelling with the Chairman. In any event, as I was lying in the hospital bed that Friday morning, the initial diagnosis was a suspected heart attack. But after an angiogram, I was told that the severe chest pains, which had left me lying on the floor at home gasping for breath at 8.00 am in the morning, were caused by a very high level of stress.[106] And, when I went to see my GP, Dr Robert Negri, he read me the "Riot Act", asking me very simply *"Is your job so*

---

[106] I recall my colleague Dr Sally Thomas telling me that this was Syndrome X, a cardiac microvascular dysfunction or constriction potentially causing angina in patients with otherwise normal epicardial coronary arteries.

important that you want to die at the office?" It was a challenging question. It wasn't so much the total amount of current work, or the fact that I had been committed to a life of managing relentless organisational change since joining RCBBV in January 1989. For most of those ten years, I had felt part of a team working in unison. But recently things had changed, and my hospital visit should not have only been a signal to take personal stock, but a message for the whole organisation to consider the importance of work/life balance.

The immediate upshot of this health episode was indicative of what I perceived to be developing in the ARCBS culture. My "incident" was immediately evident because of my absence from a NOG meeting that Friday morning. In response, and with his usual empathy, the Chairman John Hasker tracked me down in hospital. But he arrived too late because, at the earliest opportunity, and with typical bravado, I had already checked out! When I next saw Robert Hetzel, I made light of the episode, concerned that he would see it as a sign of weakness. In the following week, I continued my crazy life, with a flight to Canberra for a meeting with the Federal government, and another flight to Perth for a periodic review of the performance of the newly formed Enterprise Business Unit.[107]

In the next 12 months, the pressure of work for me and all those around me continued to mount. There was a further proliferation of national projects, the Stephen Review, persistent financial challenges, and relentless dealings with sometimes unhelpful governments. Latterly, we were consumed with the Year 2000 project in which we safeguarded ARCBS from what turned out to be a much over-rated threat to IT systems arising from the end of the 1990s and the turn of a new century.[108] In themselves, none of these issues was insurmountable. But, at this critical point in proceedings, something at ARCBS had changed. With the benefit of hindsight, there were a number of factors. Despite maintaining the structure for learning, in response to mounting external pressures we had abandoned the collegiate style of management and replaced it with an increasingly command-and-control approach. With the proliferation of roles within National Office, the organisation had adopted an employment model that required selected senior people to

---

[107] In 1997, we established a number of Business Units, Regions and Partnerships. The five Business Units were Endeavour (NSW and ACT), Bass (Victoria and Bass), Enterprise (WA and NT) Queensland, and South Australia.

[108] The Year 2000 project involved the stress testing all computer systems, at considerable cost. On the evening of 31 December 1999, the senior management team were all on call. There was hardly a single glitch.

apply for their own jobs. Whilst this was designed to drive individual performance, it undermined the authority of some key people at a critical point in the change process and weakened the team approach. And there were a number of external appointments of people whose loyalties were much more to the CEO than to the national team. The pace of change also provided little time for the team to set strategy and reflect on outcomes. As a result, people demonstrated fear of failure with the potential for covering up mistakes. Above all, instead of working on the basis of collective responsibility, the team was inclined to retreat into silos and, with a hectic schedule, the CEO had less time to share information with his colleagues, with an inclination to put pressure on anyone who did not comply with his current priorities. More worrying in a personal basis, I was beginning to behave in my dealings with some other staff in a manner that was defining me as someone that I was not – short-tempered, intolerant and lacking in humour. This was a sure sign that I should contemplate moving on and, when I discussed this with some colleagues I found that I was not alone in my concerns.

In addition to these broader cultural issues, I also experienced a rising tension in my personal relationship with Robert Hetzel. In some ways, given my position in the organisation, this was inevitable. My journey with ARCBS had started in February 1996, and I was the only employee who did not fit the mould for the current organisation. This was because I had a separate line of reporting to the Chairman, I was on a permanent contract, and I was an attendee at all Board meetings in both my Secretarial and other roles. In particular, the Board relied upon me for my grasp of financial matters, and what I reported did not always concur with the CEO's agenda. As a result, on several occasions after a Board meeting, he took me aside to indicate his displeasure at my honest but inconvenient reports. I was largely unmoved. But this adversarial counterpoint of CEO and CFO was a major change from earlier days of collegiate team-work. When my next performance review came around, in early 2000, this came to a head. In our discussion about the current state of the organisation, I touched on a number of concerns, including the need for work/life balance and Robert presented me with an ultimatum. Whilst my position as Secretary was secure, he told me that I would have to relinquish one of the two other roles. All things considered, although this would clearly reduce my scope of influence, I could see some merit in this. Planning and Finance were both important functions and, as the financial challenges were increasing, I was concerned about my ability to do justice to the planning activity for which I had already unsuccessfully requested additional resources. Anyway, after a couple of weeks of reflecting on both my own career and current organisational priorities, I opted to retain the finance role, whilst also feeling that my inability to cope with the workload was interpreted as failure.

For the next twelve months, I continued as CFO to see through the work involved in the Stephen Review, with a mounting range of submissions to Federal and State/Territory governments in which ARCBS sought to achieve suitable outcomes on both the level and basis of funding. During this period, I also spent a good deal of time with the Finance and Audit Committee following completion of due diligence reviews and implementation of risk treatment plans. At the operational level, I was as always fortunate to have the services of Rose Chai who continued with diligence in integrating financial operations. And as well as the routine work of preparing operating and capital budgets, negotiating with the Federal and State/Territory governments, presenting monthly financial reports, and ensuring financial due diligence, there was still the Funding Project. At this point, for the first time we were able to assemble a version of the budgets based on a cost recovery basis and we were generating what were called *Shadow Prices* for a given range of blood products. These were echoes of the trail breaking work done five years earlier in RCBBV.

In the meantime, the planning role was taken over by a very able woman named Dr Anna Lavelle who had only recently been employed as the Business Development Manager. Almost immediately, she was given additional resources to do the planning work. And her team adopted an innovative process of scenario planning which flushed out a range of new development options. She also designed some excellent documentation for communicating the contents of the new plan. To me it seemed a creditable outcome, although I was concerned about the ability to deliver on the strategies.

During this period, whilst the culture within the organisation was evolving towards a more directive and less collegiate model, there were also significant and not dissimilar issues involving the Board. When it was established, ARC had acknowledged that ARCBS should be governed at arms' length by a professional Board with a majority of independent members that would ensure the highest standards of governance. And ARC had the ARCBS Advisory Council as a technical/medical watch-dog. In accordance with these arrangements, the ARC Royal Charter provided ARCBS with a considerable degree of freedom to manage its own affairs. It also allowed for the payment of Board members, with the aim of getting the best people given the responsibilities and commitment of time involved. The terms of office for the inaugural Board had also been staggered to provide for an orderly turnover and continuity of membership.

At the outset, a key member of the Board was the ARC National Chairman, Ron Green. In 1999, he was replaced by Richard Morgan. I knew Richard from my days at RCBBV and I respected him. However, I also recalled his reservations about blood service autonomy because of the risk of litigation and insolvency arising from lack of medical due diligence. And with the new national body, I suspect that he did not entirely approve of the fees paid to independent members of the ARCBS Board for a governance role that went unpaid in the rest of ARC.[109] In any event, it soon became apparent that he had concerns with an ARCBS policy that failed to honour ARC principles and which would lead him to reimpose tighter control.

In pursuit of its Research and Development strategy, in 2000 the Board adopted a policy that provided for innovators within the organisation, such as members of the scientific staff, to receive some financial acknowledgement for their "discoveries". This concept was founded on the idea that, in a professional medical organisation, individual employees had a level of intellectual ownership which warranted recognition and reward that transcended the ownership of the organisation. Richard Morgan did not accept this policy. In his view, anything which employees created in the course of their employment belonged to ARC. And the idea that they should receive payment beyond their salary was contrary to the ARC principle of *Voluntary Service*. He argued this case at several Board meetings. And, at a Board dinner in Perth, attended by his predecessor Ron Green, he made an impassioned speech in which he indicated that he would not tolerate opposition on a core ARC tenet. When the Board failed to heed his warning, he set about blocking the re-appointment of recalcitrant Board members. He had the power to do this through the mechanisms for Board selection and, within eighteen months, he had removed several key players and was able to overturn the staff reward policy.

This turn of events was a significant challenge to the concept of an independent ARCBS Board. Regardless of the merits of what constituted *Voluntary Service*, the upshot of the dispute was the disruption of a

---

[109] In keeping with the principle of volunteerism, Red Cross officers on the ARCBS Board donated their fees back to Red Cross.

hugely effective team and the creation of division and discord. It also undermined the leadership of the ARCBS Chairman. As a result, and as long as the incumbents held their jobs, communications between ARCBS and ARC were significantly soured, with a fracturing of the unity of purpose to the detriment of all concerned.

Returning to my own position, at this point I became increasingly concerned not only about the increasingly top-down culture within the organisation but also our ability to respond to significant changes in the external environment. Internally, we were struggling with a range of national projects that were proving to be unwieldy and costly, such as the implementation of a new production system using French-based Progesa computer software.[110] In the meantime, it was clear that the NBA would constitute a whole new layer of oversight imposing a hugely bureaucratic level of reporting. As a consequence, and with memories of my health issue in early 1999, in mid-2000 I decided that I had had enough of being on the front line. In November 2000, I talked through my concerns with the Chairman. He listened attentively and, whilst accepting that I should relinquish the CFO role, he persuaded me to continue as Secretary, working on a part-time basis. Moving to this new arrangement gave me time to think about where life was taking me. In the meantime, the organisation moved quickly to recruit a new CFO. For a period of several months in 2001 I ran alongside the new guy, providing advice, and imparting what I could of the history and legacy. He was a quick learner and made some innovative changes although, within two years, he resigned. Not least, I think he found it difficult to fathom the complex set of relationships in dealing with governments, where Robert Hetzel's knowledge and role now went unchallenged.

So began a new period of my life in which I went through a significant transition. At ARCBS, I settled into the much more narrowly focussed role of Secretary which, although part time, continued to involve quite a bit of travel. However, I was now free to pursue other interests as related in later chapters of this book. And there were other pre-occupations. In late 2001, I had an accident stepping out of a people mover while attending a Board meeting in Adelaide. I ripped the tendons off my ankle, and had to be loaded into the plane back to Melbourne by a cherry picker! And, more seriously, in early 2002 my mother was taken seriously ill with cancer which triggered a significant change in my perspective on

---

[110] This was a controversial selection of a relatively untried system. The FailSafe system was the leading software in the field but was rejected at the last minute because of concerns about the solvency of the US supplier.

life. In the meantime, Robert Hetzel was implementing a rolling set of changes which significantly transformed the organisation. By the end of 2002, I knew it was time to step away. Fortuitously, another opportunity arose, ironically in the ARC national office. Despite the Chairman's representations, I decided to make the move and I left ARCBS in early 2003. My story resumes in the next chapter.[111]

Looking back over those seven years at ARCBS, I have to say that I take pride in my association with the formative years of what is now one of the great Australian institutions. For the most part, the people involved worked together as a highly effective team with sound leadership and a dedication beyond the call of duty. In the early days, the organisation developed and stayed true to a set of values which, even now, easily come to mind – Unity, Fairness, Service, Creativity, and Accountability. The national leaders at Head Office and in the field embraced the behaviours associated with those values with a collegiate style. And we implemented changes that were far from popular in some quarters, through the power of argument rather than line authority. However, it was probably foolish to expect this "golden" period to last for ever. As ARCBS grew and became accountable to a burgeoning government bureaucracy, the dynamics of the organisation changed. Power became centralised, and the need to drive change through persuasion was replaced by a more directive approach with which I found it increasingly difficult to identify. In mid-1999, this was epitomised in a senior management meeting one afternoon at the Victorian offices. We were contemplating the closure of the South Australian laboratories, and Marie Sellstrom, Patrick Coghlan and I counselled delay until the completion of further analysis and due consultation with those affected. Whilst Robert Hetzel accepted our view, at the end of the meeting, he said: *"This is the last time I am going to listen to you on this kind of issue."* It was a seminal moment when we moved from team-based leadership to a form of command and control.

Finally, I cannot leave this part of my life without recalling some other aspects of ARCBS days. In addition to being ARCBS Chairman, John Hasker had strong connections with Tasmanian business. He was Chairman of both an energy company called Hydro and a wine company called Pipers Brook. The latter was a particular passion, and he persuaded me to acquire some shares which I held until the business was taken over by a Belgian company some years later. In any event, in those

---

[111] Robert Hetzel would continue as CEO until mid-2009 when he returned to being a GP and established a business working as a mentor to executives.

days, Pipers Brook held its AGM in February, and at the same time organised a weekend annual dinner and musical event in Launceston. John convinced the Board that it would coincidentally have a meeting in Tasmania on the Tuesday following the weekend event. So, for several years, and at our own expense, it became a matter of course that the Board would attend the Pipers Brook celebrations. A good time was had by all!

For several years, the national office at Nicholson Street, which we named Newman-Morris House, became something of an institution.[112] In fact, I practically lived there. It was 20 minutes' drive from my place in Kew. But it was in a weird part of town. Immediately opposite was a Housing Commission block from which bodies were known to fall from time to time! And around the corner, in Rose Street, there was a brothel. Thanks to a bright idea from Rose Chai, the office became a lodging house. At one end of the building, we constructed three bedrooms with *en-suite* to accommodate the constant flow of inter-State visitors, and ARCBS staff were well known in the restaurants of neighbouring Brunswick Street. To this day, I also have another persisting attachment to that part of town. I still attend a barber in Elgin Street which is run by a wonderful gentleman from southern Italy called Lorenzo who talks at length about life, as the Pope and Carlton legend Steven Silvagni stare down from pictures on the wall.

Despite the relentless pace of our working life, we also took time out to celebrate our achievements. In particular, Robert Hetzel instituted a National Conference which took us to all parts of the country. We also had access to a variety of other external events and, in May 1999, Rose Chai and I attended the World Master of Business Conference where we listened to learning from a succession of international speakers, including US General "Stormin' Norman" Schwarzkopf talking about leadership, Al "Chain Saw" Dunlap whose ideas on "down-sizing" were not particularly well received, Australian merchant banker Rene Rivkin whose comments on wealth creation were rich considering his subsequent jailing for fraud, and Mikhail Gorbachev who talked about the new world order following the collapse of the Soviet Union. I especially remember the General's presentation and his leadership imperatives taken from the military handbook which included Rule 13: *"when placed in command, take charge"* and Rule 14: *"do what's*

---

[112] John Newman-Morris had played a key role in the development of the blood service in the 1940s and 1950s.

right". It was rousing stuff from a military mind and some of the wisest words I have heard from anyone, with relevance to all walks of life.

In concluding this period of my life at ARCBS, I have a final reflection on organisational culture and the suitability of people for their times. There is no doubt in my mind that in the early years of ARCBS, we were blessed with an amazing team of Board and executive that successfully established a new national organisation from eight very different State and Territory operating units. And this success was due, in large measure, to the collegiate nature of leadership and adherence to the model of a small and close-knit national team. However, consolidation and expansion, during a period when the organisation faced mounting external oversight, tested this culture. With mounting internal and external pressures, it became increasingly difficult to maintain the values and behaviours that had characterised the early years. Whether the transitional leadership team from those early years was suitable for, or capable of handling, the longer-term consolidation in a rapidly changing external environment is an open question. I can only speak for myself. My departure after seven years was consistent with the view that it was time for new leaders with different skills. But that is for another time and a further book!

13: Royal Charter and a Bombing

Throughout my time with the ARCBS project, I had maintained significant and harmonious relationships with people in the national office of the Australian Red Cross Society ("ARC"). In the early 2000s the notable Jim Carlton had retired, to be replaced as Secretary General by Martine Letts who had previously been the Australian Ambassador to Argentina.[113] And, in 2002, ARC elected as National Chairman a retired barrister from Queensland named Dr Rob O'Regan QC, who had been involved with my appointment as ARCBS Implementation Team Leader.[114]

In late March 2003, I was approached by Rob O'Regan for a chat about ARC plans to update the organisation's governance arrangements. I met with him and Deputy National Chairman Brian Ward whom I knew from my days at the ARC Victorian Division. Following a discussion about the need for a structure that would facilitate a more national approach to the management of the organisation, in early April I also met with Martine, who gave me a more detailed briefing on current issues in the organisation. In essence, it was clear that the national leaders saw the need for a radical change to the organisation's structure and systems of accountability, because the existing Divisional arrangements were confounding the ability to meet national objectives.

In the Australian context ARC is an unusual organisation, being one of a relatively small group of entities which operates under a Royal Charter rather than articles of association. The body was formed in 1914 as a branch of the British Red Cross Society, and established as a separate entity in 1923.[115] In 1941 it was incorporated through a Royal Charter to be governed by a Council elected by eight State and Territory bodies with the monarch of the day as Patron. Subsequently, the role of Patron was transferred to the Governor General. Under rules established by the International Red Cross, there could be only one Red Cross Society in any one country. And so one might have expected that the various entities at State and Territory level, who were responsible for the

---

[113] Born in 1935, Jim Carlton was Secretary General from 1994 to 2001, having previously been a Federal MP (1977-1994), the Minister of Health in the Fraser government in 1982/83 and Shadow Treasurer in 1985/87. He died in December 2015.

[114] Rob O'Regan was a barrister and former Chairman of the Queensland Criminal Justice Commission. He served as National Chairman from November 2000 until he was succeeded in November 2003 by another Queensland lawyer Greg Vickery, who had also been a member of the ARCBS inaugural board.

[115] The British Red Cross Society was incorporated by Royal Charter in 1908.

delivery of a diverse set of domestic services in their own jurisdiction, would be "branches" of the national organisation. In reality, these bodies behaved as if ARC was a federal organisation. They were fiercely independent, with their own Rules and policies, and at times showed only a grudging deference to the national part of the organisation. The national body had responsibility for certain national policies, international tracing, the delivery of international aid, and the advocacy of international humanitarian law. This work was financed by annual contributions from the State and Territory Divisions who, subject to resolutions by the elected National Council that met once per annum, had the ability to frustrate national initiatives. In 1998, under the leadership of Ron Green and Jim Carlton, the organisation had taken a significant step to achieve a degree of national co-ordination by establishing a National Executive consisting of State/Territory Chairpersons and national officers (National Chairman, National Deputy Chairman, Treasurer and National Youth Representative). But they had a wider vision involving a transition to a more centralised structure. In many ways, the ARCBS project was the *entrée*, and had certainly served to demonstrate that a national structure was potentially achievable and capable of bringing significant benefits in terms of efficiency and an enhanced national profile and unity of purpose.

The proposal put to me by Rob O'Regan and Martine Letts was that I should manage a project to modernise governance systems and practices, and institute a new governance structure. It was a bold venture, as the Chairpersons of the State and Territory organisations were far from persuaded about the rationale for this change, or the need to cede power to a national body. The manner in which the change in structure would be achieved would require some research and analysis. But in essence it would involve the replacement of the advisory National Executive with a Board (appointed by National Council), that would have full governance responsibility. This would facilitate a significant shift towards national leadership and control of resources. The Secretary General would become the CEO to whom Divisional Executive Directors would report, and the voluntary position of Treasurer, who had operational responsibility for finance, would be replaced by a CFO reporting to the CEO. The position of Treasurer would then morph into the chair of a Finance and Audit Committee of the Board. The way in which I was to conduct this ground-breaking project would involve my appointment as Secretary reporting to the National Chairman with a "dotted-line" to the Secretary General. And this role was seen as a relatively short term appointment, undertaken on a part time basis which might take a year or two pending a more permanent appointment if the aims of the project were achieved.

In contemplating this proposal, I was in two minds. At ARCBS, the Chairman John Hasker did his best to dissuade me. He suggested that ARC was an organisation led by people who meant well but might struggle to embrace significant change. And, given recent issues between ARCBS and ARC, I think he saw it as an act of disloyalty for me even to consider the matter. But there were other considerations. For Hasker, his ARC project had commenced in 1996. Mine went back much further. Indeed, I had been involved in blood service change management at State and National level since 1989. And, with yet another major ARCBS re-organisation underway ahead of the establishment of the new National Blood Authority in 2002, I felt that I had "done my dash" in the blood industry. Indeed, I was contemplating a life in which I would work as a consultant no longer beholden to organisational politics. From a more positive point of view, I saw the ARC project as a significant challenge, for which I was well suited. And I looked forward to working with a new set of people for an organisation whose international mission I greatly admired. It also appeared that I would be given a fairly free hand, with part-time work providing considerable flexibility. In many ways, it seemed a good way to end a journey of more than ten years with ARC on a high note and gracefully transition to the rest of my life.

After due consideration, I decided to accept the ARC offer, and in April 2003 I resigned from ARCBS. After one final ARCBS Board meeting in late April, a suitable send-off, and a short break when I spent a couple of days walking in the Mount Buffalo National Park, on 5 May 2003 I began a new phase in my life with great anticipation.

In those days, the ARC national office was in Pelham Street in Carlton.[116] It was a modern building and, given my increasing involvement with the Australian Conservation Foundation at the Green Building around the corner in Leicester Street, conveniently placed. I was given an office which sat conveniently between the Secretary General Martine Letts and the Deputy Secretary General Beryl Raufer, and I quickly became acquainted with the key staff, all of whom were supportive of my role. Martine and Beryl were both friendly and amenable people with whom I quickly established a rapport. However, of special note was a lady named Sue Miller, who would become a firm

---

[116] In recent times, ARC co-located with the Victorian Division in Villiers Street in North Melbourne. The building is now occupied by the Centre for Innovative Justice.

ally during what would turn out to be a rocky ride. She was a lawyer by training and hailed from Gippsland where she had been a community advocate. At ARC she was HR Manager, and she soon set about finding me a personal assistant.

Governance Project

At the beginning of the project, I trod very carefully with some fairly modest proposals designed to improve governance practice within the existing structure. Following discussions with the Chairman and Deputy Chairman, I completed an audit of the current governance systems using a diagnostic tool that I had developed at ARCBS. I then prepared a paper for consideration by the National Executive at its meeting in late May. Whilst ARC met many of the requirements for good governance, there were significant shortcomings which would form the basis of a project to reform systems and process. The main elements requiring attention were as follows:

a)   Development of a National Executive Accountability Statement, to provide clarity as to its role and the measures it would use to monitor its own performance.

b)   Specification of roles and responsibilities of National Executive members, and a related competency profile.

c)   Development of a Matrix of Delegations to clarify the decision-making process within the organisation and the extent to which authority was delegated to management.

d)   Establishment of an annual programme of meetings, identifying key business to be considered by the National Executive on a systematic basis.

e)   Development of policies on Conflicts of Interest and Independent Professional Advice.

f)   Completion of a risk analysis, as a basis for implementing a systematic approach to due diligence.

g)   Development of a Performance Plan for the Secretary General, and provisions for succession planning.

h)   Development of an Administration Manual for conduct of National Executive business.

In great part these initiatives reflected a similar set of policy and procedures that had been developed for the ARCBS Board, and represented a transfer of intellectual capital from the blood service to its parent body. The work involved would take up much of my time in the first six months, and enabled me to establish a level of rapport with the main players on the National Executive and their executive officers. I also reformed the methodology for presenting Board papers, with shorter documents, indication of whether matters were for information, discussion or decision, and clearly worded recommendations that enabled timeliness and accountability in implementation. These were not particularly radical ideas, but were a means to substantially change the nature of meetings with the intention of achieving more well-defined outcomes. My proposals, which included a timetable for implementation over the next six months, were welcomed and supported by the National Executive.

In the first and subsequent monthly meetings with the National Executive, I began to get a sense of ARC culture. I already knew from my days with the blood service that the organisation attracted some very passionate volunteers who were committed to both the international and the national roles. For those not acquainted, the Australian version of Red Cross had developed a distinctly different character from its British roots. The focus on international humanitarian law, overseas aid, and tracing were important. But, in establishing itself across Australia, ARC had developed a presence at State and Territory level that was more generally associated with the delivery of local community services, including the blood transfusion services. When I began my project in 2003, some of the State/Territory people were already "stung" by what they saw as the loss of their blood transfusion service to ARCBS. And the advent of a new government body (the proposed National Blood Authority), with responsibility for funding and oversight of a national blood service, was almost seen as the last straw. Consequently, at least initially and for some, any talk of further centralisation of control was anathema.

From my blood service days I had also become acquainted with eccentric behaviour by some the senior volunteers. Many of the wealthy people who donated their time to serve as officers of the organisation brought with them a command-and-control style of management, and an inclination to speak down to people who were paid. This manifested itself in an almost feudal lack of respect for professional advice provided by qualified and experienced employees. I don't think that this book is the place to comment on individuals. But I do hasten to add that these attitudes and behaviour were not universal. There were outstanding volunteers in leadership roles for whom one could only have respect for their dedication and professional approach. Perhaps it would be best to say that they were a mixed bag, and working with some of them required a thicker skin than I sometimes had. More important than all of this, however, was the history of the organisation. It is worth repeating that ARC was not a federal organisation. But through custom and practice, and perhaps as a result of the tyranny of distance, the State and Territory leaders were inclined to behave as if they were a group of tribal chieftains.

Having provided this picture of the "officers and gentlemen", it will not be surprising to hear that the people employed as the paid Divisional Executive Directors ("EDs") were also a mixed bag and often, but not always, reflected the behaviour of their volunteer leaders. In June 2002, it had been decided to establish what was called the National Management Team ("NMT"). And, when I joined the organisation, Martine Letts was seeking to consolidate her leadership of this group, with difficulty. The NMT brought together the EDs from each State and Territory and a group of managers responsible for national programmes. Given the independent inclination of the Divisional Officers, and their control of the purse strings, leadership was like "herding cats". Under the current structure, in which EDs were appointed by Divisional Executives, the NMT was very much a liaison team with the remit to provide for sharing information on national and divisional activities, discussing issues with national implications, and considering policy with the potential for national adoption. Like the National Executive, for the General Secretary it was a potentially frustrating vehicle for doing anything, not least in terms of considering the appropriate level of State/Territory contributions to national programmes, and implementing national projects including a new tracing system. The EDs took their lead from their Divisional Executives and national policy was achieved through persuasion not line authority. And, as a group, the behaviour was very similar to that of the National Executive. Indeed, in a given jurisdiction, it was sometimes difficult to know whether a particular point of view came from an Executive Director or the local Divisional Chairman. And there was no doubt as to where loyalties lay.

Returning to the governance project, in anticipation of my appointment, in November 2002 the National Executive had established a Governance Working Group ("GWG"), led by the Chair of the Victorian Division, Richard Stone. He was a physically large and friendly fellow, who was respectful and considered in his presentation, and had a somewhat discursive way of talking.[117] The other members of the team were Brian Ward, whom I already knew and trusted from RCBBV days, the ACT Division Chairman, Dr Richard Pembrey, the ACT Division ED, Tracy Hicks, the SA Division ED, Dale Cleaver, and Belinda Barnard who was the Youth Representative on the National Executive. Although we met infrequently for logistical reasons, they were a helpful and enthusiastic group who were supportive of the process and provided valuable input to the development of documentation. Not members of the group, but providing significant support, were Martine Letts, Sue Miller and the Tasmanian Division Chairman, Michael Legge.

Following the May meeting of the National Executive, Richard Stone and I prepared a discussion paper to reflect on problems with the current governance structure, to develop the case for change, to consider the options for a new model, and to present some additional ideas for improving governance practice. This paper was presented to a meeting of the National Executive on 21/22 June.[118] The paper was generally well received although I suspected that a number of Divisional Chairman were "keeping their powder dry". In any event, this started the debate in earnest with both the National Executive and the National Management Team invited to provide feedback. In the following months, there were a number of comments, particularly from those supportive of change, and I then prepared a further discussion paper for consideration by the National Executive on 28/29 September. This document consolidated all the material presented to date and characterised the current structure of the organisation as *"Autonomy with Co-ordination"*, with Divisional entities behaving like they were part of a federation, even though they were not. The problems identified with this structure included the following:

a)   The allocation of funding to the majority of operational activity was controlled by Divisional Executive Committees. This potentially confounded the ability of the National Executive to

---

[117] After a career in banking, Richard Stone OAM had a role with KPMG in which he was responsible for advising clients on corporate governance. He died in 2016.

[118] These meetings were held over a weekend to accommodate the busy working lives of volunteer participants.

implement decisions which it had made at a national level in the national interest.

b)   Assets were in the hands of Divisions which confounded optimal use from a national point of view.

c)   Members of the National Executive were also Divisional Chairman, and this presented a potential conflict of interest. This was particularly manifest when it came to decisions on the allocation of resources for funding of national programs at Divisional expense.

d)   Risk management was in the hands of Divisions, which exposed ARC to inconsistent policies and practices.

Notwithstanding these issues, it was acknowledged that the diversity and local roots implicit in the current Divisional structure provided great strength for the organisation. In particular, Divisions were well placed to recruit local members who reflected the diversity of Australia at a regional level, to develop programs suitable for local needs, to use local networks to liaise with State/Territory community leaders, and to tap into local charitable donations.

Given the perceived problems, a new vision was proposed entitled *"One organisation, responsive to community needs."* The aim was to achieve a sufficient degree of integration and national consistency to access synergy and the more effective use of scarce resources, whilst maintaining the strengths available through the community-based Divisions. The proposed change was summarised in a Governance Matrix which specified Current Practice and Future Vision. This document reflected that, whilst the role of Council would not change, there would be a significant shift from the National Executive/Divisional Executive model to a Board/Divisional Committee model. The main features were as follows.

Role of National Executive/National Board

a)   Deployment of resources according to local and national needs as determined at a national level, with a unified management structure in which Divisional Executive Directors reported to the Secretary General.

b)   Central control of all property, buildings, and facilities. This would require the clear transfer of all related deeds and authorities to a national finance function.

c)   Centralised reporting of risk management within a national policy framework.
d)   Centralised responsibility for communications.

Role of Divisions

a)   Recruitment of ARC ordinary members.
b)   Assessment of the needs of vulnerable people within their local community, and championing the allocation of resources for the delivery of services to meet those needs.
c)   Monitoring the delivery of local services to ensure that they continued to be relevant and sensitive to local needs.
d)   Fund raising, making use of local networks.
e)   Advocacy, through appropriate local networks.

Following a spirited discussion at its September meeting, the National Executive endorsed the proposals as submitted and agreed that a paper encompassing the same material should be submitted for discussion by the Council at its AGM. In the meantime, it was also agreed that Divisional Executives would have an opportunity to consider any further comments. At the AGM on 16 November, the proposals were duly received and discussed in a series of workshops. Council members were generally supportive of the proposals, and a range of helpful feedback was obtained including some interesting ideas about changing the system for electing the Council. It was agreed that the next stage in progressing the change programme would be to present the proposals more widely through a "Road Show", to be taken to all Divisions around the country. There would then be a review of progress at the National Executive meeting in February, with fully worked proposals presented to the National Executive on 1 May 2004. Subsequently, recommendations would be presented to a special meeting of Council in July/August 2004, ahead of the AGM in November when any changes to the Royal Charter and Rules would be considered.

At this point, I have to say that I sighed with great relief. The degree of acceptance and good will was considerably more than I had expected. But this was only the beginning of the journey and we pick up the story later in this chapter. In the meantime, at the AGM, there was a changing of the guard with both Rob O'Regan and Brian Ward retiring from their positions, although the Honorary Treasurer Graham Addison from WA continued. The new national officers were Greg Vickery, elected as

National Chairman, and Michael Legge, as Deputy National Chairman.[119] Whilst I was sorry to see the retirement of the team with whom I had worked for the best part of a year, these new appointments were very welcome. I knew and respected both Greg and Michael from their time on the ARCBS Board. And the new National Chairman immediately instituted a mechanism for managing business called the Chairman's Committee with membership comprising the Chairman, and Deputy Chairman, Treasurer, the Secretary General and myself. Of equal significance for the governance project were other changes in membership of the National Executive with new Divisional Chairman from NSW, Tasmania, ACT, and Northern Territory.

Other Business

Whilst the work of the GWG was unfolding, the ordinary business of ARC continued relentlessly. In 2003, there were many issues engaging the leadership team in National Office. This work included the following:

- Updating the long-term ARC strategy,
- Implementation of a new computer tracing system, for which funding from Divisions was proving to be a challenge,
- Managing the government's withdrawal of AusAid funding from various overseas projects,
- An appeal to provide drought relief, and
- The challenge of engaging with young people in an age of declining commitment to voluntary work, and
- Training of ADF personnel in international humanitarian law.[120]

Given my preoccupation with governance systems, whilst I was interested, I had relatively little involvement in these matters, although I provided plenty of input through conversations with Martine Letts and others. But I did play an active role in ensuring that ARC was appropriately informed about the aims and conduct of ARCBS affairs. And I was drawn into significant negotiations regarding the NBA Agreement which would cement the establishment of the proposed

---

[119] Greg Vickery as a lawyer from Queensland. Michael Legge AM was a fine-wool sheep-farmer from North Eastern Tasmania.
[120] ARC provided funding for the Chair of International Humanitarian Law at Melbourne University. ADF stands for Australian Defence Force.

National Blood Authority and centralised funding of the blood service commencing 1 July 2003. Implementation was being handled by a team named the Blood Review Implementation Steering Committee ("BRISC"). There were a range of important issues, including the financing of capital projects, and proposals for yet another round of efficiency dividends. But the biggest sticking point, eventually conceded by the government, was an ARC requirement for an indemnity in the event that the NBA refused to finance initiatives such as a new testing programme mandated by TGA.

Bali Bombing

Apart from these matters, by far the biggest issue during this period was the Bali bombing and its aftermath, which somewhat side-lined the governance work. This was an object lesson in the management of charitable disaster funds and would severely test the integrity, and even the survival, of ARC.

The bombing on 12 October 2002 resulted in the deaths of over 200 people, including 88 Australian and 35 Indonesians, making it the single worst act of terrorism to have impacted either country. A further 209 people were injured, including 66 Australians who suffered severe burns and complex shrapnel wounds. Almost immediately following this disaster, ARC launched an appeal with messaging that made a commitment to allocate 90% of funds raised to the victims (with an implied allocation of no more than 10% to administrative costs). And, as is usually the case in managing appeals, ARC established an Appeals Committee with responsibility for ensuring financial due diligence and processing specific applications from victims and others for allocations from the fund. This team was chaired by the then Deputy Chairman Brian Ward, with the support of the manager of overseas services, Noel Clement, and worked assiduously according to a well-tried process including appropriate assessment criteria.

By May 2003, the ARC Appeal had raised $14.3 million. However, even as I was getting my feet under the desk at ARC National Office, there were reports in the national media that the organisation had been slow to distribute funds to people requiring prosthetic limbs and surgery, and had been allocating funds to purposes other than that identified when the Appeal was launched (the relief of victims). In particular, some people questioned donations made to the Bali health system which, in part, had funded an ambulance that had failed to be delivered. And it was suggested that an allocation of funding to skin-grafting research projects in Western Australia was inappropriate.

In the next six months, a great deal of time and effort was spent not only in caring for the victims through implementation of a case manager system, and allocating funds, but also in defending ARC's reputation. Given the vitriol directed at the organisation, ARC appointed media consultants to provide advice on communications strategy with a strong message to reassure the public that the organisation had acted in good faith, both in the management of the appeal, and in the allocation of funds. Following initial communications by ARC Officers, Martine Letts was also appointed as sole spokesperson. She gave interviews and eventually issued a substantial statement, apologising for any confusion about the terms of the appeal and the intended use of funds, and providing a breakdown of how the money would be spent. This showed that almost 70 % would go directly to Australian victims and less than 3 % had gone to administration. Sadly, this did not stem the criticism. Indeed, the continuing allegations against ARC led the NSW government to launch a public inquiry under the NSW Charitable Fund Raising Act. This legislation included provisions that funds raised in a public appeal must be allocated to the stated purpose.

Confronted with mounting pressure to attack both the integrity and due diligence of the organisation, ARC employed Price Waterhouse Coopers ("PWC") to undertake an independent audit of all the funds raised and a major PR company to assist in re-establishing its position as a trustworthy not-for-profit organisation. The results of the PWC audit were published in August 2003. The main conclusion was that the funds raised had been used in a manner that matched the original intent of the appeal, and that there was no evidence of fraud or misuse of funds. But the auditors found that ARC could have managed its public communications in a more effective manner, and that two of the projects financed from the appeal fund didn't strictly accord with the stated objective of helping Australian victim and their families. These involved the allocation of $500,000 to research into skin grafts for burns victims and a Disaster Planning project for the Darwin Hospital. In response to the report, and still under attack by some in the medical profession for not allocating all of the funds directly to victims, Rob O'Regan and Brian Ward fronted the media in an ABC newscast. Rob O'Regan noted that, whilst ARC had been cleared of the allegations of wrong-doing, there was a necd to improve the organisation's processes for reporting and communication. Brian Ward referred to ARC's considerable experience in managing the allocation of appeal funds, and provided assurance that the Appeals Committee had given careful thought to the merits of the two projects which were questioned by some members of the public, with support based on the fact that they were both closely related to the welfare of victims.

Despite the outcome of the PWC Audit, and eventual exoneration by the NSW government inquiry, the debate raged on for several months. It only died down towards the end of the year when ARC issued a full report on aims, processes and outcomes of the Appeal Fund. An edited extract from the report follows:

"The Australian Red Cross Bali Appeal Fund is helping Australian victims and their families, and the people of Bali, to cope with the tremendous loss and human suffering caused by the devastating bombings. This commitment was announced at the outset of the appeal, and Australian Red Cross has not wavered from this objective. On 16 October 2002 we announced the appeal would:

- *Assist victims in Australia and their families; and*
- *Provide relief, dressing, and medical supplies in the affected area in Bali as well as to cover future needs including recovery and reconstruction.*

Since the launch of the Appeal, Australian Red Cross has provided financial assistance to 546 Australians affected by the tragedy. We are also implementing several programs to assist the people of Bali. These include programs to reinforce emergency and health services, as well as medical and livelihood assistance.

By the end of September 2003, the Bali Appeal has received a total of $15.3 million. The public donated $7.8 million (51%), the corporate sector $3.9 million (25%), and Governments $2.7 million (18%). $0.7 million (5%) were received from International Red Cross Societies and Australian Red Cross branches and units and bank interest was $0.2 million (1%).

Out of the $15.3 million received, $11.2 million (73%) has been allocated to Australia, $3.6 million (24%) to Bali and $0.5 (3%) for administration. Out of the $11.2 million allocated to Australia, $10.4 million (93%) of funds has been spent or is in the process of being spent on direct financial aid to victims and their families, $0.3 million (3%) to provide client support, referral and advocacy to victims, and $0.5 million

(4%) towards two Australian projects associated with the tragedy. A total of approximately $0.3 million remains from the initial allocation for the Disaster Preparedness project. Australian Red Cross will make public announcements in relation to these remaining funds in the future.

With the benefit of hindsight, one might wonder why this level of communication in terms of detail was not just a matter of due course. And therein lay the learning for the management of future such appeals. Clear public communication about the aims and scope of any appeal were prerequisites. In any event, after much effort to re-establish the "brand", ARC continued to be the charity of choice in managing the funds raised for major disasters. When the next disaster occurred, deriving from the need for drought relief, ARC was back on the front foot. And, by the time I hit my own personal disaster in February 2009, their systems were hugely effective and their integrity was fully restored.

Governance End Game

Whilst the national officers and senior management team were focussed on the Bali episode for much of 2003, the GWG continued to work its way through the various documents that would underpin changes to the governance structure and systems. At the suggestion of Richard Stone, this included the preparation of a Governance Charter. This turned out to be a major document of some 40 pages and 12,000 words and encompassed all aspects of the programme. Of course, the main game was the proposed changes to the structure, and we now pick up this story from where we left it at the 2003 Council AGM in late November.

The first meeting of the new National Executive in 2004 was on 29 February in Hobart. It was an auspicious gathering which included an invitation to have tea with the State Governor in Government House, a beautiful Victorian country house built in neo-Gothic style and completed in 1857. The meeting at ACT headquarters was a little disappointing from my point of view since there appeared to be signs of a little back-sliding since the change in the composition of the National Executive. This had included the somewhat disappointing loss of a supporter of the change programme, Dr William Maley.[121] Despite Greg

---

[121] Now an Emeritus Professor, Dr William Maley served as Professor of Diplomacy at the ANU from 2003 to 2021 and was Foundation Director of the Asia-Pacific College of Diplomacy (2003-2014).

Vickery's efforts to hold the line, the new team determined to put a hold on the Road Show scheduled to take place in March/April, with just a hint that the new National Executive might not be bound by the decisions of the previous team. They passed a resolution that they would like an opportunity to undertake a further review of the proposals at the meeting scheduled for 1 May 2004.

At this point in proceedings, I took stock of my personal position. The amount of work involved in the governance project, and the length of time, was proving to be considerably more than I had anticipated. And implementation of the new governance systems had created a significant operational workload. I found myself working almost full time at a time when I was developing significant outside interests. In particular, I was now Secretary of the ACF with its own significant governance project and I was on another Board. I also had a major family issue in supporting my mother who had been diagnosed with bowel cancer. I discussed these matters with Greg Vickery, and we agreed that there was merit in appointing a full time Secretary later in the year. On that basis, I gave advance notice of my intention to resign in June, with a commitment to continue working on the governance project as a consultant until completion later in the year. This proved to be a successful arrangement, with Robert Baxter being appointed to take on the full-time job of Board Secretary in July.[122]

Ahead of the National Executive meeting on 1/2 May, we had a number of meetings to consider how best to consolidate the work of the last 12 months. It was agreed to make a fresh presentation about the reasons for change and the rationale for the proposed new structure. On this occasion, I undertook to circulate another comprehensive paper to the National Executive stating the case and recording the journey to date. At the meeting, Greg Vickery would then make a presentation of the main proposals and Richard Stone and I would field questions. Thereafter, the timetable would involve the delayed Road Show to take place in May/June, with the National Executive to sign off of a final version of the proposals taking into account Divisional feedback in August. Recommendations would then be submitted to Council in November. In the event, the meeting went well and the team approved the establishment of a national Board as well as most of the other changes, subject to a further presentation at a meeting to be held on 30/31 May. However, there was some equivocation about the new management

---

[122] Robert Baxter had a military background and proved to be highly competent. However, two years later he left following the murder of his wife.

structure and the proposal to transfer responsibility for the appointment and management of EDs from Divisional Executive Committees to the Secretary General/CEO. Pending this further meeting, it was agreed to again defer the National Road Show which would now take place in June/July.

Despite the optimistic view that I had after that meeting, the meeting on 31 May would turn out to be one of the worst experiences of my life. The aim of the business was to confirm what had previously been agreed and to clarify the future management structure. But the meeting took a completely different course. One of the Divisional Chairmen attempted to amend the minutes of the previous meeting with the aim of blocking any suggestion that Executive Directors would be appointed by, and report to, the Secretary General. It was then suggested that the whole governance reform programme was unnecessary, that ARC was a *de facto* federation, and that we couldn't have staff telling the elected volunteers how to run the organisation. Recommendations designed to overturn the reform agenda were then tabled without notice, and a range of comments made which impugned the integrity of both Richard Stone and myself. And the Secretary General also came under attack, with criticism of her endeavours to obtain adequate funding for national programmes, including the stalled Tracing System IT project. Those attacked obviously defended themselves and the Treasurer made an impassioned plea in support of change, citing his long-time frustrations with the failure to co-operate in providing the funds to implement national projects. Those attempting to ditch the reform agenda doubled down and eventually Richard Stone had heard enough. He said that this behaviour from a minority of the National Executive, with no attempt to consult with him beforehand, was totally unacceptable. And he stormed out of the meeting threatening to call the media. Stunned by this extraordinary turn of events, Greg Vickery quickly adjourned proceedings to allow tempers to cool. People left the room and began to gather in small groups with Greg Vickery providing counsel. On resumption some time later, resolutions to stop the reform agenda from what turned out to be a minority of the National Executive were then put to the meeting and defeated by 7 votes to 5. But there had been serious damage to relationships which would take a long time to retrieve.

I was so shocked by the behaviour of what appeared to be a plot by certain members of the National Executive that, the following day, I prepared a detailed reflection on which I have been able to rely in preparing this account. A few days later, I submitted a considered

164

assessment to the Chairman's Planning Committee accommodating further information that had come to hand. It is not happy reading. In a nutshell, on the evening prior to the National Executive meeting, a group of five Divisional Chairmen had apparently convened and prepared a plan to overturn the governance reform programme. Two other Divisional Chairmen had declined to join this gathering and the group of five had not engaged with the Victorian Divisional Chairman Richard Stone. Whatever one may think about this behaviour, it was a salutary lesson in how volunteer leaders of charitable organisations are inclined to presume a kind of lofty prerogative without regard for due process. And it was all the more extraordinary given that the organisation in question was the Australian Red Cross Society and all that it stands for.

Despite this awful experience, the reform agenda at ARC was not lost. The people who were opposed did not give up. But, by choosing to behave in the manner they did, they lost the argument. And, after what happened, one of their number was contrite whilst another withdrew their support leaving a group of three. On 25 June, the National Executive was reconvened. The team reviewed and approved a final version of the proposals, including the new reporting relationship for Executive Directors, and agreed the material to be used in the Road Show visits to all State and Territory organisations. Thereafter, Greg Vickery assumed personal responsibility for the conduct of this activity and determined that, after such a saga, he would change the nature of the sessions to "providing information" rather than "consultation" with an emphasis on managing risk. In August, with some 20 presentations to Divisional Executives, staff and stakeholders, this process went relatively smoothly, with broad acceptance in all jurisdictions of the need for and manner of reform.

By now, the new full time Secretary Robert Baxter was on board and I slipped into consultancy mode. I was relieved that I now reported to the National Chairman and did not have to sit in meetings with some people who never had the grace to apologise for how they behaved. Perhaps their lack of respect for people they regarded as lesser mortals led them to think that they had done nothing wrong. In any event, once we had confirmed the need for changes to the Royal Charter and Rules, we also determined that it would be prudent to engage the advice and support of some legal experts in the field. Our existing lawyers were a firm named Allens Arthur Robinson ("AAR"). However, from time to time, ARC also used other lawyers and, given the specialist nature of the task, it was decided to put the matter out to tender, a process for which Sue Miller and I had responsibility. There were tenders from both AAR and Mallesons Stephen Jaques ("MSJ"). On balance, we opted for MSJ because they had specific experience in handling Royal Charters, proposed a very helpful methodology for presenting the case for change (using an Explanatory Memorandum), and also offered to work on a pro bono basis!

Over August, September and October, Sue Miller and I worked closely with MSJ in preparing the documentation to amend the Charter and Rules, and I liaised with the new Secretary, Robert Baxter, in ensuring smooth passage of the change proposals at meetings of the National Executive and eventually Council's AGM. This work continued to engage me through until the end of October when my consultancy work for the organisation finally came to an end. MSJ did an excellent job. We adopted a policy of presenting the changes as a package, since failure of one part had the potential to compromise other elements. Despite the controversy of May, and the possibility of another attempt to sabotage the reform, at the Council meeting on 27 November 2004, the changes were adopted. Interestingly, this meeting also marked the end of Martine Letts's time with ARC. Following the momentous events of 2003 and 2004 she had announced in August that, when she came to the end of her contract in November, she would be moving on. She eventually took a position at the Lowey Institute in Sydney.[123] After the AGM, Greg Vickery issued a communiqué summarising all proposals for circulation throughout the organisation. I sent my hearty thanks to Greg and the team and my sentiments were reciprocated. In the meantime, the organisation established two teams to have carriage of implementation. The Governance Implementation Committee had oversight of the changes in governance structure and systems including an update of the Delegations Matrix and the appointment of the organisation's first CFO, who was Dale Cleaver, the SA ED. And a Divisional Model Rules Working Group was established to develop a standard set of rules for use in each State and Territory. In the meantime, ARC was also busy *"doing its knitting"*, with yet another Appeal, this time in response to the Tsunami that devastated communities in the region on 26 December 2004. The stigma of the Bali Appeal was long gone. And Greg Vickery would go on to serve two terms as President of the organisation. I think the new structure served him well.[124]

---

[123] Martine Letts is now the CEO of the Committee for Melbourne.

[124] In 2005, Greg Vickery was elected to the Governing Board of the Red Cross and Crescent Movement based in Geneva. In 2011 he was elected to the prestigious Standing Commission,

I said my formal farewell to ARC at a special dinner held on 23 October 2004. I made one of my better speeches on what was effectively my retirement from paid employment, choosing to reflect on my working days going back 35 years. There were the usual kind words and I was presented with some fine-wine glasses. Interestingly, this was not the last time I heard from the organisation. In mid-2005, I was contacted by the Chairman of the Red Cross Honours Committee, John Pinney. To my surprise, it had been decided to give me the ARC Distinguished Staff Award, which consisted of a medal and citation, for my work in the establishment of ARCBS and other services to the organisation. To receive this award, I attended a special presentation at the Ridges Hotel in Melbourne on 26 November 2005. It is recognition that I treasure.

Finally, despite all the angst and controversy during my 18 months at ARC, I have to say that there were plenty of happy times and a lot of fun. To this day, Sue Miller is one of my closest friends and I keep in touch with Beryl Raufer, and Noel Clement, who is now ARC Director Australian Programs. The staff at ARC were a friendly group and we had plenty of social events, including several dinners at the home of Martine Letts in Fitzroy, and a most enjoyable Christmas party which included a visit to a Bowling Club in 2003. I also value the support and friendship provided by Michael Legge, who was there for me at times when attempts were made by certain Divisional Chairmen to bluster, bully and confound. Like Greg Vickery, he also served as a member of the International Board of the Red Cross and Red Crescent and eventually took over from Greg Vickery as President of ARC in 2011.

which in turn appointed him chairman. For his outstanding contributions to international humanitarian activity as well as the Australian Red Cross, in 2013 he was awarded an AO.

PART FOUR

WHAT ABOUT THE

ENVIRONMENT?!

14: A Green Engagement

Throughout my adult life, I have had a passion for nature. When I was a child, I lived in a rural environment with fields at the bottom of the garden and woods, parks, and ponds within walking distance. Although as an adult my work doomed me to live in cities, in the 1960s I joined Friends of the Earth. In those days, before the spectre of global warming, this organisation's main pre-occupation was recycling and that became a cause for me. As I entered politics in the 1970s, conservation and animal welfare were issues that registered in my campaigning. But environmental concerns were not at that time central to the public discourse.

When I arrived in Australia in 1986, the environment was hot news. The battle to save the Franklin River in Tasmania had just been won, and Prime Minister Bob Hawke was eulogising about green issues. This was one of the reasons that in 1987 I decided to join the Wilderness Society.[125] However, I eventually came to the conclusion that this organisation's scope of campaigning was somewhat localised, and it did not have a particularly strong organisational presence in Victoria. So, I was only involved on the periphery, patronising their shop and attending the odd meeting in Melbourne. And, with a busy working life, I had other priorities for my voluntary work, including the Australian Democrats and then beach volleyball. Indeed, drained by the stress of a heavy workload, weekends spent communing with nature on my houseboat on Lake Eildon were more of a priority than saving the planet.

Towards the end of the 1990s, I became aware of what seemed to be the main environmental campaigner *at a national level*, the Australian Conservation Foundation ("ACF"). This body styled itself as the peak environmental organisation in Australia, with a focus on influencing governments, and engaging with the bureaucracy through a range of targeted campaigns on well-defined issues. A little research revealed that it had been founded with government assistance in 1965, with no less a person than HRH the Duke of Edinburgh as one of its first Presidents. When I signed up in 1999 the current President was the lead singer of the band *Midnight Oil,* Peter Garrett. Peter had been a prominent anti-nuclear campaigner, and gave the organisation a relatively high profile

---

[125] I have belonged to the Wilderness Society ever since, supporting in a modest way their efforts to save the planet through the pursuit of diverse environmental causes.

with which I was pleased to be associated.[126][127] However, in the days before global warming was recognised as a major threat, the environment was still a relatively peripheral issue. In the next ten years, like the climate, that would all change.

Towards the end of my time at ARCBS, in the early 2000s, I had moved to working on a part-time basis. However, I did not see this as a prelude to what many people call "Retirement". The "R" word does not, and never will, belong in my vocabulary and I had no intention of ceasing work, even if some of it was unpaid. As a start, I decided to do some *pro bono* consultancy and, initially, I offered my services to the Trust for Nature, of which more in Chapter 19. I then approached the ACF. In April 2000, I wrote a couple of letters to the Executive Director, a Queenslander named Don Henry, and was eventually introduced to a woman named Lee Tan in the Asia Pacific Unit who needed some assistance in developing a work plan that would meet requirements for government funding. Conveniently, in those days the ACF was located in Gore Street, which was just a brief walk down Johnstone Street from the ARCBS offices in Fitzroy.[128] The ACF headquarters were on the first floor of this somewhat antiquated building, and consisted of a strange collection of enclosed spaces around the periphery and a large meeting room in the centre. I began to work with Lee Tan in April, on a project which lasted for several months, and produced an Operating Plan. The main focus was to promote and strengthen the environmental content of AusAid programmes in PNG and East Timor, and to influence environmental policy in Indonesia.[129] Lee Tan was a remarkable woman, who bravely ventured into remote parts of PNG and other countries in the region. She regaled me with many stories about her adventures, in which she often went in fear of her life, dressed as a local, and with her laptop hidden under a cloth in a basket. Sadly, with the termination of

---

[126] In late 1984, Peter Garret was a parliamentary candidate for the Australian *Nuclear Disarmament Party* which obtained 7.2% of the vote in the Senate election. With a personal vote in NSW of 9.6%, Garrett nearly got elected. Although several Senators were elected under the NDP banner, their political campaigning evaporated in the early 1990s with the emergence of the Green Party. Peter Garrett is now the ACF's Patron.

[127] Midnight Oil performed at the Opening ceremony of the Sydney Olympics in 2000 singing *Beds are Burning* and displaying *Sorry* signage. His campaigning for indigenous rights continues to this day.

[128] Given ACF's subsequent involvement with Al Gore, the location of the offices in the 1990s is an interesting coincidence.

[129] Until 2013, AusAid was the organisation responsible for delivering most of Australia's non-military overseas aid and had a requirement to consider environmental issues.

AusAid funding, her programme was eventually wound up. But her work epitomised the outward focus of the organisation.

In the course of attending the ACF offices, I met several other folk, including the General Manager Michael Fogarty and his partner Anna Molan who had responsibility for HR. With my knowledge and background, I eventually provided assistance to Anna on a number of HR-related issues including OH&S policy and then, one day, Michael indicated that the ACF had need of someone to assist with reforming its governance arrangements. I gave him a detailed account of my experience in this field and, a couple of weeks later, I was invited to a meeting with the President. When I first met Peter Garrett in early August 2001, I was impressed. He was a larger-than- life character with a charisma that matched his public persona as a rock star. He was tall, with a bald head that glowed in the firmament of the office, a relatively soft but persuasive way of talking, and a sharp intellect consistent with his legal training. He told me about his commitment to pushing the environment to the top of the public policy agenda, and outlined the need to modernise the ACF's governance arrangements that were no longer fit for purpose. In particular, he shared his frustration with not only the systems, but also the structure. He then introduced me to Don Henry and several other senior managers, with whose professionalism I was duly impressed. At the end of that meeting, I undertook to submit a scope of works to meet his needs for governance reform. I got onto this straight away, and obtained an immediate response. In a letter dated 8 August 2001, he formally engaged me to undertake a fairly wide-ranging governance project in which he would be the sponsor, and my main contacts would be the Executive Director, General Manager, and ACF's legal counsel.

Thus began a period in which the ACF became a central part of my life. Indeed, as the years rolled on, the people there almost seemed like family. My work on "governance arrangements", which eventually involved major constitutional reform, led to a role on the Governance Committee, the Executive Committee and the Board which would engage me for more than 13 years until I retired from active engagement in September 2014. And, as with so many other voluntary activities in which I have been involved over 50 years, the content and value were just as significant as any of the work undertaken in paid employment.

The governance project got under way in earnest in October 2001, with completion of a risk analysis using a team-based Australian

Standard 4360 programme.[130] I had some considerable experience with this model from numerous exercises undertaken during my time at the blood service. The team for this programme consisted of the Executive Committee of Council which was a body of eight people. And, ironically, for the first meeting I turned up on crutches having just ripped the tendons off my ankle in an accident whilst on ARCBS business in Adelaide! The members of the Executive, including Vice Presidents Penny Figgis and Peter Christoff, were a lovely group of people, many of whom would become firm friends in the years that followed. At first, they were a little circumspect about working with me, given a perception that I came from a "corporate" background. But the President's imprimatur gave me sufficient legitimacy to proceed, and we soon had a lengthy list of risks and consequences. I then compiled the usual questionnaire in which participants identified the impact and likelihood of the specified risks, and prepared a report to be used as the basis for developing a risk treatment plan.

The results of the risk analysis were inwardly focussed and quite revealing. The top five risks were a surprise, given my naïve expectations about what I saw as a progressive environmental organisation.[131] They were all HR-related issues including insufficient pay, inability to attract people with appropriate competencies, unsustainable work practices, resources insufficient to meet workload, and poor succession planning. The next five risks related to funding issues, lack of strategic planning, perception of ACF as being politically affiliated, vicarious risks arising from partners in environmental campaigning, and poor communication with the public.

Suitably impressed by what had been articulated in this initial exercise, the Executive Committee decided to extend the analysis to the whole of Council which was the organisation's 36-member governance body. Their analysis embraced the findings of the Executive Committee, but threw up a number of more externally-focussed risks, including the following: perception that integrity was compromised by being associated with certain corporate entities with which projects were being undertaken, supporter base lacking diversity, legislative threat to charitable status with potentially adverse financial consequences, and concern that the effectiveness of the environmental movement was

---

[130] Now superseded by ISO31000, AS4360 provided a methodology for assessing and treating organisational risk, using a database of similar exercises in other businesses.

[131] At this time, the ACF employed around 80 mostly young people and had an annual turnover of around $10 million.

compromised through being fractured. These comprehensive exercises were systematically followed through with the development of risk treatment plans, which we completed mid-year 2002. And, in the next twelve months, the results of this work significantly informed the organisation's planning and budgeting, particularly in respect of HR issues.

Interestingly, during the risk analysis exercise, concerns about the governance structure and systems did not rate as a significant or urgent issue. However, a review of governance arrangements was a central part of the remit provided by the President, and this became my next focus. To facilitate this work, in September 2001, the Executive Committee re-established the Governance Sub-Committee with Vice President Peter Christoff as the chair. Peter was a Melbourne University academic who had previously been on the Board of Greenpeace. He was an engaging fellow with a considerable intellect and a feisty nature. The terms of reference for this committee were approved in November and I joined the team early in 2002. Thereafter, it had responsibility for oversight of a governance programme, which included the preparation of a Council Accountability Statement, development of a Delegations Matrix to clarify the respective roles of Council and management, completion of a Council skills audit, development of policy statements on Corporate Governance, HR, and OH&S, and other material for inclusion in the Annual Report. I also commenced the development of a Council Administration Manual, including induction material for newly elected Councillors.

Given the scope of work, the Governance Sub-Committee soon started to meet on a regular basis. Initially, we had lengthy and sometimes inconclusive meetings held during breaks in the Council's two-day weekend gatherings which were held three times per annum. But, given the workload, we were soon meeting by teleconference. Under Peter's leadership, the committee embraced the governance programme with some enthusiasm, including a fairly wide-ranging discussion about structural issues such as the size and role of Council. It also commissioned me to commence a long process of reviewing the regulations (interpretations of the Constitution) and administrative guidelines. This body of policies and procedures consisted of some 40 items, many of which were outdated or redundant. Maintenance would become a never-ending task with which I was engaged for the next 12 years!

Naturally, as the work of the risk analysis and then the broader governance programme unfolded, I became a regular attendee at meetings of Council. When I first started to attend these gatherings, I found them to be quite daunting. The Councillors were an extraordinary collection of environmentalists from across the country, with concerns about many and diverse causes which they pursued with commitment and passion. They sat around a huge rectangular table, hastily assembled by attendees just before the meeting, with proceedings chaired by the President who gazed upon the host of *greenies* with a hawkish and discerning eye, and administration coordinated by the indomitable Fiona Rae, who was Don Henry's PA.[132] And it soon became clear that the body had an almost cranky dynamic, which derived from widely conflicting views on certain key environmental issues. Sometimes, debate would boil over, with passions flaring. And there was also a clear tension between certain older Councillors and the management team, the subtleties of which were initially lost on me but slowly emerged.[133] In any event, given the intensity of discussion, and what I saw as the importance of the environmental issues, when it came time for me to speak on the governance-related agenda, I always felt that I was detracting from the real business of the day. However, although my stuff caused some Councillors to go bleary-eyed, I was always treated with courtesy and consideration.

After a couple of years, during which time my original programme of improving governance *systems* was largely completed, and following the 2003 Council election, in 2004 responsibility for what by now had become the Governance Committee of Council passed from Peter Christoff to Ross Tzannes. Ross was a NSW Councillor and a practising lawyer. He was also an eminent person for his work outside ACF, with an AM for his contributions to ethnic affairs in NSW and involvement in various cultural activity, including the Australian film industry. Over the next ten years Ross was to become a great friend and a close confidant on governance matters and much else. And, under his leadership, in November 2004 the Governance Committee was commissioned to undertake a full review of the governance *structure*, which would

---

[132] Fiona ("Fi") Rae was a bundle of energy with brightly coloured hair and a personality to go with it. She was amicable but did not suffer fools gladly, worked long very hours, and sometimes vented her frustration during Council meetings with noisy outbursts from the kitchen.

[133] Amongst other things, one senior Councillor, Geoff Mosley, had been the Executive Director at a time when the current Executive Director, Don Henry, was a Councillor. There was clearly some history between them.

become the core of my work in the organisation over the next five years.[134]

Given my on-going commitment, which had now extended way beyond the original remit established by Peter Garrett, at this time it was decided that I would be appointed to the vacant position of Honorary Secretary, reporting to the President.[135] This was duly enacted at the November 2004 Council meeting, as a result of which I became a member of both the Executive Committee and the Finance Committee.[136][137] Interestingly, at around the same time, Professor Ian Lowe was appointed by Council to succeed Peter Garrett as President. This was the beginning of a highly successful and amicable relationship which would last for the next ten years.

The review of ACF's governance structure was no mean task. The last major change had been implemented in 1990, when the current State-based system of electing Councillors for three year terms had been introduced.[138] Since that time, there had been only minor amendments to the Constitution. When we commenced the review in 2005, the current structure provided for the governance body (Council) to be elected by ACF members triennially using a system of Quota Preferential voting, with representatives from each State and Territory in a model rather akin to that used for the Australian Senate. As a result, the Council consisted of some 35 elected Councillors and a President appointed by Council to which the Executive Director was accountable.[139] However, responsibility for operational matters was delegated to the Executive Committee, and a range of other Council committees established for purpose including development of environmental policy. Apart from the Finance Committee, which had external members with specialist

---

[134] Terms of reference were approved in April 2005.

[135] The ACF Constitution provided for an Honorary Treasurer and Honorary Secretary. The organisation had ensured that the former of these positions was always filled by a person with appropriate financial credentials. Considered to be of lesser importance, the Hon Sec position had been left vacant since 1976, with the Executive Director undertaking the role by default. My predecessors as Hon Sec were Messrs Ratcliffe (1964-68) and Wilson (1974-76).

[136] I would always regard this membership of the Executive Committee as the first of three terms on "the Board" of the organisation. My latter two terms were November 2007-November 2010 and November 2010-November 2013.

[137] At the time, the Finance Committee, chaired by the Hon Treasurer, had an operational role with membership consisting of a core group of councillors and a number of external financial specialists.

[138] Previously they had been elected for two-year terms.

[139] The President had to be an ACF member, and could be a Councillor. However, in practice, the person appointed to this important role was usually a notable non-Councillor nominated for the purpose by a committee of Council.

knowledge, membership was confined to Councillors with management in attendance.

In discussions at meetings of the Governance Committee, it became apparent there was a wide diversity of views about the effectiveness of this governance structure. A significant majority believed that the Council had too many members to function effectively in performing any role, never mind governance. In particular, there were concerns about inadequate oversight of the management team, a slow and cumbersome system for policy formulation, the failure of systems designed to provide for Councillor accountability to members, and a lack of appropriate skills amongst Council members to fulfil the governance role. However, there was another view that, however imperfect it might be, ACF was a grass roots "democracy", with Council being an assembly directly elected by and accountable to ACF members, and that this body must retain the governance role. And this became a *cause célèbre* for resisting change.

To inform the review of the governance structure, it was decided to undertake some research into how other "Not-for-Profit" organisations were currently structured. For this analysis, the Governance Committee engaged a fellow named Paul Flowerdew, who was one of Peter Christoff's post-graduate students in the Department of Resource Management at Melbourne University. Terms of reference for the project included the completion of a survey based on a range of parameters for measuring the evolution of governance structure and systems over the last five years. And we identified a group of some 20 organisations with whom to benchmark, which included entities with a variety of humanitarian and environmental missions both in Australia and overseas. Paul's job was to make contact with these bodies and obtain from them a commitment to engage in the survey, with the benefit to them of receiving a report on alternative governance structures and systems in which the identity of participating bodies would remain anonymous.

While Paul was slaving away with his benchmarking exercise, the Governance Committee began to develop a Governance Options Discussion Paper, the contents of which would eventually be informed by the results of Paul's research. This became a major document for consideration by Council with the potential to radically reform the ACF's constitution. At the same time the committee addressed a number of other *"sticky"* issues. These included the reform of the convoluted processes for developing environmental policy, development of a system for reviewing Council performance using the Council Accountability

Statement, and the role of ACF branches which had been introduced as a means of generating support for campaign activity at a community level but whose activities were giving rise to vicarious risk. The future of branches was a particularly long-running saga which, given the relatively small contribution of those bodies to the organisation's mission, consumed an exorbitant amount of time. But our dedication to giving the matter due care and attention was very much a reflection of the organisation's values and its commitment to community engagement. I also continued the programme of pruning the accumulated body of regulations and administrative guidelines. By now, to accommodate this extensive agenda, the Committee had established a programme of monthly teleconferences, each of which extended for several hours and supplemented the face to face meetings during Council weekends.

In October 2005, Paul Flowerdew completed his research, and he provided a report on his findings to a meeting of the Governance Committee on 15 November 2005. The results made interesting reading, with most benchmark partners making major changes in their governance arrangements over the last five years, and a clear movement towards two-tier structures with Council-type bodies elected by members, and skill-based Boards appointed to fulfil the governance role including oversight of management. With these findings to hand, the Committee completed the first draft of the Governance Options Discussion Paper.

At this point, it is worth recalling the basis and nature of the ACF Council who were ultimately responsible for approving any governance changes. At its inception, ACF had been founded as a body designed to inform the body politic about environmental issues which, as the name implied, were considered to be centred on "conservation". Later, in 1989, the organisation had amended its constitutional "Objects" to reflect a broader agenda of achieving the "ecological sustainability of the planet". Under the model established at its foundation in 1966, ACF was a representative democracy in which Councillors were elected by members. In 1974, the organisation had introduced proportional representation for its elections, and in 1990 the term of Councillors had been extended from two to three years with Senate-like electorates to elect five Councillors for each State, two for the ACT, and three for the Northern Territory and other Australian jurisdictions. The Council met up to three times per annum and appointed an Executive Committee, currently consisting of eight Councillors, to *advise* Council on management issues.

The people elected through this system were a wide range of men and women from quite diverse backgrounds and with a spread of 50 years in the age profile. In particular, there were a small number of Councillors, such as the noted environmental campaigner and author Geoff Mosley, who had been active in the organisation since its inception in 1966. They formed a relatively tight-knit group of elder statesmen who regarded themselves as guardians of the values and traditions of the organisation. And they were largely resistant to any significant changes, particularly if they had the potential to undermine the supremacy of Council and what they saw as the fundamental democratic and community-based nature of ACF. In contrast, there was a group of environmental activists in their 20s and 30s for whom the current structure was excessively bureaucratic and unwieldy in delivering timely responses to a rapidly changing external environment. The remaining Councillors were a mix of people from many walks of life with an interest in or passion for a variety of environmental causes. With this membership, Council meetings could be fractious and frustrating, not least for ACF staff who sat in attendance in seats located behind the main table. And some members of Council had no understanding of the appropriate interface with staff, with a propensity to interfere in operational matters which were the province of the management team. At times, this did not make for a happy organisation.[140]

At the Council meeting in November 2005, Ross Tzannes reported on progress in reviewing the governance structure and systems, and alerted the Council to the results of the Flowerdew research. In particular, he noted the direction of change in the governance structures of a number of organisations towards smaller governance bodies and improved accountability. At this stage, he was careful not to commit the Governance Committee to any particular model, but promised to provide a set of governance criteria and options for consideration at the next meeting. The response of Council was predictably diverse, with those opposing change firing some warning shots.

In early 2006, the pace of work accelerated, and I took up residence in ACF offices with a desk of my own and a commitment to work on a *pro bono* basis for at least a couple of days a week for the next two years. Apart from the governance project, the administration of new

---

[140] On one occasion, Peter Garrett became so frustrated with the fractious debate over ACF's dealings with corporate entities that he walked out and only returned after tempers had dissipated. On another occasion, one of the older Councillors took a "pot shot" at the Campaign Director, Denise Boyd, for having the temerity to do some knitting as she listened patiently to a Council debate.

governance systems was taking a lot of time, and I felt a mounting responsibility towards Council for ensuring due process, including compliance with the Constitution and regulations.[141] I also took on the role of Returning Officer for the Council elections due in 2006.

In late February the Governance Committee had a special face-to-face meeting in Melbourne to talk through the detail of the options for governance change. And the Committee completed a further version of the Governance Options Discussion Paper, which now encompassed a Vision Statement, a section on the evolution of ACF's governance arrangements, an assessment of issues arising from the current governance model, design criteria for an effective governance model, and options for future structures. Option A envisaged a minimalist approach, leaving the governance responsibility with Council, whilst strengthening the delegation to the Executive Committee. Option B involved retaining the Council as the governance body, but reducing its size to deliver more effective operation. Option C envisaged a two-tier model in which an elected Council appointed a Board to which governance responsibility was transferred. And Option D provided for a directly elected Board with the Council abolished. The paper also provided an implementation timetable with the aim of concluding constitutional changes and transition arrangements at a Special General Meeting towards the end of the year. At the same time, the Committee initiated a process for consultation on governance issues with ACF members and staff.

By early March, based on feedback from members, staff and Councillors, the Committee came to the view that Option C was the preferred model. Under this model, the Board would have oversight of management, and would approve the three-year strategic plan and the annual plan on which the budget was based. Council's role would focus on setting *strategic direction* through a Ten Year Strategic Plan, development of environmental policy, membership engagement, and appointment of the Board including performance review. It would also have input to, but not the final say on, the three-year/annual plans. Notably, the Committee decided not to deal with the delicate subject of reforming the branch system, because we thought that this issue had the potential to divert attention from the main objective.

---

[141] At this time, the ACF had an in-house lawyer named Charles Berger who focussed on the legal aspects of campaign work. However, at the Executive Director's behest, he also provided legal opinion on governance matters. At times, this had the potential to confound my rather more pragmatic advice to Council. But, with the support of the Governance Committee, my view usually prevailed.

The Governance Options Discussion Paper was duly presented to the next meeting of Council on 18 March 2006, with a lively discussion and a largely positive reception. Although some members favoured the directly elected Board envisaged in Option D, the majority of Council saw the merit of the two-tier structure envisaged in Option C and, perhaps for reasons of self-interest, there was little support for the reduction in the size of Council proposed in Option B. A vociferous minority supported the minimalist approach in Option A, at the same time declaring implacable opposition to Option C which they saw as a usurpation of the democratic basis of the current ACF constitution. When it came to a vote, after a very lengthy debate in which a recorded vote was demanded by the opponents to change, Option C won the day. Forthwith, the Committee was authorised to present detailed proposals for changes to the Constitution which would give effect to a structure based on that model, subject to a vote of ACF Members at a Special General Meeting.

Shortly after this meeting, Geoff Mosley resigned from the Governance Committee and indicated that he would mount a campaign urging ACF Members to vote "No" to the proposed constitutional changes. Although the Committee was sad to lose his contribution, and the historical perspective that he brought, his departure was a relief as it enabled the team to focus on the job at hand. And there was much to do, since amendments to the Constitution required legal input from both our internal legal counsel and external legal advisers.[142] Along the way, we took the opportunity to make a number of other changes to the constitution designed to meet recent amendments to incorporation legislation, and to improve the effectiveness of operations.[143] We also settled the composition of what was to be an eleven-member competency-based Board, with the President acting as chair, six other Councillors (the two Vice Presidents and four others elected by Council), and the ability for Council to appoint up to four co-opted members to facilitate the establishment of a team with the range of skills to meet an agreed competency profile.

Given this workload, in May the Committee had another face-to-face meeting to consider all the changes in fine detail as well as a timetable. In the process of our deliberations, the team addressed a nagging issue

---

[142] ACF's external legal advisers were Arnold Bloch Leibler who generously provided regular *pro bono* advice.

[143] ACF is incorporated in the ACT, and the ACT government had recently amended the relevant legislation.

regarding the rules for voting on constitutional amendments. At that time, voting was confined to those physically present at a Special General Meeting, with each attendee permitted to cast up to five proxy votes. In a national organisation with thousands of members, this effectively disenfranchised most of the membership who could not physically attend the meeting. Accordingly, we decided to extend the system of proxy voting, with a provision for every member to vote by proxy. To implement this change, there would need to be two Special General Meetings, at the first of which members would vote on the new proxy system which would then become applicable at a second Special General Meeting, when the substantive changes to the constitution were considered.

At the meeting of Council in June, I presented an Explanatory Memorandum providing a detailed account of all the proposed changes to the constitution. After some debate, Council resolved to recommend adoption of the amendments, with a small group opposing. Notice of the Special General Meetings to consider the proposed changes, together with an explanation of the rationale for change, was then issued to all members. At this stage, those opposed to the changes exercised their right to mount a "No" campaign". Under the constitution, and at ACF expense, this entitled them to present a written case for voting against the changes. This they did with a paper which attacked the proposals on the basis that they would undermine ACF's democracy. As Honorary Secretary, I issued a riposte.

After a brief campaign, the first Special General Meeting, relating to the change in the Proxy system, was held on 18 August at the State Library in Sydney. Whilst the "No" campaign made a concerted effort to defeat this proposal it was passed by 290 to 20. The second Special General Meeting, to consider the substantive changes to the constitution, was held at the Melbourne Town Hall on 1 September 2006. At this meeting, the "No" Campaign made a final effort to stop the changes with a resolution that "The Motions Be Not Put". This was defeated and, in a series of subsequent votes which covered the changes relating to governance, legal compliance, and administrative efficiency, approximately 93% of members voted in favour.

Our job done, the Governance Committee breathed a huge sigh of relief. Whilst, ahead of the voting, we had good reason for optimism, the achievement of at least 75% support for changing the constitution was quite a hurdle and the opposition was resolute.[144] For me, after the furious debate to amend the Royal Charter in a similar cause at the Australian Red Cross Society in November 2004, not to mention the less contentious project at the Boat Club, these constitutional battles were beginning to become too much of a good thing. But I was well pleased with the outcome at the ACF, as I truly believed that it would deliver a stronger and longer-living organisation.

Implementation of these changes to the governance structure presented considerable challenges, and the aftermath would linger on for several years. The motions passed at the September meeting had included a transition process to allow for the completion of the 2006 Council election, with the newly elected Councillors to meet and appoint the inaugural Board at their first meeting in November. In the meantime, the members of the old Executive Committee of Council fulfilled the Board role in a caretaker capacity.[145] Unfortunately, as with so many of the best-laid plans, this process was disrupted because there was a hitch in the NSW Council election, as a result of which there had to be a re-run which involved a relatively lengthy process of postal voting.[146] So the people serving on the caretaker Board continued in office until the next meeting of Council scheduled for March 2007. At that meeting on 31 March, the new Board was finally appointed with the election of two Vice Presidents and four other Councillors. At the same time, the Honorary Treasurer was elected as one of the co-opted members. At this stage, this left up to three vacancies for other co-opted members. Before proceeding with these appointments, it was agreed that Council should approve a Board Competency Profile and I would then complete a skills analysis of the Councillor members of the new Board, to identify a potential skills gap which would inform the appointment of the other co-opted members. To have carriage of all this work, Council appointed a Nominations Committee with whom I worked over the next few months. It was easier said than done, and the appointment of co-opted members was not completed until November 2007.

---

[144] Interestingly, Don Henry said to me at the time that, given the depth of feeling amongst some of the older Council members who opposed the change, he never thought we'd succeed. And, as he freely admitted, he had much to thank us for, since reporting to the 36-member Council had at times been a nightmare.

[145] This interim Board actually had its first meeting on 14 September 2006, following the successful outcome of the Special General Meeting.

[146] Biographical details relating to one of the candidates had been omitted in error by the printer and it was deemed that his candidacy was compromised. The re-vote vindicated his concern.

Apart from mechanics of implementation, there were other issues. The new structure, in which Council had ceded governance responsibility to a skills-based Board which it appointed, had been supported overwhelmingly by ACF members. However, there was lingering opposition to this change amongst some members of the newly elected Council and, in part, this was fed by a perceived lack of clarity about the respective roles of Council and Board. The Board moved quickly to address this issue by requesting the Governance Committee to develop a schematic that identified respective roles. The Committee duly established this document, with content that reflected the intent of the constitutional changes. But it left a couple of grey areas – strategic planning, and approval of environmental policy. Interpretation of well-meaning words would nag away for several years and, in both areas, we eventually established processes to satisfy most people.[147]

As Honorary Secretary, my main agenda during the remainder of 2007 and beyond was to introduce a whole set of systems designed to bring the Board up to an acceptable level of good governance practice. The principal elements that were rolled out in the next couple of years included a Board Accountability Statement, a Board Performance Review mechanism in which Council had a deliberative voice, policies on a Code of Conduct/Conflicts of Interest and a Board Member's entitlement to independent professional advice, a revised Delegations Matrix, a CEO Performance Plan, completion of a Due Diligence Review, introduction of a Deed of Access and Indemnity to provide a degree of personal protection for Board members in the event of litigation relating to ACF's activities, and preparation of a Board Administration Manual and Induction Pack. The Board also established a number of committees. The Finance Committee of Council became the Board's Audit Committee with financial management responsibility transferred to the Executive Director, a Business and Performance Committee was established to manage Board business, and the Governance Committee became a joint committee of Council and Board.

During this time, I reflected on the services required to support the Council and Board. Over the last three years, I had shared a mounting administrative workload with the Executive Director's Executive Assistant and, by late 2006, I was working on a voluntary basis several

---

[147] In the end, it was agreed that Council should determine the content of the Ten-Year Plan and the Board should determine the content of the Three-Year and Annual Strategic Plans with Council input. As regards environmental policy, in frustration with the slow pace of Council work, the Board developed a provision for developing "policy positions" which address short-term needs.

days a week. Clearly this could not continue indefinitely and, with the help of the ED's Executive Assistant, an excellent woman named Suzanne Toumbourou, I developed a proposal for the appointment of a Board and Council Assistant. The Board and Council approved this appointment in September 2007 and Christine Zarb Guthrie joined the administrative team in November 2007.[148]

Relieved of the weight of administrative workload, I was available for appointment to the Board. At the November 2007 Council meeting, I became one of three new co-opted members. In the next six years, I served two terms on the Board, continuing in my role as Honorary Secretary, but also now contributing in a broader sense to the delivery of the organisation's mission. The work involved was both challenging and enlightening for someone with my background and interests, and the opportunity to contribute at such a senior level was beyond anything that I could have envisaged when I had that first conversation with Peter Garrett in 2001. We pick up the story of life on the Board in the next chapter.

---

[148] Suzanne had been appointed to replace Fiona Rae two years previously.

15: Never a Dull Moment

When I joined the ACF Board in November 2007, I did not kid myself about my environmental credentials. I sat at the table with some outstanding scientists and campaigners, by whose knowledge and experience I was often overawed. However, I brought another skill set, relating to governance, planning, and financial management, which was a worthy if secondary contribution to the achievement of the organisation's mission. At the outset, I should also say that I was fortunate indeed to be in the company of President Ian Lowe, Executive Director Don Henry, and Vice Presidents Peter Christoff and Katherine Wells, who together were an outstanding leadership team.[149] In my first three years on the Board, I was also accompanied by a number of other remarkable people from across Australia, including South Australian academic and lawyer Robert Fowler, WA ACOSS Director Irina Cattalini, accountant Kester Brown, Queensland campaigners Rosemary Hill and Nikki Parker, indigenous leader Chrissy Grant, and the philanthropist and farmer Mark Wootton.[150] Mark would prove to be a significant fellow-traveller because we had similar views about the respective roles of the Board and management, and the need to be agile in advocating changes to government policy. What made this team such a delight to work with was the diverse nature of the group and its ability to work in a collegiate manner. The tone was very much set by the President who encouraged real debate on policy, with a calm, rational and good humoured style. And we made excellent use of pre-meeting dinners to address difficult issues, but also discuss a wider set of important matters such as cricket and footy! During our less formal proceedings, I was especially pleased to have the opportunity to become acquainted with Chrissy Grant, who was the first indigenous person that I had ever known on a personal basis.[151] To attend Board meetings in Melbourne, she had quite a journey from rural NSW, and she shared with me some home truths about indigenous culture and ways of life in the

---

[149] Professor Ian Lowe AO is Emeritus Professor of Science, Technology and Society and former Head of the School of Science at Griffith University, as well as an adjunct professor at Sunshine Coast University and Flinders University. He was named Humanist of the Year in 1988, and has held many other positions, including membership of the UN's Intergovernmental Panel for Climate Change for the SW Pacific.

[150] ACOSS stands for the Australian Council of Social Service.

[151] Chrissy Grant is an Aboriginal Elder (Kuku Yalanji from the Jalunji-Warra clan) and a Torres Strait Islander (Mualgal from Kubin on Moa Island). She has worked for many years as a consultant to indigenous communities on cultural, natural resource management, heritage, and conservation issues.

remoter parts of Australia, which changed my views about the history and rights of aboriginal people.

Apart from addressing the considerable programme and systems which went with implementation of the new governance structure, during 2007 the Board quickly got into its stride on the core business of the organisation, which was to support the management team in pursuit of the organisation's vision and mission. During its first term from 2006 to 2009, there were some 20 Board meetings with a hugely diverse agenda and some challenging moments of internal tension and debate. And there were a number of major events on the national and international scene in which ACF would play a significant role.

In late 2006, Australia was governed by an ageing Coalition government under Prime Minister John Howard, which was at times openly hostile to the environmental movement and sceptical about global warming.[152] During the Howard years, if ACF had any ambitions to pursue its environmental agenda from within the corridors of power, we were dreaming. However, on the international scene, climate change was becoming a significant issue. And a majority of the Australian population had come to acknowledge that the problem that had a solid basis in science and the potential to make life on Earth rather unpleasant. The United Nations Framework Convention on Climate Change ("UNFCCC") Kyoto Protocol, designed to mitigate global warming, was due for ratification and some firm commitments on emission reduction targets by late 2007.[153] And, there was a groundswell of public opinion in support of action. Ever the pragmatist, Howard saw the writing on the wall as far as his electoral prospects were concerned. So, in January 2007, he installed Malcolm Turnbull as the *Minister of the Environment and Water,* and the government made an "in principle" commitment to the implementation of a market-based Emissions Trading Scheme ("ETS"), which could be presented as consistent with neo-liberal economic philosophy. This shift in policy wasn't couched in terms of recognising the danger presented by fossil fuels, with many of the Coalition's backers having significant vested interests which would be adversely affected by implementation of an emissions reduction policy. But it was a recognition of the mood overseas and locally. And the new direction of government policy was obviously welcomed by the ACF and other environmental lobby groups, with the prospect of a bipartisan

---

[152] Howard had been elected in 1996, and his government had little regard for the environmental lobby which was characterised in Australia's conservative media as left wing and ideological.

[153] The Kyoto Protocol was signed into existence on 11 December 1997.

political approach since the ALP also embraced the need for policies to address global warming. In the meantime, the ACF had signed an agreement with Al Gore to roll out what was called *The Climate Project*.[154] An account of this highly successful grass-roots initiative, which would be a major feature of ACF activity throughout my time on the Board, is given in the next chapter.

Apart from climate change, in 2007 the Board also dealt with a succession of issues both environmental and organisational. On the environment front, there was a major concern about Federal Government plans to revise the Environment Protection and Biodiversity Conservation ("EPBC") Act and switch responsibility for regulation from the Federal to State/Territory governments.[155] This had the potential to compromise the ability to manage landscape ecology on a national basis. Like many issues, it was a *sleeper*, sitting as a proposal somewhere in the bureaucracy. And we spent many years successfully resisting any legislative change although, sadly, ten years later, this delegation of responsibility to States and Territories would eventually be enacted by a Coalition government. A related issue was the health of the Murray Darling River system. This major waterway, extending from Queensland through NSW, Victoria and South Australia, had been slowly degraded from decades of poor irrigation and farming practice, with environmentally disastrous results not least at the basin in South Australia where there was virtually zero flow into the sea. To his credit, Howard recognised the need to deal with this problem with an in principle $10 billion Water Plan announced in January 2007, in which he committed the government to address the "over-allocation" of water flows with a requirement that the States would hand their control over water to Canberra. In subsequent years, the design of the Murray Darling Basin Plan ("MDBP") would become the subject of much environmental lobbying including significant input from the ACF, with the aim of delivering additional environmental flows and a range of actions to address inefficient irrigation practices.

Another major issue on the Board agenda was the philanthropically funded North Australia Program. Don Henry and a number of Board members had a strong personal commitment to this activity, which was designed to protect the environment through working with traditional land-owners in the face of burgeoning development. Although there

---

[154] This agreement was signed on 12 October 2006.

[155] EPBC stands for Environment Protection and Biodiversity Conservation.

were projects across the nation, the most important centres of action were in the Cape York Peninsula in Queensland, and the Kimberleys in WA. In both cases, ACF was party to extended negotiations which eventually led to significant expansion of national parks, protected landscape, and modified development activity that was respectful of both Indigenous rights and the long-term health of the environment.

During this time, there was also pressure for the ACF to become involved in action to protect Tasmanian and Victorian forests, oppose the potentially polluting Tasmanian Pulp Mill proposed for the Tamar Valley, and seek the termination of the coal industry. Whilst ACF made a modest attempt to engage with Tasmanian issues, this ground was largely ceded to the Wilderness Society. As regards coal, there was a concerted push from some members of Council to make coal a central part of campaign activity, both in respect of coal exports and the continued operation of coal-fired power stations in Australia, especially at Hazelwood in Gippsland where the ACF was party to legal action aimed at closing the antiquated power plant.[156] But, in those days, Don Henry held the view that a campaign on the lucrative and labour intensive coal export industry was premature. Not least, this was because such a campaign had the potential to undermine the pursuit of the ACF's main objective of delivering an ETS by drawing the organisation's public narrative into arguments about jobs versus the environment.

Within the organisation, during this first term, the Board had a mounting concern that many of ACF's suite of environmental policies were either redundant or out of date. The development of environmental policy continued to be a Council matter and, in the last three years, it had completed just three new policies, on Water, Population, and Climate Change. Not least, this slow rate of progress was due to the convoluted process which involved infrequently convened Council committees and lengthy consultation with a membership base spread across the country. And a good deal of the Board's time was put into trying to negotiate with Council the streamlining of this process, not to mention the initiation of up-to-date policy on other contemporary environmental issues.

In my first term on the Board we also concerned ourselves with defending the ACF's independence and ability to lobby for environmental causes. There were two dimensions to this - ACF's links to business, and the attempt by some politicians to stifle ACF advocacy with the threat of removing its charitable status if its campaigns were

---

[156] Hazelwood Power Station was eventually closed in 2017. I witnessed the demolition of its 8 signature towers on 25 May 2020.

perceived as "political". On the business front, for many years there had been a simmering issue within the organisation regarding ACF projects with external bodies, including industrial corporations. The purists on Council would have preferred that the ACF had nothing to do with the likes of BHP, energy companies, or indeed any organisation involved in development with whom an association might be perceived as compromising ACF's integrity. This view certainly coloured the organisation's policy on investment of its own reserves for which there were very strict ethical tests. However, when it came to influencing public policy on the environment, the Board and management team saw merit in forming partnerships with corporate players willing to acknowledge an environmental responsibility. This policy was manifested in initiatives like the Business Leaders Round Table in which the ACF had a dialogue with several corporate entities to develop environmentally responsible corporate policy, an agreement with AGL on promoting investment in, and use of, renewable energy, and several other business relationships that were designed to achieve targeted and measurable environmental outcomes.

As regards threats to ACF's advocacy role, this issue would simmer throughout my time on the Board, particularly with a Federal government proposal to legislate a new body to monitor the activities of charitable organisations. In the meantime, there were more subtle external threats to ACF's authority and influence. In particular, the Board noted with concern an attempt to muddy the environmental waters by the formation of a right-wing front-organisation called the AEF which never really gained traction but sounded sufficiently like the ACF to potentially undermine ACF's integrity.[157]

During this period, whilst *The Climate Project*, which focussed on global warming, was top of mind, ACF developed a number of initiatives designed to address environmental issues in a way that had meaning to people's everyday lives. In terms of being seen to practise what we preached, since 2002 we were fortunate through our supporters to be based in offices on the first floor of the Green Building in Carlton.[158]

---

[157] The AEF was established in 2004, at the instigation of the Institute of Public Affairs, financed in part by the mining industry. Get-Up labelled it a fake environmental group. True to this characterisation, the AEF was and is skeptical on climate change, in favour of logging, against wind energy, opposed to the Murray-Darling Basin Plan, and against World Heritage status for Tasmanian forests.

[158] The Green building was conceived by ACF and constructed by an ethical investment consortium which purchased the site in Carlton and transformed an existing brick warehouse. The result was one of Australia's most sustainable office buildings, which was opened in October 2002.

This small office block had been constructed on a sustainable basis with a water recycling plant, solar energy, high-rated insulation, a roof-top garden, and bicycle racks rather than an underground car park. And we leveraged the premises to pursue a practical environmental agenda, with Open Days when literally thousands of people came and inspected green building operations. Meanwhile, the campaign team under the very able leadership of Denise Boyd implemented a number of other programmes designed to demonstrate the impact on the environment of the ordinary citizen's personal way of life, and to urge them to take action for their own and the greater good. These included the Greenhome Project, the Consumption Atlas, and the launch of the *"Who On Earth Cares"* ("WOEC") Website. The Greenhome Project provided a range of information relating to the environmental footprint of goods used in every-day life, with a focus on practical suggestions for the family about home insulation, waste disposal and recycling, implementation of renewable energy, and environmentally friendly transport options. The Consumption Atlas provided the ability to identify the environmental footprint of, and level of pollution associated with, your home and suburb through on-line access to a huge database of environmental information. The WOEC website, which had a range of citizen-oriented environmental messages, was fronted by the actress Cate Blanchett. Although this didn't have any ACF branding, Cate was appointed by ACF as an Environmental Ambassador and proved to be a powerful advocate.[159]

Throughout my first term, the Board also committed a great deal of effort to the more routine work of reviewing the Annual Plan and Annual Budget, driving a significant improvement in the presentation of financial statements, setting policy for financial reserves that ensured solvency, effective deployment of some substantial bequests, and fund-raising. As regards the Annual Plan, the Board's collective mind was particularly exercised over Key Performance Indicators, the identification of which proved to be somewhat elusive. This was because, unlike most corporate entities producing goods and/or services, the outputs and outcomes arising from advocacy and lobbying were very difficult to measure. In settling the Annual Budget, the main issue was finding a "sweet spot" where estimates of fund-raising were concerned. In particular, the marketing department was heavily committed to a

---

[159] Cate Blanchett was eventually appointed as an Honorary Life Member for her selfless dedication to this and other initiatives in the face of considerable ridicule in the right-wing media for what was characterised as *frippery*.

strategy using what was called the *Face to Face* programme. This required a significant investment in employing sub-contractors, suitably trained and vetted to undertake the work, who would recruit ACF members by approaching the public on the street. These new members would make immediate commitments to financial donations deducted automatically from their bank account. There was much discussion about the vicarious risk of using "environmentally illiterate" contract staff to contact the public, not to mention the real rate of return bearing in mind the propensity for significant attrition.[160] And the Board was particularly concerned about our dependence on this source of income, whilst other lines of revenue generation, such as appeals, became increasingly challenging, especially after the "Great Financial Crisis" of late 2008.

Finally, towards the end of my first term on the new Board, in 2009 there was preliminary discussion about updating the longer-term Strategic Plan which was due for a major review by Council. This exercise had the potential to significantly impact the shorter-term operational plans for which the Board was responsible, and also highlighted a significant issue arising from the new governance structure. As will be evident, the Board consisted of seven members who were also Councillors and up to four independent co-opted members. For most of its business, the Board could focus as a team in determining policy and approach. However, when dealing with matters where there was an interface with the Council, the Councillor members had a potential conflict of interest. The most obvious example was the Council's role in reviewing Board performance, and that was easily addressed by the Councillor Board members relinquishing their Council hats during the review process. However, the planning work had the potential to muddy the waters. As Councillors, the Councillor Board members had a very real interest in setting the long-term Strategic Direction as reflected in the 10 Year Strategic Plan. But, as Board members, they had a role in determining priorities and allocation of resources that would be manifested in campaign activity as reflected in the Annual and Three Year Plans. The fulfilment of both roles proved to be challenging and, as a co-opted member, I became increasingly conscious that I had a particular responsibility to represent an "independent" perspective and maintain the integrity of the process.

Returning to the mission of the organisation, as an advocacy body, by far the biggest part of the Board's efforts in those first three years was

---

[160] Of those signing up to make a donation, some donations would be cancelled immediately, and there was an accelerating rate of cancellations thereafter.

dedicated to the interaction with the body politic. And, as a policy framework, the Board adopted and regularly updated a Political Strategy. In its advocacy role, the ACF sought to establish meaningful relations with both the Federal and all State/Territory governments, with the aim of gaining commitments to adopt our environmental policy. And we did this without regard to the party political nature of the governments. We would speak with anyone willing to listen. And these efforts were ongoing through regular contact with a range of politicians and bureaucrats. The bulk of the work was in the hands of the Executive Director, the President, and other specialist staff members, including a liaison officer permanently located in Canberra. However, for each election, ACF raised the stakes with a budget allocated to establish what we saw as the key environmental issues in the given jurisdiction. During an election campaign, we would then issue a scorecard for the main parties, to inform the public about their respective environmental credentials. Given the short-term nature of many State/Territory parliaments, this was an almost ongoing exercise. And during my first term on the Board there were elections in every jurisdiction, including the federal General Election on 24 November 2007.[161]

In the run up to the 27 November election, the Board approved an ACF manifesto entitled *"National Agenda for a Sustainable Australia"*. Of its kind, it was one of the most comprehensive and professionally produced documents that the organisation had ever published. The document covered all the elements in the ACF's vision for an environmentally healthy future. But the main issue, front and centre, was global warming, and a vital part of delivering the organisation's message was The Climate Project. I have no doubt that our campaigning in that election, focussed on marginal electorates, had a substantial impact, which would have not been lost on any astute politician. But, with all the main parties in apparent agreement on the need for action to address climate change at least, the campaign augured well.[162]

With the election of the Rudd ALP government, and a Senate that had a fine balance in terms of the likely support for environmentally progressive policy, the ability for ACF influence had been greatly advanced. Back in March 2007, Rudd had addressed what was called *The*

---

[161] In an interesting turn of fate, Kevin Rudd became Prime Minister in an election held on the same day as I was appointed to the ACF Board. And the ALP government would be in power until September 2013, with my final term on the Board ending two months later.

[162] After the election, in February 2008, the Board commissioned a review of ACF's election performance, with external input. The report reflected well on Don and his team.

National Climate Summit in which he made a speech identifying climate change as *"The Great Moral Issue of the Day"*. Now we were about to find out whether this was a commitment carved in stone, or etched into the beach to be washed away by the next tide. The initial signs were very encouraging. The ACF's very own Peter Garrett was appointed as *Minister of the Environment Heritage and the Arts*, and the doors of ministers and bureaucrats were suddenly thrown open, with an invitation not just to be heard but to participate.[163] And economist Professor Ross Garnaut was appointed to develop detailed proposals for implementing the government's climate change policy. In the meantime, Kevin Rudd signed the Kyoto Protocol.[164]

In April, and mindful of the UN meeting on Climate Change scheduled for December in Copenhagen (the COP15 meeting), Council adopted two important policy positions on Climate Change Policy which would become the touchstone for subsequent events:[165][166]

a) To Avoid Dangerous Climate Change: *All actions should be taken by signatories to the UN Framework Convention on Climate Change ("UNFCCC") to limit the rise in global temperatures to no more than 1.5°C above pre-industrial levels and then trend down to 1°C consistent with 350ppm of CO_2 in the atmosphere.*

b) To Mitigate Through Emissions Reduction: *Australia must adopt legally binding emission reduction targets, with caps and timeframes, consistent with Article 2 of the UNFCCC, to protect Australia's fragile ecosystem.*

Consistent with this policy framework, the Board considered recommendations from management on targets for emission reductions compared with 1990. And the figure of 30% by 2020 was established as the benchmark. The Board also supported the inclusion of neighbouring underdeveloped countries in our campaign, with policies such as reduced deforestation in Indonesia and PNG. Armed with these and other policies, the President Ian Lowe and Executive Director Don Henry were given a fairly free hand by the Board to engage with the government in

---

[163] Rudd had appointed Garrett as Shadow Minister for Climate Change, Environment and Heritage and Shadow Minister for the Arts in December 2006.

[164] Rudd formally signed the Kyoto Protocol on 7 December 2007.

[165] These are shortened versions of two longer motions.

[166] COP 15 refers to the 15th Conference of the Parties to the UNFCCC.

what was already a tortuous process of developing an Australian climate change policy capable of being approved by the Australian Parliament. Their efforts were not helped by some Liberal and National MPs, and the mining lobby, who started to question the adverse impact of an Emissions Trading Scheme on business, jobs, and the cost of living. The Greens also started to show signs that they might not be very flexible in their commitment to the letter of UN policy on emissions reduction targets.

On 4 July 2008, Ross Garnaut presented his preliminary proposals for implementing an ETS.[167] The Garnaut Report confirmed the threat of global warming as being *"without reasonable doubt"*. And it recommended medium to long-term frameworks and policies to provide for *"a reasonable contribution by Australia to international action in improving the prospects for sustainable prosperity"*. Specifically, it proposed a 10 year plan with carbon pricing designed to recognise the real cost of carbon to the health of the planet, and to reduce greenhouse gas emissions in a measurable way to contain increases in global temperatures with modest economic impact. In Garnaut's modelling, it suggested that by 2020 Australia would need to reduce emissions by 25% on a 1990 base if the country was to play its part in restricting carbon pollution to 450ppm of CO_2 in the atmosphere which equated to keeping global temperature rises to no more than 2°C.[168] The core elements of implementing this policy involved establishing a model that put a price on carbon, and an emissions trading scheme that would enable this to be factored into the cost of all parts of the economy including energy generation, energy intensive industries, and transport. The policy also had the benefit of raising revenue which could be invested in renewable energy, and eventually alleviate the short-term increase in costs for energy dependent industries. Consideration was also given to compensating low-income families that would suffer modest increases in the cost of some goods by appropriate adjustment to personal income tax.

In the second half of 2008, while everyone was digesting the Garnaut recommendations, other events unfolded. In the United States, following years of financial deregulation by successive administrations, a crisis in the subprime mortgage market developed which would culminate on 15

---

[167] The final report was issued on 30 September 2008 and, ten years later, its predictions on the mounting environmental crisis are largely accurate.

[168] The 450ppm and 2°C parameters should not be lost on the reader. ACF's policy was considerably more challenging with targets of 350ppm and 1.5°C.

September with the collapse of the Lehman Brothers investment bank. This triggered the so-called Global Financial Crisis ("GFC"). Then, in November, there was an election in the USA with a result that gave cause for hope of effective action on climate change and many other causes. Barack Obama was elected as US President to succeed the climate sceptic George Bush. It was a time when the world took a deep breath and, following our own election in 2007, what we called *"the forces of darkness"* seemed to have been vanquished for a time at least. On 21 January 2009, I remember watching the inauguration of this new champion of progressive politics, with the words from his campaign *"Yes We Can"* ringing in my ears.[169] I felt energised, and listened intently to the inspiring words. But my sense of elation would be short-lived. Less than three weeks later, a series of personal traumas intervened. On Saturday 7 February, my son Andrew and I had a near-death experience during which our house in Callignee was burnt to the ground. And, on the same day, my mother was rushed to hospital with a stroke arising from her cancer treatment. These events, and the subsequent trauma of rebuilding the house, would change my life for ever. And, for several years, they would be a burden which affected every part of my existence and tested my character in manifold ways, not least in fulfilling my role at the ACF.

The response of my ACF colleagues to the Callignee bushfire was unqualified sympathy and support, and this probably contributed significantly to my resilience and recovery. In particular, I vividly remember receiving calls from the President and Vice Presidents as I was walking the devastated landscape, trying to come to terms with the almost desert like terrain which had so recently been lush forest. And, in response, I continued my journey in the organisation with little interruption. Indeed, even as I was taking up residence in my shed for several weeks, I fronted at the next ACF Board meeting which was held on 13 and 14 February, determined that the forces of nature would not deflect me from my responsibilities. As it happened, that Board meeting was held at a critical moment in Australian history. In response to the Garnaut Report, the government had published a White Paper on climate change called the Carbon Pollution Reduction Scheme ("CPRS"). And in response to the GFC, it had also announced a $42 billion economic stimulation package, which included significant input from the ACF for government investment in a $3 billion home insulation programme.

---

[169] It was 20 January 2009 in Washington.

Despite its best intentions, these two initiatives would eventually conspire to produce an unhappy political outcome for the government.

The CPRS was of course a beast with which the ACF was well acquainted. Indeed, its development owed much to ACF and its allies in the Southern Cross Climate Coalition ("SCCC"), working with ministers and bureaucrats.[170] Inevitably, as a policy developed in a political climate where there was an imperative to achieve bipartisan support, it contained some compromises. And the provisions were the subject of considerable flux. In the early months of 2009, Executive Director Don Henry and President Ian Lowe kept the Board informed about progress, and the Board expressed its concerns that some of the key parameters were not consistent with ACF's own analysis and policy. At this point, and given that the government seemed determined to proceed with the current scheme or an even more compromised version, it was noted that there were three options for the ACF:

a) Continue working with the government, with the aim of seeking amendments to the relatively weak terms during the legislative process.
b) Seek to delay the legislative process until the latest data on climate change was issued at the Copenhagen Conference in December 2009 which might push the government into adopting more ambitious terms that were closer to ACF policy.
c) Signal that the ACF would not support the CPRS with the current settings.

At the February 2009 Board meeting there was an energetic debate in which we were mindful of the many arguments and factors in play. To begin with, ACF policy was very clear, and there was little appetite for compromising on the action which would eventually be required to address the current scientific evidence on climate change. However, there was some understanding that it might be necessary to achieve the required outcome in stages, and compromise ACF policy for the sake of achieving some real immediate action on climate change, as opposed to standing out for tougher action which might never be legislated. The Board also recognised the potential for a significantly divisive debate between environmental organisations. In particular, the WWF were supporting the current relatively weak government proposals whilst

---

[170] The SCCC consisted of the ACF, ACOSS, the ACTU, and the Climate Institute headed by John Connor, who had previously been a senior manager at the ACF.

others were vehemently opposed.[171] The Board was also conscious of the need to maintain public support with careful messaging, at a time when the main defenders of the big polluting industries such as coal were redoubling their efforts to spread doom and gloom about the economic consequences of switching to renewable energy. Having regard to all these considerations, the Board endorsed a strategy in which the ACF and its SCCC allies would continue to work with the government with the aim of delivering a CPRS which was consistent with ACF policy. And, if the government seemed unable to deliver, then Don and his team were urged to advocate a delay in the legislation until after the Copenhagen Conference.

Having taken this position in February, negotiations with the government continued without any clear outcome evident. However, things were about to become more challenging. At its meeting on Friday 3 April 2009, the Board was briefed on a proposal, to be considered at the Council meeting scheduled for the following day, in which the ACF policy on climate change might be tightened. This obviously had the potential to make it even more difficult for ACF to support the government's position. The Board resolved to await the outcome of the Council's deliberations, with some diversity of views about the extent to which the ACF should compromise its own agenda by supporting government policies that were less than perfect.

At its meeting on 4/5 April, Council with its seven Board members present had a very lengthy debate on climate policy, and were of course made aware of all the same factors and constraints that had been considered by the Board. Eventually, there was unanimous support for a tightening of policy which made the chance of Don Henry and his team achieving a CPRS outcome that would meet the expectations of those Councillors unwilling to compromise even more challenging. The terms of this policy read as follows:

"ACF supports all actions and targets initially intended to limit the increase of the average global surface temperature as close to 1.5°C above pre-industrial levels as possible, and to then over the longer term stabilize global average temperatures at 1°C above pre-industrial levels and atmospheric concentrations of greenhouse gases at 350ppm or less. ACF asserts that Australia must set legally binding emission reduction

---

171 The WWF is the World Wide Fund for Nature.

targets, with caps and timeframes that will ensure that Australia plays its full part in the achievement of Article 2 of the UNFCCC, particularly taking into account Australia's status as a developed country, its high level of emissions, and the Australian environment's high levels of vulnerability and sensitivity to global warming."

Noting this position, in the weeks that followed Don and his team continued to work with the SCCC and the government on the content of the CPRS legislation. During late April, the government was still considering a range of options, with the aim of tabling a Bill in Parliament in mid-May. But then, on 3 May, they suddenly finalised their position with policy settings which were far less ambitious than those recently adopted by the ACF. And they decided to present the environmental lobby groups with a *fait accompli*, and a Press Conference scheduled for the next morning that allowed little time for lobbyists to consider their position or consult with colleagues. That evening, denied time for due process within the ACF, Don Henry found himself in the unenviable position of having to decide whether to support the government or walk away. He consulted with the President and, with no time to consult with the Board let alone Council, they determined to stand with the government whilst reserving their ability to argue the case for tightening the policy as it went through the legislative process. On 4 May 2009, with members of SCCC including Don Henry in attendance, the government proceeded with its press conference to announce the terms of its climate change policy which had very modest objectives in terms of reducing carbon emissions. This was to be incorporated in a Bill to be presented to Parliament on 14 May.[172]

In the next ten days, the response to the SCCC support for the government's relatively weak policy, announced without prior warning, caused a degree of consternation amongst some ACF supporters, the broader environmental movement, and the Greens political party. Within the ACF, several Council and Board members were quick to register their deep concern with the President, and letters threatening to resign were received from ACF members. In response to the growing furore, on 16 May the Board met by teleconference for a discussion about the circumstances which had led to the Executive Director's public

---

[172] The CPRS Bill was passed by the House of Representatives on 4 June, and went to the Senate on 15 June 2009. It was defeated on 13 August when the Greens declined to support what they saw as an inadequate scheme and insufficiently ambitious pollution reduction targets. The same thing happened again in November/December 2009.

endorsement of policy far removed from that adopted by Council. The meeting was tense. But, bearing in mind all the circumstances, the Board determined to endorse the actions of the President and Executive Director on the understanding that ACF would continue to work for modification of the CPRS to reflect the ACF's adopted policy. The Board also commissioned Vice President Katherine Wells and me to undertake a review of governance issues. [173]

Whilst the divisive debate over the CPRS was unfolding, the ACF also received some good news. For several months, we had been negotiating with the Green Building Partnership for the renewal of the rental agreement covering the lease of our offices in Leicester Street, Carlton.[174] However, in April 2009, Board member Mark Wootton indicated to the Board that he and his wife Eve Kantor would like to donate the building to the ACF as a treasured asset in perpetuity.[175] Needless to say, whilst building management was not a core activity, the Board welcomed this proposal, and Project Spring was established to work through all the details. This was an extraordinary gift of great generosity and, notwithstanding our current "little local difficulties", showed an enormous faith in the values, integrity, governance and professionalism of the organisation. Completion of the transfer was set for 1 July 2009, and implementation was a significant piece of work led by ACF's Hon Treasurer Kester Brown, which included the transfer of tenancies, establishment of new building service contracts, transfer of staff, development of a 60L Building Charter, and the establishment of Management Committee to be chaired by Kester. In another piece of good news, again despite the ructions over the CPRS, Don Henry was deservedly nominated as *"Not for Profit CEO of the Year"*, perhaps also reflecting a broader community acknowledgement of the endeavours and achievements of the ACF and its leader.

On 25/26 July 2009, Council met and had its first opportunity in full session to consider the CPRS drama. The atmosphere was tense, with a rumour circulating that Dr Bob Brown, the leader of the Green Party who

---

[173] At its meeting in June, the Board agreed a number of changes to current processes, including the strengthening of the Board's Reserve Powers, the ability to establish a Board emergency committee capable of being convened at short notice to consider urgent matters on a delegated basis, a decision to codify the power of the President, and the development of a procedure for rapid briefing of Councillors on urgent matters.

[174] The Green Building Partnership was between Green Projects Pty Ltd and Surrowee Pty Ltd and was the body that funded the acquisition of the property.

[175] Mark Wootton once told me that this donation would never have occurred had it not been for the 2006 changes in the constitution, which were regarded as a quantum step in improving the organisation's governance and financial due diligence.

also happened to be an ACF Honorary Life Member, had been refused an opportunity to address the meeting and rally the organisation against the policy. Both the Board and the Executive Director were under considerable pressure, and Don Henry made a robust defence of his actions in all the circumstances, with tacit support and assurances from Councillors who were Board members. In particular, Don indicated that, despite the way in which the government had presented the CPRS announcement, the SCCC and others had not endorsed the policy unconditionally. And he explained that the ACF and all the other parties were continuing to work with the government to improve the terms of the proposals. He also noted that the waters had been muddied with an advertising campaign, organised by certain fossil fuel companies, which had been referred to the ACCC for false and misleading statements.[176] As regards the attendance at the Council meeting of Dr Bob Brown, he indicated that, once ACF's policy on climate change had been clarified with him, his request to address Council had been withdrawn.[177] During the ensuing debate, it emerged that there was considerable angst amongst fellow environmental organisations. In particular, in protest at what was said to be ACF's *treachery*, some members of the environmental movement had indicated their intention to break away from the long-standing Mittagong Forum.[178] In the event, Council accepted Don's explanations, but there was a clear message that many Councillors were uncomfortable with the ACF's operating *"within the tent"*. This would have ramifications for Don's future scope of operations.

The July Council meeting was the final gathering of the people elected in 2006, and my energies now switched to the next set of Council elections with nominations due to close in August. In the meantime, the Board paused for breath. At the meeting in September, it reviewed its plans for participation in the forthcoming COP15 meeting in Copenhagen, on which many hopes for locking in international efforts to deal with global warning were pinned. It approved a proposal to review organisation structure, and commenced a significant review of the Executive Director's contract following his completion of ten years'

---

[176] ACCC is the Australian Competition and Consumer Commission.

[177] Once it was explained to him that the ACF support for the government's Bill was conditional on certain changes to the legislation, Dr Bob Brown did indeed withdraw his request to address Council. His attendance would also have posed significant political risk, potentially compromising the ACF's party political neutrality. At the very least, had he attended, representatives of other Parties would also have had to be invited.

[178] The Mittagong Forum was a gathering of environmental groups from around the country who met to share intelligence and consider matters of mutual interest. The group was wound up in December 2009.

service.[179] In particular, it was determined to adopt modern parlance for the role by changing the job title from Executive Director to CEO, and to complete a performance review later in the year. Finally, the Board also considered a number of matters that they would wish to take up with the new Councillors who were due to take office in November. In particular, it was decided to prompt Council into a review of the long-term Strategic Plan, streamline its process for developing and reviewing environmental policy, and improve its systems for engaging with ACF members.

At its final meeting on 20 November the Board approved proposals, for submission to the newly elected Council, on a review of the long-term Strategic Plan review. It was also briefed on progress to resolve a serious dispute over a project to develop a Gas Hub at James Price Point in WA. This presented a classic issue for the ACF and the broader environmental movement, with tension between development interests and environment protection, and conflicting positions taken by local indigenous groups. On the administrative front, the Board also committed to the completion of a Due Diligence Review by management to give assurance to the Board on a range of operational matters. Finally, at this meeting, I took leave of absence from the position of Honorary Secretary. The workload of several years combined with the personal traumas earlier in the year had taken its toll, and I was fortunate in coming to an agreement with Vice President Katherine Wells, who undertook to fulfil the role for six months from February to August 2010.

The results of the Council elections in late 2009 threw up a significantly different group of Councillors. Indeed, the election itself, the conduct of which was again my responsibility as Returning Officer, was quite a spirited affair - with a number of candidates clearly expressing their concerns about recent ACF actions and the perception that we were too close to the government of the day. As a result of this campaigning, and reminders to vote, there was quite an increase in the turnout. And some notable people were elected, including Richard Denniss of the Australia Institute, climate campaigner Phillip Sutton, the Executive Director of the WA Conservation Council Piers Verstegen, and an environmentalist named James Pilkington from the Northern Territory. In subsequent months, due to vacancies and the changed circumstances of some newly elected Councillors, a number of other

---

[179] Don Henry had joined the organisation in 1997. There was some debate about whether it was appropriate to renew his contract for another five years or, given current "industry" practice for long serving leaders, a shorter period.

significant people were elected by default, including the author Jonathan King. The changes to Board membership were less dramatic. Initially, there were just a couple of new people, with Alex Gordon (ACT) and Steven Ross (NSW) replacing Katherine Wells and Rob Fowler. However, in the next twelve months, both Gordon and Ross stood down for personal reasons. Consequently, in November 2010, Jonathan King was appointed to the Board and Rob Fowler re-joined the team. During 2010, Mark Wootton also stood down, to be replaced by an environmentally minded physician named Grant Blashki.

The next three years would be quite a roller coaster for both the ACF and the politicians that we sought to influence in the cause of enlightened environmental policy. In particular, public policy on climate change would bring major political trauma. In September 2008, Malcolm Turnbull had become Leader of the Opposition in succession to a couple of weak stop-gap leaders, and the Coalition had confirmed the previous Howard government's support for the implementation of an Emissions Trading Scheme. However, there were many in the Liberal and National parties who were still unconvinced by the science of climate change, and there was considerable in-fighting over the Coalition's position on the government's CPRS. On 1 December 2009, Tony Abbott instigated a Liberal Party leadership spill, with Malcolm Turnbull defeated by one vote. As the new Opposition Leader, Abbott immediately called a secret ballot on the Party's support for an emissions trading scheme. The Liberal Party voted to reverse its bipartisan support for government policy, in favour of some other policy for managing climate change that was yet to be agreed. This would be the beginning by the Coalition of a relentless policy of opposition to real action on climate change, which remains an unresolved issue to this day.[180]

Undaunted by this development, Prime Minister Kevin Rudd soldiered on with his commitment to some form of the CPRS. And, in December, world leaders gathered in Copenhagen for the latest UN Climate Summit. ACF was represented at this gathering by Ian Lowe, Don Henry and his team, and there were high hopes of an accord on real international action to set targets for reducing carbon emissions. In the event, the gathering failed to deliver a meaningful agreement, mostly because the timing just wasn't right for a number of the key players. As a result, wording in the final communiqué recognised the scientific case

---

[180] In 2018, the Turnbull Coalition government endorsed what was called the National Energy Guarantee ("NEG") policy which contained elements of what could become an ETS. But it and Turnbull were ditched. In the meantime, the clock on climate change continued to tick.

for keeping temperature rises to no more than 2°C, but did not contain commitments to emissions reduction targets to achieve that goal. However, the meeting did lay the ground for firm commitments by major polluters which were achieved at subsequent meetings, culminating in the December 2015 Paris Agreement.

Back in Australia, in January 2010, Rudd again submitted the CPRS legislation to the House of Representatives, where it was passed on 2 February. However, the Bill stalled in the Senate where it sat languishing until the next election.[181] Notably, Rudd did not choose to use the further rejection of the Bill by the Senate as a trigger for a Double Dissolution election. In the meantime, February opinion polls showed that, whilst Rudd was still popular, support for the government was in decline for a number of reasons. In particular, there were problems with some of the government's initiatives designed to deal with the GFC, including the home insulation programme for which Peter Garrett was responsible, health policy, and Rudd's personal leadership style. And, after the failure of Copenhagen, the public were tiring of the relentless campaigning on climate change. In particular, there were signs that they were responding positively to the belligerent style of the new Opposition Leader who suggested that there was no need to wreck the Australian economy for a cause for which there was no international agreement. With the government starting to show signs of division, on 24 June 2010, there was a leadership spill in which Rudd was replaced as Prime Minister by Julia Gillard. I was overseas at the time and, like many other Australians, I was deeply shocked. On assuming power, Gillard committed the government to a significantly revised agenda, and called an election for 21 August.

For the 2010 election, the Board approved a policy position that confirmed the current ACF position on climate change and a number of other key environmental issues. On the latest scientific evidence, global warming was accelerating, and Council had tightened our position even further with wording that reflected a target to cut Australia's greenhouse pollution by 40% of 1990 levels by 2020. In the course of the election, Abbott pursued the Gillard government relentlessly over its modest climate change policy, conjuring up the spectre of what he called a "Carbon Tax" that would increase the cost of living. Cornered in an interview just a few days before the election, and mindful of the intention to implement an ETS which would include a *"price"* on carbon, she said

---

[181] The Bill would lapse on 28 September 2010, following the government's decision to call an election.

she would never introduce a "Carbon Tax". The result of the election was a hung Parliament, with the ALP hanging on to government with the help of a Green MP and three Independents.[182] And the language that Gillard had used about not introducing "a Carbon Tax" would come back to haunt her. What followed was a tortuous struggle between a Government committed to take serious action on climate change and an Opposition determined to discredit climate science, block climate change legislation, and bring down a minority government characterised as a Labour-Green coalition.

Against all odds, the government would endure for its full three-year term, including nearly the whole of my second term on the Board. In the process, much progress would be made in establishing the following public policy consistent with Australia's international commitments to combat dangerous global warming:

- A price on carbon leading to an ETS,
- Creation of the Climate Authority, to monitor the impacts of the policy,
- Establishment of the Clean Energy Finance Corporation to provide seed funding to support embryonic wind, solar and other non-fossil fuel renewable energy generation,
- A Renewable Energy Target,
- Establishment of the Australian Renewable Energy Agency ("ARENA"), to coordinate renewable energy programmes.

From an ACF point of view, we were still welcome in the corridors of power, and Don was applying himself diligently and tirelessly to improving the institutions and systems required to achieve an effective climate policy.

Whilst all of this was going on in the external environment, the ACF was getting on with its knitting. In particular, with the departure of the long-serving Michael Fogarty who, for several years, had been Marketing Director with a focus on Fund Raising, Don Henry proposed another organisational review. He obtained Board support for the appointment of a Chief Operating Officer ("COO") with responsibilities not dissimilar to the role of General Manager once held by Fogarty several years previously. The rationale was to enable Don to focus on his

---

[182] The position in the House of Representatives was ALP 72, Coalition 72, Greens 1, Independents Wilkie, Windsor, Oakeshott, Katter, and a WA Independent National MP.

external advocacy and relationship-building role. In March 2010, the seasoned professional Danny Vadasz joined the organisation and, in the next three years, he would streamline and enhance the organisation's administrative structure and systems. Most notably, he recruited a highly competent Finance Manager named Mal Lewis who would transform the quality of financial reporting. And, with increased transparency, the Board was able to grapple with some important financial issues which had previously been elusive through lack of appropriate information. These included the efficacy and probity of the Face-to-Face fund raising system, the level of reserves required to ensure solvency, and the financial performance of various programmes compared with budget. The organisation's financial health had of course been substantially strengthened by the donation of the Green Building, which brought not only a boost to the balance sheet but a new stream of revenue arising from the leasing of office space to organisations such as Birds Australia, and a solar energy company. In May, the long-serving and highly-regarded Treasurer, Kester Brown, retired. He was succeeded by Todd Davies, who would be an energetic and innovative contributor over the next three years.[183] The Board also finally completed the first ever Due Diligence Review, which sought to provide the Board with assurance on a range of key operating parameters. Mid-year, the Board revamped the structure of its agenda with business ordered in a manner that ensured that appropriate time was given to key decisions in the early part of a meeting.[184] We also worked with Council in adopting the following new and amended policies statements, guidelines and regulations:

- A new policy, *"Free/Prior/Informed Consent"*, was designed to ensure that there was due process in obtaining indigenous support for environmentally sensitive development,
- The regulation *"Role of State Forums"* was amended to improve Councillor engagement with ACF members,
- A new regulation, *"Approved Campaign Structures"*, provided for greater input by Councillors in campaign work managed by staff,

---

[183] Kester Brown served as Treasurer from 2002 to 2010 His length of service was only matched by Geoffrey Goode, who served from 1976 to 1984 and continued to support the organisation for many years including the conduct of the count for Council elections.

[184] From its inception in 2006, the Board had established an annual agenda in which Key Business such as Annual Plan, Budget, Campaign Performance, Political Strategy, Communications Performance, and Strategic Alliances were scheduled. The new scheduling provided that the order of business reflected Matters for Decision, Matters for Discussion, and Matters for Information.

- A new guideline, *Policy Positions,* was established to enable the adoption of brief statements of principle, for areas of environmental policy where more comprehensive policy statements had yet to be agreed.

Council and the Board were also exercised about the report by Allan Hawke of the EPBC Act published in October 2009. This review, ten years after the enactment of Australia's principal environmental protection legislation, was scathing in terms of the failure to achieve the desired protection of the nation's flora and fauna. There were many flaws, including the piecemeal approach to managing threats to the environment and failure to recognise cumulative impacts, the ability of States to pass other Acts which over-rode the EPBC Act, and a poor application of the process for establishing and resourcing species recovery plans. Sadly, despite ACF efforts, led by Rob Fowler, to ensure a meaningful response, successive governments did virtually nothing to fix the problems that would see a mounting tide of threatened species and habitat.

As planned in late 2009, the Board also made good on its commitment to initiate a review of the long-term Strategic Plan which would become operable for the period 2011 to 2020. Whilst this was a Council matter, the Board facilitated the exercise, with the allocation of a significant budget to engage an external consultant to facilitate the review. The process was led by the Council's Strategy Policy Liaison Committee ("SPLC"), which was chaired by Board member Councillor Rosemary Hill, with Director of Strategic Ideas, Chuck Berger, leading the management team.[185] They considered a number of external consultants and settled on Chris Tippler.[186] Tippler had a reputation for enabling organisation to re-envision themselves, with a focus on sustainability and effective people-management. Indicative of his style, in the preface to his book on strategic planning, he expostulated *"In travelling with me I ask only that you bring an open mind and a willingness to travel".*[187] These precepts would be very much evident in his approach with the ACF although, sadly, Council dispensed with his services before he

---

[185] Chuck had moved to this role from his position as Legal Counsel. His new job title was always mystifying to me, as it suggested a somewhat ephemeral role, rather than one that would deliver a strategic plan.

[186] Chris Tipler was based at Melbourne University and owned a business called Corpus Rios that facilitated innovative strategic planning reviews.

[187] The book entitled *"Corpus Rios"* was published in 2010 by Rios Press in Victoria.

completed the project, preferring to internalise the exercise in its final stages, not least because of the cost.

The Strategic Planning review began at a Council meeting in July 2010 with the adoption of a timetable which, given the infrequency of Council meetings, was spread over a fairly lengthy period. In the next six months, it was agreed that there would be a review of the organisation's vision, mission and values, and in the first half of 2011 Council would then identify critical issues, review strategies, and assess resource implications. The main project got under way at the Council meeting in November 2010, with briefings from staff on a variety of material, including theories of change, the changing business of advocacy, ACF's current reputation and competencies, and current trends in the external environment. Chris Tippler then commenced a programme in which he invited Council to conjure up a *"Realistic Imagination of Success"* and identify some *"Powerful Ideas"*. Following this briefing, Council broke up into four groups which developed responses to questions posed by Tippler. The material generated was challenging stuff, which flushed out many and diverse ideas relating the ACF's core business. Indeed, these deliberations touched on all the current challenges and tensions within the organisation, including matters such as

- The balance between advocacy, campaigning and community engagement,
- The extent to which the organisation should be an agent of transformative change,
- The importance of communications skills and methodology in delivering a radical narrative,
- The risk of being captive of the political system, and
- The need to embrace a sustainability agenda that was broader than climate change campaigning.

With much work behind the scenes in the following three months, in April 2011, Council was presented with a major document identifying five options for "desired futures", the efficacy of which was tested against the organisation's vision, mission and values. Specifically, these were "Influential Operator" (the current mode of operation), "Transformative Agent", "Disruptor", "Political Intervener", and "Clarion Caller". After much debate, Council resolved that the long-term plan should be based on ACF becoming a *Transformative Agent*

208

(pursuing a positive and hopeful vision for transformative change to a fully sustainable society), and a *Clarion Caller* (committed to work with boldness, urgency, and clarity, in mobilising capacity). With this as the over-arching construct, the SPLC and management team now proceeded to develop the wording of the full long term plan which was eventually adopted by Council in November 2012. It would set the organisation in new directions. Whilst advocacy would continue to be an important role for the CEO, and conservation was still evident as a theme in much of the organisation's activities, the narrative for campaigning and community engagement was now clearly couched in terms of *transformation towards a sustainable society*.

Returning to the external environment, in 2011 the minority ALP government proceeded with its plans to tackle climate change. On 24 February, Prime Minister Julia Gillard unveiled a plan for the introduction of a price on carbon to take effect on 1 July 2012, with transition to an Emissions Trading Scheme in 2015. She also announced the intention to introduce a new mining tax to enable the government and Australian community to tap into the enormous revenue going to largely overseas shareholders as a result of the recent commodity boom. Her commitment on the carbon price was instantly condemned by Tony Abbott as a breach of faith and, for the next eighteen months, we would hear the continually repeated Coalition mantra that they were going to "Axe the Tax". In the ensuing months, the legislation would travel through the House of Representatives and the Senate. This time, Gillard negotiated with both the independents in the lower house, and the Greens in the upper house, to ensure passage. And it eventually passed the Senate on 8 November 2011, by a vote of 36 to 32, with Green and some other cross bench support. However, it was a far from perfect mechanism, not least because the carbon price was scheduled to start at $23 per tonne compared with the current market price in Europe at about half that figure. But in the first six months from 1 July 2012 the provision raised $3.8 billion. At the same time the Treasurer, Wayne Swan, delivered significant compensating tax relief for the lower paid through a very substantial increase in the personal income threshold. And significant funding began to flow into support for investment in renewable energy.

In the meantime, the ACF Board was dedicating a great deal of effort to translating the content of the aspirational 2011-2020 Ten-Year Plan into a Three-Year Plan and an Annual Plan. To fulfil this requirement, the Board established a Strategic Planning Implementation Team to identify meaningful strategies, review resource requirements, and develop performance indicators. It was onerous work which resulted in a good deal of intellectual debate amongst Board members about methodology. And we established a number of *ad hoc* teams to work on some contentious issues. I was engaged in a lengthy discourse with Rosemary Hill over models of what we called "collaborative engagement". And I worked with the COO on the development of a Capabilities Statement, which encompassed some challenging outcomes in terms of reconfiguring the competencies and compliment of staff required to deliver the new strategies. As always, the identification of meaningful performance indicators was a difficult task to which we repeatedly returned without ever really being satisfied.

During this time, the Board approved a major shift in the political strategy adopted by Don and his team. In response to concerns that the ACF was perceived as a creature of the ALP, not to mention the Greens, it was agreed that Don should operate *"out of the tent"* as far as lobbying the government was concerned. Instead of joining government teams to negotiate outcomes which had the potential to compromise ACF policy commitments, he would now seek common ground with other environmental organisations whilst continuing to lobby for adopted ACF policy. The organisation would also pursue programmes designed to "hold the public's attention" which included a relaunch of *The Climate Project* as "The Climate Reality Project", the promotion of the new strategic agenda in a document named *Better than Growth*, and the pursuit of other environmental agendas, including the establishment of the Murray Darling Basin water management agreement, the pursuit of World Heritage status for a number of key land masses, support for the development of an effective Forest management policy for Tasmania, and conservation of various other land threatened by development, often working with indigenous groups. By pursuing these agendas, the ACF re-established good working relations with a number of the environmental groups who had become disaffected over the CPRS incident. And the outcomes were significant, as the minority government managed to deliver the real and ground-breaking climate change systems referred to earlier.

Meanwhile, the Council and Board continued to reflect on the mechanics of the Constitution. In the new Board's second term, this led to a number of modest changes which delivered clarity and more effective operations. At the 2010 AGM, we provided that the President would ordinarily be appointed in Council's mid-term so that he/she had

had time to become acquainted with ACF's agenda and culture. And, at the 2012 AGM, amendments were approved to allow Councillors who moved inter-state to continue representation of the original State subject to certain provisions, and to enable electronic voting in Council elections. The Board also completed a review of its own performance, updated the Risk Analysis, and approved a major shift in the ACF membership system to address the long-term decline in membership and accommodate by some changes in the tax law. In particular, the Board agreed to the introduction of a $10 membership fee, for which ACF delivered specified benefits such as the right to vote in Council elections and receipt of the Habitat Newsletter, with the ability to make tax-deductible donations over and beyond that fee. Finally, in the latter part of this period, the Board approved a number of administrative innovations. In September 2012 we replaced the time-consuming practice of circulating a hard copy of Board papers, which were delivered to our homes about a week before each meeting, by an electronic version which we were able to access via an ACF-supplied IPad. Initially, this proved a little challenging for some. And I recall one Board member casting his equipment to the floor and demanding hard copy forthwith! But actually it was a long-overdue innovation for an organisation which prided itself in environmentally friendly practices. We also experimented in video-conferencing, with Board members tuning in to Board meetings from remote locations. This proved to be less successful, with our in-house technology far from "state-of-the-art". In particular, I remember on one occasion that Rosemary Hill, who was keen to use this technology to avoid a long and expensive haul to Melbourne from northern Queensland, spent most of the meeting with her face at the horizontal! More generally, it proved difficult for those tuning in to participate in meaningful discussion and the practice was discontinued.

In the second half of 2012, at a time when I was experiencing the unexpected onset of Post-Traumatic Stress Disorder, which I largely kept to myself, I hit a significant disruption to my work.[188] The circumstances were sad and serve to remind one how easy it is to underestimate the importance of inter-personal relationships in organisations where there is strong involvement by volunteers. Since joining the ACF team I had had a remarkably smooth run as far as my dealings with ACF staff were concerned and, in all my work, I had found people to be co-operative and

---

[188] PTSD is a condition that can arise up to five years after a major trauma. It hit me in 2012, after the completion of the rebuilding of the house destroyed in the 2009 fires.

friendly, without exception.[189] Not least, this applied to Don Henry himself, who was an exceptionally polite and considerate fellow, and his successive Personal Assistants Fiona Rae and Suzanne Toumbourou. Indeed, during the critical period of governance change, Suzanne had been a tower of strength as well as a lovely person with whom to deal. And, in mid-2007, Don and Suzanne had been supportive in the appointment of a Council and Board Assistant ("CBA") to provide administrative support. Subsequently, for several years, and eventually on a part-time basis, this person had fulfilled a valuable role in supporting my work as Honorary Secretary as well providing back-up to the CEO's PA. However, in 2010, the incumbent had had some health issues and during 2011 I had found it necessary to resume some administrative work. But this couldn't continue for ever and, in February 2012, I wrote to Don indicating my concerns which he undertook to address. In the meantime, Suzanne Toumbourou had left the organisation to take up a position in Eco Trust. A few months later, and before I had been able to establish a rapport with Don's new PA, I was shocked to be informed that the CBA role, on which I relied to deliver a service to the Council and the Board, had been made redundant. Not surprisingly, in the absence of consultation, I was not happy. Not least this was because I was in the midst of organising the 2012 Council elections. And management's plan for continuing the administrative support to the Council and Board now appeared to rely on the CEO's new PA, who already had her hands full with work for Don. I raised my concerns with staff, and Don's new PA did her best to cover key aspects of the CBA role with the assistance of contract staff to assemble meeting papers and take minutes. In the meantime, I was permitted to engage someone to help me with the elections, and recruited a bright young American student named Adam Cauley. So, we muddled through. But I was struggling.

After concluding the election in November 2012, and with my own health problems, I indicated that I could not continue as Honorary Secretary without administrative support. In particular, we were struggling to produce minutes, were slow to submit annual returns to the authorities, and Councillors were complaining to me about inadequate administrative support at the very time when a new Council was coming on board. In response to my concerns, a new part time administrative

---

[189] From my experience, the organisation employed people whose dedication to the cause meant that pay was not top of mind. In return, the organisation had a fairly benign culture of flexible work practices and assumed mutual support.

position was created which was significantly different from that which had been made redundant. In frustration, in February 2013 I took my concerns to the Board and, with several new Board members, I did not get a particularly sympathetic hearing for what was rightly considered to be a management matter. On reflection, I realised that I had broken one of my own cardinal rules by stepping over the line between Board and management, although the relatively "hands-on" role of Secretary which I had held for more than a decade had muddied waters. To cut a long story short, eventually a new Council and Board support person was appointed reporting to the CEO's Executive Assistant rather than the Honorary Secretary. She started employment in March and was happy to take advice from me on Board matters. But my relationship with the organisation had been soured and I started to realise that it might be time for me to move on.

Notwithstanding this sad interlude, I did serve out my term as Board Member (and Honorary Secretary) due to end in November 2013. The new Council elected in late 2012 proved to be an interesting group, with quite a strong intake of younger people. And this gave rise to the appointment of some new and younger Board members. Piers Verstegen had been on Council for several years and was an excellent addition to the team with a firm commitment to ensuring that the ACF embraced the new transformational agenda. Jimmy Cocking was an enthusiastic environmental campaigner from the Northern Territory, with a sharp intellect and magnificent dreadlocks.[190]

It didn't take the new Council long to pick up on concerns amongst older members about a lack of clarity and purpose in the role of Council. And, with the long-term Strategic Plan having just been updated, the work of Council did indeed seem to be very narrow with Board oversight, development of environmental policy, and engagement with members being the main activities. As a result of these concerns, in April 2013 Council quickly established a committee called the Transformative Council Working Group ("TCWG") with terms of reference "to examine mechanisms to improve the operation of Council". Whilst the scope of this group's work was fairly narrowly defined, as time passed they expanded their remit. And it was clear that there was an agenda by some to develop some radical proposals, including a change to the governance structure.[191]

---

[190] Jimmy is now a Vice President and will complete his third term in 2021.

[191] This would manifest itself in a new governance project in 2014, after my retirement.

The Board's work during the final year of my term was busy and varied. Externally, 2013 was a year in which "the forces of darkness" would achieve an ascendancy. In March, there were rumblings about a range of policy issues within the government, and Rudd made a challenge for the ALP leadership. He failed, and promised not to do it again. But, with the relentless negative campaigning by Abbott, the government's popularity continued to languish. In April, due the constrained economic activity associated with the GFC, the carbon price in Europe collapsed from an average of $12 per tonne to $3.34, and the Treasurer announced that revenue from the carbon price would fall way short of projections. As a result, it would be necessary to defer for twelve months some of the income tax cuts the government had promised in the Budget. In late June, Rudd again challenged for the ALP leadership and, in a ballot on 27 June, he prevailed. Almost immediately, he ordered a review of climate change policy and, on 14 July 2013, he announced that the government would replace the fixed carbon price with a price set by international markets, and move to an emissions trading scheme in 2014, which was a year earlier than previously planned. Abbott's response to all of this was to accuse the government of trying to fool the public, and he committed a future Coalition government to abolishing the carbon price altogether.

In August, Rudd called an election which was held on 7 September. During the campaign, Rudd recovered some of the public support lost by Gillard. But Abbott was relentless in his attacks on the government and, to reassure the public of his climate change credentials, he announced that he would continue a commitment to reducing carbon emissions. However, instead of using the ETS, he announced that the Coalition would establish what he called a *Direct Action* policy. This would involve paying companies to be energy efficient, the creation of a Green Army to plant 20 million trees, and other anti-pollution measures. The result of the election was a foregone conclusion, with the Coalition achieving a 30-seat majority in the House of Representatives. The ALP recorded its lowest two-party-preferred vote since 1996 and the lowest primary vote since 1931. Kevin Rudd announced his resignation as party leader and confirmed that he would not run again in the subsequent leadership election. And sadly, ACF's great champion, Peter Garrett, retired from Parliament. On taking office as Prime Minister, Abbott announced almost immediately that he would repeal the Carbon Price/ETS legislation by Christmas. However, this was easier said than done because, until the new friendlier Senate took office on 1 July 2014, he did not have the numbers in the upper house.[192] The repeal legislation was eventually passed by the Senate on 17 July 2014, in fairly unusual circumstances as far as the ACF was concerned. In the run-up to the Senate vote in July, the Coalition government's ability to repeal the Carbon Price/ETS depended on the three votes of the Palmer United Party, controlled by billionaire businessman Clive Palmer. As it happened, Palmer was supportive of renewable energy, and a deal was struck in which he would vote for the legislation to repeal the ETS if the government retained the Clean Energy Finance Corporation, the Renewable Energy Target, and ARENA. The ACF played a part in the negotiations and garnered a press conference on 26 June 2014 at which Palmer's conditions were announced. As it happened, at that very time, Al Gore was visiting Australia in support of the Climate Project and he and Palmer stood together at a press conference in support of renewable energy. It was a strange moment. And, afterwards, there was speculation as to who was using whom! From our point of view, in all the circumstances, the environment was the winner.

Whilst this sequence of events unfolded on the national stage, with the ACF doing its best to defend all that had been achieved on climate change under the six years of ALP government, other business manifested itself. Following persistent efforts from a number of Councillors, significant resources were allocated to a campaign against coal exports. Also, following the significant change in its membership, the Board committed serious time to developing their teamwork, with a weekend retreat at the offices of Board member Grant Blashki. The main agenda for this meeting was to focus on how best to translate into operational activity the transformative agenda in the new Long Term Strategic Plan. The outputs from our deliberations were significant, as we clearly identified the Goals/Outcomes for inclusion in the Three-Year Plan and Annual Plan that would deliver on the *Transformative* Strategies in the Ten-Year Plan.[193] The Board also addressed a number of administrative issues, including the re-scheduling of the financial year-end to facilitate better management of budgeting and cash flow, and the results of an audit of all Regulations and Administrative Guidelines.

---

[192] The Senate numbers in September 2013, reflecting the 2010 election were Coalition: 34, ALP: 31, Greens: 9 and two others (Nick Xenophon and a representative of the Democratic Labour Party). From 1 July 2014, the Senate numbers were Coalition: 33, ALP: 25, Green: 10, PUP: 3, Others, including Xenophon: 5.

[193] The Goals/Outcomes were Safe Climate, Healthy Eco-systems, Leadership, Living Sustainably, and Indigenous Rights. The 10YP Transformative Strategies were "The Big Picture", "Engagement", "Advocacy", and Collaboration'".

As my time on the Board was coming to an end, the new Abbott government was getting into its stride. And we waited with interest to see what the Coalition's Direct Action policy for addressing climate change would actually look like. When the details were announced, we had serious doubts about its ability to adequately address even the most modest of emissions reduction targets. In the meantime, the Board approved a new model for The Climate Reality Project ("TCRP"). Previously, this work had been financed by funding from Gore's charitable trust. Now ACF would manage the Australian programme on a franchise basis from the international TCRP board, of which Don had been appointed a member. Funding of $200,000 was advanced to finance the training of another 200 presenters.

At the 2013 AGM, I retired from the Board and, to my surprise and delight, I was awarded Honorary Life Membership. The presentation, made by Ian and Don, was a proud moment, and I was very much aware that I was joining a pretty exclusive club.[194] To be honest, I took the view that my contribution to the environment did not rate with most of the other Honorary Life Members. But I cherished the association with such laudable people. In my response before a packed meeting I paid tribute to both Ian and Don. I was fortunate indeed to serve during their time.

As it happened, just before the AGM, a volunteer to take over as Honorary Secretary emerged, which was a great relief as we had been struggling to find a successor. And, following an interview, Jonathan Anstey was appointed at the first meeting of Council in 2014. Although I was no longer a Board member, to facilitate an orderly changing of the guard, I continued my membership of the Governance Committee. Mid-year, I was disturbed to hear that there was talk of further constitutional changes, with a smaller Council and a directly elected Board, to which I was opposed. And, after all my years of *pro bono* work, I was disappointed to hear that there was a proposal to engage external consultants to undertake a governance review at a cost of $50,000. With these concerns, and mindful that I might now be an obstacle, I decided that I should also resign from the Governance Committee. Interestingly, after serving for 10 years, the President Ian Lowe also retired from office in 2014. His time as President was the longest uninterrupted period of

---

[194] There are only around 20 living Honorary Life Members at any one time. The list of people so honoured includes the actress Cate Blanchett, Penny Figgis, Geoff Mosley, Mark Wootton and Eve Kantor, environmentalist and retired leader of the Greens Dr Bob Brown, the Hon Peter Garrett, and Emeritus Professor Ian Lowe.

any holder of the office.[195] And, in the following twelve months, Don Henry retired. It was indeed the end of an era.

When I look back on those years, I do take some pride in all that was achieved. In my late fifties and early sixties, I had had the rare opportunity of applying all the knowledge and skills acquired during a lifetime of managing change, to an organisation in which I truly believed. Of course, the structure and systems which the governance team and Board instituted were not perfect, and would continue to evolve as circumstances changed. But the ACF became a more resilient organisation, with sound finances, more focussed campaigning, greater unity of purpose, and improved accountability. These were and are the conditions for a long life and enduring existence in an increasingly hostile external environment. And Australia in the 21st Century is a better place for having a strong environmental lobby with the ACF in the vanguard.

---

[195] In the history of the ACF since its formation in 1964, up to and including Ian Lowe, there were nine Presidents. Ian served for the longest uninterrupted period. However, Peter Garrett served for more years in two periods between 1988 and 1993 and 1998 to 2003. The other Presidents, in order, were Sir Garfield Barwick, HRH the Duke of Edinburgh, Mark Oliphant, Nugget Coombs, Murray Wilcox and David Yencken.

16: The Climate Project

One of the most important projects with which the ACF was engaged during my time with the organisation was what was initially called *The Climate Project* ("TCP"). In my view, it is the epitome of successful work in the space that the ACF sought to occupy – mobilising public opinion to influence government policy. The genesis of this project was in a distant land. In the years of the Clinton administration, Al Gore assumed a special remit for developing policies to address Climate Change.[196] Through the influence of his parents, he had had a longstanding interest in the environment and had published a book on the subject entitled *Earth in the Balance* which was published in June 1992.[197] With the US environment portfolio, he was an important player at the UNFCCC negotiations in 1997 that established the Kyoto Protocol. In November 2000, he ran for President and was defeated by the narrowest of margins in questionable circumstances. Afterwards, it initially appeared that Gore was on the scrap heap of history. However, he was not done by a long chalk. After licking his wounds, he decided to devote a significant effort to campaigning on environmental issues.

In the early 2000s, Gore started to update and present a slide show on climate change that he had first assembled in the early 1990s. This presentation endeavoured to make a compelling case for the view that humans are the cause of global warming and that, unless urgent action was taken, there would be irreversible changes to the planet's climate that would make human life on Earth intolerable. Gore started to tour with this slide show, in the USA and overseas, sharing the information he had compiled with anyone prepared to listen. And, in the spring of 2005, he made a presentation to a large gathering in Los Angeles organised and hosted by environmentalist Laurie David. Afterwards, David suggested that Gore should transpose the slide show into a movie and, after some persuasion, a production team was assembled. The film entitled *"An Inconvenient Truth"* was eventually released in May 2006 with a screening at the *Sundance Film Festival*. This was followed by a book of the same name, with all proceeds going to a not-for-profit organisation whose principal mission was to finance activities designed to encourage bold action on global warming. The aim of both the film

---

[196] Some of this material is taken from the book written by Al Gore entitled *"An Inconvenient Truth"* (Bloomsbury Publishing, London, 2006).

[197] *"Earth in the Balance – Ecology and the Human Spirit"* was written by Al Gore (Houghton Mifflin, Boston, 1992).

and the book were to re-capture public imagination at a time when much of the energy and commitment generated in developing the Kyoto Protocol were waning, even as the date in 2007 for setting firm targets for emissions reductions was looming.[198]

Whilst Gore was developing the film and book on global warming, he was also attending international gatherings of environmentalists, including IPCC meetings.[199] At one of these meetings, in early 2006, ACF's Executive Director Don Henry met and formed a working relationship with Gore. Subsequently, Gore agreed to visit Australia and promote his material. In the course of discussions, Gore shared with Henry a model for promulgating his message using "ordinary folk" who were trained to present his ideas using the slide show and responding to questions arising from the audience of citizens who had bothered to attend. This model had proven to be highly successful in the United States and they believed that, with some modification to the slides to provide a southern hemisphere perspective, it would easily translate to Australia. Following further meetings, during which Don Henry became an accredited adviser to Gore, in late 2006 the ACF established a contract to implement *The Climate Project*. This was submitted to the newly established ACF Board in October and received wholehearted support. There was a significant match with the ACF's strategic plan, and it was absolutely mainstream activity for an advocacy organisation.

In Australia, the basic concept of the TCP was to recruit a large number of individual citizens, from all walks of life and across a wide demographic in terms of age and location, and put them through a training course in which they would be given the skills to make a presentation at a public meeting using the Australian version of the Gore slide-show. This project was financed through a significant financial allocation from ACF's budget and a generous contribution from Al Gore's philanthropic fund.

The adoption of this programme in Australia was timely. In the early 2000s, the country had languished under a conservative government that

---

[198] In 1992, the UNFCCC committed signatories to reduce greenhouse gas emissions in recognition of man-made global warming. This commitment was extended by the Kyoto Protocol adopted on 11 December 1997, and required signatories to set internationally binding emission reduction targets. The protocol came into force on 16 February 2005 and currently has 193 signatories. In 2012, Australia was one of 37 countries to sign the Doha Amendment to Kyoto committing signatories to measurable greenhouse gas reduction targets. Subsequently, a further 32 countries have followed suit. In a separate UNFCCC Paris Agreement concluded in 2015, 195 nations agreed to establish plans and regularly report on their contribution to mitigate global warming.

[199] IPCC stands for Intergovernmental Panel on Climate Change.

was hostile to the environmental lobby and had declined to sign the Kyoto Protocol in keeping with a commitment made to President Bush in 2001. Significant members of the government denied the science of climate change, and the party was wedded to support from the coal and gas industries. At the same time, climate change was not top of mind for the ALP. However, as the ACF was preparing itself for a launch of TCP in 2007, a Federal election was looming. Ever the pragmatist, Prime Minister John Howard changed tack. In January, he started to talk about the possibility of some form of market-based emissions trading system. And, in the meantime, although there was some resistance from the trade unions, the ALP led by Kevin Rudd began to advocate the need for action on Climate Change and Australia's formal endorsement of the Kyoto Protocol.

In 2007, the TCP was geared up for implementation with over 250 presenters trained and suitably inspired following the visit and participation in a major gathering of budding presenters addressed by Gore in Sydney. As part of the program, ACF was not only a party to the training but played a key role in supporting the TCP presenters before, during, and after specific presentations. In particular, the ACF provided resources to organise the multitude of public meetings in community halls and at the premises of a huge number of community organisations across the nation. The scope was considerable with the potential to complete over 500 presentations in the run-up to the election.

With climate change now having real traction with the public, the ACF was mindful of the potential impact of the TCP in key electorates in the 2007 election. To this end, an analysis of marginal seats was undertaken with the aim of identifying those which presented the best chance of influencing the result in terms of electing an MP prepared to support action on global warming. As was always the case for any campaign by ACF, this was not "party political". The ACF was seeking to highlight an important issue with long-term implications for the health and wealth of the nation, and cause political candidates to make commitments regardless of their political persuasion. So, as the TCP was rolled out in 2007, ACF made sure that special attention was given to key seats in terms of deploying the number and scope of presentations. I well remember this hit list identified on a white board in Don's office. It was real environmental political activism. And, as the results of the subsequent election would demonstrate, it worked.

As it happened, we were fortunate that the election in 2007 was not called until the end of the year, with Election Day on 24 November. I would not wish to claim that ACF's campaign was the main determinant of the outcome. Howard had been in power for eleven years and, in the final term, he'd had a majority in the Senate that led him to overstretch himself with the Work Choices legislation. In that sense, he probably brought about his own downfall. But the environment played a part, and Kevin Rudd and the ALP came to power, with the Coalition losing 23 seats including most of those on the TCP hit list. It was a telling moment. In the Half Senate election, the Coalition lost overall control with the outcome reflecting a fine balance made up as follows: Coalition 37, ALP 32, Greens 5, Nick Xenophon, and one Family First senator. The scene was set for a very interesting three years the full story of which from an ACF point of view was covered in the previous chapter.

Following the success of the TCP in the 2007 election, the programme went from strength to strength. In the next several years, many more presenters were recruited and trained, with each presenter committing to several presentations. And the programme complemented the work of other climate change activist groups including the Youth Action on Climate Change, the Australian Youth Climate Change Coalition, and the Climate Action Network. Al Gore continued his international work with the TCP spreading all around the world. In November 2012, he screened a "24 Hours Forum" with over 17 million viewers and 150 million followers on Twitter. And he was a significant player in obtaining the commitment of developing countries to the Paris Agreement.

After several years of successful achievement in spreading the message in Australia, in 2013 the TCP was revamped using a franchise model in which the ACF would have the rights to use the slide show in Australia for an extended term. And the programme was rebadged under the name *The Climate Reality Project*. ACF would also become a party to implementation of the programme into the Asia Pacific region with Australia supporting the roll-out in India, Indonesia and several other countries.

At the time of writing this book, the Climate Reality Project is no longer an ACF programme. But the work continues with activities across the globe. ACF has focussed its resources on more immediate local concerns.

17: Environmental Challenges of the 21st Century

As we have seen, in the early years of the 21st Century I became seriously involved with the environmental movement through engaging with the Australian Conservation Foundation. Hitherto, I had the knowledge of the common man or woman. As the years ticked by thereafter, I became informed. And concern about every aspect of the environment is now an abiding interest. In this chapter, I provide an Everyman's Account of current concerns.

Connectedness

I have to begin this commentary by declaring an interest. As a human being, I would like my family and successors to enjoy the diversity of environment that I have experienced. But I do so in the belief that human beings are a dispensable item. The planet Earth does not need us. And if we are not prepared to accept that we are connected to everything around us, we probably deserve to become extinct.

With that perhaps depressing note, you might think that I am about to dig my grave and climb into it. But actually I am an optimist. Despite what humans have been doing to the planet in the last 250 years of industrial development, I think there is a chance for the human species to live in balance with nature. But we have to recognise that we are not above the environment but are a part of it. It seems so simple, but not many people get it. And perhaps we need to build into our education system a mandatory course in which children are given an understanding of this basic existential fact. Unfortunately, this flies in the face of more pressing concerns for human beings living in the 2st century. In the West, we seem consumed with education that is designed to turn us into worthy capitalists. And some of the world, we still have peoples who are committed to their interpretation of the word of God. In yet others, there are still authoritarian regimes in which people are subject to other propaganda designed to ensure the continued power of demagogues and dictators.

Despite these deep flaws, I think we are capable of building a free and open society in which we engage in productive work that understands the finite limit of resources. And I think that we need to lead our lives in a way that recognises that everything is connected to everything else, and that when we harm one part of the total system of existence, we are harming all parts including ourselves. If that were our starting point for a discussion about "the environment", we might get somewhere in living in harmony with our surroundings and each other.

Finite Resources

The history of our planet is dotted with instances where the existence of certain creatures is threaten by the finite nature of the environment in which they reside. And this is as true of humans as it is of other creatures many of which have become extinct because their habitat disappeared. Sometimes, a species will decline because another supersedes it in the course of evolution and natural selection. At other times, extinction has been brought about by natural changes in the climate. And there are many other causes of extinction such as the planet's being hit my meteorites. But we are the only species that has tested the planet's finite resources to its limits by ruthless exploitation of all the resources on which we can lay our collective hands. And the threat that this poses to our existence is not exactly a new message. I started to gain an appreciation of this when I was in my late teens. In my first year at university, I studied politics, and one of the simplest philosophical ideas that penetrated my cortex was the wisdom of knowing your limits. And when I was studying economics, I remember Malthus's book on the *Principles of Population* (1798) and the impact of over-population. In the late 1960s, the Club of Rome produced many warnings, and its treatise entitled *Limits to Growth* which was published in 1972 had a profound effect on me. But who was listening to all these messages? Not many, I think. And those in power, whoever they were, had other agendas. They were committed to boundless growth.

So a second message to teach our children is that, although human ingenuity will lead to improvements in productivity and innovation that will enable us to get more from less, there is a finite limit to most things derived from the world around us.

Pollution

In the last 200 years, as man has moved from his agrarian roots, pollution in many forms has started to overwhelm us. For me, Carson's book in 1962, *The Silent Spring*, was an early warning sign if ever there was one. Her message about the impact of using pesticides was seminal. In the 1970s, I joined Friends of the Earth because their message of managing waste through recycling made so much practical sense. And, when I came to Australia, the country had just made a giant step by stopping the Franklin Dam which had the potential to destroy a great source of biodiversity. But in the meantime, our seas and oceans have become clogged with plastic waste.

In the 21st century, we have accumulated so much information about the pollution and environmental damage caused by our industrial activity and way of life that you would imagine that we would want to do something about it. Yet we still burn fossil fuels for energy, drive cars that poison the air, and cast plastics into the ocean. Where I live for some of the time, the Latrobe Valley is one of the most polluted places on the planet. I live on a nature reserve. So I could turn a blind eye. But 10 kms away are open cut mines, and power stations burning brown coal, belching steam but also polluting gases into the atmosphere. 20 kms to the west is the relic of a decommissioned power station, where the soil has been made toxic by coal ash. There is talk of drilling for gas, which may pollute our water table. And the people in neighbouring towns have lived with poor air quality for decades. All of this is done in the name of industry and jobs, without regard for the long-term consequences. If you challenge the apparent right to exploit the earth, you are demonised as "left wing", or "greenie". Nothing can be allowed to stop the pursuit of economic gain and short term private interest in the name of a warped version of the public good. This has to stop. And those who can see the truth of what is being done in our name need to speak often and loudly.

Climate

Inevitably, this line of argument brings me to what Kevin Rudd called the *Biggest Moral Challenge of Our Time*. Given the history of the Australian government in the last ten years, how hollow this sounds. We have done little or nothing to respond to a growing mountain of scientific evidence. And we still allow voices steeped in personal gain from dangerous economic activity to be heard and to prevail. And what makes it worse is that those like former Prime Minister Tony Abbott, who assert that "the so-called science of climate change is crap", make it their business to personally vilify those who presents the facts. I have read several books on the psychology of climate change deniers. They are a motley crew and it is difficult to change their beliefs. Although they would have you believe otherwise, science has no currency with them. In a democracy we must allow them a voice, but listening to them saps energy and diverts from the urgent need to act. Their ignorant minority views, wrapped in the language of caring for jobs and livelihoods, must not be allowed to dominate public policy.

I take solace that, at this difficult time in human history, the younger generation are leading the way. And the most recent efforts of school students is heartening. It is extraordinary that those who would wish to deny the need for change have the brass to say that these well-meaning young people shouldn't fill their heads with ideas that give them sleepless nights. Such ignorance! They have a right to speak up, because we are destroying their lives and future by pursuing short-term economic gain without regard for the connectedness of everything, the limits to natural resources, the pollution we cause, and the global warming that will make Earth's climate uninhabitable for humans.

Conclusion

I have no easy answers to these challenges. But I do know one thing. People in my generation must speak out. Failure to advocate change in public policy and practice, after all the advantages that we have enjoyed in the last 50 years, is a dereliction of our duty to our fellow human beings.

PART FIVE

GOVERNANCE AND RISK

18: Board Time

As I was coming to end of my days at ARCBS, I gave some serious thought to becoming both a professional non-executive director and a consultant. I had been a member of the Australian Institute of Company Directors ("AICD") since the early 1990s; but I had never attended their professional courses because I thought it would add little to the years of practical experience I had accumulated in both the UK and Australia. I also had a mild distaste for the networking dimension of the AICD, which seemed to be an organisation which people used to obtain Board membership more through who you knew than what you knew. Nevertheless, I had retained my AICD membership because it gave me access to their intellectual capital. I hasten to add that I also read widely in the field of governance and risk management and had accumulated a library of relevant reference documents.

By far the most significant role I would play as a non-executive director was at the ACF as related in the previous section of this book. However, I have been on the board of several other bodies which I record below.

Arthritis Victoria

The first organisation whose Board I joined as an independent non-executive director was Arthritis Victoria. Proving my point about "who you know", I became acquainted about a vacancy through the then CEO, Shirley Caulfield. I had known and come to admire Shirley from my time at RCBBV when she had been the ARC Victoria Director of Voluntary Services, and in August 1999 she encouraged me to submit my Resume to the President of the Board, Bruce Dyson. I then met with him and he showed particular interest in my governance work, indicating that the Board was keen to review its role and performance. My nomination was put to the Board and in October 1999 I was offered a position which I duly accepted.

Arthritis Victoria was a charitable organisation that belonged to a family of state and territory Arthritis organisations affiliated with Arthritis Australia as the peak body.[200] It had been founded as the Rheumatism and Arthritis Association of Victoria by an eminent

---

[200] Some years later, Arthritis Victoria pulled out of this affiliation, and reconstituted itself as Musculoskeletal Australia.

physician, Dr Leslie Koadlow AM, who was Honorary Life Governor of the organisation as well as a Board member.[201] It was an organisation with significant standing in the community, with an annual revenue of around $3 million that was largely financed by fund raising and donations. This funding was used to finance a range of activities designed to educate, inform and support people with musculoskeletal conditions, and fund-related research programs. And the delivery of many of the support services depended on the deployment of volunteers.

Board meetings were held in the evening, and I attended my first meeting on 5 October 1999 at their premises in Kooyong Road, Elsternwick. At the opening of proceedings, I was greatly disappointed to hear that Shirley Caulfield had resigned and would be leaving after a handover at Christmas. However, as she explained, she was herself a long-suffering victim of rheumatoid arthritis and needed respite. Leigh Garwood had been recruited to replace her. The Board was an interesting group of around 15 individuals with a mix of medical and business backgrounds. For the first few monthly meetings I kept a low profile, listening and learning about the culture. And, from what I could see, the Board was fairly hands-on with relatively little emphasis on strategy and development. However, in early 2000, as mooted by the President in my initial conversation with him, the Board commissioned a strategic review which included a review of the role and performance of the Board. And, with his agreement, in April I submitted a Discussion Paper in which I presented proposals for improving governance policy and systems designed to achieve a quantum step in the Board's operations. To my disappointment, this input was not welcomed with any enthusiasm. But in May the Board commissioned a confidential Board Members' Survey, undertaken by Shirley Caulfield, in which individuals were invited to present their views in anonymity. The results were not encouraging. There was an acknowledgement that it might be helpful for the Board to have an Accountability Statement, as mooted in my Discussion Paper. But there was little support for the rest of my suggestions, including the conduct of a risk analysis, development of a manual of delegations to clarify decision making, introducing a policy on conflicts of interest, establishing a system for Board appointments based on relevant competencies, and introducing regular reviews of Board performance. At the meeting of the Board on 22 June, after some discussion on both

---

[201] Dr Leslie Koadlow AO died in 2011. He was married to Elsie Koadlow OAM who was a noted psychotherapist. Both families came to Australia from Poland on the same boat in 1927. Elsie Koadlow died in 2012.

my Discussion Paper and the results of the confidential Board Members' Survey, it was decided that my proposals were too elaborate for a small organisation and that "if it's not broken, don't fix it." I was disappointed and, although I received some support from the President, it was clear that most of the Board could not see the merit of a system where there were clear lines of responsibility and accountability that would cut across their ability to have a personal hand in the management of the organisation. In 2001, the dismissal of my proposals would come back to bite the Board with a vengeance.

In the next twelve months, I regularly attended Board meetings and built up a fairly comprehensive understanding of the organisation, its staff, and its challenges. During this period, my first impressions about the Board were largely confirmed. There were a couple of directors, a doctor and a scientist, with whom I developed a rapport. And they were sympathetic to the need for improved governance systems. They also shared with me concerns about the financial literacy of some Board members, lack of team work, and poor attendance by several directors, which meant that they contributed relatively little to proceedings and laid themselves open to liability for decisions that they did not fully understand. I also had a concern about the approach adopted by the Founder. Given his great knowledge and experience, he would have been a worthy patron; but I thought his inclination to intervene in management and operational issues was more akin to the behaviour of the owner of a small business.

At its meeting on 28 June 2001, the Board was alerted to an HR problem in the Fundraising Department. The CEO attempted to give comfort to the Board that he had the matter in hand. But the Board determined to intervene by appointing a team to assess whether management was following due process. They then appointed a committee to advise the CEO on how to handle the matter. By early August, it then became evident that at least one member of the Board had a significant conflict of interest through his relationship with a member of staff who was involved in the dispute. And there was also evidence that other members of the Board had relationships with staff which affected their ability to be even handed. Eventually, these matters became the subject of legal action against the organisation and potentially the Board. And some Board members then sought to position themselves to absolve themselves of culpability.

By November 2001, I had come to the firm view that this Board was floundering through lack of governance systems. I had several private exchanges with the President, and proposed that the Board have a session on governance to address a range of issues arising from the HR dispute. I also discovered from the Vice President, who was close to many of the staff through a long association with the organisation, that Board members were continuing to interfere in operational matters. At its meeting in December, the Board deferred consideration of my proposals for addressing the governance problems and, over the Christmas break, I had a long think about the state of the organisation. The Board had demonstrated an unwillingness to recognise and deal with a significant governance problem. And I had few allies on the Board to support my views. So, in January 2002, I resigned.

In the aftermath of this sad sequence of events, the President stepped down, and his successor engaged a consultant with a legal background to undertake a thorough review of the organisation. I was invited to make a submission, which I did in August 2002. I identified a number of significant issues, including lack of governance policy and systems, Board interference in operational management, lack of stakeholder liaison, the need to strengthen the HR function, and the need to appoint a Board with a sufficient range of competencies. I believe that the consultant reported in October 2002. But whether my views carried any weight, I do not know. I was not briefed on the outcome.

This experience was an object lesson in what can go wrong when there is an absence of good governance, not to mention the potential perils for a CEO in such an organisation.[202] To some extent, I felt that I had let the organisation down by failing to stick it out. But the high-handed and wilful actions of some people, for whose actions I was ultimately liable despite my representations, left me no alternative but to step away.

Research Infrastructure Support Scheme ("RISS")

After the disappointing experience at Arthritis Victoria, and with an expanding role at the ACF, I did not rush to seek another Board position. However, in early 2007, my colleague and friend from ARCBS days, Patrick Coghlan, persuaded me to become involved with a newly formed organisation called RISS. RISS was being established to foster the building of collaborative relationships in support of research projects, to

---

[202] Leigh Garwood left the organisation at the end of his contract in 2004. He went on to be the CEO of Seeing Eye Dogs and then Vision Australia, where he served with distinction until he died in 2017. He was widely respected and well regarded.

advise people seeking TGA GMP compliance, to manage Funds provided by the Commonwealth government to invest in research infrastructure, and to finance the preparation and distribution of related educational material.

In its infancy, this looked to be a very exciting venture, and Patrick was keen for me to contribute my governance and planning experience. In April 2007, I accepted an invitation to join the Board. After some delay, we had an inaugural meeting on 16 August at which I immediately felt some disquiet about the viability of the venture. At the outset, it was reported that the Victorian government had withdrawn its potential involvement. And, given the nature of the business, I had some reservations about the independence of the Chairman given his recent role as head of the TGA. It was also disconcerting that even the proposed administrative support was in doubt, with ARCBS proving slow to confirm a fee-for-service arrangement. With all these concerns, many other calls on my time, and even before my directorship was confirmed by the regulatory authorities, in September I resigned.

On reflection, this involvement was a mistake. Again, I had allowed myself to be drawn into a responsibility through someone I knew, without prior due diligence. Interestingly, to give credit to all those involved, RISS did go on to become a viable organisation.

Land Covenanters Victoria

One of the most frustrating experiences as the owner of a property with a Trust for Nature covenant ("TfN"), is the relative isolation one feels from all the other similarly covenanted properties. This is a function of the covenanting organisation. TfN do not have the resources to provide significant ongoing support.

In 2020, I had reason to liaise with the TfN legal officer Cecilia Riebl about a Land Tax matter and received sympathetic support. In mid-2021, Cecilia alerted me to the fact that there were plans to establish a new organisation to bring together all covenanted property owners in an association that would both advocate for the cause and provide a vehicle for mutual support. I quickly became actively involved, and at a special general meeting in October 2021 the organisation was established. I agreed to serve on the Board, and the organisation has made a flying start with a Web Site established in December and significant plans in hand to expand the initial membership to include a majority of the more than 1,200 covenanters in Victoria. There are a range of projects designed to advocate biodiversity, recruit all covenant holders to join the organisation, develop systems for mutual support in maintaining properties, pursue changes to legislation to provide incentives for adopting covenant, and achieve consistent treatment of properties by local authorities. It is early days, but this has already been proven to be one of the most productive teams that I have joined, and this is no doubt driven by a unity of purpose, and the shared values of participants.

19: A Line of Consultancy

Whilst my attempts to be a non-executive director met with limited success, the other activity to which I gave serious thought was consultancy. In particular, I believed that there was considerable scope for developing and implementing governance systems in not-for-profit organisations. In the first decade of the 21st century, I established a business entity through which I offered my services to a number of organisations. I also worked as an associate with a company called *Growing Your Knowledge* ("GYK"). In this chapter I provide an account of work undertaken on my own account which ran in parallel with my involvement with the ACF as reported in previous chapters. An account of my work through GYK is given in the next chapter.

Trust for Nature

My first venture into the world of consultancy, even before I became involved with the ACF, was with the Trust for Nature ("TfN"). Impressed by their mission to support the proliferation of privately owned nature reserves protected by covenants, in March 2001 I approached them with an offer to provide some professional services. Since I had no previous experience, I offered to work on a *pro bono* basis. The response was positive, and I soon commenced activities.

The sponsor for this work was the CEO, Michael Looker, and he requested that I begin by providing advice on HR.[203] Working with the Office Manager, Paula Thomson, we talked through the contents of their current HR Manual, identifying areas where there were gaps, particularly in terms of compliance with the relevant Awards. Specifically, I was then asked to assist in the completion of a number of HR policies in preparation for the renegotiation of the work-place agreement later in the year. The policies on which I worked covered the following areas: Occupational Health and Safety, Induction, Recognition of Trade Unions, Smoking, and Privacy and Employee Records. In undertaking this work I liaised with the Department of Natural Resources and Environment, to ensure that TfN were compliant with government requirements. And I was fortunate to encounter a very helpful

---

[203] Michael Looker eventually became Director of Regional Strategies for the Asia Pacific at The Nature Conservancy. In 2019, he was appointed as the Chair of an organisation named Conservation Coaches Network, which shares conservation learning and standards.

compliance officer, Barbara Hall.[204] The work was completed in October.

In the meantime, I had discussions with Michael Looker on the completion of a governance programme. He was interested and indicated that he would discuss it with the Chairman of the Board whilst I was overseas on a trip to the UK.[205] On my return, Michael introduced me to the then TfN Chairman, Brian Snape, who was broadly supportive, subject to more details about how the work would be undertaken. However, the Board was undergoing a restructure and he suggested that we delay the main project until October, when I would be invited to attend a Board meeting. Meanwhile, it was agreed that I would commence a risk analysis, which would involve the management team.

This was the first time that I'd designed this type of programme for a small organisation using the learning from the extensive work completed at ARCBS. Working with a five-person team we commenced the analysis in October, with a plan designed to deliver a list of top risks and risk treatment plans by February. The first brainstorming session went very well with enthusiastic participation and, following a subsequent ranking stage, we came up with our top eight risks. They were revealing to the team, encompassing security of funding, OH&S, stewardship, legal compliance, and IT capability. Following feedback by the Board, the team then worked through the development of Risk Treatment Plans, and I left them with a schedule involving a regular annual update.

In October, I met the Board, which now had several new and younger members. At this meeting, I received a mixed reception to my governance proposals which included a review of the first draft of a Board Accountability Statement that I had submitted. Some of the older Board members were wary and concerned about what they saw as a somewhat bureaucratic approach which might confine their ability to act. However, they could see the benefit of putting in place some documentation to underpin the Board's integrity. The younger members were keen to proceed. After some discussion in my absence, they indicated that they would commence the governance programme with a special meeting in December. It was left for the Chairman, Michael and myself to meet and agree a programme which would initially focus on

---

[204] Barbara Hall was the Manager Statutory Authorities with responsibility for liaison with organisations like TfN that received government funding for specified programmes such as the TfN's Revolving Fund.

[205] On this trip, at Michael's suggestion, I visited two major environmental projects in the UK – the seedbank at Wakehurst Place in Sussex and the Eden Project in Cornwall.

developing the accountability statement.

Sadly, at this point, the project stalled. When I next met with Michael Looker he told me that the Board was not yet ready to embrace the kind of far-reaching governance programme that I had proposed. They thanked me for my proposals and indicated that they would give serious consideration to some of the ideas in the New Year. But they would be doing this in-house.

My reflection on all of this is that, whilst I had established a good rapport with the CEO, I had invested insufficient time in convincing the Board about the benefits of improved accountability. It might have been much better to have started with something less complex like the development of a Corporate Governance statement, a performance plan for the CEO, or perhaps some policy statements on such issues as conflicts of interest. It seemed that I had frightened the horses and this was learning for any future similar venture.

In the meantime, all was not lost. In the course of working at the organisation, I had learnt a great deal about the Trust for Nature covenant system. In late 2000, Andrew and I pursued our dream of acquiring a conservation property. As related in Chapter 21, that would lead to the purchase of a nature reserve on which we placed a TfN covenant.

Westgate Community Initiatives Group

As my role as a consultant became known by word of mouth amongst friends, in early 2003 I was approached by a colleague from RCBBV days, Mary Price, to assist in raising governance standards in a small community organisation for which she did voluntary work in Footscray. Mary indicated that they were prepared to reimburse me for completing an audit of their current governance practices and some follow-up action. In April, I met with the Management Committee and we agreed to proceed with the audit with a report to be prepared on options for follow-up activity. Given the nature of the organisation, and its largely voluntary basis, in a memorandum of understanding in May, we agreed a level of fees well below what I would ordinarily charge. Nevertheless, this was my first-ever paid consultancy.

I completed the audit through a series of interviews with key players and delivered a report in which I identified a number of gaps in their systems. In August, I met with the team and they decided that, as a first step in improving their governance, they would undertake the risk analysis that I had recommended. We commenced this process in

September, and identified nine significant risks which led to considerable debate within the team. However, just as my hopes was raised about doing some serious governance work, the Management Committee decided that they did not have the time or energy to proceed any further. I suspect that they were pre-occupied with operational matters. Anyway, I left them with a range of material on which they could do further work if and when the spirit moved them. This included generic versions of an Accountability Statement, Delegations Matrix and Conflicts of Interest policy.

ACCA

In 2006, I was approached by a lady named Francesca Manglaviti, the newly appointed CEO of an organisation called the Australian Crohn's and Colitis Association ("ACCA"). My name had been passed to her by an ex ARCBS colleague, Dr Anne Fletcher (of which more in the next chapter), as someone who might be able to advise on governance matters.[206] This would lead to the most comprehensive piece of consultancy work undertaken as a lone consultant on a remunerated basis.

ACCA is an organisation that provides support services, advice and encouragement to people suffering from Inflammatory Bowell Disease and to their families. The organisation also operates as an advocate for suitable treatments and raises funds for research. In my initial discussion with the CEO, she indicated a wish to undertake an audit of the organisation's governance systems and practices. I met with her in June at their offices in Mooroolbark and I introduced her to what I was now calling the Wigginton Governance Matrix. Given the modestly funded nature of the very worthy organisation, I undertook to undertake the audit, a risk analysis, the compilation of a Board Administration Manual, and the development of some governance policies, for a discounted fee.

I started this six-month project by sending a briefing and proposal to the Board which we discussed at a meeting in July, with the aim of completing work in November. I then proceeded with a presentation to the six-member Board in August about the nature of "governance" and the kind of policy, systems, and practice that would deliver good performance. Subsequently, I completed a full audit of the organisation's current governance arrangements and, in September, I took them through

---

[206] The organisation is now named Crohn's & Colitis Australia.

the results. I have to say that the response of the Board to all of this was both welcoming and constructive. There was a firm commitment from the Chairman, a man named Bruce Tobin, and most members of the Board, although one member expressed concern about maintaining what he saw as a relatively onerous set of arrangements.

In September we had our first session of the risk analysis programme and the Board were highly co-operative in brain-storming and completing the subsequent questionnaire. In October, we reviewed the results which encompassed a list of 20 significant risks. Some were existential, such as the failure to secure sufficient funding, or to protect the organisation's intellectual property. Others were operational, such as insufficient IT systems, and the vicarious risk arising from false or misleading advice. The learning was salutary, and the team then applied themselves to developing appropriate risk treatment plans to mitigate or remove the risks. In the meantime, I developed a Board Accountability Statement, a Board Administration Manual and policy statements on Independent Professional Advice and a Code of Conduct and Ethical Behaviour. All of these documents were sent back to the Board in October and November, when I had a final session to wrap up the project. The material was well received and adopted with minor amendments.

As a general statement, I think this was the most successful small project in which I engaged as an independent consultant. More than anything, I put this down to both the willingness and commitment of the Board, who had initiated the work, and my own level of professionalism which had been honed in previous projects. The success was certainly borne out by the fact that in early 2009 I was invited back to undertake a project on Board Performance. Unfortunately, I was in the midst of recovering from the fire and I had to decline.

Reform of Rules

The final field of my consultancy work has involved the updating of organisational Rules, all of which has been undertaken on a voluntary basis. This has been a substantial body of work, enabling a number of community not-for-profit organisations to comply with the State legislation governing incorporated associations. The first of these exercises were completed at the Darlingford Waters Boat Club and the ACF, as mentioned in previous chapters. However, a couple of others are worthy of mention because they were not so successful for reasons I will explain.

Traralgon Bridge Club

During my time living in Traralgon in 2009, I joined the local Bridge Club, playing with an excellent player and delightful fellow named Michael Zarb. In the first couple of years, when I was recovering from the fire, I steered clear of doing anything other than attending on Monday nights to play bridge. But, eventually, as knowledge about my background and experience became known, I was prevailed upon to join the committee. At the time, there was an imperative to update the Club Rules, in response to a change in regulatory legislation, and they asked me to undertake the work.

The Traralgon Bridge Club had been formed in 1993, and the existing Rules dated from 2007. They were rudimentary, as the organisation had adopted the "Model Rules" of the time, as provided under the Victorian Incorporated Associations Act 1981. In 2011, this Act had been updated to include a number of new provisions, designed to improve governance practice, including the following:

- Membership entitlements,
- Procedures to deal with grievances, disciplinary matters, and resolution of disputes,
- Measures to achieve improved financial accountability,
- Policy on conflicts of interest,
- Procedures for dissolution of the organisation.

In undertaking this project, I initially turned to some new "Model Rules", as provided in the legislation, which already included wording to reflect the above matters. However, there was provision to submit *Modified Rules*, to accommodate additional measures consistent with the legislation. Building on my previous experience with small organisations in achieving due process, I saw this as an opportunity to establish a higher standard of governance for the Club. Accordingly, I modified the Model Rules to include a number of additional measure including the following

- A limit on the length of Officers' terms,
- Enhanced procedures for the orderly conduct of meetings,
- A provision to conduct elections by postal ballot, and
- The facility to use emails for communications.

The most contentious of these proposed changes was the use of postal ballots. As with many small organisations, the Club was used to conducting elections at the AGM, with proceedings often involving last minute arm twisting. Postal ballots enabled a more orderly and considered approach as well as enfranchising those unable to attend the AGM. After several discussions, the Committee were persuaded of the merits of all these changes, and the Club approved the new Rules at the AGM in 2012. Paperwork was sent to the authorities and we all assumed that we were home and hosed. In the meantime, the Club operated with the Modified Rules. Then in 2021, it was discovered that they had not been approved by the authorities. To my great disappointment, a new Club committee decided to adopt the Model Rules instead of resubmitting the Modified Rules citing that they were simpler to follow. You can't win them all!

Traralgon South and District Association

While the Bridge Club was a disappointment because the organisation would not accept my case for enhanced governance, the history of adopting new rules for the Traralgon South and District Community Association ("TSDA") is a different story. A full account of my involvement with that organisation is given in Chapter 29. But, in a nutshell, even though this organisation adopted Modified Rules with enhanced governance, this did not in itself guarantee systematic accountability.

20: Growing Your Knowledge

By far the most significant pieces of consultancy I have undertaken involved my contribution to the work of another consultancy organisation. In 2005 I was approached by a colleague from ARCBS days, Dr Anne Fletcher, to become an associate of Growing Your Knowledge ("GYK"). GYK had been formed by Anne and her lawyer husband Gerald in 2002, with offices in Mosman, Sydney.[207]

In mid-2005, Anne was tendering for a project commissioned by the Commonwealth Government to review the Australian Stem Cell Centre ("ASCC"). Founded in 2003, this body was based at Monash University in Melbourne, and operated as a medical R&D organisation which focused on regenerative medicine through the use of stem cells.[208] The organisation was financed by both the Commonwealth and State governments with funding that was subject to periodic renewal. And the aim of the project was to ascertain whether the venture was achieving its objectives and was worthy of continued Government funding. The review encompassed governance, operational management, strategic planning, and scientific outcomes. There was also a requirement to assess performance against international benchmarks. To undertake this exercise, Anne assembled a team of people with a wide range of competencies. My contribution related to my knowledge of governance, risk management, planning and finance. Other associates included Julie and Roger Bayliss who had many years' experience as Senior Trade Commissioners with the Australian Government and Gordon Smith who was a qualified accountant and company secretary. I was excited by the chance to be involved in working with this team and I gladly accepted the offer. I prepared an updated CV, which was included in the tender documentation.

The bid for the project was successful within some fairly tight financial limits, and with completion scheduled for December. The deliverables were both a Management Report and a Scientific Report with findings and recommendations. The published scope of works was designed to assess whether the ASCC had:

---

[207] An immunologist, Anne Fletcher had been a senior manager at the ARC NSW Blood Bank, before succeeding Dr Patrick Coghlan as the ARCBS Director of Intellectual Capital. Between 2005 and 2012 she was an ARCBS Board member.

[208] One of ASCC's founders was Dr Alan Trounson, a scientist who was on the team that delivered Australia's first IVF baby in 1980.

241

a)   Established a sufficient organisation to manage its operations,
b)   Met KPIs and Milestones designed to demonstrate achievement of the objectives in its strategic plan,
c)   Complied with ethical and biological standards,
d)   Established and implemented appropriate governance arrangements, giving special regard to whether the Board comprised persons with appropriate skills,
e)   Made progress towards becoming self-sustaining,
f)   Met legal and contractual obligations,
g)   Employed a sufficient number of appropriately qualified staff,
h)   Established an appropriate standing in the international community,
i)   Appropriately accounted for the changing nature of the external environment, and
j)   Met scientific and research targets.

It was also a condition of the project that any findings would be strictly confidential, "in perpetuity", with all documentation collected by the consultants to be destroyed at completion of the project. This restricts what I am able say about the contents and outcomes of the project, but does not preclude some comments about the nature of the work and the methodology used.

The project commenced in late July 2005, with a briefing at the ASCC premises at Monash University. At a meeting in Sydney in early August, the team then went through the Terms of Reference and allocated tasks. For the review of governance and risk management, I worked with Julie Bayliss employing the Wigginton Governance Matrix.[209] This provided a 23-point basis on which to examine the organisation's governance structure, systems, and practices. Roger Bayliss, Gordon Smith and I undertook an assessment of the financial management systems and funding model, Gordon reviewed financial performance, and Roger and I reviewed the organisation's strategic planning. In the meantime, Anne and Julie were engaged in a mammoth exercise to assess the scientific outputs of the organisation through the recruitment and convening of a Panel of international scientific experts in the field. Gerald assessed legal and regulatory compliance. And Julie worked with Anne on

---

[209] This is a tool that I established in 2003, for undertaking governance reviews.

benchmarking with international organisations and assessing the ASCC commercialisation model.

As will be evident, in the time frame, this was an enormous workload. And one of the key requirements for our work was the maintenance of a log which reflected the content of our interaction with all the parties involved. The other members of the team were based in Sydney, so I took responsibility for local liaison with the Monash Medical Centre. As regards my area of work, ASCC management were most obliging and, through a series of fact finding visits, I was provided with all the material that I requested. This included a very wide range of governance documentation such as the results of risk management exercises, the Deeds that constituted the structure for the organisation's operations, and the current version of the strategic plan. On 23 August, the ASCC team had a critical meeting with the Board at their premises in Collins Street, Melbourne and afterwards Roger and I met with the Chair of the Audit Committee. On 9 September, Anne convened the international Science Panel whose proceedings lasted for a week. And, on 11 October, we all attended the AGM and Stakeholders' meeting.

During October and November, I worked with Roger and Julie in preparing our sections of the main report, which was a challenging exercise given our different styles of writing. The first full draft of the Science Report was concluded in late October and the first draft of the main report was finished on 4 November. These drafts were circulated to key people to check key facts, and the final versions of the documents were then delivered as scheduled on 2 December. It was an amazing effort.

As mentioned above, the confidentiality clauses in the contract for this work preclude any comment about the outcome of the Review or even the culture of the organisation. What I can say is that it was a hugely rewarding experience. I found the collegiate nature and intellectual rigour of the team highly stimulating. And, of course, we did far more work than was reflected in the budget. Therein lies a potential issue with any consultancy project of this nature. You don't get the work unless your tender is competitive. But, if you have integrity, it is difficult not to go that "extra mile" to ensure a professional outcome with sensible recommendations. In any event, I believe that the Report was well received by the Commonwealth government and this is certainly borne out by the fact that, three years later, the GYK team was invited to revisit the organisation and complete a further review.

The second review was commissioned by the Commonwealth government in early 2008, with completion due in September. The aim of the project was to assess the organisation's progress since the review in 2005, and to examine the extent to which recommendations made in the earlier review had been fulfilled. Anne assembled the same core members as in the first review, and the project got under way with a four day meeting at ASCC premises in April. Again, an account of the contents and outcomes is constrained by confidentiality clauses in the contract. But it is safe to say that it was a significantly more intense and comprehensive exercise involving a close interaction with senior management and the Board as well as the key stakeholders in the organisation. Following completion of the review, the Report contributed to some serious outcomes.[210] Amongst other things, the Board fired the CEO over the commercial direction of the organisation and its ability to achieve self-financing by 2011. Subsequently, the whole Board resigned citing differences of view with stakeholders and potential conflicts of interest. Audits of public organisations are not for the faint hearted!

---

[210] These statements are based on a report in the *Sydney Morning Herald* on 6 September 2008 and an article in the magazine *Fierce Biotech* on 9 September 2008.

PART SIX

BACK TO NATURE

21: Hunt for Paradise

Having spent my early life close to nature, urban life has never been my idea of paradise. As a young Australian actor, Sean Keenan, once said: *"Being in the city makes me want to curl up and die"*. From the very start of my time in Australia, largely thanks to the McArthur family, I quickly learnt to appreciate the great Australian outdoors and I spent a good deal of my leisure time on bush walks. And this is an interest that I have shared on a regular basis with Andrew. We have visited many wild places, travelling in all directions from Melbourne.

In the early 2000s, as I was thinking about ways of engaging with environmental causes, I also gave thought to a more practical contribution to conservation. With some spare cash to hand, Andrew and I came up with the idea of acquiring a nature reserve. And a model for conserving land with significant biodiversity was readily to hand. The Trust for Nature ("TfN") had a portfolio of conservation properties for acquisition through their "Revolving Fund".[211] They also facilitated the purchase of privately owned conservation blocks through the organisation's web site. So this was an obvious place to start our quest.

In the second half of 2001, Andrew and I visited a number of properties provided through the TfN system. Towards the end of the year, we identified a block in Gippsland. The land in this part of Victoria is reminiscent of England, with farms located on rolling hills, albeit with native vegetation. The TfN block at 200 Sheens Road sat to the east of Mirboo North on the Boolarra Road. It was a property of 300 acres and on the market for $139,000 which very much suited our financial capability. After a couple of initial visits to the property, Andrew and I formed the view that this was "the place". It had outstanding biodiversity and was relatively free of weeds. And it sat nestled between farmland and property leased from the State government by HVP which had previously been State Forest.[212] Access was via an unsealed road and, within the property, there were extensive walking tracks. We camped on site, and one morning I had my first encounter with a lace monitor![213] Following extensive exploration, we formed the view that a house could be located on a northern boundary with views across adjacent farmland.

---

[211] The Revolving Fund is financed by the State government who make an annual grant for acquisition of suitably biodiverse vacant blocks. The TfN then attaches a covenant to prevent future development before on-selling to private landowners.

[212] HVP is a company named Hancock Victorian Plantations Holdings.

[213] A lace monitor is a tree goanna lizard.

In early 2002, I began the process of due diligence on this property and at an early stage discovered a snag. TfN's Vendor's Statement issued indicated that there was road access. However, this was incorrect. The unsealed access road passed through HVP's property and they were reluctant to grant right of passage. I took this up with TfN and there began a long process, involving HVP, the local Council, and the Department of Primary Industry, in which we attempted to address the matter. This exercise continued throughout 2002 and, when I look back, I cannot believe that we were so patient. But we rated the land very highly. Eventually, in November TfN took the property off the market pending resolution of the access issue. In early 2003, we made one final attempt to acquire the property. But it was to no avail, and we moved on.[214]

Around this time, Andrew was working for an organisation that did environmental audits, assessing the impact on flora and fauna of potential development proposals. And he had a project that took him down to Sea Spray in Gippsland. One sunny afternoon, I visited him there to consider whether we wished to persist with our dream. It was an important decision, involving a substantial commitment of time in search of a suitable property. After some deliberation, we agreed that we should give it a go and thus began a new adventure.

As with most things that Andrew and I did together, we set about the property search in a systematic fashion, adopting a set of selection criteria as follows:

a) Verified outstanding biodiversity, with little or no weeds.
b) Minimum of 120 acres.
c) No more than 3 hours' drive from Melbourne.
d) With a dwelling, or capable of having a house.
e) $250,000 with a house or $150,000 without.
f) Mountains or coastal aspect desirable.
g) Adjacent to other reserves to facilitate landscape ecology.

Armed with this specification, in mid-2003, we began our search, casting a very wide net and including properties beyond those listed by TfN. We undertook out first sortie in May 2003, and covered blocks in Daylesford and Castlemaine. And the search continued for about three years, as we travelled west to Colac and Apollo Bay, north to Mansfield

---

[214] TfN eventually retained the property and named it the Grieve Nature Reserve.

and Benalla, southwest along the Grand Ridge Road, and into east Gippsland including properties in Briagolong and Gormandale. There were many false trails but several properties became the subject of significant evaluation. And we were particularly drawn to the rainforest in the Strzelecki Hills where there were a number of blocks with outstanding biodiversity embedded within logging tranches. But there were always drawbacks, not least access, and topography for building a house. In the meantime, I had decided to sell the houseboat on Lake Eildon and this released another $120,000 which extended our budget to around $350,000.

In December 2006, we investigated a couple of properties in Gippsland, and took the opportunity to visit local estate agents on the off-chance of finding something not listed on the internet. We called into Stockdale & Leggo in Traralgon, and encountered a knowledgeable fellow named Leon Hammond.[215] We explained our requirements and, as was usual with estate agents, he immediately enquired as to what type of business we were intending to establish. When we told him we were looking for a block for conservation, he looked bemused. But then he had an idea. The previous year, a block of 240 acres had been on the market for $395,000 but had failed to sell. It was in Redhill Road Callignee and was owned by a company that had acquired the land for extraction of gravel for road building. However, the owners had never got round to clearing the forest and were now winding back their activities. So they wanted to sell. He described it as open bushland with some deep gullies, and without a dwelling. Although it was way beyond our budget, Andrew and I expressed interest and decided to take a look. The entrance was off a sealed road opposite a rural housing estate and, as we walked through the forest down the main track going westwards, Andrew was impressed. Although there was evidence of some dumping including a rusty old car, there appeared to be few weeds, and abundant biodiversity. We spent a couple of hours, finding several tracks going through the forest and it seemed to fit the bill. By now, it was late afternoon and we just made it back to the office in time to touch base with Leon. We discussed the price, indicating that it was beyond our budget. But Leon told us to leave it with him. In fact, he didn't even know whether it was still on the market. And, if it were, perhaps the owners might have a different view about price given that it had previously failed to sell. We drove back to Melbourne.

---

[215] Leon was actually the founder of the business and was just working part time. Not long after, he acquired the Traralgon Vineyard.

A few days later, I called Leon to ask what the owners had to say and he reported that they now wanted $440,000! I was downcast. But Leon said "hold on". He was dealing with the family of two old gentlemen who were trying to dispose of unwanted assets. The aged owners were reluctant to sell, but the younger members of the family were keen to get their hands on some cash. And he suggested that we should make an offer just to see whether, given little interest from other parties, they would bite. We decided on an offer $250,000, and left it with Leon. With Christmas upon us, we heard nothing. Then in January I received a call. To our surprise, the owners had come back with a revised price of $260,000. It seemed too good to be true. The next weekend, Andrew and I revisited the block for a more thorough assessment before deciding what to do. In Andrew's view, whilst the price was significantly higher than that for the Mirboo North property, it had comparable biodiversity. And it had the benefit of an adjacent sealed road along a one-kilometre frontage. We agreed to the price and, on 3 March, we signed the contract to proceed, with settlement due for 30 April 2007. But then we hit a snag. In the course of due diligence, it emerged that the vendors who had signed the contract were not the same as the owners listed on the title deed. They had failed to keep this information up to date and, whilst it was easily fixed, this potentially invalidated the contract. The vendors were slow to correct their error and, when the date came for settlement, they failed to settle. We were aghast and, given that purchasers are entitled to walk away, our solicitor asked us whether we still wanted to proceed. We were adamant, and began rigorous representations. To cut a long story short, the vendors did eventually update the title deed. But not until after we had served a writ! The property finally transferred into our ownership on 12 July 2007.

With a great sigh of relief, we almost immediately moved to establish a TfN covenant to protect the property from development. This is a lengthy process requiring an audit by TfN, and signature by the Minister. This was finally concluded on 31 July 2008.

22: Building a House

Having acquired the property in Callignee, the next phase of this environmental project was to establish some form of permanent residence on "the block" as Andrew called it. The rationale for this was both to have a base from which to fulfil our responsibilities in managing the land, and the means to enjoy the quality of life that living next to the forest would bring. We considered various concepts, including a caravan, but quickly came to the view that we needed something more permanent. Under the TfN covenant, 0.7 hectares could be designated as the domestic area, within which we could clear the forest and establish a house and other infrastructure.

The next step was to identify a site for the house. I was keen to find a location which would provide a view of the surrounding hills including Mount Baw Baw to the north. But we also had to take into account the newly adopted "Fire Management Overlay" ("FMO") which was a set of rules designed to ensure that any house would be defendable from bush fire. The FMO was based on parameters such as the slope of the land and the proximity of the forest, and we were also keen to have access to the kilometre of sealed road running down the eastern boundary of the block. Adjacent to this stretch we identified half a dozen options, and then engaged with a group of people that the local planning authority (Latrobe City Council) identified as interested parties to conclude an assessment.[216] This team rejected all the sites bar one which was a relatively flat area of forest next to a spur heading west and about 220 metres above sea level. It didn't offer me the distant views of mountains that I wanted but, as Andrew always said, I had a great view of forest!

The next job was to clear the trees and bush covering the domestic area. The estate agent put us in touch with a woodman named Colin Pattinson whose family had been logging and caring for forests in the Strzelecki hills for several generations. In November 2007, in less than a day he had cleared around 0.4 hectares leaving a huge pile of logs in one corner. As it happened, I didn't get to observe this work. On the previous evening, Andrew and I were staying in a local motel and, at 7.00 am I received a call from a hospital in Melbourne telling me that my mother was seriously ill. I quickly jumped on a train for my very first V Line trip, leaving Andrew with the car to proceed with oversight of

---

[216] This group consisted of a Planning Officer, and representatives of the State Government and the Country Fire Authority.

the tree felling. Fortunately, as regards my mother, it was false alarm.[217] And, in many ways, I was almost glad not to see the carnage on site. A post script to this exercise is that, a few weeks later, some local lads decided to set fire the pile of logs and, even before we had taken up any kind of residence, the Country Fire Authority ("CFA") attended to extinguish a significant blaze. It was an omen.

Whilst planning preparation of the site, we assessed options on the house and related infrastructure. After some lengthy investigations we agreed that the best approach was to acquire a "kit home" which would be fabricated in Melbourne and transported in sections for installation on site. We also needed water tanks sufficient to cover domestic and fire-fighting requirements, a septic tank, a seriously large shed for storing equipment, and access to power. For the water and sewage systems, Colin Pattinson put us in touch with a plumber named Owen Burns who turned out to be an incredibly helpful and competent guy.

The power supply proved challenging, with the options of connecting to the grid or establishing an off-grid solar system. Connection to the main grid was prohibitively expensive, with the local power company quoting $37,000 to establish a new pole and underground cabling over several hundred metres. Consequently, the installation of solar panels and batteries became a viable option. During our long quest for a property, we had already encountered blocks with off-grid power systems. But we were apprehensive because, in 2007, the solar power industry was in its infancy. Over several months we investigated a number of small solar-power companies and, at the time, there was no one available in Gippsland apart from an embryonic business in Yarragon. But there were several small companies operating in and around Melbourne. We obtained quotes from several operators, including Going Solar which was by chance on the Ground Floor of the ACF's Green building. We also discovered that, in the event that connection costs at a remote location were prohibitively expensive, there was Commonwealth Government scheme to provide funding to cover 50% of the cost. Since the estimates for installing our 5 KWH system were generally in the order of $40,000 to $50,000, it was not difficult to take the virtuous option and establish a fully self-sustainable system at a net cost to us of around $25,000.

Even as we were considering signing a contract with Going Solar, their representative Jarrod Tewierik contacted me to say that he had set

---

[217] V Line is the regional railway company in Victoria.

up his own company. Engaging him seemed a relatively high risk approach, given that he was just starting up. But he demonstrated both knowledge and attention to detail, and spoke with great passion about what he was doing. He was also a former boyfriend of Andrew's partner Siobhan! After checking out a few of his existing customers, we concluded that he knew what he was talking about and would deliver a quality system. Thus began a long-term relationship which delivered a highly effective system. This encompassed solar panels to be installed on the roof of the shed, industrial-grade batteries installed in a small shed within the main shed, a regulator, an inverter, and cabling to the house. Jarrod's system also involved a 5KW generator as back up with software to check the charge in the batteries each evening and automatically run the generator to bring the charge to 100%. In some ways, the most challenging part of adopting this approach was obtaining the Commonwealth government scheme (RRPGR).[218] This required the preparation of significant documentation to demonstrate that the alternative to solar energy was expensive, and that the property was to be a permanent residence. I made this commitment in good faith, transferring to the local electoral register and relocating my driving licence.

Of course, the most important part of the building project was the house. Having decided on a kit home, we evaluated alternative suppliers located both in Melbourne and in rural Victoria. There were several contenders, but we eventually settled on a company named Kentucky Napier based in Bayswater who had several house designs for assembly in the city and transport to a remote location.

Like so many things to do with housebuilding, the establishment of the house did not quite go according to plan. Kentucky Napier provided the facility to customise one of their models to suit customer requirements in terms of layout and site. The model we chose, the Barwon 130, had three bedrooms, including one with en-suite, a main bathroom, a laundry, three living areas and a veranda around two sides. We went through several iterations of the design, with Andrew determining the finer points including bay windows, steel railings and other features. The resulting cost was $167,000 installed, (plus $17,000 for a number of variations during the project, including hard wood for decking, steel hand-rails, special fascia, back stairs, and mobile crane for installation) and the contract was signed on 27 October 2007. With the

---

[218] RRPGR stands for Renewable Remote Power Generation Program.

Callignee House 2008

site being cleared in November, it was all systems "go".

The building project was scheduled for completion within 220 days. With a start before Christmas, and delivery of the house in early May, completion of the project was due on 3 June 2008. In the early months of 2008, Andrew and I made regular visits to the construction site in Bayswater and were pleased with progress. And then in early May we were informed without notice that the house had been installed on site in Callignee with final works to be completed on location. This raised concerns. In particular, the decking had not yet been stained, with the potential for weathering in the Callignee climate, and the railings had not been installed. And clearly, further works would now be undertaken by subcontractors without the supervision available in the city.

In the following weeks, our worst fears were now realised. The most serious issues were poor quality of workmanship with installation of the steel railings and damage to the unsealed decking from the use of an angle grinder. Commencing in early June, thus began a protracted series of letters and meetings which, over the next four months, gradually turned into a dispute. By far the biggest issue was the slow deterioration in the condition of the decking. In the end, after a site meeting and a showdown in Kentucky Napier offices with a member of the Napier family, we came to a compromise and agreed to a set of actions to address the defects. They then made attempts to address the

253

imperfections, but we were far from satisfied.

In the meantime, the solar system had been installed, and all other services completed. So, with a great sigh of relief, on 7 October 2008, the Certificate of Occupancy was issued and we were "good to go".

Shortly after, we formally took possession and arranged to have a range of furniture installed. As it happened, my mother had recently moved into a Nursing Home and we had access to most of her furniture, goods, and chattels, including a somewhat tired lounge suite, dining table and chairs that had come from England, a drinks cabinet, cutlery china and glasses, and pictures.

So I began what would be a relatively short period of country living. Summer was around the corner and the angst arising from the dispute with Kentucky Napier gradually dissipated. Christmas arrived with the usual celebrations in Melbourne and, on 20 January I have a fond memory of sitting in the living room watching the inauguration of Barak Obama. It all seemed like a new beginning with much to look forward to. Within two weeks, my world would change for ever.

23: The 2009 Fire

In February 2009, Andrew and I experienced a major natural disaster which was to have a huge influence on our lives for quite a few years. When we acquired the property in Callignee in 2007, we always knew that there was potential for a fire. Indeed, as you take the turn off the Hyland Highway towards Callignee, there is a sign on the left which states that *"You are entering a fire prone area. High Risk of Fire Danger."* I'm not sure how many people actually notice that sign. But, anyway, we were more than aware of an ever-present danger. So, when it came to establishing a house, the specification included fire-resistant building materials, a significant water supply in metal tanks, and fire-fighting equipment, with a hose and dedicated water pump.

In the period just before the extraordinary events of 7 February 2009, I had already acquired some training in how to manage a bush fire. On Redhill Road, I was instrumental in forming what was called a Community Fireguard Group. This was a neighbourhood support initiative fostered by the CFA, with people from neighbouring properties convening to plan a collective response to local bush fires. In our group, which covered properties over a five-kilometre stretch, we had people with a range of properties and circumstances including some who had lived in the district for more than ten years and were well prepared. Nevertheless, we all went through CFA training, including the use of a video taken during the Canberra fires of 2007. This showed residents coping with and surviving a relatively slow-moving fire. We were taught the basics of preparing our property beforehand, wearing the right clothing, retiring into the house as the fire front came through to avoid radiated heat, and emerging to fight off ember attack. It all seemed very manageable and gave us a false sense of security.

In the first few days of February 2009 it had been incredibly hot. Andrew's birthday is on 6 February and I was in Melbourne to attend a family dinner which we held at a restaurant in St Kilda. Given the heat, we were happy to be indoors. On the morning of the fire, I received a call from my neighbour in Callignee, Louise Mann, to tell me that there was fire in the area. The exact status was unclear, except that it was about 20 kms away to the west on a day when there was a strong north-westerly wind. The temperature was in the 40s, with very low humidity, and the bush was tinder dry. After the call from Louise, I called Andrew and we decided that we should go to Callignee to defend the house. We left Melbourne at about 1.00 pm and sped along the Princes Highway towards Traralgon. At Labertouche we hit a road-block and we diverted our journey south, taking the road through Leongatha and then down the Strzelecki Highway. As we approached Morwell, we saw a huge wall of flames on the western side of the hills between Churchill and Callignee. Undaunted, we proceeded into Traralgon and drove out to Callignee encountering very little traffic, no road blocks, and an almost eerie calm.

We arrived at the house around 3.00 pm and began our preparations. This involved clearing the decks of flammable materials, installing buckets with mops and water on the decks, moving furniture into the centre of rooms, donning personal protection gear, putting the car in the shed, removing essential items such as my computer to the car, and hosing down the house and surrounding land. Then we just sat it out, anticipating that something would come but not knowing quite what to expect.

By 6.00 pm, there was an increasingly dense smoke haze, and a distant rumbling noise. Then, during the next hour, we experienced the most amazing fire storm. First, as we stood watching on the deck, it started to grow very dark and a few embers started to fall. Then, on the ridge to the north-west of the house, there was a glow of light which turned to yellow, and then orange. At around 6.40 pm we retreated into the house as a wall of red rapidly grew before our eyes. By 6.45 pm, all the trees around the house were burning and there was a deafening roar akin to the sound of a jet engine. Then the fire front arrived at the clearing and hit the house. By now, the flames were at least 100 feet in the air, spread across a wide front from our vantage point, with a lethal burning gas enveloping the whole house in flames. At this point, we realised that this was no ordinary bush fire (According to the CFA, aerial imaging showed that the temperature was in excess of 1300°C).[219] As we watched from inside the house, the flames hit the windows, and within two minutes, the aluminium frames began to melt, and the glazing cracked. Andrew attempted to apply the fire hose, but then the water pump failed. As the windows came crashing down, and the fire entered the house, we retreated into the laundry at the rear of the house closing a central fire door behind us.

We stayed in the laundry for approximately 10 minutes, lying on the floor and trying to get oxygen as the tiled floor heated up from flames beneath the house. Smoke entered the laundry and I was close to losing consciousness. I remember saying that I couldn't breathe and Andrew

---

[219] A "normal" house fire burns at around 900°C.

decided we should evacuate. At around 7.05 pm, he took my hand and led me through the back door and down the steps which were already on fire. We ran across to the shed and opened the west facing roller door. As I slammed the door closed, I recall that there were items in the shed that had already ignited which Andrew extinguished. We climbed into the car where we lay down covering ourselves in blankets.

For the next 15 minutes, we waited inside the car. Although by now the fire front had passed through, the heat from the fire consuming the house was horrendous. At a critical moment, I remember a huge explosion. This turned out to be one of the LPG bottles which stood vertical adjacent to the house. It literally blew its top, an event which the gas company told me later was a very rare event reflecting extremely high temperatures. Meanwhile, the shed was rattling as it was shaken by a fierce wind and bombarded by a torrent of embers falling like a heavy hail storm on the roof. Miraculously, the steel shed withstood both the battering and the temperature, although a side door blew off leaving us exposed to the south. As I lay on the back seat, I do recall thinking that this might well be the end of my life. But we stayed conscious inside the car by talking to each other and breathing the small supply of air within the enclosed space. At one point, another fire started up in the shed with plastics self-igniting. We briefly left the car to extinguish the flames.

Callignee House after 2009 fire

257

By around 7.20 pm, the storm had begun to lesson in intensity. We left the car, and tentatively stepped through the hole in the side the shed where the door had blown off. We cautiously investigated our surroundings. The house was fully gone with the crumpled roof sitting on the ground. There was fire in the trees all around and the understorey was burning like tinder.

As we were taking in the scene of total devastation, we heard voices. Having survived their own inferno 2 kms away, our neighbours, Louise and Tony Mann and their two teenage sons Scott and Christopher were walking down Redhill Road and had arrived at our property. We embraced and then together we walked the 3 kms down the hill to the outskirts of Traralgon South. There were burning trees on either side of the road. And we had to step over burning trunks and branches which lay scattered across the road. As we progressed, we saw that most of our neighbours' houses were on fire. The air was thick with smoke and we were choking. Miraculously, we arrived at the bottom end of Redhill Road where it crosses the Stoney Creek. This was the northern edge of fire and we suddenly emerged into a relatively normal atmosphere to find a CFA truck parked across the road at the junction. People greeted us as we emerged from the smoke, and I shall never forget the look of amazement on the face of the CFA captain Pieter van der Liest. I'm sure he thought we would all be dead. For a moment, I was choking and I had to lie down in a cylindrical bus shelter to recover my breath. In the meantime, Pieter radioed our survival back to CFA HQ and, a few minutes later, a vehicle picked us up and took us to the CFA shed where paramedics gave us a medical check. Then we were then taken into the fire station, for rest and water whilst the police took our names and address. We borrowed a telephone, and I rang my mother's number at her Broughton Hall nursing home in Melbourne, only to find that she had been transferred to hospital with heat exhaustion. I explained the circumstances to a nurse who said she would let my mother know that Andrew and I were safe. Andrew then rang Siobhan.

Following our survival, what then transpired is a remarkable journey of recovery. At around 9.00 pm Andrew and I were loaded onto a bus and whisked away to the Relief Centre in Traralgon which had been established in the Arts Centre in Grey Street. We attended a desk where Red Cross registered us as survivors, and issued each of us with a blue slip of paper which became our identity card. We were then driven by a volunteer to emergency accommodation at the Traralgon Motel on the edge of town. We flopped down in Room No 6 and it started to dawn on us how incredibly lucky we were to be alive. We again contacted the most important people in our lives and shared with them our relief at having survived. After the telephone calls, we started to relive the experience of the fire, remembering details and sharing how we dealt with each event. We talked for several hours, listening intermittently to ABC radio (am as the FM channel was down because the transmission tower on Mt Tassie had been destroyed). The broadcast gave the latest information on how events were unfolding across the State. Then we went to bed. Sleep was fitful, and intermittently Andrew listened to the radio as news came of 173 deaths and the loss of thousands of houses across the State.

In the early hours of Sunday 8 February, just before sunrise, we were awake and talking. For the first of many mornings I broke down. Amazingly, Andrew stayed calm and comforted me. And we started to consider what we would now do and how we would cope. Annoyingly, in a forgivable oversight, we had left our telephones, wallets and keys in the house. We had no money and only the personal protection gear in which we were standing. Andrew went to the Reception of the Motel to enquire about whether we had to pay for our room. The owner told us that the Council would be paying for several days' accommodation and, in an incredible act of kindness, she then offered to lend us her husband's car. We had breakfast and then drove down to the Relief Centre. We checked in and were interviewed by a number of people all of whom were very sympathetic about our temporary status as refugees. In particular, a representative of the State Department of Human Services ("DHS") arranged an immediate emergency grant with a cheque for $427. Amazingly, Andrew did not qualify for this grant because he was not a permanent resident. Since we were penniless, we were in desperate need of this cash and the DHS lady telephoned Kmart to arrange for them to cash the cheque. She also suggested that we should visit an Op Shop who would give us some fresh clothes.

We then departed in our borrowed car to obtain some essential personal materials. Kmart said that they could only cash our cheque if we bought something and that condition was easily met as Andrew selected some cheap underwear. Armed with our new wealth, we set off for the pharmacist. In particular, Andrew needed some medication for his Graves disease and I needed stuff for my eyes. Amazingly, the pharmacist was most unhelpful with Andrew's medication, applying a bureaucratic rule which meant that we had to pay for a full bottle of medicine but only receive three days' supply with the need to return in 3 days' time. At this stage, it was clear that some people in Traralgon were unaware of the tragedy that had befallen those in the sticks! Then we went to the Op Shop. The staff were very kind, and insisted on giving us three sets of clothing without charge.

By now, we were hungry and we decided to have lunch at Iimis restaurant in Traralgon. It was a busy Sunday and amazingly, we were offered a free meal. After lunch, we made the first of many attempts to visit Callignee. We couldn't get past the police road block at Loy Yang Power Station and returned to the Relief Centre for an evening snack.[220] We then returned to our motel for recuperation.

The next day (Monday 11 February) we went to town to begin a slow process of resuming a semblance of normal life. The ANZ bank accepted my blue Red Cross document as identification and gave me $500 from my current account. They also organised replacement credit and savings cards for both of us. We visited Subaru to ascertain their willingness to help with assessing the car for insurance purposes, and returned to the Op Shop for more clothes. We again visited Iimis where we were given a free coffee and a voucher for $30 by the very kind Russian owner. We then returned to the Relief Centre and were given further information about the support available to survivors. Not for the first time, we bumped into the Manns, and the Evans.

Louise told us that our shed (and car) was reported to be gone. Next, we attended a Centre Link interview and I was offered a grant of $1,000 to be paid into my bank account, and told that a further $20,000 might be available subject to a means test which in the event excluded me. We were also given a voucher to use in Kmart for more clothing. En route, we bumped into our neighbours Jo and Peter Evans. Their house had been destroyed and we were much relieved to find them alive. In the early evening, we again drove out to Callignee and this time managed to get through to Traralgon South where we were delighted to meet up with some of the CFA guys. In the course of our chat, they suggested that Redhill Road might be open. So we jumped into the car, only to be stopped by a policeman at the Koornalla junction. He said the road had been cleared of debris but was still closed. But then he decided to turn a blind eye and let us through providing we were back in half an hour. We drove up to the property, seeing for the first time the desolation along the way. 200 Redhill Road was like a bomb scene. However, we found that

---

[220] The police road blocks, which were instituted for both safety reasons and because the district was potentially a crime scene with 11 local deaths, would be a running sore for the community for some days.

the shed was still standing, with the car intact and my computer still sitting where I had left it on the back seat. We returned to the road block and that evening went to the Sari Indian Restaurant where the generous owners offered free drinks and a half-price meal.

That night, I slept fitfully, continuing to mourn the loss of house, contents and the bush. First thing the next morning, after calls and breakfast, we visited Eureka Sheds to discuss securing the shed. They were very helpful and particularly happy about the fact that their product had withstood the holocaust! We also visited the GIO office to pursue the insurance claims, did some personal shopping, and acquired a new telephone and camera. At 1.00 pm we attended a meeting for survivors.[221] The mood in the room was sombre. The briefing by the authorities received a mixed response. Some survivors expressed their appreciation for the support being provided. But others were angry, with concerns about lack of warning before the fire and frustration about being denied access to properties.

After the meeting, we again went out to the property. The road blocks were all gone. Several people visited us, including the press. We had the bizarre experience of being interviewed and photographed amidst the ruins. Then we walked through the property and took photos. I was deeply disturbed by the desolation. Afterwards, we returned to the Relief Centre for food. I was in a grave mood and my inability to cope with what I perceived to be the loss of the forest, the house, and my mother's furniture overcame me. Andrew was like a rock. He took hold of me, shook me, and impressed on me that this was Australia, and that the bush would recover. And, as far as the house was concerned, we could build again.

The next morning, Wednesday, the shock was finally wearing off. Andrew and I had a long chat and we planned the next steps in our recovery which involved a return Melbourne. After another free breakfast at Iimis, and visits to GIO, Eureka Sheds, and Col Pattinson, we bought flowers to give to both the hotel and restaurant owners. We then hired a car from Budget, returned the borrowed car to the motel and checked out. We left Traralgon at 3.00 pm that afternoon and we were welcomed home by Siobhan and Britt. I was able to get into my house in Kew with a spare key that was hanging in the back patio, and I then went to visit my mother in hospital. She was in remarkably good form. I retired totally exhausted.

---

[221] GIO is the name of an insurance Company.

On Thursday 12 February I awoke late and started the process of trying to deal with my mother's illness and the need for an inspection of the property by an Insurance Assessor. By mid-day, GIO had come to the party and I was put in touch with a Jim McFee who agreed to conduct the inspection forthwith. I picked up Andrew and we met up with the poignantly one-legged Mr McFee at 3.00 pm who immediately commenced his review of the damage to the property. In the meantime, I slipped into the car which started first time. The insurance assessment didn't take long, with Mr McFee indicating that an immediate grant would be given to help us along. After some discussion on points of detail, he said that he would write a formal report, and send it to GIO for a formal decision on a total write-off. At 5.00pm, with Andrew driving the Subaru, I returned the hire car to Budget who only charged us for one day.

After staying overnight at the motel in Traralgon, the next day (a Friday 13th) we returned to Melbourne in the singed Subaru with drooping melted wing mirrors to be welcomed by family once more. And on the Saturday I attended a meeting of the ACF Board in Carlton. Members of the Board were amazed at my survival, and at my appearance so soon after the event. Thus are legends made!

24: Down but Not Out

In the immediate aftermath of the fire, the desire to stay close to the seat of the disaster in Redhill Road was strangely overwhelming. But there was also my mother's illness in Melbourne to consider. So, the next four months were actually a wretched time as I commenced an existence where I was torn between the two locations. It was also a period when I began to keep a log. At first, it was just a natural inclination of mine to keep a record of events. But eventually, after taking advice from a trauma counsellor at Relationships Australia, keeping a daily account of everything that happened became a systematic coping mechanism on the road to recovery.

Following the return to Melbourne on the Friday after the fire, to address my compulsive attachment to the property at Callignee, I determined for a time at least to take up residence in the shed on the block. Having taken my Subaru car in for its damage assessment in Melbourne, I then returned to Callignee with some bedding, water tanks, and other basic survival equipment.

Fringe Dweller

For the next few weeks, and in weather conditions that were mild, the shed became my temporary home. I swept it out, set up table and chairs, and dragged into use an old but perfectly serviceable mattress that had survived the fire leaning against the wall at the back of the shed. It was the weirdest form of camping. Whilst I could relieve myself a few steps distant from the shed, I found that the public toilet next to the Traralgon South Community Hall was functioning, although it lacked for loo paper most of the time. And by now, a local Relief Centre had been established, with people from various agencies available to provide advice on all sorts of recovery matters. On the first of several visits, I found a guy who had information on insurance policies. To my amazement he told me that, in addition to a payment of $26,000 to support renting a property for a period, under the insurance policy we qualified for a 25% supplement on the total sum insured because the house had been written off. I broke down in tears with what was very good news in terms of financing a recovery. The insurance company also released an initial payment of $30,000 to cover recovery expenses. Meanwhile, the local water authority visited the property and tested the water in the tanks. They declared it potable which meant I had a normal water supply whilst camping out.

Back at the shed, I received a visit from the police. At this stage in proceedings, the access roads were closed except for residents, with my blue Red Cross identity paper providing entry to what was still regarded as a crime scene.[222] I provided a full account of all that had happened and was later required to attend the police station and sign off the statement. The next day, some people in grey overalls appeared. They had American accents and they told me that they wanted to do some soil tests. I agreed, and they went onto the property. Then they disappeared, never to be heard of again. I stayed on the block for the rest of the week and did the first of several media interviews with a lady from AAP.[223] At the weekend, I returned to Melbourne.

Whilst in Melbourne, I met up with Andrew and had the first of many more considered conversations about the events of 7 February. Amongst other things, we decided to prepare a submission to the Royal Commission and we mapped out the main points. Whilst in the city, in a bizarre episode, I also found myself at Epworth Hospital in Richmond. As I was coming out my house on Saturday night, I found a young man lying in the street suffering from a stab wound. I got him into the car and took him to the Emergency Department. After quite a wait, his injury was found to be non-life threatening but he was whisked away to be admitted overnight. His name was Peter, and I never saw him again. On the Monday, I was also informed by the insurance assessors that the car was a write-off and not road-worthy. By a great stroke of luck, I mentioned this to my bridge partner Gill Lavers and, in an act of great kindness, her husband Doug offered to lend me one of their cars, a Hyundai 4WD.

On Tuesday 24 February, I returned to Callignee in the borrowed Hyundai, and in the afternoon I was visited by a man from Telstra who was undertaking a systematic review of all telephone lines. Seeing that I was camped out in the shed he said that he'd provide me with a temporary line. At no charge, he dug a small pit at the entrance to the property to locate the copper cable, and then he trailed a wire up to the shed and connected me to a handset that he provided. At this stage, whilst most of the local population had removed to neighbouring towns, there was all sorts of activity down Redhill Road which I was keen to monitor. In particular, the Council were working on the roads, clearing dangerous

---

[222] With 11 people dead, and arson the likely cause, the authorities were still undertaking a systematic review of all properties in search of possible further victims.
[223] AAP is Australian Associated Press.

trees, and re-establishing drainage. And there was evidence of contractors venturing along the northern track. Interestingly, I was never contacted by the local Recovery Committee and I only found out about its existence years later. In the meantime, the insurance company were keeping in touch and on 24 February, just 17 days after the fire, confirmed the full payment to be made. They also indicated that I would get a brand new car, with a courtesy car to be provided as and when I wished to pick it up. In the meantime, I took the opportunity to take stock and grieve. I walked the length and breadth of the property in its now denuded state, discovering old roadways, stumbling upon the skeletons of animals, and investigating the far western boundary in Koornalla on foot.

Of most remarkable note were the multitude of trees still standing and the evidence of trees near the top of the property having their tops blown off by the force of the fire storm. On several occasions I would receive telephone calls and begin the never-ending story telling. And, on a couple of weekends, Andrew visited and we walked to the far south-west corner to find the ancient corner post of the original Crown property. Amazingly, by now, the first green shoots had appeared from the ground. The following weekend I again went to Melbourne to complete our submission to the Royal Commission. On Monday, I returned the Lavers car and picked up the Subaru courtesy car, a Liberty.

In the first week of March, the family joined me in Traralgon to go hunting for a rental property. Traralgon was the obvious place, given the rail connection to Melbourne and there were plenty of options. In the following week, I settled on a Unit in Hickox Street. And on 13 March I picked up the new Subaru Forester. In the same week, Grocon, the company engaged by the State government to undertake demolition and clearing of sites, were in touch. They provided a date for completion of their works. After a last night of sleeping at the property, on 24 March, even as the Council issued a notice condemning the shed in Redhill Road and evicting me, I moved into my rented accommodation. So I began a new phase in what would become a lengthy period of recovery.

Down but not out in Traralgon

Were it not for the fire, Traralgon is not a place that I would ever have chosen to live. I have nothing against small towns of 20,000 people. And Traralgon is a pleasant town with a lively pulse. It's just that such places fall short of the amenities available in cities, and living there has all the

265

irritations of proximity to other people. But these were not normal times and I was easily reconciled to a suburban existence. And there was an imperative to continue a local presence because Andrew and I were already planning the rebuilding of the property in Redhill Road. In particular, I needed to be on hand not only to monitor the building projects but to oversee very significant other works on the Callignee property undertaken by a range of organisations. The most significant of these was Telstra, who were keen to install optic-fibre cable in the underground channels which ran along both the eastern and northern boundaries of the property. Given the post-fire terrain, free of vegetation, they saw it as a unique opportunity to implement long-planned works.

The unit in Hickox Street had a comfortable living room, a couple of bedrooms and all mod cons. It also had a lock-up garage which would become an important storage point. At $450 per week, it was good value. It was a long time since I had been a tenant, and I had to get used to the idea of being beholden to a landlord. But, in the circumstances, Stockdale & Leggo were fairly amenable. And the neighbours were quiet and kept themselves to themselves. The location was pretty handy for both the shopping centre across the Princes Highway and the railway station which was a 10-minute walk away. In the initial days, I continued my journeys to Melbourne by car to visit my mother. But, when a free rail-pass became available, Andrew and I eventually set up a two car arrangement with his "retired" Suzuki coming back into service and located in Kew so that I had a car at each end.

When I look at my notes for the time, there was no shortage of things to do and, in that first month of suburban living, I had a lengthy agenda arising from the fire. This included the following:

a)   Conduct of a survey of the boundaries, with a local company undertaking to complete the works at cost.
b)   Organising a range of fencing projects, with each of the main four boundaries requiring a different approach determined by respective neighbours.[224]
c)   Securing rights to the unused government road that ran along the northern boundary.
d)   Planning for replacement of the shed.
e)   Sourcing an architect and builder for the new house.

---

[224] To the north, the boundary was with a farmer, to the west, there were a number of small holdings, to the south there was HVP, and along the east was the reserve adjacent to the sealed Redhill Road managed by the Council.

f)   Preparing for a meeting with the Royal Commission.

g)   Auditing the solar-power system which eventually involved removal of the batteries and invertor to Melbourne for testing and safe keeping.

h)   Clearance of dangerous trees.

i)   Demolition of the house and site clearance, and

j)   Audit of the water tanks and septic tank.

In no time, it was April when Andrew and I attended the preliminary hearing of the Royal Commission. On 14 April, all insurance monies were received, just nine weeks after the fire. This was also the day on which I was for the first time contacted by my Council appointed Case Manager, a fellow named Adrian Giannini. This would be the start of a remarkable relationship that would last for 18 months. Adrian was a Youth Counsellor working for the Berry Street family-support organisation, and had been temporarily redeployed to join a team of Case Managers giving one-on-one support to fire victims. He was a short guy with a dapper beard who lived in Boolarra and had had his own close encounter with the fires which passed near his home a week before the Churchill fire. In his spare time he was a musician. His support during what was the most difficult period in my life was outstanding. He provided sensitive and helpful personal counselling as I began to work my way through the post disaster trauma. And over the next twelve months he provided a huge amount of advice about my rights and entitlements, including access to all sorts of charitable gifts and, biggest of all, an allocation of $75,000 from the Victorian Bushfire Relief Fund.[225] Entitlement to this latter charitable donation was far from straightforward. Allocations were made only to people who had lost their principal residence and, on an initial reading by those in authority, the house in Callignee was a holiday home. But, as established in Chapter 22, Callignee was my permanent residence. I had established it as such when applying for the Commonwealth grant for the solar power system. And I had taken up residence six months before the fire. Eventually, after at one stage receiving a communication that I was suspected of trying to make a false claim, the authorities relented and the payment came through. As I was trying to settle in Hickox Street, another disaster struck. As will be recounted in Chapter 29, on 20 May my mother died after her long struggle with cancer. One consequence is that I had to

---

[225] This relief fund, which eventually reached $350 million, had been established to support fire victims and was managed by the Australian Red Cross Society.

hurriedly remove her final effects from her Broughton Hall Nursing Home to Hickox Street. Andrew was a huge help as we hired a van, and transported most of her worldly goods for storage in the shed.

Whilst living in Traralgon, I visited the property in Callignee nearly every day. There was so much going on there. And it wasn't all work. When hanging out at the shed, I continued to receive many visitors. This included a coach load of football entities travelling with a Channel 10 journalist and photographer. On board was none other than the Coach of the Essendon Football Club, Kevin Sheedy, accompanied by Adam Ramanauskas, John Barnes, and Collingwood player Brodie Holland. Kevin and I had a most enlightening chat as we lent on the remnant of the wooden boundary fence (which stands to this day), and Adam gave me a much needed hug.

Whilst all of this was going on, I did manage to find some leisure time consistent with my existence in Traralgon. In particular, I joined the Traralgon Bridge Club which had recently relocated to a site adjacent to the Traralgon Recreation Reserve. I also enrolled at a gym in Churchill at the Council Leisure Centre. And, a stone's throw away, there was a pleasant walk around the Railway Reserve.

On 19 October, Andrew and I attended the formal hearings of the Royal Commission, which were held at the Traralgon Winery owned by no less than the retired estate agent from whom we had purchased the Callignee property, Leon Hammond. It was a traumatic experience in which both I and Andrew gave evidence. I was cross examined by counsel representing the State government who was at pains to obtain an admission that we had chosen to defend the property despite warnings from the government of the dangers presented. He also drew attention to the inadequacy of our water pump despite an acknowledgement that we had otherwise made appropriate preparations. At the end of my evidence, the Chair asked me about the state of the reserve. At this point, I broke down, unable to contain my grief and I was excused. Afterwards, I was interviewed by the media giving the first of many interviews over the next twelve months.

Much of my time in the following eighteen months were spent on the commissioning and building of the new house on the property and an account of this is provided in the next Chapter. In the meantime, I had other pre-occupations. In the second half of 2009, I had to go through a long and tedious process of winding up my mother's estate. In the spring, I was contacted by a group of ornithologists who completed the first of several bird surveys. As temperatures rose in January 2010, smoke started to rise from the ground in one of the gullies. At first we thought this was probably a vestigial burning of a root system. But attempts by the CFA to extinguish the fire were unsuccessful. Eventually, Loy Yang Power station came to the rescue. They sensitively excavated the ground and found a seam of coal/peat which was capped at no expense. In April, I gave an interview to the local newspaper on the recovery of the nature reserve and, in May, the Council wound up the Case Manager's work. In June I took a holiday in the UK and, on my return, I found the shed infested with mice which required urgent treatment. Meanwhile, the property was blooming with all manner of new growth including an amazing array of Xanthoria Minor with creamy white stems. In October, I attended a very interesting Council briefing on the establishment of what was called a LEAP programme of which there is more in Chapter 29. Finally, in April 2011, my time at Hickox Street came to an end. The new house in Callignee was not ready for reasons that will be explained in Chapter 25. So, for a while, I had to make do with commuting to Callignee from Melbourne. It was the end of a strange era of living in limbo.

25: Paradise Regained – At a Price

Within a few short months of the 2009 fire, Andrew and I began to think about our future on the block. Still in shock, there was a point when I wondered whether we had tempted fate by enforcing the deal to purchase the land with reluctant vendors. Were we really destined to own this piece of land and had we brought misfortune upon ourselves? For a short while, while in a more rational frame of mind, Andrew was also ambivalent. But the doubts we both experienced soon passed, and were replaced by a kind of compulsion to face disaster with defiance. Although there was certainly conversation about whether we wanted to put ourselves in harm's way again, we both came to the view that we were determined to build again and do it better than before.

So it was, from a very early stage, that the toe-hold we had on the property became the grim but poignant foundation of a new beginning. In particular, with the shed quickly replaced by a new construction of identical design, the water tanks and septic tanks intact, and the first signs of life from the devastated vegetation, it seemed that all was not lost. And once the site had been cleared by Grocon on 2 May, it was like we had a new "green field", although at this stage all you could see was grey/black ground with a whiff in the air of sulphur and ash.

The new housing project commenced with a considerable stroke of good fortune. Following the fires, the Building Designers Association of Victoria offered to provide free architectural services to all those wishing to rebuild. In mid-April, we took them up and received offers to complete a design from six architects. We proceeded to interview, in what was a strange reversal of the usual supplier-client relationship. And it was with some embarrassment that I had to inform five of the applicants that we had decided not to take up their generous offer! We engaged a fellow named Zol Nagy who had offices in Clayton. And we met with him for the first time on 8 May, just three months after the fire.

Zol was a charming and mildly-mannered chap in his late 30s with an existing track-record in innovative design. Every conversation with him was an enlightening experience as his creative mind engaged with our dream of what we wanted. After specifying our requirements, he made a site visit and then began the lengthy process of producing a series of alternative designs for the house that would fit within the dimensions and topography of the Callignee building site. This went through several iterations, and we didn't reach the point of signing off the design and specification until late October. More than anything, this long gestation period was a function of both our uncertainty about the design and the need for features that made the building as safe as it reasonably could be in resisting a future bushfire. As regards safety, the building materials were key, and Andrew in particular spent a huge amount of time researching options, with me following up on many leads. The outcome was a house with a number of important structural features including the following.

a)   A concrete base rather than the perishable wooden stumps used with the first house.
b)   A steel frame in place of the previous wooden frame.
c)   Hebel (aerated concrete) panel walls, with metal cladding instead of hardi-board used in the previous house, and stone sections.
d)   A colour bond roof, as before, but with metal as opposed to plastic fitments for venting.
e)   A silicon wrap around the roof space, designed to withstand 1,000 degrees.
f)   Steel pillars around a decking made of fire-resistant Black Butt wood, which was our only real design weakness in terms of fire vulnerability.
g)   Windows with high-grade double-glazing for heat resistance and insulation.
h)   Fire-resistant metal shutters to cover all the glazing.
i)   High fire rated insulation in the walls and roof.
j)   Fire-resistant bamboo front door and internal connecting door.

The specification for the prospective builder included an extensive set of requirements for internal fixtures and fittings, the colour scheme, plumbing, electrical circuits and much more. Zol Nagy patiently worked through all our needs and came up with an elegant design that more than matched our dream.

Whilst designing the building, there was also a need to obtain a new Building Permit. Since the original build, the government had ramped up the regime for allowing development in fire-prone areas. The new system was called BAL ("Bushfire Attack Level"), and required that building materials must meet certain minimal standards consistent with an assessed level of risk for a given site. In the case of 200 Redhill Road, there were some issues in terms of proximity to the bush and the slope of adjacent land. But, after several adjustments to the position of the house, we secured a BAL 29 rating. In broad terms, this meant that we had to build with materials that would withstand 290°C for one hour. Our specification more than complied with this provision. Indeed, the main building materials were consistent with the higher BAL 40 rating, and the silicon lining in the roof was BAL Flame Zone (meaning it could withstand 1,000°C for one hour).

Whilst we were still working on the specification, and obtaining the Building Permit, I began to identify a range of local builders willing to build in the bush. There was quite a field, and I short-listed and met about five to whom I sent the specification and a request for a tender. For most of them, the custom-built nature of the house was quite a challenge with one fellow refusing to build with a metal frame, and others struggling to reconcile a custom build with the more conventional "off-the-shelf" model. As we were to find out, the custom build, albeit accompanied by the most detailed and clearly written specification, would provide a challenge to any local builder. It required a very special level of supervision and attention to detail, particularly with many aspects of the build in the hands of sub-contractors.

After a pretty frustrating process of vetting, one company appeared to stand out, in terms of well-presented estimates, affordability, and an apparent understanding of the nature and scope of the build. Cavalier Homes were based in Traralgon and quoted $261,000. Following a final meeting with them just before Christmas, we signed a contract on 20 January 2010 with completion scheduled for 16 November 2010. In the event, we did not complete our dealings with this organisation until twelve months later at a VCAT hearing in November 2011, although I was able to take up a form of residence in April of that year.[226]

The story of what went wrong with the building of the new house could be the subject of a book all of its own, and it would not make happy reading. The kind of issues that arose have cropped up in many episodes of the TV programme *Grand Designs* and, given the circumstances of two people recovering from the trauma of fire, it was astonishing that we survived without serious health issues (although I did suffer some PTSD following completion).[227] The main factors were that in quoting for the project (in cost and time frame) the company did not take into account the complexity of the build, and the site manager lacked diligence in reading the specification, placing orders, supervising sub-contractors, and liaising with people that we engaged for specialist works. This

---

[226] VCAT is the Victorian Civil and Administrative Tribunal which mediates civil disputes.
[227] PTSD is Post-Traumatic Stress Disorder.

combination of factors led to incorrect orders, insufficient supply of materials, mistakes and the need for reworking, and ultimately a major delay in completion and a significant blow-out in the cost. The problems were many and varied, and including the following.

a) The number of Hebel panels required was under-estimated, and installation and rendering was piecemeal with a need to rework.

b) The quantity of colorbond sheets required was insufficient and, when installed, the frame and sheets did not cover the building requiring a late roof extension.

c) The kitchen fittings failed to accommodate a waterfall feature and drawers had to be remodelled.

d) Tiling of laundry, bathrooms and kitchen was botched, with the wrong tiles and grouting. It had to be redone.

e) Trenches for plumbing compromised electrical cabling.

f) Cavalier refused to undertake a number of works such as retaining walls and porch steps although they were in the specification.

g) The decking did not comply with fire regulations and had to be ripped up and done again.

h) The electricians came all the way from Pakenham and did not complete their works in a timely manner.

i) The architraves and skirting boards were not as specified.

j) The vents and other fittings on the roof were not steel but plastic and had to be replaced.

k) Downpipes were the wrong profile.

l) Ceiling fans were not installed as specified on plans.

m) Delays in supplies made it necessary to extend the period during which scaffolding was required.

o) There was damage to window frames in course of rendering.

p) On completion, the builder left a quagmire of clay and mud around the house with inadequate drainage.

Being a witness to all these errors was painful in the extreme, causing endless discussions about how to respond between Andrew and me which tested our relationship. But at least I was able to keep an eagle eye on progress. Strictly speaking, clients are not allowed on a building site unless they are accompanied by the Site Manager. But in his frequent absence this was impossible to enforce. I should also add that the poor performance did not apply to all works. A great deal of the work was carried out in a timely and proficient manner.[228]

In any event, as milestones came and went, it was clear that the deadline for completion would not be met and the list of defects was growing. Christmas came and went and, in March 2011, we presented a preliminary Defects List. Almost immediately, the company issued a formal extension notice citing unhelpful weather and interference by the clients as the reasons for delay. As a consequence, we had the first of several meetings with Cavalier management in which we pointed out that they had frequently failed to follow the specification and that our repeated intervention had been necessary to ensure compliance. Then we were hit with a real shock. Cavalier issued us with several Notices of Variation with demands for additional payments.

In the next few weeks and then months, debate over the delays and variation claims continued, even as a range of works were in hand to complete the project. And by mutual agreement on 6 June 2011 I was unofficially allowed to take up residence, following my removal from the rented property in Traralgon which was originally scheduled to meet the November 2010 completion date. In August, the Certificate of Occupancy was issued. Eventually, with an impasse on the mounting variation claims from Cavalier, things came to a head. On 19 August, they issued a formal statement of claim for payment of variations of $30,960.08, with an offer to settle for $20,000 if we paid in the next few days. We rejected this claim and eventually made a counter claim for $24,932. For several weeks, there was an impasse. Then, in September, they issued us with a VCAT notice for formal mediation.

The reference to VCAT was quite a shock, but we should have anticipated it because it was normal practice in troubled building projects. The battle lines were clearly drawn and, unacquainted with VCAT proceedings, I felt the need for some legal support. We engaged a barrister, Tim Whitehead, who provided advice, and accompanied us at the VCAT hearing which was held at 10.00 am on 8 November 2011 in Melbourne.

The VCAT process was interesting. The two parties were established in separate rooms, and the mediator engaged in a form of shuttle diplomacy in which we gave him our views about the Cavalier claim and he took our argument to them who then gave a response. We had assembled an argument to deal with each of the elements in Cavalier's claim and we knocked them off one by one. We were greatly assisted by

---

[228] The concreter was highly competent but had a grouch. He did not appreciate the shape with many non 90° angles!

the fact that I had a blow-by-blow account in the daily log that I had maintained throughout the period. It strengthened the mediator's resolve in sustaining our case. We had a break for lunch and then the bartering continued. By 3.30pm we had got Cavalier to reduce their claim to $5,000 and were contemplating pursuit of our claim on them. But, on his latest visit, the mediator told us that the other party was getting very tetchy. He said that, in his experience, there usually came a point where the party that was conceding had had enough. He sensed this was the point and, all things considered, we took the view that $5,000 was worth it to bring the whole saga to an end. So we settled. And this wasn't just the end of the building battle. In a way, it was also the conclusion of the saga which had started with the fire on 7 February 2009. I was greatly relieved. And Andrew and I retreated to a coffee shop to lick our wounds. I think we felt vindicated, although I had the legal bill to settle. But it had been worth standing up to negligence and incompetence as a matter of principle. Now some form of normal life could resume.

PART SEVEN

A PARENT LOST AND A PARENT GAINED

26: Eunice's Twilight Years

One of the most difficult things about migration is the people that you leave behind. For me, my mother Eunice was obviously an essential other. And when I left England in 1986 she was nudging 70 years of age. In the immediate years that followed, we spent significant time together alternating between England and Australia. As she used to say, we actually spent more time together than if I were living in the UK.

As my mother aged, we got to the point where there was a need for a serious family discussion about her dotage. These deliberations focussed on who would take responsibility for her welfare in her final years, with the suitability of alternative locations also a factor. Ultimately, it was her call and, in late 1994, she decided that she would like to migrate to Australia on the basis of living close to but not with me. This was of course easier said than done. In her late 70s, her age and the upheaval involved might have precluded such a move. But, after all the years of being a War Widow and fending for herself whilst raising two sons, my mother was a fearless and intrepid lady. And she had no significant health issues apart from a niggling back and a little osteo-arthritis. So, in early 1995, she made application to migrate and, under the points system applicable at the time, she was successful.[229] This triggered a huge amount of work at her end, putting her house on the market and packing up. She also had to cope with saying goodbye to a lifetime of friends acquired in Nottingham and around the UK. It was brave stuff for a 78-year-old. Eventually, with the assistance of my brother, her home in Nottingham was sold to a couple from Hong Kong – a sign of the times, as that territory was about to be transferred back into the hands of People's Republic of China. And she finally left the country on 26 September 1995, never to see those shores again.

Meanwhile, in Australia, I began the process of finding Eunice somewhere to live. It was a time when prices had not yet gone through the roof and there were plenty of options. It didn't take long to find 10 Edgevale Road Kew, which was just two kilometres from my place in High Street. It was a two bedroomed bungalow opposite a reserve, and sat on a rise, with both a front and a secluded back garden. And it was on the corner with Barkers Road with a short walk to a milk bar and, across the road, a café and convenience store. It was a bit of a trail up to

---

[229] Given good health, financial independence, and one of two sons living in Australia as a permanent resident, she qualified under the family reunion scheme.

the centre of Kew for shopping and other amenities. But my mother was fit and well. The asking price for the house, over which we did not quibble, was $150,000 and was more than covered by the sum received from the sale of her home in Nottingham. Possession was scheduled for 22 December.

After a period of living with me in High Street, which included visits to the quarantine centre in Fairfield for TB tests, numerous orientation activities, and a very memorable Christmas lunch with friends Ruth and Bill Duffy at their home in Carlton, Eunice moved into 10 Edgevale Road on 28 December 1995 and would live there happily for the next 13 years.[230]

When I look back to those days, I never cease to be amazed by my mother's resilience. She took to living in Kew like a duck to water, although she quickly made a significant decision which had the potential to be a little isolating. She had one look at the preponderance of trams and special road rules in Melbourne, such as "hook turns", and decided to give up driving. This meant that, for local travel, she depended on trams, discount taxis, and lifts from me and others. More than anything, her ability to assimilate was based on the fact that she had an outward going and friendly personality. And, amongst people of her own age group, she was almost universally welcomed. Contemporary middle-class people in Kew mostly identified as being British and were delighted to be acquainted with a real English lady. My mother joined in a number of local activities. From her visits to stay with me over the previous ten years she was already known to the clergy and congregation of the local Anglican Church, Holy Trinity. And she quickly became a regular attender, getting to know the vicar and others who were only too pleased to give her lift to and from Sunday services. She also joined the Kew Bridge Club, which in those days was located up some stairs above a shop in Cotham Road. And, ever mindful of keeping fit, she joined the local Leisure Centre where she went swimming every week. She also made regular visits to the city by tram to visit the department stores and stop for a spot of lunch, making friends along the way. And she also discovered an excellent Council service that provided a lift to and from the local supermarket in Kew. During the course of a year, we went on several overnight trips, visiting national parks, and other tourist

---

[230] The migration health checks and related arrangements for a person of Eunice's age were significant. In addition to the Fairfield screening, we also had to lodge a bond which was held by the government for three years as surety against a Medicare claims.

locations.[231] And commencing in 1996, we re-established a traditional family Christmas, with roast turkey and plum pudding despite the warm summer weather. On these occasions, for a good many years, we would be joined by Andrew and eventually Brittany with the full works of a Christmas tree with piles of presents.

Having said all this, it wasn't all plain sailing. When she purchased the Edgevale Road property, she had a beautiful native garden and patio at the rear, with table and chairs under the shade of a Jacaranda tree. However, she decided that she wanted plants and flowers to remind her of England. And one day I found that her gardener had ripped out a significant number of beautiful natives and planted roses and other British plants. It was one of the few cases when she and I had a falling out which I instantly regretted. It was the only time she said she wanted to go home and we soon made up. She also had minor issues with the neighbours. The house immediately to her rear was rented by students and, over the years, some were a little noisy. But with growing deafness she became oblivious. Later, there was a lad with a dog that barked all day. Mind you we saw the funny side of that. The surname of the student was Yap and he lived in Barker's Road. My mother also woke up one day to find that her letter box had been blown up during the night. I explained that this was a rite of passage for the local youth. She also had a constant battle with people parking their cars immediately outside the house because it blocked her view of the reserve. Her politely worded notes, requesting that the owners of 4WD vehicles desisted from parking their "bus" in front of her house, were the cause of some amusement by local people.

During the early days of living in Kew my mother was fiercely independent. However, in late December 2001, when she was approaching her 85th birthday, she developed a severe gastric condition which lasted for several days during the visit of family from England (my brother's first wife Margie, and her grown-up children Alex Wigginton and Julia Stannard). She made nothing of it and soldiered on. Then, in May 2002, she collapsed in the street, with nausea and diarrhoea. She was rushed to St Vincent's Private Hospital for tests, and was diagnosed with an ulcer and an early-stage lymphoma. When I visited her, she turned to me to say that "*this was it*", and that "*I've had*

---

[231] One of her favourite spots was Mount Buffalo National Park, and we stayed at the Chalet on several occasions. During the day, she would stay in the comfortable public rooms at the Chalet, while I went out bush-walking. In the evening we'd dine, with fine wine, and a game of scrabble to follow in one of the sitting rooms with a log fire burning.

had a good innings", clearly indicating that there was no place in her mind for any treatment or recovery. Not surprisingly, I was deeply upset, and I well remember that shortly after I had to go to Darwin for an ARCBS board meeting. As I sat one evening in my hotel room, I received a call from my nephew Alex and was overcome with grief.

Despite our initial response, Eunice's cancer diagnosis was not the end of the story by a long chalk. Her condition was stabilised and, after extensive screening, she returned home and came under the care of an oncologist named Alan Zimet. Mr Zimet prescribed a programme of chemotherapy to be administered through six doses over about six months. And he suggested that, if the treatment was successful, she might expect at least five years of remission. After some investigation of what was involved, Eunice agreed to this treatment, attending the Outpatient Ward at the Epworth Hospital in Richmond. And, as the months unfolded, she responded very well. Mind you, she did have some side effects, including loss of hair. As was so typical of her, she made light of it as we went shopping to buy a wig. In any event, by late 2002, Mr Zimet advised that she was in remission with a requirement for monitoring every six months. And so, duly chastened, she resumed normal life. However, she did make one definitive statement. If the cancer returned, she would never have chemotherapy again. But we agreed that we'd face that bridge when we came to it. In the meantime, she agreed that following her reprieve we should take the opportunity to make a record of her life and times. I conducted several interviews and, in the course of her recollections, she reminisced about my father. This led to some investigations about his military career and untimely death. We were able to get a copy of his military record and a map reference for the crash of his plane in Burma. But this revealed little of his activities. And the references to his crash and burial left unanswered questions apart from a statement that he was "Missing in Action". We left it at that.

In the next five years, as Eunice's life extended towards her ninetieth year, she continued to do all the things that she had done before, with the help of a cleaning lady and a gardener. Reluctantly, she adopted a stick for when she went walking, and in her 90s she eventually graduated to a mobile walking frame. However, she kept up her swimming, walked around the block every day, and we continued our trips to all corners of Victoria. In January 2007, we had a 90th Birthday Party at Edgevale Road with 25 guests and catering by the café across the road. It was a happy day, with Eunice surrounded by a lovely cross-section of people that she

281

Eunice's 90th Birthday

had come to know, and amusing speeches. Andrew broke from his holiday on Kangaroo Island to join us, and grand-daughter Julia and her partner Mark were visitors from England.

As it happened, Eunice's 90th birthday celebration turned out to be a watershed. In August 2007, she had a gastric turn. Then in September, whilst staying at an Anglicare Nursing Home called Broughton Hall as her house was being restumped, she had breathing problems with water on the lung. In October, Mr Zimet had diagnosed a return of the lymphoma and, in response, she quickly reiterated her opposition to further chemotherapy. However, Mr Zimet told us that the treatment for lymphoma had improved radically since 2002 and that there was now a drug which stimulated the body's immune system to fight the cancer cells. In a private aside which was challenging, he also told me that, if Eunice did not take the drug, she didn't have long to live. In what was a great challenge for both of us, Eunice and I discussed the position. I would say to her that it was her decision and I would respect how she felt. And she kept saying to me *"I don't want you to be upset when I die. You won't be upset, will you?"* This was a question to which there was no correct answer.

After some reflection, in early November, Eunice decided to give the new treatment a go and she seemed to cope with the first dose. At the time, Andrew and I were in Callignee preparing the site for the new house. At 7.00 am one morning, I got a call from a hospital to say that Eunice was in hospital and fighting for her life. Leaving the car with Andrew, I jumped on the train and rushed to her bed side. Not for the first time in this final period of her life, it was a false alarm. She had reacted badly to a change in her blood-pressure medication and, thinking that she was dying, she had physically resisted resuscitation! She survived this incident, but she lost some ability to speak properly for a few days as the result of a mini stroke. Afterwards, she recuperated in the Caritas Christi Palliative Care unit in Studley Park Road, and we reviewed whether she wanted to continue with the chemotherapy. It was a strange place to be discussing a matter of life or death. Nearly all the other residents were in their last days, with successive co-habitants in her shared room expiring during the night. After two weeks, she walked out alive and relatively well.

At this point it was too early to say whether the treatment was working and, having started, Eunice decided to continue. Given the impact on her general health and need for intensive care, after each dose she had a further period of recuperation at the hospice. At one stage, she had minor surgery to insert a pace-maker because of heart issues. By April 2008 the course of six doses had been completed and she had returned home. We then had a general review of her condition with Mr Zimet who told us that the cancer had not disappeared but was getting no worse. In all the circumstances, he advised that we monitor the status every few months before attempting any further treatment.

During this challenging period, we gave serious consideration to whether Eunice could continue independent living. In the previous six months, we had already made several modifications to the house, she had registered with a rapid response service with an emergency button on a chain around her neck, and we had organised "Meals on Wheels". But on a number of occasions she fell out of bed and, on more than one occasion, I was called to Epworth Hospital as she had called an ambulance. Miraculously, she never broke a bone. The problem was that, although she had all her mental capacities, these incidents of physical incapability were undermining her confidence. So, with the costs well within her means, we investigated the possibility of her moving into a retirement home with access to supported living. There were quite a few options, with some providing different levels of independence as a person's health and need for support evolved. Having already stayed there during her re-stumping episode, Eunice was attracted to Broughton Hall and she went on the waiting list for a room. In the meantime, we put Edgevale Road on the market. It didn't take long to find a buyer. By this time, a room had become available at Broughton Hall and she moved into Room 131 on 20 June 2008, with most of her house contents transported to the new house in Callignee.

So began the final phase of Eunice's life which lasted less than twelve months. Her bed-sitting room with en-suite had sufficient space for a lounge chair, desk, and china cabinet, with favourite pictures on the wall. The facility was reasonably well managed with a dining room and lounges. And there was a private suite that you could hire for family and other gatherings. In the grounds there were seats and walking paths. However, it did feel a bit like an open prison. Doors for leaving the building had locks with exit codes and gates from the garden to the street were similarly secured. And, more importantly for Eunice's mental state, the other inmates were a motley collection of humanity. There were some younger disabled folk who were friendly enough and seemingly out of place. But the majority were elderly and in varying states of mental decline. Eunice found a few people with whom she could commune, but the company of people with advanced dementia at meal times was especially depressing. And strange things happened. One day, on her return from lunch she found an elderly lady sitting in her room who had to be ejected. And on another occasion some cash from her purse went missing, which was reported without resolution.

During this time, I visited several times a week, and took Eunice out for trips to cafes and to visit friends. But, as the months unfolded, the disease began to take hold. She never lost her mental capacity, but the environment, and the weight of sickness and drugs to maintain a stable condition, began to take its toll on both her physical and mental health. We spent Christmas at my unit in Kew and, with a little help and advice, I did the cooking. Then, on 7 February, came the fire at Callignee. On that same day, Eunice was rushed to hospital and put into intensive care for several days. The first I knew of it was when I contacted her to tell her that Andrew and I had survived the fire. It was not a good day.

The decline and death of a parent, particularly when you only have one, is a seminal moment. It was a wretched time. While I struggled to recover from the trauma of the fire, Eunice was beginning to fade and I felt like I was between a rock and a hard place. I remember saying to her that she was losing weight, and even suggested that she might be starving herself, which she vehemently denied. With the benefit of hindsight, what I now believe is that the morphine she was being given to cope with pain was slowly closing down her bodily functions. And I sometimes reproach myself that I did not do enough to engage with what was happening to her. In any event, the final weeks of her life are burnt into my memory. There were frequent visits to the nursing home, and sometimes the hospital, and lonely trips back and forth down the Princes

Highway to check on the Callignee property. In late May, the end came in a graceful way that reflected Eunice's indomitable character. The day before she died, we played our last game of Scrabble in the games room. At 5.00 pm, I left the Nursing home. Soon after I arrived home, I got a call saying that I had better come quickly because my mother was about to die. I rushed to the nursing home and went to her room. There she was, sitting up in bed. She smiled, with her bright blue eyes and, as I sat in the chair next to her bed, she leaned over and with typical humour said *"I think I got ahead of myself there"*. After an hour or so of our usual chatter, I left her for the night and, on the way out, a nurse pulled me to one side. She told me not get my hopes up. Before a person dies, they often rally just one more time. The next morning, Wednesday 20 May, I got another call to say that Eunice was slipping away. I rushed to her bedside to witness her final moments. She was unconscious and I said my goodbyes. Then, even as I briefly sat with her holding a still warm hand, I felt that the person that I had known all my life was no more. Before me was a lifeless body and the spirit had moved on.

The immediate aftermath was swift and relentless. As is the normal course of events after a death, vacant nursing home rooms are quickly on the market for occupation by another. Eunice's body was immediately removed to a mortuary, and I was given 48 hours to remove her effects. With Andrew's help, on the Friday we hired a van, loaded up, and drove to Traralgon where her belongings were deposited in the shed adjacent to the unit I had hired after the fire. In the meantime, I had contacted my brother Michael who decided to fly to Australia for the funeral which was scheduled for the following Tuesday. Thanks to my mother's practical approach to life, the work required in preparing for the church service was minimal. About six months before she died, she had insisted that we visit a Funeral Director, and had already determined the model of her coffin, arrangements for the service and cremation, and even the hymns and music. These included the 23rd Psalm (the Lord is My Shepherd), Corinthians 1 Verse 13 which is a reflection on Love, and some favourite poetry. The Service was held in Trinity Church and was attended by a considerable group of friends as well as the immediate family. As is the Australian custom, at the rear of the church was a table on which was displayed pictures and belongings from various stages in Eunice's life. This included unfinished knitting, spectacles, examples of her embroidery, and pictures she had painted. And during the service, at which both Michael and I spoke, she had organised the playing of the hymn Finlandia by Sibelius which to this day still brings tears to my eyes whenever I hear it. The reception was held in the church rooms and, in the evening, the family went out to dinner in Camberwell. A few days later, I received the ashes. In due course, as agreed with my mother, these would be split into three parts. A third was deposited in an unmarked spot in the memorial garden next to the Holy Trinity church in Kew, where we had a brief commemoration service. Later in the year, I took ashes to England and this second tranche was buried under the chestnut tree outside Eunice's office at Nottingham University. The Anglican Chaplain conducted a brief service. Later, with my nephew Alex's help, we got permission to install a wooden seat just beyond that tree with a plaque commemorating her life and time at the University. The final part of her ashes remains to this day in Kew, awaiting delivery to the same spot in Mewaing, Myanmar where my father lies.

Finally came the execution of Eunice's will. With the international dimension, resolution consumed a lot of time and effort over many months. But eventually it was done, with disbursement of funds completed on 19 December 2009. Residual effects were stored away in the house at Kew and life continued as it must. Grief was slow to ebb, and I did my best to fulfil my mother's wish *"not to be upset"*. But you never stop grieving a beloved parent who is no more. The best I could do was to frequently recall what a great human being she had been.

As we will see in the next two chapters, despite my mother's death, her spirit lived on. And when I eventually got round to examining her personal effects I was in for a surprise. Eunice left behind quite a few engaging questions and just enough information to seek and find some answers. The results of my investigations would bring a whole new meaning to my life.

27: The Mists of Time

After the fire, and the death of my mother, I was far from well. Both events had taken a big toll, with moments when I felt depressed and hopeless. I took professional advice, and the early commitment to rebuilding the house had provided a consuming focus in which Andrew and I persisted for the best part of three years.

In early 2012, with completion of the VCAT hearing over the housing dispute, I came to a grinding halt with another bout of PTSD. To recover, I just sank back into enjoying the property at Callignee, participating in some community work, watching some local footy at the weekend, and catching up with family and friends in Melbourne. There was a lot to do in completing all sorts of loose ends at the house, and by now the regrowth of vegetation on the block required urgent attention as it threatened to envelop the walking tracks. I continued to work at the ACF and visited my nephew Alex and his wife Julia who were currently living in Newport, NSW. And later in the year I went to Nepal and Bhutan for spiritual renewal, with an uplifting visit to the Tiger's Nest.[232]

Towards the end of 2012 I started to recover and decided it was time to go through some of my mother's belongings that were variously located in Kew and Callignee. One item was a metal box around 30 cm by 15 cm with a key and a handle on the top. I'd been aware of this container of "relics" for some time, and I knew it was a place where my mother kept personal items including letters, military insignia, and other papers. In fact, I'd known about this box from childhood days when our home in Ranelagh Grove Nottingham contained a variety of things associated with my father. The artefacts included his pipes, parachute, brief case, Sam Browne leather strapping, compass, and personal army knife. Anyway, I found this box in the shed and opened it up. As I examined the contents, I started to think about the parent that I'd never known. And, with a trip to the UK planned for 2013, to attend the 500th Anniversary of the founding of my school in Nottingham, I decided that I should pay a visit to the British National Archives ("BNA") to see if I could uncover more history about my father and his wartime exploits. In June 2013, whilst staying with my nephew who had returned from Australia and was now living in Richmond, I duly made the first of what would be many visits to the BNA.

---

[232] The Tiger's Nest is a remote and lofty monastery located near Paro, constructed in 1692 near the cave occupied by Guru Rinpoche who brought Buddhism to Bhutan.

The BNA is a modern building off the South Circular Road, not far from Kew Gardens. My first visit was exploratory and I had no idea what I would find. I recalled the data I had obtained ten years earlier about my father's military record, his posting as *"Mission in Action"* following a plane crash in Burma, a burial at *"Pongyichaung"* in a place called Mewaing, and his name etched on a column at the main cemetery in Yangon. And I began by searching records relating to the awarding of OBE medals. As I leafed through papers referring to my father, I stumbled across a reference to an organisation called the Special Operations Executive ("SOE"). At this point, it meant nothing to me, but I asked the staff and they directed me to a collection of documents which gave an account of SOE activities in various theatres of the Second World War. It slowly dawned on me that this organisation was not part of the British regular army. On this first visit to the BNA, I also took the opportunity to trace some family history through official records of Births, Deaths, and Marriages. I didn't make much progress but began to find my way around the system.

In the next few weeks, I had two strokes of luck which proved hugely valuable in pursuing my research. During this visit to the UK, I met up with two old friends from university days, Dick Gupwell and Roger Mallion. I told Dick about my SOE discovery and he came up with the name of a woman he knew at the Burma office of the EU, Sally Stein (now Sally McLean), and a colleague of hers who was a retired London University historian named Colonel Sam Pope, both of whom had knowledge of SOE in Burma. Then, on my return to Australia, I caught up with my friend Robert Agnew. On telling him about my interest in Burma, he shared with me that his son Toby used to play football for Macedon with a chap named Tom Kean who now lived in Burma. Toby had recently bumped into Tom on a visit to Wilson's Prom National Park and discovered that he worked as journalist in Yangon.

In the months that followed, I followed up both of these leads, and results of my initial enquiries at the BNA. Dick's contacts provided me with amazing material about SOE activity in Burma. And Tom Kean would prove an enormous help in engaging with present-day Myanmar. And, having discovered the existence of SOE, I started to acquire a library of books about the work of that organisation. In several accounts, I came across references to my father, and it slowly dawned on me that I was on the cusp of revealing what might be an amazing untold story. It was at this point that I decided to write a biography of a man who was virtually unknown to me. It would be a fulfilling voyage of discovery in which I would eventually find a parent that I thought I would never have. It would change how I thought about myself, as well recording for posterity, in the book entitled *"Wig's Secret War"*, the story of a remarkable man.

This was not my first attempt at writing a book. But the history of the blood service, completed ten years before, and based on manifest records and recent memory, had never been published. This was a more daunting task. I started with a skill set that was rudimentary, and very little knowledge of the publication process. That is not to say that I was lacking in ability to write intelligible English. But the style developed in my business career was vastly different from that required in writing a biography.

For the uninitiated, and the benefit of any aspiring writer, I'd like share a little about the journey. The compilation of the biography of a deceased person requires significant detective work on the facts and events associated with the subject's life. In the case of my father, I started with an almost blank sheet. I began with his war-time record, and uncovered a set of official documents designed to obfuscate. In time, I penetrated the strange language used for alluding to covert activities and eventually discovered that, whilst retaining a military rank, my father ("Wig" as I will call him hereafter) was subject to another and clandestine system of designation. To follow the track of his early career in the regular army, I went to many sources. In particular, during my visits to the UK, I visited the Royal Military College at Sandhurst, and the regimental headquarters of the Sherwood Foresters in Nottingham.[233] Through these sources, I was able to trace my father's enlistment, officer training, and life in Britain during the eighteen months' period before deployment to North Africa in 1942. This culminated with his participation in the battle of El Alamein.

The references in military records to covert activities began in late 1942. First he was in Cairo, then there was a transfer to Italy, and finally he was posted to Calcutta. And with each step he was promoted, quickly reaching a military rank of Lt Colonel. To investigate his covert activities, I obtained a pass to enter the secure area of the BNA where, over two years, I spent several months going through hard copy SOE records. I also visited the archival section of the Imperial War Museum in London where there were recordings of interviews with retired SOE officers. On one such a visit, I had a quite extraordinary experience as I

---

[233] The Sherwood Foresters no longer exist as a separate entity having been integrated into the Mercian Regiment.

started to listen through headphones to the recollections recorded in the 1960s of a man who had worked in the SOE Cairo office in 1942. As I sat quietly at a desk, the man began to talk about my father as if it was only yesterday. I could not contain myself and caused quite a disturbance as I uttered an expletive! The work at the BNA was less exciting and more akin to searching for needles in haystacks. But the papers contained many references to my father in Cairo, where he learnt his trade, Italy where he became the leader of air operations in southern and Eastern Europe, and then in Calcutta where he was responsible for similar SOE activity in Burma.

Wig's work in the Far East was of special interest because it led to his untimely death, with 7 September 1945 now registering a special date in my own life. Apart from tracing SOE activity in Burma in 1945, my focus went to the village of Mewaing near the hills where his plane crashed in September 1945. The story of my research into this event is the subject of a detailed account in several chapters in *Wig's Secret War,* and the truth of what happened could never have been achieved without the assistance of some remarkable people, including my local "agent" Naw Jercy and her son Ephraim who undertook several field trips to the location of the plane crash and the burial site.

The other aspect of events in Burma related to the assertion that my father was *"Missing in Action"* ("MIA"). From the early days of my investigations, I felt uncomfortable about this assertion, and I was determined to prove otherwise. I was supported in this by relatives of a number of other casualties from the plane crash with whom I had contact through web sites and blogs relating to wartime air crashes. I was also fortunate to stumble across a very special American who specialised in war-time air-exploits named Matt Poole. He had relevant local maps and even a picture of the plane that crashed. In any event, at the BNA I eventually uncovered a classified official report on the air crash which verified all the relevant details including burial in the grounds of the Mewaing monastery. This enabled me to convince the Commonwealth War Graves Commission to reverse their assertion that my father was MIA. And it led to the establishment of a very special memorial at the Taukkyan War Cemetery which will stand the test of time.

Whilst much of my research was spent on the war-time years, I did not neglect the rest of my father's life. This would prove to consolidate my growing sense of connection with him. Mind you, for anyone seeking to uncover the background of a previously unknown person, a word of warning is required. With my father, research in the census returns and records of Births Deaths and Marriages threw up some surprises and required true detective work down many false trails until the only explanations left for inconsistencies had to be the truth. In a nutshell, the family version of my father's early life with wealthy parents proved to be untrue. He actually obtained his surname from his unmarried mother Hilda, and his father was unknown. The Wigginton clan came from the village of North Luffenham in Rutland where there were family records going back several centuries. Intriguingly, though, despite a modest background, my father went to a private school, learnt to speak "properly", and paid his way into Sandhurst military college, with the help of an unknown benefactor. And he had a previously unknown brother, Edward, whose family I eventually tracked down.

Information about other aspects of my father's early life, at school and at work, were easier to trace. Through records maintained by his school and employer in local Nottingham Archives, I was able to trace his education and work before the war. His work in logistics (scheduling trams) was of special interest to me, since that figured strongly in my own early business career. And I also uncovered evidence of his sporting activity, with rowing, rugby, tennis and running all pastimes that he had in common with his sons.

Through all this detective work, which included many more lines of investigation, I was able to piece together a picture of a most remarkable man of whom I was genuinely proud, and with whom I was able to strongly identify. He was a man with charm and humour, with resilience and courage. The only regret in all this was that my mother was not around to corroborate at least some of what I had uncovered. But then I wondered how much she actually knew. Perhaps my father had kept secrets from her. He wasn't destined for covert services for nothing!

Whilst uncovering the details off my father's personal life, I was conscious of the need for context. This would consume a good deal of research as I knew relatively little about covert activities in the Second World War. Fortunately, in the modern era, there is increasing interest in the work of the SOE, with many books written by those directly involved. I was also fortunate to contact and meet several scholars currently working in the field including an Oxford don, Roderick Bailey. For the wider war-time context, I was lucky to be introduced by a friend Rod Burgess to a Professor of History at Aberystwyth University, Martin Alexander. He had a special interest in modern covert activity and a wider knowledge of the Second World War. These and other individuals directed me to many sources to establish an authoritative account of the history of the war with relevance to my father's SOE activities.

A key aspect of writing a book is the delivery of a manuscript capable of publication in terms of content, length, and readability. Whilst I had no trouble with the content, the length was a significant issue. The first draft of the manuscript reached over 160,000 words and the appendices were significant. This was far too long and, with the help of several editors, I eventually cut this back to 100,000. As writers will tell you, this process is like "killing babies". It's painful and immensely time consuming. In the case of this book, it went on for six months as I gradually approached a tome of publishable length.

Towards the end of my writing phase my mind turned to publication. After trying to find an agent, and exploring self-publishing, I came across an author named Jennifer Elkin who had been through the same experience with a book she had published on the work of her father as a member of one of the Special Duties squadrons deployed by SOE. She put me in touch with Simon Hepworth, who had a special interest in publishing RAF-related books. Simon bravely took me on with a royalties contract, organised the design of the cover, and came up with a name for the book. The learning was enormous and I was very fortunate to have him. When we eventually published in 2017, we launched the book in a restaurant in Wakefield. Subsequently, I pursued various avenues for marketing, assisted by several newspaper articles in Myanmar and the UK, and using a web site I established for the purpose. The sales have been steady and, by 2021 the number was well over 300.

With the journey complete, there was one last thing. I did not write this book for financial gain and, now knowing what sort of man he was, I decided that my father would be happy for proceeds to go to a needy cause. The perfect vehicle was Help for the Forgotten Allies ("H4FA") which raises funds to support surviving Karen guerrillas. This is managed by Sally Kean, and I make regular donations to this charity in honour of my father and to acknowledge the Karen people who so nobly supported the British in the war.

Finally, it is worth reiterating what I said at the outset. Before this journey, I had a single parent who was recently deceased. The writing of the biography not only put on record the achievements of a remarkable man; I now have a second parent to cherish. And the whole experience has given me a taste for writing which will last for the rest of my life.

28: Reconnecting with British Roots

The writing of the book about my father triggered a major change in how I felt about myself. Since migrating to Australia, I had made significant efforts to assimilate and to put behind me the British roots that defined who I was in the first half of my life. Indeed, my advice for a happy life to anyone who migrates is that you must let go of the past and embrace the new culture and nationality. The alternative is to become an unhappy ex-pat who, in Australia, the locals will brand as a whinging Pom.

I had applied this approach to my existence for 30 years with some success. In the early days, I made strong efforts to connect with the relatives already living in Australia. And, even in the early years of living as a permanent resident, I really can't remember anyone referring to me as being "British" in anything but the friendliest of terms. I never sought to speak to people about my British background although, to this day, my accent and vernacular sometimes betray me. I have always been proud to inform people that I am a patriotic Australian citizen, for thirty years I have travelled on an Australian passport and, most important of all, since the early 1990s I have supported the Australian cricket team! For 25 years, I have also barracked for an AFL footy club (Essendon Bombers) which is a prerequisite for living in Victoria. Interestingly, despite the persistence of her English accent, the arrival of my mother even bolstered my definition of myself as one of the 30% of Australians born overseas, and another 20% of Australians with at least one parent born overseas. After all, Australia is an immigrant nation, and all but the original inhabitants are descended from those who have arrived since 1788.

The uncovering of my father's past, and a number of other factors that have emerged in recent years, have brought about a significant change in that outlook. And it may also be the case that, as I have got older, I have started to reflect on my whole life not just the most recent part of it. In any event, I have changed the way I think about myself.

When I think about what constitutes identity, it has many dimensions. When you are a child, and the captive of a family and to a lesser extent a school environment, it is inevitable that you have a relatively strong and focussed view about who you are. In my case, I was one of two sons from a middle-class British mother with a relatively narrow heritage because the wider family only included an aunt and uncle. My father was deceased and, although my mother made strenuous attempts to honour and cherish his memory, his presence was minimal apart from a few of his belongings. My father's parents were dead and apparently he had no siblings. And, on my mother's side, my grandfather was long gone and my maternal grandmother died the same night that I was born. Apart from the sister who lived in Nottingham, my mother had three siblings, but they were distant. I had an uncle living in Sussex whose existence did not emerge until I was a young adult, and I had an uncle and aunt who lived in Australia.

As a youngster, I carried with me some pride in being British but in an understated way. In our family, there was no jingoism. On the contrary, my mother fostered an interest in the world outside Britain. We belonged to the Experiment in International Living, with foreign students staying in our home, and I was encouraged to collect foreign postage stamps to develop an appreciation of the world beyond.[234] From a young age I regularly corresponded with my Australian cousin Ian, and my mother also took every opportunity to take my brother and me abroad, including visits as a child to France and the Netherlands.

As a young adult, this sense of being a citizen of the world was expanded. Still at school, my first independent overseas trip involved a grand tour of Western Europe with three school friends in a campervan. And as a student in the 1960s, I visited both the Soviet Union/Eastern Europe and the USA. I was also strongly influenced by a love of my European heritage, bolstered by membership of the British Liberal Party which embraced the European venture. It was no flight of fancy that I was at the forefront of advocating British membership of the Common Market in the 1970s.

Given our background, both my brother and I easily accommodated the idea of living overseas. In the 1970s my brother lived in New York to pursue a career in architecture, and he would probably have stayed there had it not been for the Vietnam War. I felt a special connection with Australia, fostered by friendship with my cousin Ian. And it's no great surprise that, given my disgust with the direction of UK politics and society in the 1980s, in 1986 I left for the Antipodes.

So why have I reconnected with my British heritage? The discovery of the origins and life of my father brought an understanding of a part of me that would for ever be British. Before his death aged 31, my father spent a significant part of his adult life in foreign parts, but he was a very

---

[234] The Experiment in International Living was established in the USA by Dr Donald Watt in 1932 with the aim of fostering international student exchanges to foster peace and international understanding. Today, it operates in more than 150 countries.

British person. And the research into his early life revealed a history that connected me to a particular part of England, going back many generations, of which my mother had no knowledge. The discovery of grave stones in a Rutland cemetery going back centuries is a very strong kind of grounding. This research also extended the family to encompass my father's previously unknown brother Edward and his family. And an interest in genealogy led to uncovering my mother's roots going back to some Scottish heritage of which perhaps she had some knowledge since I was sent as a boy to learn Scottish dancing. After all this research, I now had a sense of belonging to Britain which comes from connection to the land. In comparison, even after 30 years, my roots in Australia are more ephemeral, notwithstanding that the most important relationship in my life now is an Australian named Andrew. And even Andrew has English roots through his mother.

The second factor in my reorientation certainly derives from getting older. For several decades in Australia, through my work and other activities, I have acquired friends from all walks of life. And the acquisition of the property at Callignee has provided a special connection with a particular piece of land. But I have always been conscious that present "ownership" does not provide roots. More important, as I have got older, I have realised that most of the long-term relationships in my life are with British people. Inevitably, the contemporaries that you meet and become friends with at school, at university, and in other aspects of your early life, become important because of a shared journey of personal development. And my sense of being British has become all the stronger by writing my first memoir, *For Goodness Sake*.

A third important element of British connection is my brother's family. Whilst I have never had a strong relationship with my brother, I have always maintained close ties with his first wife, and had a particular bond with his daughter Julia, and son Alexander Wigginton. And the publication of my father's biography has facilitated a reconnection with my brother and his second wife and their children. As I reached my 70s, all of these blood lines have begun to take on a stronger meaning. And my connection with Alex has gone further. Following the five years he spent living in Australia, his family have become significant others. And when they returned to England in 2015 a part of me went with them.

The final part of this reorientation derives from Australian politics which has become increasingly insular and inward-looking. In particular, I have experienced some despair about the continued re-election of a deeply conservative political elite who seem to embrace a view of

Australia in the world that is beginning to look like Thatcher's Britain. When I migrated to Australia, there was talk of a republic, and meaningful recognition and reconciliation with the country's original inhabitants. And the public discourse embraced many views that I shared and valued, including environmental awareness, the need to cherish social capital, and the importance of public good as opposed to the pursuit of personal wealth. It was also an outward-looking country that embraced multiculturalism, and accepted responsibility for other less prosperous nations in the southern hemisphere. Following the election of John Howard in 1996, this began to change. I will return to this subject in Chapter 31. But the politics of the last twenty years in Australia, and particularly the last 10 years, have left me deeply disenchanted with the direction of the country. Perhaps I was naïve to think that Australian culture would continue the enlightenment of the Hawke and Keating years. But the decline of the progressive side of politics is deeply disillusioning. And I feel betrayed by the narrow minds of many current Australian politicians who have little vision or competence.

Having said all this, Australia is still my home and is likely to remain so for the rest of my life. In many ways, the decline in the British body politic with the departure from the EU is even more depressing. More importantly, I have a commitment to the people in this place that I think of as family. Nevertheless, I will endeavour to cherish those who I love in foreign parts, and see them as long as I am able to travel. I am now truly a creature of two continents and cultures.

PART EIGHT

NEVER TO RETIRE

29: Squeaky Wheel

When Andrew and I purchased the block in Callignee, we had a very clear vision. As it said in the strategic plan for management of the property: *"We must convince each generation that they are transient passengers on the planet Earth. It does not belong to them. They are not free to doom generations yet unborn."* The aim of the purchase was to do something practical for the environment by actively conserving a piece of land with significant biodiversity. And, in 2007, that was certainly what brought us to the foothills of the Strzeleckis. But the fire in February 2009 interrupted our mission and diverted me onto different paths which would include many achievements but also some grief.

In the aftermath of the fire and the death of my mother in 2009, my world was dominated by a programme of recovery. In Melbourne, whilst I remained as a member of the ACF Board, I did not have the fortitude to continue with consultancy work. So my world became centred on Callignee, which became a focus both in re-establishing a foothold on the nature reserve and coming to terms with loss and grief.

As I was languishing in rented accommodation in Traralgon during 2010, it came to my notice that the local Latrobe City Council were endeavouring to introduce a community-based programme designed to encourage local residents to take responsibility for their own safety and wellbeing. In late 2010, I attended a seminar organised by the Council at the Quality Inn in Traralgon. Council officers introduced attendees to the concept of Local Emergency Action Plan ("LEAP") groups. And, at the end of the meeting, I signed up to establish such a team in the Callignee area. This was my first venture into voluntary community work as opposed to political activism, and there was much to learn.

Emergency Committee

The first meeting of our local LEAP team took place on 16 November 2010 at the newly rebuilt Callignee Community Hall. This was attended by a number of local people who would eventually figure strongly in the work of the group, including the captains of both the local CFA brigades. And we had direct support from Council through the Council's Community Recovery Coordinator, Deb Brown. The activity was auspiced by the Victorian Bushfire Recovery and Reconstruction Authority ("VBRRA"), and funded by the Victorian Bushfire Appeal Fund. According to the programme, the aims of the team were *"to build community capacity and readiness for future disasters"*, which would include the development of a community Emergency Response Plan to complement the Council's Plans. At that meeting one of the people at the Council's seminar, Graham Bolton, assumed the role of convenor. He was a thoughtful guy with whom I had had some contact during the early days of recovery in 2009. And he was a member of the Callignee CFA brigade. He applied himself diligently to chairing the meeting and I volunteered to be the secretary. So began what turned out for me to be a journey of some nine years' community work.

In our initial deliberations, the team considered the broad terms of reference issued by the VBRRA, and identified the main elements of a plan that would involve mapping the local community and its assets, preparing a Community Emergency Handbook ("the Handbook"), and fostering the establishment of Community Fireguard Groups. In early December, Council provided a Workshop to provide LEAP teams with basic training about the management of meetings and, to assist our deliberations, we were offered the support of a facilitator named Steve Pascoe who subsequently attended a number of meetings.[235] Early in the New Year, we adopted formal Terms of Reference. And in March we named ourselves the Local Safety Network to better reflect the scope of our activities.

In the next twelve months the team implemented all of the items in its initial plan. But the business that consumed the most time and effort was the development of the Handbook, which was designed for distribution to all members of the community. And the team was fortunate to have access to some ground-breaking work undertaken by a similar team in Yinnar led by a fellow named John Harris.[236] Our version of this document ended up being some 44 pages in length. And the drafting of content was at times tortuous, given the differences in style and views of its authors. The main elements were as follows:

a)   Description of the community, which included a map showing the history of fire in the district,

b)   Recognition of the risk posed by fire and other emergencies,

c)   Preparation of a household Fire Plan,

d)   Establishment of a Community Fireguard Group,

---

[235] Steve Pascoe was from Strathewen, a town between Yarra Glen and Kinglake, and a survivor of the fires which devastated that town in 2009.

[236] The Boolarra Yinnar and Districts Local Emergency Action Plan became available to the Callignee team in November 2010.

e)   Deciding on whether to Stay or Leave when faced with a fire,
f)   Planning for emergencies other than fire,
g)   Support for people with special needs, and
h)   The role of emergency agencies.

In addition, for distribution to all community members, the team prepared a large fridge magnet with emergency numbers, and a local map provided by the Council to show residents how their property was positioned in its local landscape.

Development of the Handbook went through around 15 versions and the final draft was completed in June 2011 when we went out to tender for a printer. We also established a network for distribution ahead of the 2011/12 Fire Danger Period. We made a point of personally hand delivering the Handbook, magnet and map rather than just leaving the items in their letter box, to ensure that they received proper attention. And the material was very well received, with positive feedback from across the community.

Whilst the team was focussed on the Handbook, Graham Bolton maintained links with the Council's Emergency Coordinator, Lance King. And, at the instigation of Brendan Scully who was VicPol's community liaison person, the team received a formal invitation to attend meetings of the Municipal Emergency Management Planning Committee ("MEMPC"). Graham and I attended our first meeting on 6 September 2011 where we reported on our activities and circulated the Handbook, which was very well received. For me, this would be the beginning of eight years' work with the MEMPC, attending four meetings per annum to provide community input to the Council's emergency management planning work. And, in my case, it involved contributions as a community representative to a number of other Council-based emergency-management activities. This included membership of the CERA Risk Management team run by the SES, a project team to implement a Council-wide emergency communications system (designed by Attentis), and the Council's Recovery Sub Committee.[237] Participation in the work of these groups became a significant body of work in its own right, involving a substantial commitment of time.

Returning to the Local Safety Network ("LSN"), having completed the first Handbook, the team considered whether there was further work

---

[237] CERA stands for Community Emergency Risk Assessment. SES is the State Emergency Service.

that warranted continuation of the group. It was broadly accepted that we had only just begun; but there was concern that we were largely a self-appointed team with little accountability. With my background, governance was something that I was particularly concerned about and, following a model established by Council, we concluded that we should become part of the local community association, the Traralgon South and District Association ("TSDA"). This would provide for appointment by, and accountability to, a body elected by the community. In May 2012 an approach was made to the TSDA and, at that organisation's AGM in July, it was agreed that the LSN should become a sub-committee of the association with a new name, the Callignee and Traralgon South Emergency Committee ("CEC"). At this point Graham Bolton decided to step down, and the TSDA appointed Stuart Strachan as Convenor with Callignee CFA Captain Ian Ewart as Deputy. I agreed to continue in an administrative role. Stuart Strachan and I also both agreed to serve on the TSDA Committee to ensure reporting and accountability to an elected body.

In the following several years, the CEC went from strength to strength. A small but loyal and persistent team burrowed away pursuing an emergency management agenda with relentless vigour. The scope was considerable and included the following:

a) Development, production and distribution of seven Community Bushfire Preparedness Brochures.
b) Development, production and distribution of two Community Calendars.
c) Development, production and distribution of a 2nd edition of the Community Emergency Handbook in 2014.
d) Convening of community meetings at which emergency agency representatives explained their roles.
e) Completion of a Community Risk Analysis, development of Risk Treatment Plans, and periodic update of this Analysis with input to Council's CERA risk management programme.
f) Partnership with Forestry organisation HVP in an Arson Prevention Programme involving erection of posters around the community during the Fire Danger Period.
g) Membership of the MEMPC and its project teams to provide community input.
h) Submission to Emergency Management Victoria of community views on the Leave and Live Policy.

i)   Development of community messaging videos on fire planning which were screened on Channel Nine.
j)   Fostering a Project at Kurnai College in which a student developed a video for use in educating teenagers about fire planning.
k)   Promotion of a property signage system, with installation of a uniform sign with number and name of street.
l)   Development and implementation of a Neighbourhood Support system.
m)   Fostering of Community Fireguard Groups, with five eventually being established in the district.
n)   Community mapping.
o)   Audit of Community Critical Assets.
p)   Assistance to the Council in fostering the establishment of emergency planning committees in other communities in the Latrobe Valley.
q)   Consolidation of the Recovery Action Plan developed and implemented by the Community Recovery Committee.
r)   Participation in numerous emergency management related conferences and seminars to provide community input.
s)   Establishment of the Latrobe Community Emergency Management Forum ("LCEMF") as a gathering for small-town emergency management committees to share learning.

Through this very significant body of work there was growing recognition in the community, at Council, and amongst the emergency agencies. And the team gradually became the "go to" organisation for community input on these issues. In large part this was due to the leadership of the Convenor, Stuart Strachan, and the great teamwork displayed by our loyal band of committee members. From my perspective, this was voluntary community activity at its best.

Despite its extraordinary achievements, in 2019 this team hit troubled waters. There were people in the community who either did not value, or perhaps even resented, its significant contribution to community wellbeing. From my observation it was a manifestation of the Australian "Tall Poppy" syndrome. And the demise of the CEC unfolded in a way that was both hurtful to its members and damaging to the community.

In early 2019, the community reached an important milestone with the 10th anniversary of the 2009 fires. And the TSDA established a working party to plan commemoration of the disaster. The events went well, and I attended both a memorial service and a community dinner where I sat with my neighbours Louise and Tony Mann to reflect on all that happened to us on 7 February 2009. As part of the media coverage for our community's commemoration, the TSDA's officers were interviewed for a write-up in the local newspapers. The aim was to reflect on the recovery and resilience of local people. When the article was published, there was hardly a mention of the CEC. I was surprised and somewhat affronted. I raised my concerns with TSDA officers, and they shrugged their collective shoulders saying that they had told the Press about CEC activities and it was a matter for them to decide what they reported. In sadness, and with family health issues a preoccupation at the time, I took leave of absence from the TSDA Committee.

In April, I went overseas and, whilst I was away, there was a disturbing development. Even as I was sitting one morning in my cottage by the side of Loch na Keal on the island of Mull (where I was doing research for a book), I received an email from Stuart Strachan to tell me that the TSDA had instituted disciplinary proceedings against him. He was unsure of the reason. However, he had been seeking to uphold the application of local planning law, and this had led him to challenge a number of local planning applications in which farm land would be used for residential development. In the process, he had put a number of people off side.

On my return from overseas in July, I attempted to mediate in a situation that had the potential to undermine the CEC. I was unsuccessful and, already having my own concerns about the TSDA on a range of other matters, including their financial due diligence, I resigned from the TSDA Committee. Meanwhile, the attempt to "discipline" Stuart Strachan continued, with a number of delays and obfuscation by both parties, and Stuart seemingly suspended from the TSDA Committee. Then, whilst Stuart was overseas on holiday in August, the TSDA escalated their attempts to sanction him. They expelled the CEC from the TSDA. This was done without notice, and without prior consultation. And the reason they gave for the expulsion, alleged risk arising from CEC activities, seemed spurious.

When I was informed of this egregious decision, I was attending an international conference on Disaster Management in Melbourne. I was shocked. And, when I challenged it, the TSDA doubled down and continued to relentlessly pursue Stuart Strachan regardless of the mounting collateral damage. Initially, I was visited by an officer of the organisation at my house in Callignee who tried to persuade me into abandoning support for Stuart. I offered to mediate but, before I could take any action, the TSDA renewed their disciplinary proceedings against him. I then appealed in writing to the TSDA President requesting that they intervene because of the potential damage to community relations. I got no reply. Then the TSDA Committee turned on me. In early October, I was called at 8.40 pm in the evening, and three members of the committee tried to bully me with a variety of accusations and allegations. This unexpected impugning of my integrity caused me considerable trauma. And, in the immediate aftermath, I took my concerns to a doctor who advised me to walk away because it was fruitless to try and negotiate with mindless aggression.

In the weeks that followed, the TSDA persisted with their aggressive tactics towards Stuart Strachan. They also held their AGM at which they not only failed to make any mention of the expulsion of the CEC, but confounded Stuart Strachan's attempt to continue as a member of the TSDA Committee. And just before Christmas (8 months after their original attempt to sanction him) they finally convened a meeting of a Disciplinary Committee. It stalled, with those who had agreed to act as "independent" arbiters withdrawing. At around the same time, I wrote to the TSDA President again appealing a personal intervention to reinstate the CEC and address a number of other concerns that I had raised with her. My appeal fell on deaf ears.

After Christmas 2019, things went quiet. But in January 2020, the TSDA Committee re-instigated disciplinary proceedings against Stuart. And in February, I wrote to the Secretary citing my own distress at being bullied and requesting an apology. They chose to publicise this communication and then attempted to get me to retract my complaint! At this stage, I resigned my membership of the TSDA. And shortly thereafter Stuart Strachan did likewise.

This sequence of events was deeply upsetting. Not only had the reputation of the CEC been trashed; I had lost all sense of having quiet enjoyment of the property in Callignee. And all because I had sought to defend an individual and a committee that had made a major contribution to the community over many years.

To his credit, in the weeks that followed, Stuart Strachan was undaunted and proceeded to re-establish the CEC as a separate entity. But I had had enough. In my view, the CEC had now lost its social licence, and the community was deeply divided which would seriously undermine any attempt to undertake locally based emergency management activity.

Thus ended a significant chapter in my life, and there was a sad upshot. For more than 10 years, I had organised an annual meeting of neighbours who were formed into a Community Fireguard Group to share fire defence plans. One member of the team was also a prime instigator in expelling the CEC. The Community Fireguard Group folded.

The TSDA

Despite the sad story outlined above, my involvement with the TSDA Committee had had its better moments which are worth a brief mention. I actually first got involved with this community association in 2008, when the location of the local refuse tip was a burning issue. And I even got elected to the committee just before the fires in 2009. At that point my membership went into hibernation. But in 2012, representing the CEC, I re-joined and made a significant commitment to the administration of the TSDA Committee. In particular, I introduced systems for the orderly conduct of meetings, I rewrote the Rules to comply with new legislation for incorporated associations, I conducted a community survey designed to inform future planning and development, I introduced a Council issue-tracking system to improve the accountability of Council officers in response to matters raised by community members, I completed an organisational risk analysis, I promoted occupational health and safety, and I arranged for the amalgamation of the TSDA and the Hall Association. I also wrote policies on a range of matters, I drafted letters for signature by officers, and I interceded in disputes between members. And I did my best to raise the standard of financial reporting, although my attempts were resisted by successive Treasurers. In summary, I left the organisation in a better state than when I joined it.

The way in which all of this came to an end was unfortunate. But, in community organisations, when there are divisions between committee members something has to give. Given what happened to the CEC, my resignation was inevitable.

Conclusions

With my departure from both the TSDA and the CEC, my community activism in Callignee largely came to an end. Perhaps fortuitously, shortly after the final episodes in what had become a very sad story, in

February 2020 the world was hit by the Covid-19 virus in which citizens had to self-isolate and community activity was suspended. In the weeks that followed, I was able to reflect on all that had happened. And I was struck by how an apparently civil society could so easily slip into confrontation and discord. I was also concerned at how I had allowed people behaving badly to define who I was. I reset my mind to focus on living peacefully with my immediate neighbours with a hope that at some point there would be a reconciliation between the warring parties. In the meantime, I recalled why Andrew and I had acquired the conservation property in Callignee in the first place. In many ways, the fire in 2009 and its aftermath had hijacked our environmental agenda, and I realised that it was time to get back to the real reason for owning the nature reserve, which was conservation for future generations. When we started to emerge on the other side of the pandemic, I found myself in a different place. And I resumed the agenda that Andrew and I had originally adopted, conserving nature and advocating sustainability.

30: A New Compulsion

The writing and publication of *"Wig's Secret War"* instigated a new chapter in my life. The daily sessions sitting in front of my laptop, and occasionally looking out into the bush to see kangaroos munching at the grass, had become a new form of existence. There were several dimensions to this. I had always enjoyed putting pen to paper, and prided myself in being able to write decent English. But in writing the biography, I had had to acquire some new skills. It was a big step to convert the informative style I had developed during my business career to presenting words in a manner that would capture the imagination of the reader. And, from reading other authors, I had gained some insights into the devices used to engage and enchant. Also, in writing the biography of a deceased person, I had developed a taste for detective work, with all its mystery, intrigue, and revelations. A candle had been lit and burnt brightly.

For Goodness Sake

Following *Wig's Secret War*, my first instinct was to write something about my mother, whose life as a widow was a model of dedication and fortitude. However, I had included something about her in my father's biography and there was a more pressing compulsion. For the benefit of my family if nothing else, I decided to write about my own life. Given my relative lack of fame, this would seem to be a somewhat fanciful venture. But I sensed that there was learning from a diverse and largely fortunate life that I would like to impart. And once I started to write, it quickly became apparent that my existence fell into two distinct parts; living in Britain and living in Australia. In *For Goodness Sake*, I wrote about life in Britain, from 1945 to the mid-1980s.

In assembling an account of anyone's life, you need sources. For an autobiography, there is personal memory; but casting back to childhood and young adult years is easier said than done for someone in his 70s. However, I had one thing going for me. Since the 1960s, I had maintained a diary and, situated in Kew, these documents were not consumed in the 2009 fire. So I had a significant source of information, which included contact lists, dates of meetings, and records of events. During my life, I have also been in the habit of recording my reflections about the world, as well as anecdotes about incidents in my own life. And these notes, some hand written and others typed, sat in filing cabinets waiting to be explored.

So began an intense period of writing in which I revisited every part of my early life, seeking to remember what had happened, when and where. Strangely, recollection of my childhood was not as difficult as I expected. I literally sat down and plumbed the depths of my memory. And, to provide context, I linked events in my personal life to the history of the time, including the difficult years of post-war recovery in Britain, key international events, and the unfolding of domestic politics. I also found it relatively easy to recall school days, and the highs and lows of my nuclear family life. Above all, for these early years, I was able to identify the way in which my view of the world had been formed from the influences around me.

My reflection on days of learning at university brought back especially happy memories. For Baby Boomers, tertiary education was free, so there was no pressure to get a job apart from during holidays when I earnt some cash for travel. And, particularly in the humanities, studying for a degree was an opportunity to reflect on the human condition. In a world of full employment, it certainly wasn't about obtaining a qualification for work. And, in the absence of any responsibilities or parental control, there was plenty of time for fun.

When I moved on to my working life, which commenced in the mid-1960s, there was absolutely no shortage of material for inclusion in a book. I was fortunate to have had a career with many jobs in a major international company through which I had been given significant responsibility from an early age. I was also given some unusual opportunities, including a two-year management development programme that gave me the chance to reflect and consolidate learning, which is rarely offered to people in the modern era. And I benefited from living in all four corners of the United Kingdom, cherishing the connection with Scotland which would become important to me in later life.

Whilst work dominated many of my waking hours, I was fortunate to have been raised in a family that believed that you should give time and commitment to voluntary work. And, through both my natural inclination and academic studies, this included politics. When I look back, there is virtually no time when I wasn't interested in *current affairs* and, as a young adult, I quickly became an activist. In my 20s, this drew me into a separate world that ran parallel to my business life and gave me a rich counterpoint to the pressures that come from earning a living. Through political activism I found a vehicle to express my views and potentially change society. At times it was heady stuff. But I felt empowered and full of life.

Of course, life is not a bed of roses and the good things in life are interspersed with periods of darkness. In the early 1980s, I certainly had my personal setbacks, both with physical health, my political career, and through dances with death. And at work, as my career progressed, I encountered and became a player in the takeover battle between Imperial Group and Hanson Trust. This proved to be pivotal, with high drama, and a lost cause that had a silver lining. Suddenly without employment, I found myself temporarily ship-wrecked, and a free agent to seek pastures new. Given the enormous impact of takeover and redundancy, not many people have the opportunities that I had to start again and make a new life by migrating to Australia.

After about two years of intermittent writing about this early part of my life, in the first half of 2018 I had completed most of the manuscript for the first memoir. I then started to think about who might wish to review the content before I went to publication. Fortunately, writing about events more than 30 years ago, most of the critical comments were about people in leadership roles who were no longer with us. But I genuinely wanted some validation from friends and colleagues for things I had said. So I began a very long process of editing which eventually involved several people.

The publication of the book proved to be easier than I expected. In late 2018, I approached Simon Hepworth, who had published *Wig's Secret War,* and he said that he was up for it. However, he was pre-occupied with several other books and I had to join a queue. In the event, we didn't get under way until I visited Simon at his home in Merthyr Tydfil in April 2019 when we agreed a timetable. Back in Australia, in July we settled the title, the index and a few other details, and publication proceeded in August. Surprisingly, it began to sell and I soon got several enquiries through my website as well as feedback from unexpected quarters. In any event, regardless of eventual sales, my family and friends now had a record on which they could reflect and I felt that my work had served its purpose.

Woods, Roos, and Cougars

In the middle of 2018, while I was in the final stages of completing *For Goodness Sake*, I was mindful of what I would do next. I had a number of ideas, including a historical novel set in the 17th century, and a book on the island of Mull. In the meantime, I had developed a link with my local country football club in the Gippsland township of Churchill, the Churchill Football Netball Club. It's a strange thing, but I had an almost obsessive attachment to this place because it lent its name to, and was the origin of, the fires that ravaged the property in Callignee in 2009. And going there was a bit like returning to the scene of a crime! In any event, as the new house in Callignee was being constructed in 2010, I started to follow my local football team. On a Saturday afternoon, I would park my car next to the oval at Gaskin Park to watch the game, with youngsters barracking from the back of Utes, the honking of horns in celebration of a goal, consumption of meat pies, and idle chatter with other spectators. Eventually, I attended the Club's AGM, became a member, and met Mark Answerth. Mark had played for the club, was a past President, and was currently chairman of the Past Players Committee. I had several chats with him and, discovering that I was a writer, he suggested that I might like to write a history of the organisation.

This new project, with Mark as my sponsor, started in June 2018 and would become a consuming passion for much of the next three years. At the outset, Mark briefed me by saying that the Club's history went back several decades and that there had been Premierships in the 1950s. However, through reports in local newspapers, it soon emerged that the club's history went back to the 19th century, with reports on games played by the Hazelwood football team, and even a team picture emerging from way back in 1888.[238] Copies of the newspapers were recorded on microfiche, with the antique reels of negatives for back projection available in a local library. With this and later hard copy records, I was able to construct an entire history of all the games played by the Club, including not just the senior team but also the reserves and the Under 18 thirds. Thus began many months of research. It was laborious work. But it was also exciting to find reports on the club's history including a report on the formation of the Club in 1890. And I eventually found a booklet recording a complete history of the league in which Hazelwood had played between 1946 and 1983.

As the record of the football club emerged, I started to get an appreciation of the history of the district in which the Club was located. I made it my business to get in touch with local historians to trace the arrival of Europeans in Gippsland. Through the Morwell Historical

---

[238] The town of Churchill was originally called Hazelwood, with the name changed in 1965 to honour Winston Churchill.

Society I was fortunate to find a historian, Robert De Souza Daw, who had been working on the history of local families and had an excellent knowledge of the early days of European settlement. And he pointed me to a number of other sources which enabled me to piece together the development of the local community from the 1840s to the current day. I also researched the history of the game, and met a wonderful guy named Col Hutchinson who was the AFL's official historian. He gave me a detailed account of the evolution of the sport from its earliest days and put me in touch with other sources.

In undertaking this project, I was aware that I wasn't just recording the history of football but also netball. I was determined to do justice to this sport, encompassing the other half of humanity, but this was challenging. The newspapers were less diligent in reporting the game, and detailed information on matches was only available for the last 10 years, through the League's website. Nevertheless, through various detective work, I was able to trace the history from the 1990s.

From the start, this project also had another dimension. From the beginning, Mark Answerth encouraged me to meet retired players with the aim of obtaining their knowledge and insights about the various teams over the years. In my very first interview I met Eric Rowley who at the time was 104 years old. He had played for the Morwell team in the 1930s, and was the Coach and Captain of Hazelwood in 1946 when the Club re-formed after World War Two. His memories were golden. That first interview in August 2018 was the beginning of a marathon that encompassed more than 130 past and current players, officers, staff and supporters. The personal histories were fascinating, with some anecdotes that would curl your toes. But many were worthy of including in the book.

The work of writing this book continued throughout 2019, and in December Col Hutchinson pointed me towards a publisher named Geoff Slattery in Melbourne. Mark and I met with him and we established a timetable for publication in 2020 which would mark the 130th year since the Club was founded. Unfortunately, this plan was derailed by the arrival of the Covid-19 pandemic in February 2020. So, we delayed until we could organise a proper launch, with publication eventually achieved with much fanfare on 30 April 2021 at a function attended by some 100 people. This project not only delivered an important record of achievement for the Club. It provided a reference point for young and old that gave local people a pride in who they were. And the experience left *me* with a great sense of belonging to a whole new tribe.

There's More

By now it had become very clear that I could not exist without having a writing project, and many ideas were filling my head. With the end of the football book looming, I had two more in store. The first was the current offering, and the next was a book on the island of Mull.

If you've got this far, you have already read most of the most recent project, *Don't Look Back*. The book I am writing on Mull crept up on me. From the time I first visited the island in the 1960s, I was spellbound. And through periodic visits over the years my attachment had grown to the point where it had got under my skin. In 2019, I spent 6 weeks on the island, doing research and conducting interviews. In the course of that wonderful trip, I soon found out that six months would not be enough. So I booked a second visit of six months for 2020. Sadly, the Covid-19 virus put paid to that, and my further research and interviews were delayed until 2023. In the meantime, it had become clear to me that this would be a book about "the evolution of community". And from my previous experience in life, including involvement in campaigning on political and social issues in two different cultures, there was no shortage of material as reference points for what I might write about life on an island stretching back into the mists of time.

PART NINE

THE LIGHT OF EXPERIENCE

31: Australian Society

In this final section of the book, I aim to provide a reflection on both the society in which I have lived for 35 years, and some learning about life and the spirit of things. In this chapter, we begin with some observations about Australian current affairs.

The Body Politic

Since Ronald Horne coined the expression in 1964, Australia is often characterised as "The Lucky Country". The full quote from his book is that *'Australia is a lucky country, run by second-rate people who share its luck',* and this refers to the wealth of environment and resources that Australians enjoy and the poverty of political leadership. Things haven't changed. But, during my time, Australian society has been through a significant transformation.

Before migrating, I had followed Australian politics and society through the eyes of Australian friends and relatives, and had obtained a view that the country was prosperous, socially conservative, fiercely egalitarian, and obsessed with sport. I had been acquainted with the constitutional trauma of the Fraser and Whitlam years, and my cousin Ian enlightened me about the deeply conservative regime of Joe Bjelke Petersen in Queensland, where public gatherings were banned and homosexuality was still a crime. It was also apparent that Australia had an excess of government, with a federal parliament, state/territory parliaments and a plethora of local Councils. Barely a year went by when there wasn't an election somewhere.

When I settled in Melbourne in 1986, things seemed to be on the move, with a federal Labor government led by Bob Hawke and Paul Keating. Whilst the country was following the international trend towards deregulation, in the first ten years of my time in the country there appeared to be a progressive agenda, including the introduction of universal health-care under Medicare, a comprehensive social contract with the unions, tighter OH&S laws, introduction of compulsory superannuation, recognition of Native Title, and an active environmental policy. All of this was happening at a time when, in the UK, Thatcher was ruthlessly pursuing neo-liberal small-government economic policy, with cuts in public expenditure, deregulation, attacks on organised labour, and the suggestion that the poor were responsible for their own demise. It was a great relief to get away from all that libertarian stuff, and at times I even saw myself as a political refugee. Mind you, as mentioned earlier in this book, the style and manner of politicking in the Australian parliament was in marked contrast to the orderly and largely well-mannered proceedings of the British counterpart.

Whilst I approved of most of what the Labor government was doing, in the early days the main focus of my own political activity was an involvement with the Australian Democrats, who seemed to perform a useful role in modifying the political debate through holding the balance of power in the Senate. In the meantime, the Liberal Party was wrought with internal strife between what were called the liberal "wets" and conservative "dries". The member for my local seat of Kooyong was Andrew Peacock, who appeared to be something of a dilettante.[239] For a time, he was a relatively progressive Leader of the Opposition, but he was hotly opposed by the deeply conservative John Howard. Howard was a suburban solicitor and came from a small business family in the Sydney suburb of Earlwood where my Uncle Ernest lived.[240] Despite a lack of charisma, he was the beneficiary of the eventual turning of the political tide and made it to The Lodge in 1996.[241]

With the advent of Howard and his Treasurer Peter Costello, Australia was subjected to a version of neo-liberal economics. Howard had been a somewhat lacklustre Treasurer under Prime Minister Malcolm Fraser, and his elevation heralded a long period when there was little sign of statesmanship from the political leaders of the country. For people with a progressive point of view, the Howard years (1996-2007) were marked by some far from heartening outcomes including the following:

- Privatisation and poor regulation of the aged-care sector, which has come back to haunt us during the Covid-19 pandemic,
- Reduced investment in higher education and research (leading to that sector's reliance on overseas students, which has also brought huge damage during the Covid-19 crisis),
- Equivocation on multiculturalism, which gave heart to the extreme right-wing One Nation party of Pauline Hanson,

---

[239] Kooyong was the seat in Melbourne held for many years by the founder of the Liberal Party, Robert Menzies. It is now represented by the current Treasurer of Australia Josh Frydenberg.

[240] In the Website Sydney Suburbs Review, Earlwood is described as a "largely quiet and peaceful suburb, but also rough and ready".

[241] The Lodge in Canberra is the Australian equivalent of the British 10 Downing Street, being the home of the Prime Minister.

- Politicising of immigration policy, leading to the cruel incarceration of thousands of refugees for many years on off shore islands,
- Backtracking on the Kyoto Protocol to tackle climate change,
- The tricky undermining of the 1999 referendum on the republic, and
- An unsuccessful attempt to undermine workers' rights through the Work Choices legislation.

Howard also had little experience in foreign policy and appeared to give little thought to the consequences of committing Australian troops to other people's wars. In particular, this played out in his unreserved support for George's Bush's invasion of Iraq after the 9/11 attack on the USA in 2001. Mind you, to be fair, during his time in office the Australia economy did flourish. There was a sustained period of growth, fed by demand from developing countries for Australian commodities, and taking advantage of the deregulation implemented by Hawke/Keating. And he did do some positive things. After the massacre at Port Arthur in 1998, he bravely introduced tougher gun laws. And his Treasurer Peter Costello implemented significant financial reform, including the introduction of a GST in the face of considerable opposition from the Labor Party, and the establishment of a sovereign Future Fund. Belatedly, Howard also embraced the idea of an Emissions Trading Scheme to address the threat of global warming. But could you ever trust a man who, when answering a question, looked at you with his head to one side and his eyes askance suggesting that he was about to play loose with the truth.

In 2007, after Howard had over-reached with his Work Choices industrial relations legislation, and on a tide of optimism from the progressive side of politics, a new Labor government was elected. "Kevin 07" Rudd became Prime Minister, and Howard lost the seat of Bennelong in inner Sydney to an ABC journalist Maxine McKew. What some people characterised as his "1950s" style regime was swept away and, in the early days, it seemed that the country was about to take a quantum step forward with significant social, economic and environmental reform. But in 2008 the world was hit by the Global Financial Crisis. In response, the new Australian government adopted a classic Keynesian approach of increased public expenditure, focussing on investment in education, transport, and health programmes. The country avoided a recession, but, with burgeoning public debt, the government was blown off course. And, in late 2009, the body politic was transformed with a radical change in the leadership of the

Opposition Liberal Party. After Howard's departure in 2007, the Liberals had been led by Brendan Nelson, who had struggled. A year later, he was replaced by the relatively progressive Malcom Turnbull. Turnbull was popular with the public but less popular with some people in his own party and, with adverse opinion polls, in a Party Room spill on 1 December 2009, he in turn was overthrown by the deeply conservative Tony Abbott in a vote of 42 to 41. This signalled a major shift in both Liberal policy and tactics. Up to this point, and with Liberal support, Rudd had invested much of his credibility in dealing with what he called "the great moral issue of our time", global warming. With the ascendancy of Abbott, the Liberals abandoned meaningful policies to address climate change. Under sustained pressure, Rudd abandoned his climate policy and, for this and some other poor performance issues, Labor's standing in the polls plummeted.

In 2010, with an election looming, the Labor Party dumped Rudd, with Julia Gillard elected by the Party Room as leader and Prime Minister. In the August election, she survived but with a minority government. The next three years were a catalogue of vicious adversarial politics. Gillard did her best to pursue a progressive agenda, introducing a carbon price to deal with global warming, making a huge investment in education, committing to a national broadband network, and establishing a national disability insurance scheme. But public debt continued to rise, and Australia was buffeted by volatile international economic conditions. Under Abbott, the Liberal Opposition became hugely effective in selling a negative story about the government's perceived failings and, when it seemed that Labor's fortunes were desperate, there was another leadership spill with Kevin Rudd returning as Prime Minister. In the election of 2013 he didn't save the day, but he did reduce the size of the inevitable Liberal victory.

2013 saw the start of what I regard as the worst period of government in my time of living in Australia. Instead of building on the work of the previous government, Tony Abbott proceeded to dismantle many of Labor's progressive policies, including the Carbon Price.[242] In 2014, Treasurer Joe Hockey brought down a budget that sought to pursue a full-blooded neo-liberal economic policy. Many of the measures never got through the Senate. But he did some serious damage, including an

---

[242] With several months before the new Senate took office, the ALP managed to block repeal of the carbon price. However, when the new Senate numbers came into effect on 1 July 2014, the government tried again and, on 17 July, the repeal Bill passed with the support of the cross-bench which included three Palmer United Party members.

end to financial support for the motor industry. Within a short period, Australia's three car companies announced their intention to withdraw from Australia, and the country was doomed to lose not only vital engineering skills and infrastructure but also an estimated 100,000 jobs. This policy was the single largest piece of vandalism of any government in my time. Hockey did not last long, and was eventually appointed as US ambassador. He was replaced as Treasurer by Scott Morrison who came from a marketing background and had little experience in economics and finance. As Treasurer, he proceeded to make some poor decisions. In 2015, he approved the implementation of the so-called "Robo-Debt" system to claw back allegedly false welfare payments from the poorer members of society using a computer-generated means test.[243] He was also responsible for giving permission for a "commercial" company called Landbridge, controlled by the Chinese Communist Party, to take control of one of Australia's strategic assets, the Port of Darwin on a 99-year lease.[244]

As Abbott seemed to abandon the norms of cabinet government, he took upon himself a range of decisions which saw his standing in the opinion polls take a major dive.[245] In late 2015, Malcolm Turnbull challenged his leadership and defeated him in a party ballot. But, in so doing, he created many hostages to fortune, becoming a prisoner of the Liberal Party's right-wing. In July 2016, he called an election and narrowly scraped back into power with the public now expecting that he would become his own man. But, with Abbott lurking on the back benches, aided and abetted by ex-policeman Peter Dutton who was Immigration Minister, he struggled to adopt a progressive programme. In particular, an energy crisis was looming as the government failed to plan for the replacement of coal-fired power stations, and the government implemented a half-baked version of the national broadband network which was already creaking at the seams. To give him some credit, Turnbull did facilitate a public vote and legislation on introducing same-sex marriage, and he tried to address the climate issue. His Environment Minister, Josh Frydenburg developed a policy called the National Energy Guarantee which was designed to introduce a form of emissions trading scheme to drive the transition to renewable energy. But

---

[243] This was eventually the subject of a class action and was withdrawn.

[244] Five years later, in 2020, he openly attacked the Chinese government, driven by the Trump re-election agenda, and would have the gall to criticise the Premier of Victoria for having a "heads-of-agreement" with the Chinese for future infrastructure investment.

[245] This included his "captain's call" of awarding a knighthood to the Duke of Edinburgh.

the right wing of the Liberal Party, aided and abetted by the National Party, would have none of it. Eventually, it all came to a head with a leadership challenge led by Peter Dutton. Given his lack of charisma, apparently callous attitude to refugees, and poor performance as a minister, his appointment would have been the kiss of death for the Coalition at the next election. What actually happened, during a series of votes over several weeks in August 2018, is the subject of some speculation. In any event, Scott Morrison managed to appear as a "clean skin" and emerged as a compromise candidate.[246] Not surprisingly, Turnbull then resigned from Parliament, triggering a by-election won by an Independent.

The new government, led by the man I call "Motor Mouth" Morrison because of his assertive fast talking and propensity to govern by grand announcements, was a team of compromise candidates with an apparent paucity of policy. There was talk of an election in the autumn and this was eventually called for May 2019 when I was overseas. Anticipating this timing, I had organised to have my voting papers sent to the island of Mull and I duly voted hoping for an end to the ineffective Coalition government. The government itself was also expecting defeat, and had gone to the election with a limited agenda. As it turned out, it survived with a majority of one, due at least in part to attacks in Queensland on the impact of Labor's progressive policies, including a campaign by Clive Palmer which characterised the ALP leader Bill Shorten as shifty. With suitable evangelical vigour, Morrison heralded his re-election as a miracle.[247]

For the next six months, with no agenda for government, Morrison fiddled around with ideological bills on protecting religious rights and cracking down on unions. Whilst there was a lot of hot air, in both cases the legislation struggled, with much opposition from a sceptical Senate. Then, as the summer approached, the country was hit by two major disasters which would fill the political void and test Morrison's mettle. Following the relentless drought and ever-increasing temperatures, in late 2019 the country was hit by the worst bush fires on record. Despite this, as Christmas approached, Morrison slipped away for a quiet family holiday. Discovered on a beach in Hawaii, he quickly returned with

---

[246] There is a lovely picture during this crisis, in which Morrison has his hand round Turnbull's shoulders saying "I'm your man". The story is that, whilst openly supporting Turnbull in leadership polls, he quietly encouraged his supporters to vote for Dutton.

[247] Morrison is an Evangelist. Although he espouses Christian values, his personal beliefs are unclear.

considerable condemnation for negligence. Then, in February, the world was hit by the Covid-19 virus. This time, although he was slow to take it seriously, the health fraternity prevailed upon him to act. Just in time, he banned flights from China, created an all-party National Cabinet and implemented a lockdown. His approach paid dividends and, before we knew it, he had adopted Keynesian economic policies to deal with the economic consequences. Australia started to shine as a country that had adopted appropriate measures, and Morrison was rightly credited with adopting a statesmanlike role. Sadly for him, as the pandemic persisted, the glow began to fade. He never fully grasped the need for a national quarantine facilities to manage the return of overseas travellers, his government's poor regulation of the privatised aged-care sector led to hundreds of deaths, his plan for the supply of vaccines proved insufficient, and the program for implementing inoculation was slow and disorganised. As the country grapples with the Omicron variant, it remains to be seen whether he will recover from these failings. In the meantime, the government has failed to establish a meaningful policy to tackle climate change, with the absence of a plan to achieve an orderly and just transition from coal and gas to renewable energy. He has also struggled to act convincingly on a series of issues relating to the treatment of women. His integrity has also been the subject of some damning assessments by journalists. His best hope of re-election is to focus on the economy and security issues. As this book is published, it remains to be seen whether recent events in the Ukraine or some other shock will save his bacon.

Finally, I need to say something about politics in country Victoria. The Federal seat of Gippsland has been held by the National Party for many years. This reflects the largely agricultural nature of the area, the socially conservative character of the people, and a tacit agreement with the more city-based Liberals not to contest the seat. The National Party is a strange beast, reflecting a mixture of agrarian socialism in which there is advocacy for government support to the farming sector, and conservative social policy. The Nationals morphed out of what was called the Country Party, which is probably a more appropriate name for them given their absence from city-based electorates. In the 21st century, in which Australia desperately needs a more progressive social policy and strong action to tackle global warming, they are an anachronism, but they will not be easily dislodged.

At State level, the Nationals also have a strong influence in Gippsland although the industrial electorate of Morwell, in which Callignee is located, is held by an Independent. Sadly, both sides of politics have neglected the district which has low economic growth, declining industries, relatively high unemployment, and some serious social problems. The area is desperately in need of progressive political leadership and investment in modern technology and industries. With a local interest through the property in Callignee I feel a moral responsibility to do something about this. But it's difficult to know where to start. If only I were twenty years younger!

And one last thing about Australian politics. It has always struck me that Robert Menzies stretched credulity when coining the name Liberal Party for the collection of politicians that he assembled in August 1945. This has never been a true liberal party. Although it has included some who had liberal values, it has always been the party of the "haves" serving the interests of the big-end of town. And, increasingly, it has espoused libertarianism and small government. In many ways, it is epitomised by John Howard who, even to this day, is wheeled out to share with us the benefit of his wisdom as a self-styled elder statesman. I think a name change to the "Conservative Party" is warranted, to leave the term "Liberal Party" to those in the UK and Canada who actually do embrace more progressive values.

Society and Culture

Before migrating, with a typically jaundiced British view, I used to laugh about the juxtaposition of the words "Australian" and "culture" in the same sentence. One of the best things about the last 35 years has been the revelation that Australia is actually a very civilised, sophisticated, and multicultural kind of place. But there also some serious issues. It's a mixed score card.

Native People

Australia has an unresolved issue with its native peoples. Before the arrival of Europeans the continent was inhabited by aboriginal nations whose ancestors go back at least 60,000 years. There is much debate about the nature of aboriginal society prior to occupation by European settlers. But there is no doubt that, in the 18th century, the British forcibly occupied their land and many colonists subsequently cast them as unsophisticated savages. The principal reason for invasion was to incarcerate people transported from Britain for committing mostly minor crimes borne of poverty. As time has passed these convicts and their keepers have given birth to a multicultural nation of immigrants who call Australia home. These people largely live in ignorance of the original inhabitants. So, there is unfinished business in acknowledging the true history of the continent and embracing the now greatly reduced number of original inhabitants and their culture.

Some non-aboriginal Australians wish to deny this history and it truly astonishing that aborigines were not recognised as citizens in their own land until the 1970s. However, there is a growing mood for change. Sadly, in the meantime, current generations of native people suffer greatly from some of the things the invaders brought with them to Australia. As a result, Aborigines live twenty years less than the rest of the population because of poor health, are twice as likely to be in prison, and have lower education achievement.

In the 21st Century, the state of native peoples is an international scandal of which the country should be ashamed. In 2017 there was a great conference of aboriginal peoples. They produced the Uluru Statement which sought to address previous wrongs with a range of initiatives, including the establishment of an Aboriginal Assembly to advise the Australian government of the day, the development of treaties recognising the original inhabitants, and more effective action to correct previous wrongs. To date, the response of the Coalition government has been slow and ineffective. We need a radical change of heart.

The Arts

On a more positive note, Australia excels in artistic endeavour. From my own experience in Victoria, although the impact of Covid-19 has been challenging, the arts flourish. There are concerts of classical music given by the Melbourne Symphony Orchestra, performances by the Australian Ballet, all forms of popular music delivered at major events and in pubs, live theatre, art exhibitions, and the Melbourne Comedy Festival. There is also an abundance of authors, artists, and designers that bear witness to the Australian experience. Across the country the film industry is alive and kicking.

Australia is also fortunate to have some of the best restaurants in the world and a thriving wine industry which matches any country in the world.

Immigration

Over the last twenty years, one of the worst stains on Australian society has been the handling of refugees. It is not that Australia fails to meet its international obligations to provide shelter to those in need. But, thanks to John Howard, the influx of boat people has been politicised. It started in August 2001 with the misrepresentation of the facts regarding the arrival of a Norwegian ship called the MV Tampa and the false claim that refugees had thrown their children overboard. And it quickly escalated, via the Border Protection Act, into "the Pacific Solution", involving off-shore processing of people called "illegal" asylum seekers. This was justified on the basis that "stopping the boats" saved lives potentially lost at sea. It ended with thousands of men, women and children incarcerated in off-shore camps in Naura and Manus Island for years without entry or hope. And the policy has been maintained by both the major political parties, vying with each other to show who can be tougher on the unfortunate victims. It is time for a serious re-casting of immigration policy based on a regional approach. We must close our off-shore camps and rediscover our compassion for the disadvantaged oppressed.

A Sporting Nation

In Australia, sport is like a religion. And nowhere is this truer than in Victoria. You can hardly spend a day in Melbourne without sport coming up in conversation, and the vast majority of people are only too keen to tell you which AFL team they support. The interesting thing about this phenomenon is that, whilst support for a team reflects tribalism, the passion is not taken to the violent extremes experienced with other sports in many other countries. You can attend a footy match and find yourself sitting in comfort next to a supporter of the opposing team without rancour. Mind you, when it comes to behaviour on the field, it's a different matter. Indeed, Australians are renowned for sledging on the cricket oval. But that betrays a competitive streak in the Australian psyche which should never be underestimated. Despite this sometimes unattractive character, sport binds the country and society together, not least in rural communities. I cherish this aspect of Australian society.

Nationhood

During my time in Australia, the question of the links to Britain have often been the subject of considerable public debate. There are strong ties between many Australians and people in the UK, and the desire to maintain some sort of link is understandable. However, the constitutional link through a foreign head of state is anachronistic. To an immigrant like myself, the fact that many local people cannot see this is bemusing. We do need to determine the means by which the head of state is selected; but that is not a difficult detail to resolve. The main issue is that we need an Australian head of state! In a similar vein, in a country that prides itself in being multicultural, Australia has a national flag whose form is dominated by the flag of another country which is a constant reminder of invasion and colonialism. Despite the attachments of old soldiers to the Union Jack, it is time for a change. We need to find a new symbol of who we are.

Another issue that bemuses most immigrants is the basis for some of Australia's public holidays. If everyone in Victoria wants to have a day off for a horse race (Melbourne Cup), or the AFL Grand Final, that's OK with me. But the celebration of the Queen's Birthday in June (she was born in April) is bizarre. And the date chosen for Australia Day, 26 January, is also an anachronism. The voyages of Captain Cook and the botanical work of Joseph Banks are important aspects of our history worthy of recognition. But Australia needs a national day that truly celebrates our rich history of native peoples, complemented by multicultural immigration over 200 years.

Finally, I also have some misgivings about Anzac Day, with which many immigrants find it difficult to identify. Until John Howard began a nationalistic campaign to revive this commemoration, memories of Gallipoli were slowly disappearing into the mists of time. Remembrance Day on 11 November is a universal day with which **all** Australians can identify for honouring the fallen including all those who identify with the Anzac tradition.

Media

When I settled in Australia, one of the few things that I missed from Britain was media diversity. Even in the 1980s, the range of alternative newspapers was limited. Over 35 years, the media landscape has deteriorated significantly as the numbers of owners and diversity of views has shrunk. It has not helped that successive Coalition federal governments have reduced the real value of funding for balanced public broadcasting by the ABC. The one ray of sunshine has been the emergence of access to electronic media which, in my case, means the news provided by organisations such as the Guardian Australia. But the preponderance of newspapers owned by the conservative side of politics, and the spread of lies and misinformation on-line, is very worrying. As evidence I cite a widespread view in some parts of Australian society that the Covid-19 virus is a hoax, vaccines damage your health, and global warming is a left-wing conspiracy. We need new mechanisms to temper freedom of speech with a requirement that public communications are based on facts and empirical evidence.

Regional Australia

As a Melbourne resident, you could be forgiven for thinking that Australia is a predominantly middle-class country with minimal poverty. And this impression is bolstered by the fact that the Victorian capital has frequently been voted by an international panel as *"The World's Most Livable City"*. But in the last ten years I have spent significant time in a rural community, and have encountered real poverty. Many country residents experience a lower standard of living, a shorter lifespan, poorer diet and health, and lower educational standards. City people live in blissful ignorance of this, which is allowed to continue because *"out of sight is out of mind"*. In a hugely wealthy country there needs to be a major change in how we view our regional communities, with better infrastructure and public services.

Climate

Australia has a wealth of renewable resources which will facilitate an end to our dependence on fossil fuels for energy and transport. We have the brains and ingenuity to develop new industries that will conserve our natural environment for future generations, creating new jobs to replace those that are lost. There is a need for urgent action from the federal government to embrace renewable energy, and the longer we delay, the more painful it will be to make the inevitable change to industry and communities. Fortunately, action is being taken at State level by governments of all political persuasions. But the absence of meaningful public policy at a national level in 2022 is a scandal.

32: The Spirit of Things

I was brought up in a household where engagement with organised religion was recognised as a natural part of life. Although I was sent to a Sunday school run by the Methodists, our family attended the early 13th century St Leonard's Anglican Church in the village of Wollaton, on the edge of the city of Nottingham. And my values were obtained from a mother who had a strong Christian faith and who provided some administrative support to the local vicar. As a young teenager, I was confirmed into the church in a ceremony conducted by the Bishop of Southwell, and I maintained my faith through my teenage years. At one stage, I even toyed with Catholicism, enrolling for a course of leaflets on the "true faith". I think I was attracted by the ritual and the universality. But as a teenager I found the need for confession, and Papal infallibility a bit much to swallow. In my early 20s, when I lived in Glasgow, I was an acolyte in a Scottish Episcopal church. In the meantime, my mother became secretary to the Anglican Chaplain at the University of Nottingham for whom she worked for many years. And, when she moved to Melbourne, she attended Holy Trinity church in Kew, Melbourne until she went to meet her maker. These connections reinforced my own attachment to the Anglican denomination.

Given this background, the change in my views may be surprising. It was a slow process, in which I became increasingly concerned about the attitudes and practices of church-goers in a society where there was considerable social injustice. In particular, I was struck by the hypocrisy of some people that I met in politics who claimed to believe in Christian values but pursued polices designed to reward greed in the name of personal freedom. Mind you, this disenchantment did not immediately lead me to question my beliefs. But it did cause me to question many of the tenets of Christianity, and I eventually came to the conclusion that much of the church's teaching had failed to keep up with the rapidly changing world. In particular, it seemed that like many followers of Islam, the Christian dogma was rooted in medieval times. The precepts had been designed by those appointed with religious authority to control the minds and lives of the people through fear, and were based on maintaining an almost feudal compliance. And religious leaders relied on ancient scriptures, which had been interpreted by interested parties long ago, and translated for use by distant peoples living in other times.

My reservations did not stop there. It was evident that the mono-theistic religions dominant in the western world, all of which came from the Middle East, were steeped in a creation myth, with the dominant concepts of "Good" and "Evil", "Heaven" and "Hell", "Original Sin", and guilt derived from man's inclination to defy God's will. And implementation of their various creeds, with crusades, jihad, fundamentalism, and an obsession with the need to own and control "the Holy Land", had led to amazing acts of wanton destruction in the name of the one true faith, with women cast into inferior roles, and many others condemned as outcasts and/or beyond redemption.[248]

In my 20s, I made it my business to study other religions. In the 1960s, there was no shortage of options to accommodate the human need for some form of spirituality in their lives. In particular, through the travels of the young, people in the West were exposed to eastern religions which were based on a very different way of thinking about the place of humans in the scheme of things. And that is where I began to seek and find a different way of thinking about spirituality which had more meaning for me in the modern world.

I have to admit that, although I liked the concepts of animism, karma, and the circular nature of life, I never really engaged with Hinduism. Perhaps I was lazy. But the system of beliefs seemed to be as complex as the architecture of the temples. And, with its multiplicity of gods, it seemed too fanciful, with far too much baggage from the days when science held little sway in human thinking. That is not to say that I didn't respect the underlying acknowledgement of the relationship between humanity and nature. Sikhism had an appeal, with its teaching that humans create their surroundings as a reflection of their inner state. However, the set of ideas that really spoke to me, in terms of its relevance to the modern world, was Buddhism. In particular, this philosophy offered a vision that helped me to integrate my views about spirituality and the connectedness of everything. It promoted the idea of inner reflection, compassion, and respect for the environment. And it was free of the guilt and judgementalism of the Middle Eastern religions which are dominated by religious leaders who assume an authority to tell people what to think.

In the 1970s and 1980s, when my life was largely consumed with work and various forms of community activism, thoughts of religion and spirituality took a back seat. Whilst I was driven and sustained by the values I had acquired in my youth, this did not translate into religious

---

[248] In the modern era, the teachings of evangelical churches are a particular concern to me, with beliefs in fanciful ideas such as the virgin birth and resurrection. And I find it worrying that some of our current political leaders belong to such organisations.

observance. However, as I reached middle age, I became more reflective, and spent a significant amount of time reading and soaking up spiritual writing, which appealed to my thoughtful and sometimes ascetic nature. And, eventually embracing Buddhist philosophy, I even started to declare myself a Buddhist in the census return!

There were many aspects to this growing commitment to the Buddhist way of thinking, and I am by no means convinced by all the teaching. For example, I was never sold on the idea of reincarnation, which seems to be a fanciful if well-intentioned way of connecting man to nature which has no basis in scientific evidence. This is not to deny the spiritual nature of all living things and even inanimate objects. However, the commitment to compassion reflects my views about healthy and peaceful human relations rooted in social justice, and the concept of man being part of the environment has a strong appeal consistent with the fundamental spiritual views embraced by First Nation peoples around the globe. And I was particularly sold on the Four Noble Truths as a construct for explaining the human condition. Without expounding that whole philosophy, these tenets are as follows:

- Suffering is endemic.
- The causes of suffering are delusions and non-virtuous acts.
- To achieve happiness you must eliminate delusions and pursue virtuous acts.
- A virtuous life is achieved through the practices that collectively are called Dharma, as shown below.

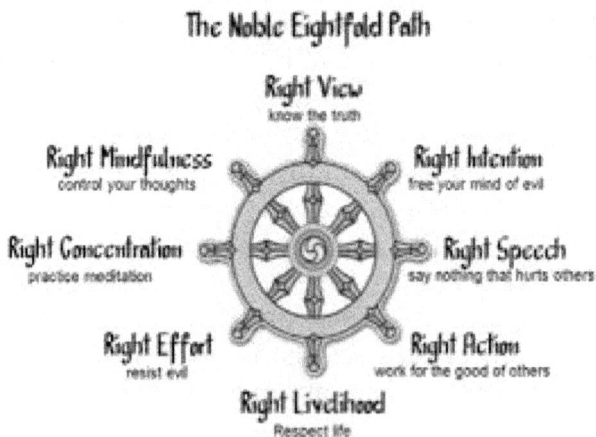

The Noble Eightfold Path

Right View
know the truth

Right Mindfulness
control your thoughts

Right Intention
free your mind of evil

Right Concentration
practice meditation

Right Speech
say nothing that hurts others

Right Effort
resist evil

Right Action
work for the good of others

Right Livelihood
Respect life

The important thing about all these ideas is that they involve taking charge of your own life, taking time for reflection, and understanding why we are the way we are. They do not rely on looking to some supreme being, or its representatives on Earth, for prescriptions on how to lead your life. And the insight into the relationship between humans and nature dovetails beautifully with my awareness about environmental issues, including the existential crisis arising from greedy and wanton exploitation of the planet's resources.

As with many things in life, my own enlightenment about environmental issues crept up on me. I was fortunate to acquire a love of nature at an early age. And, by the time I was a teenager, I had developed a natural affinity with and respect for all living things. As a young adult in the early 1970s, I became a member of *Friends of The Earth*.[249] In those days, before climate change became a major issue, their strongest campaigns were on the need to respect the finite nature of the world's resources and recycle man-made products. At the same time, I was aware of the more aggressive campaigning approach pursued by Greenpeace.[250] I applauded their motives, but I was less convinced by their direct-action. Nevertheless, in my political campaigning with the British Liberal Party, I always had a place for environmental issues in my campaign literature.

When I moved to Australia, my link with environmental organisations changed. In the 1980s the Wilderness Society was in the news over its successful campaigns in Tasmania involving the use of federal government powers to reverse local plans to build the Franklin Dam. I became a member. And, in the 1990s, I signed up with the Australian Conservation Foundation, which seemed to be the leading environmental campaigner in Australia. For ten years, the ACF would then become one of the most important things in my life. And I became steeped in their philosophy and thinking about the nature of the physical environment. In particular, after years of exposure to all the scientific evidence and all the persuasive argument about environmental issues, I became convinced of the need to transform society to a new kind of existence that was not based on consumption and growth. And, at the same time, I

[249] Friends of the Earth was established in California in 1969 by David Brower and David Aitken and quickly became established in USA, UK, France, and Sweden. Their advocacy focuses on the social, political and human rights contexts of environmental issues, and their campaigns now mostly take place in the United Kingdom, with a few activities in USA and Europe and an international office in Amsterdam.

[250] Greenpeace was founded in 1971 by Canadians and, in its early days, was noted for its direct action anti-nuclear campaigns, including opposition to French nuclear tests in the South Pacific Ocean.

deepened my understanding about the way in which humans are connected to, and are part of, the environment in which they live.

With this practical experience, and the Buddhist philosophy, in the early years of the 21st century, a clear view about the place of human beings on planet Earth emerged. And my commitment was bolstered by visits to the Kingdom of Bhutan, a constitutional monarchy where national success is measured by Gross National Happiness, and all their energy comes from renewable sources.[251] I also started to try and lead a life which was consistent with what had become a deeply held set of beliefs. My outlook encompasses the following key elements.

a) Much of the pain we experience comes from within. It is borne of unrealistic expectations and attachments, unbridled passions, building walls not bridges, denial of our true selves in the face of pressure from other people and circumstances to be something we are not, denying or misrepresenting the truth, and living with a closed mind.

b) Bad things happen, not necessarily of our making, and character is defined by how we cope with adversity.

c) The impact on others of the way in which we choose to express ourselves is at least as important as the content of our thoughts and feelings. We need to be mindful of this in our physical, spoken and written exchanges with other humans.

d) True value lies in the spirit of things. It does not derive from an economic calculation, nor is it a quality to be the subject of judgemental comparison.

e) Social harmony is achieved through seeking the best in people, encouraging positive thoughts and actions in others, playing to people's strengths not their weaknesses, and subsuming personal interests to the greater public good.

f) Wisdom comes from knowing your limits, and this applies to both our personal existence and the operation of the societies within which we live.

g) Human beings are part of the physical environment in which we exist. Whilst we are social animals, and our commitment to education, work, health, and leisure requires social interaction and leads us to live in cities, we derive physical health, peace of mind, and perspective through being close to nature.

---

[251] Located in the Himalayas, Bhutan obtains energy from hydro-electric schemes and even exports surplus energy to India.

Now in my 70s, I do wonder whether acquisition of this knowledge at an earlier age might have changed my life. But that is to devalue the learning that comes from experience. In any event, as a closing note, I would urge the reader to lead a life in which they not only seek to change the world but also the way in which they choose to experience it. This is truly an agenda for the achievement of a happy life.

Glossary

AAP	means	Australian Associated Press
ACCA	means	Australian Crohn's and Colitis Association
ACF	means	Australian Conservation Foundation
ACOSS	means	Australian Council of Social Service
ACTU	means	Australian Council of Trade Unions
AHMAC	means	Australian Health Ministers Advisory Council
AIDS	means	Acquired Immune Deficiency Syndrome
ALP	means	Australian Labor Party
ARC	means	Australian Red Cross
ARCBS	means	Australian Red Cross Blood Service
ARENA	means	Australian Renewable Energy Agency
ASCC	means	Australian Stem Cell Centre
AVF	means	Australian Volleyball Federation
AVP	means	Association of Volleyball Professionals
ABVPA	means	Australian Beach Volleyball Professionals Association (Also AVPA)
BNA	means	British National Archives
BRISC	means	Blood Review Implementation Steering Committee
BTS	means	Blood Transfusion Service
BVPT	means	Beach Volleyball Professional Tour
CEC	means	Candidates Endorsement Committee (Ch4)/ Callignee & Traralgon South Emergency Committee (Ch29)
CERA	means	Community Emergency Risk Analysis
CFA	means	Country Fire Authority
CJD	means	Creutzfeldt Jakob Disease
COP	means	Conference Of the Parties
CPRS	means	Carbon Pollution Reduction Scheme
DHCS	means	Department of Health and Community Services
DHS	means	Department of Human Services
DWBC	means	Darlingford Waters Boat Club
EPBC	means	Environment Protection and Biodiversity Conservation
ESU	means	English Speaking Union
FIVB	means	Fédération Internationale de Volleyball
GFC	means	Global Financial Crisis
GMW	means	Goulburn Murray Water
GWG	means	Governance Working Group
GYK	means	Grow Your Knowledge
HDV	means	Health Department Victoria
HESTA	means	Health Employees Superannuation Trust of Australia
HSUA	means	Health Services Union of Australia
HTLV	means	Human T-Lymphotropic Virus
ICRC	means	International Committee of the Red Cross
IPCC	means	Intergovernmental Panel on Climate Change
KPMG	means	Klynveld Peat Marwick Goerdeler
LCEMF	means	Latrobe Community Emergency Management Forum
LEAP	means	Local Emergency Action Plan
MDBP	means	Murray Darling Basin Plan
MEMPC	means	Municipal Emergency Management Planning Committee

MSJ	means	Mallesons Stephen Jaques
NAT	means	Nucleic Acid Testing
NBA	means	National Blood Authority
NCSC	means	National Companies and Securities Commission
NHMRC	means	National Health and Medical Research Council
OH&S	means	Occupational Health and Safety
PWC	means	Price Waterhouse Coopers
RCBBV	means	Red Cross Blood Bank Victoria
SCCC	means	Southern Cross Climate Coalition
SEATS	means	Stock Exchange Automatic Trading System
SMG	means	Sports Marketing Group
SOE	means	Special Operations Executive
TfN	means	Trust for Nature
TGA	means	Therapeutic Goods Administration
TSDA	means	Traralgon South and District Association
UNFCCC	means	United Nations Convention on Climate Change
VBRRA	means	Victorian Bushfire Reconstruction and Recovery Authority
VCAT	means	Victorian Civil Administration Tribunal
VMG	means	Venture Marketing Group

Acknowledgements

In preparing this second part of my memoirs, I have sought to ensure that the account of my life is an accurate reflection of the events and the facts. To this end, in some cases I have circulated the relevant chapter to the people about whom I have written for input and comment. However, the account I provide in this book is entirely of my own making and, apart from my son, I have not sought approval from any other party.

I would like to thank a number of people who have provided generously of their time in reviewing the material and providing their own recollections. Of special mention, I received enormous help from Dr Roger Mallion who undertook a comprehensive review of the manuscript providing valuable input and comments, querying my use of Australian vocabulary, and sorting out my wayward approach to compound nouns. For the three chapters on the blood service, I am indebted to Dr Patrick Coghlan for his review and input in remembering the details of events. For the chapter on the Australian Red Cross Society, I am grateful for the input and comments of the previous President of the organisation Greg Vickery. For the chapters on beach volleyball, and boating on Lake Eildon, I am grateful to Robert Agnew for his comments. For the chapters on the Australian Conservation Foundation, I received helpful input from Denise Boyd, Professor Ian Lowe, and Ross Tzannes.

Finally I again owe a huge debt to my publisher Simon Hepworth who has encouraged me in my endeavours and has delivered my latest offering with great care and attention.

Bibliography and Sources

Author	Title	Publisher	Place	Date
Carson	The Silent Spring	Houghton Mifflin	Boston	1962
Club of Rome	Limits to Growth	Potomac Associates	Falls Church Virginia	1972
Gore, Al	Earth in Balance - Ecology and the Human Spirit	Houghton Mifflin	Boston	1992
Gore, Al	An Inconvenient Truth	Bloomsbury	London	2006
Sykes, Trevor	Lessons from the Crash	Australian Financial Review	Sydney	2012
Tippler, Chris	Corpus, Rios	Rios Press	Melbourne	2010
Various	NCSC 9th Annual Report	Australian Government Publishing Services	Canberra	1988
Wigginton, Gavin	For Goodness Sake	Ad Astra	Merthyr Tydfil	2019
Wigginton, Gavin	Wig's Secret War	MTW	Merthyr Tydfil	2017

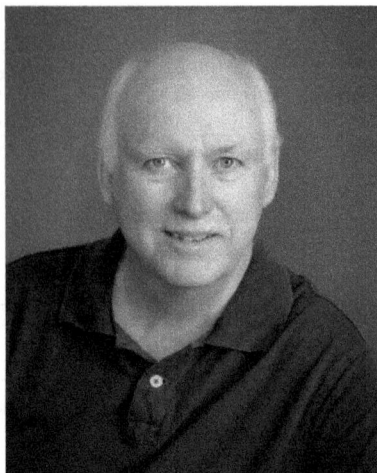

Gavin Wigginton was born in Nottingham in 1945. He is a sometime graduate of the Universities of Wales (in Swansea) and Hull. In the late 1960s he commenced a career in the private sector of British industry, with roles as an internal consultant, HR manager, and corporate planner.

Since 1986, Gavin has lived in Australia. After a time with the National Companies and Securities Commission, he was for 15 years a senior manager with the Australian Red Cross Society's blood service. In 2005 he was awarded the Society's Distinguished Staff Award. More recently, he has been a management consultant specialising in governance and risk analysis and has served on the board of a number of not for profit organisations.

Gavin has been an active environmentalist for most of his adult life, and for ten years served as Honorary Secretary and a board member of the Australian Conservation Foundation. He is an Honorary Life Member of the Foundation.

Nowadays, Gavin is an author, specialising in biography and social history.

INDEX

www.ingramcontent.com/pod-product-compliance
Lightning Source LLC
Chambersburg PA
CBHW070340090426
42733CB00009B/1236